Shojo Beat

VAMPIRE KNIGHT

Story & Art by
Matsuri Hino

Vol. 18

The Story of VAMPIRE KNIGHT

1 Cross Academy, a private boarding school, is where the Day Class and Night Class coexist. The Night Class—a group of beautiful elite students—are all vampires!

2 Four years ago, after turning his twin brother against him, the pureblood Shizuka Hio bit Zero and turned him into a vampire. Kaname kills Shizuka, but the source may still exist. Meanwhile, Yuki suffers from lost memories. When Kaname sinks his fangs into her neck, her memories return!

3 Yuki is the princess of the Kuran family—and a pureblood vampire!! Ten years ago, her mother exchanged her life to seal away Yuki's vampire nature. Yuki's Uncle Rido killed her father. Rido takes over Shiki's body and arrives at the Academy. He targets Yuki for her blood, so Kaname gives his own blood to resurrect Rido. Kaname confesses that he's the progenitor of the Kurans, and that Rido is the master who awakened him!

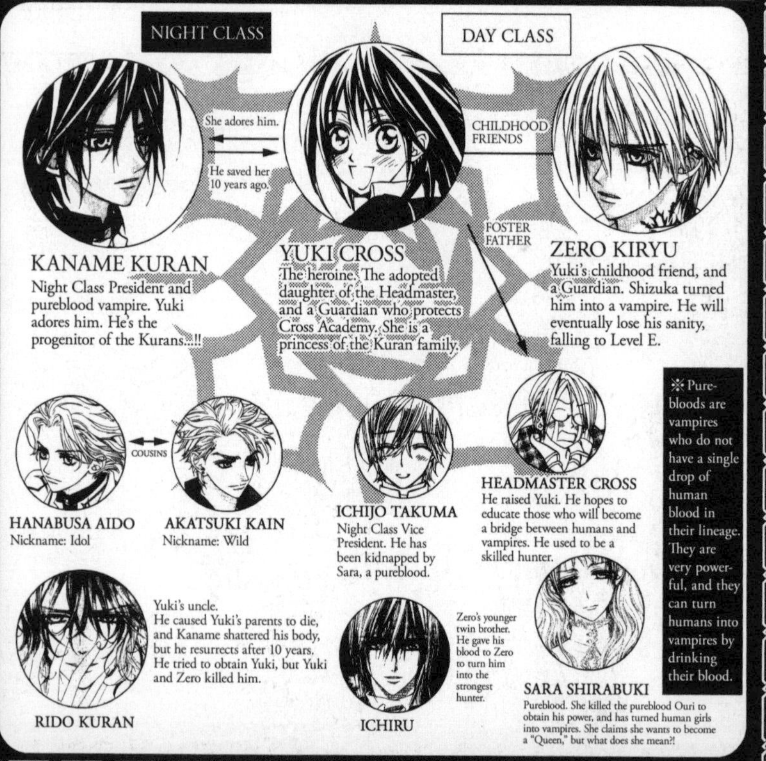

NIGHT CLASS
DAY CLASS
She adores him.
He saved her 10 years ago.
CHILDHOOD FRIENDS
FOSTER FATHER
KANAME KURAN
Night Class President and pureblood vampire. Yuki adores him. He's the progenitor of the Kurans...!!
YUKI CROSS
The heroine. The adopted daughter of the Headmaster, and a Guardian who protects Cross Academy. She is a princess of the Kuran family.
ZERO KIRYU
Yuki's childhood friend, and a Guardian. Shizuka turned him into a vampire. He will eventually lose his sanity, falling to Level E.
※ Purebloods are vampires who do not have a single drop of human blood in their lineage. They are very powerful, and they can turn humans into vampires by drinking their blood.
COUSINS
HANABUSA AIDO
Nickname: Idol
AKATSUKI KAIN
Nickname: Wild
ICHIJO TAKUMA
Night Class Vice President. He has been kidnapped by Sara, a pureblood.
HEADMASTER CROSS
He raised Yuki. He hopes to educate those who will become a bridge between humans and vampires. He used to be a skilled hunter.
Yuki's uncle.
He caused Yuki's parents to die, and Kaname shattered his body, but he resurrects after 10 years. He tried to obtain Yuki, but Yuki and Zero killed him.
RIDO KURAN
Zero's younger twin brother. He gave his blood to Zero to turn him into the strongest hunter.
ICHIRU
SARA SHIRABUKI
Pureblood. She killed the pureblood Ouri to obtain his power, and has turned human girls into vampires. She claims she wants to become a "Queen," but what does she mean?!

4 Cross Academy turns into a battlefield. After fierce fighting, Yuki and Zero succeed in defeating Rido, but then Zero points his gun at Yuki. No matter what their feelings are, their fates will never intertwine. Yuki leaves the Academy with Kaname, and the Night Class at Cross Academy is no more.

5 A year has passed since Yuki and Zero's parting. Kaname and Zero have become the representatives of each group respectively. Meanwhile, Sara Shirabuki begins to make suspicious moves by creating more servants of her own. Yuki tries to live together with Kaname, but he slays Aido's father and disappears. Yuki is taken captive by the Hunter Society, and reinstates the Night Class at Cross Academy to maintain order. Meanwhile, Kaname starts getting rid of purebloods.

6 Sara manages to enter the Night Class and tells Zero about Kaname's sin: It was Kaname's plan to turn Zero into a vampire who could kill off the entire race. Kaname enters the Hunter Society headquarters to kill Sara. Zero and Kaname begin a fierce battle, but Ruka—who has always been loyal to Kaname—protects Zero. Now Yuki and Zero must face Kaname and stop him!

BUT I...
RUKA DIDN'T HESITATE
...SO I WON'T EITHER!
I STILL BELIEVE ONE DAY...
...I'LL FIND THE PATH OUT OF THIS DARK FOREST.
KANAME!
Yuki and Zero are the last line of defense! What is Kaname's true intent?
MY BURDEN IS GONE.
I'D NEVER BE ABLE TO CAPTURE YOU...
...IF I THOUGHT ABOUT WHAT I WOULD DO WITH YOU AFTER-WARDS.
THE SUN WILL SHINE DOWN ON THIS
AND THEN...

VAMPIRE KNIGHT

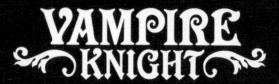

Contents

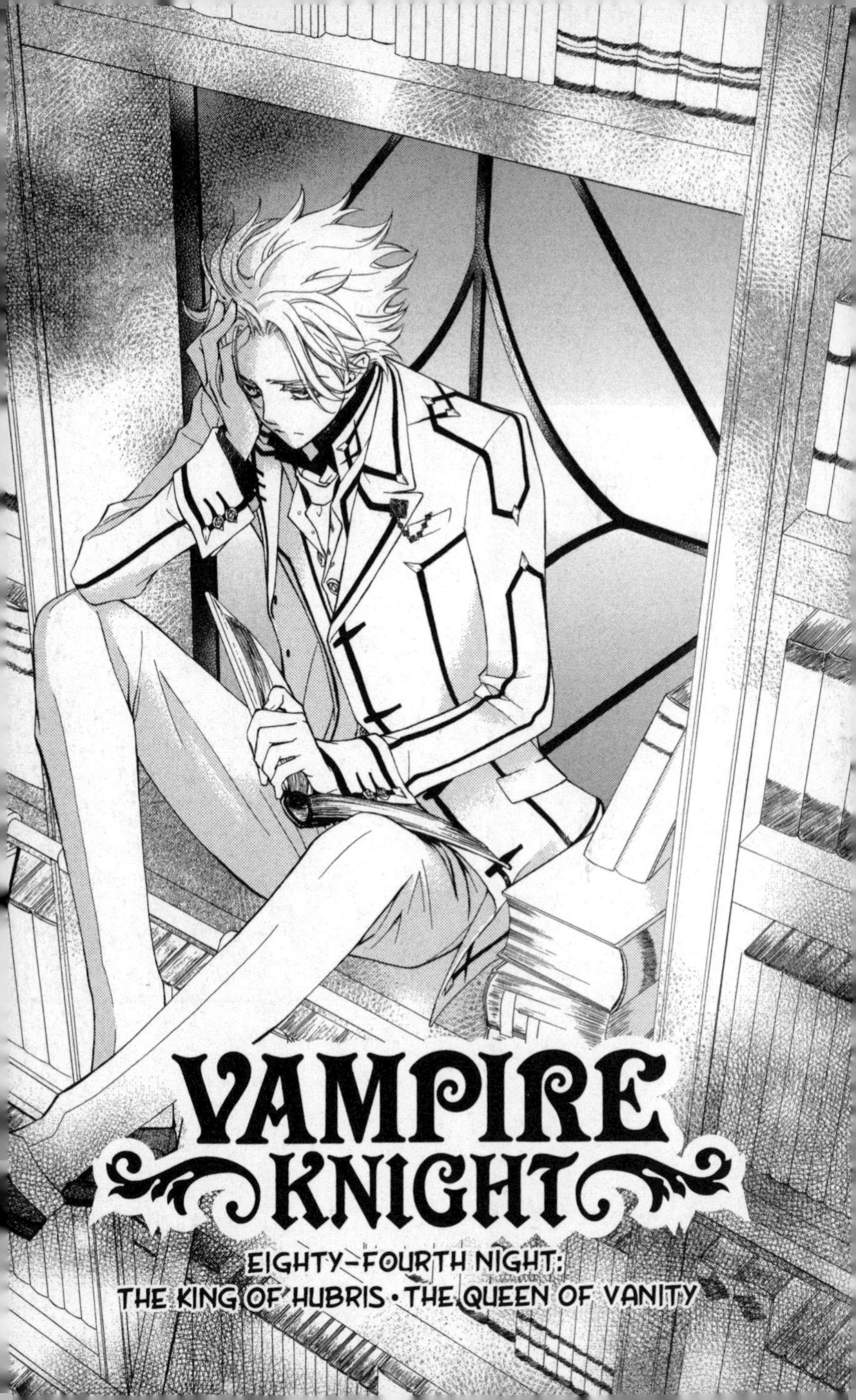
VAMPIRE KNIGHT
EIGHTY-FOURTH NIGHT:
THE KING OF HUBRIS • THE QUEEN OF VANITY

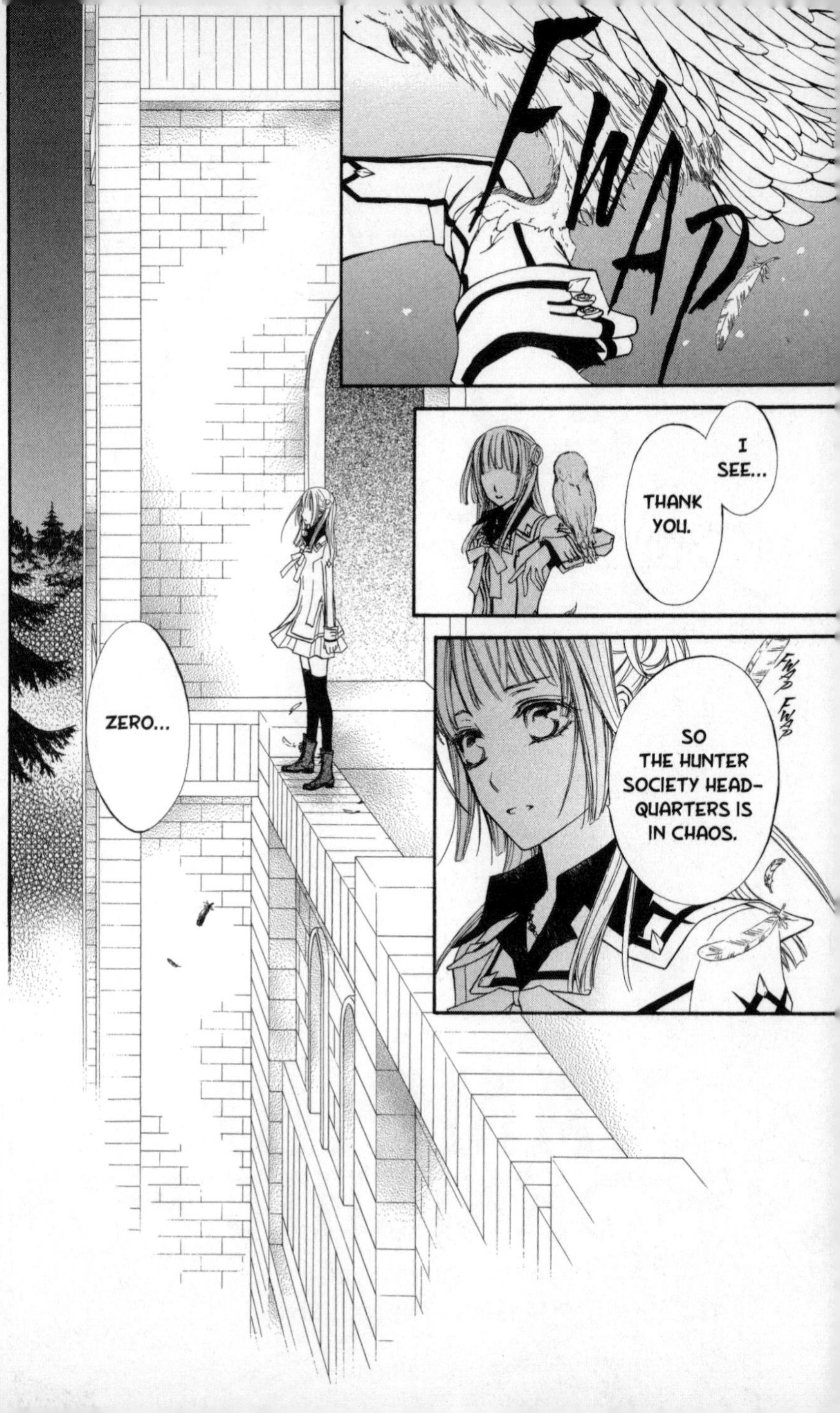
FWAP
I SEE...
THANK YOU.
FWAP FWAP
SO THE HUNTER SOCIETY HEAD-QUARTERS IS IN CHAOS.
ZERO...

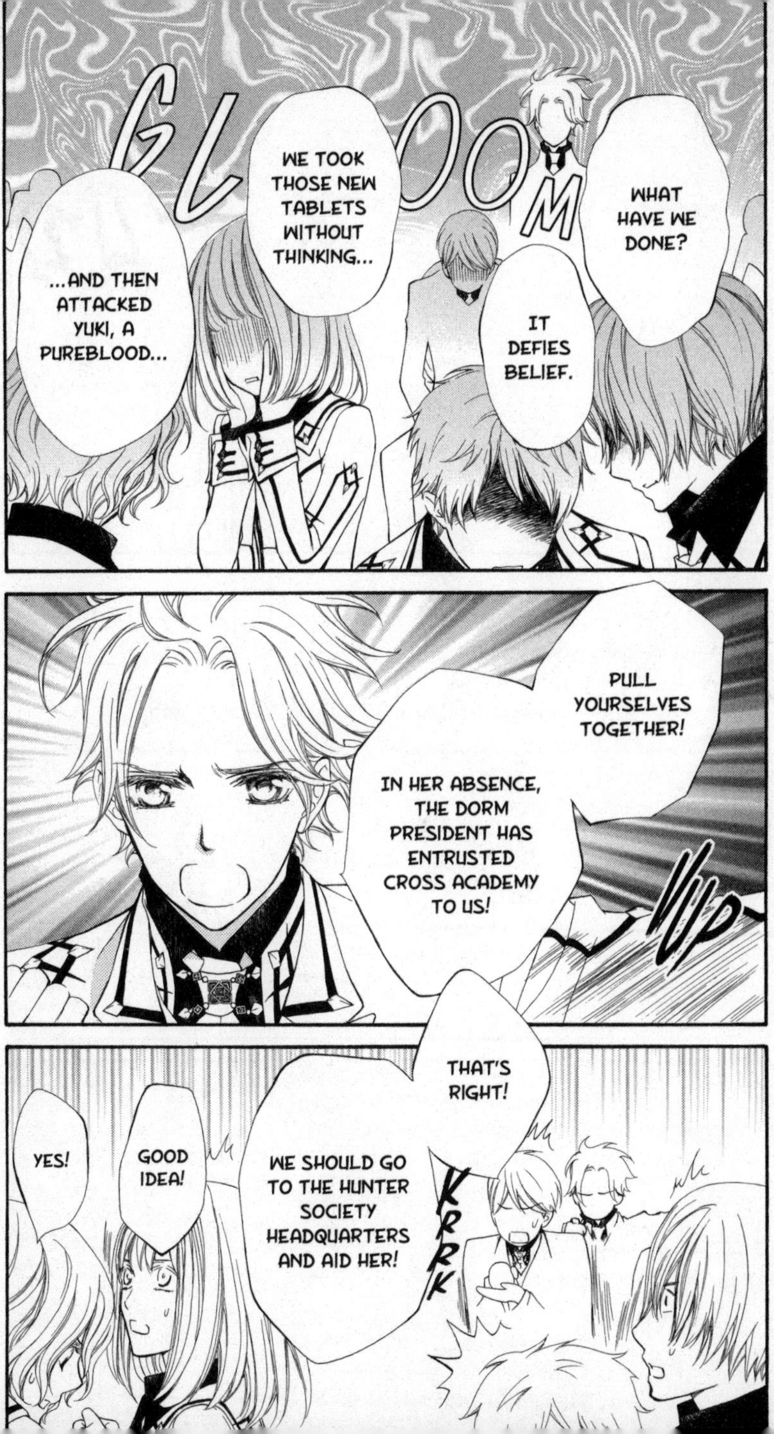
WHAT HAVE WE DONE?
IT DEFIES BELIEF.
GLOOOM
WE TOOK THOSE NEW TABLETS WITHOUT THINKING...
...AND THEN ATTACKED YUKI, A PUREBLOOD...
PULL YOURSELVES TOGETHER!
IN HER ABSENCE, THE DORM PRESIDENT HAS ENTRUSTED CROSS ACADEMY TO US!
THAT'S RIGHT!
WE SHOULD GO TO THE HUNTER SOCIETY HEADQUARTERS AND AID HER!
KRRK
GOOD IDEA!
YES!

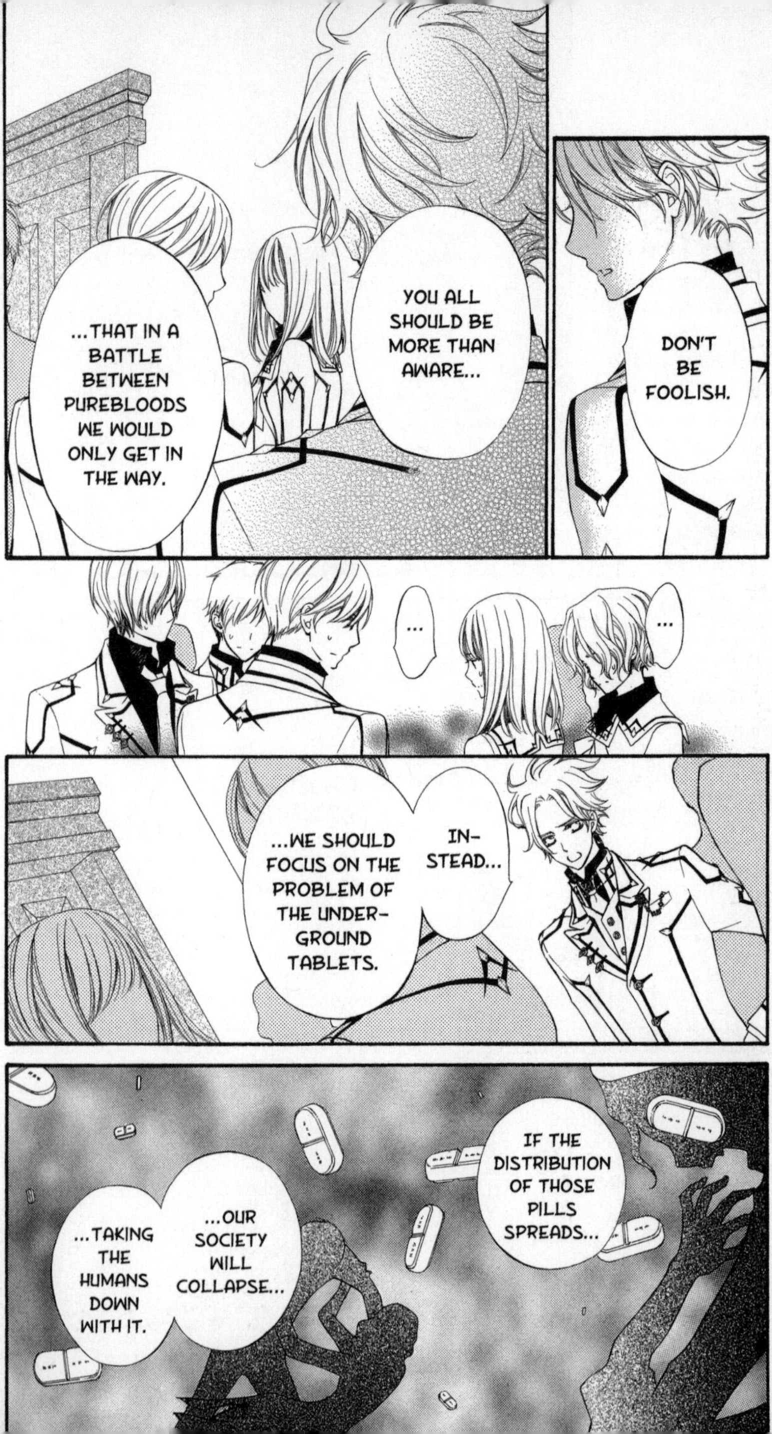
DON'T BE FOOLISH.
YOU ALL SHOULD BE MORE THAN AWARE...
...THAT IN A BATTLE BETWEEN PUREBLOODS WE WOULD ONLY GET IN THE WAY.
...
...
IN-STEAD...
...WE SHOULD FOCUS ON THE PROBLEM OF THE UNDER-GROUND TABLETS.
IF THE DISTRIBUTION OF THOSE PILLS SPREADS...
...OUR SOCIETY WILL COLLAPSE...
...TAKING THE HUMANS DOWN WITH IT.

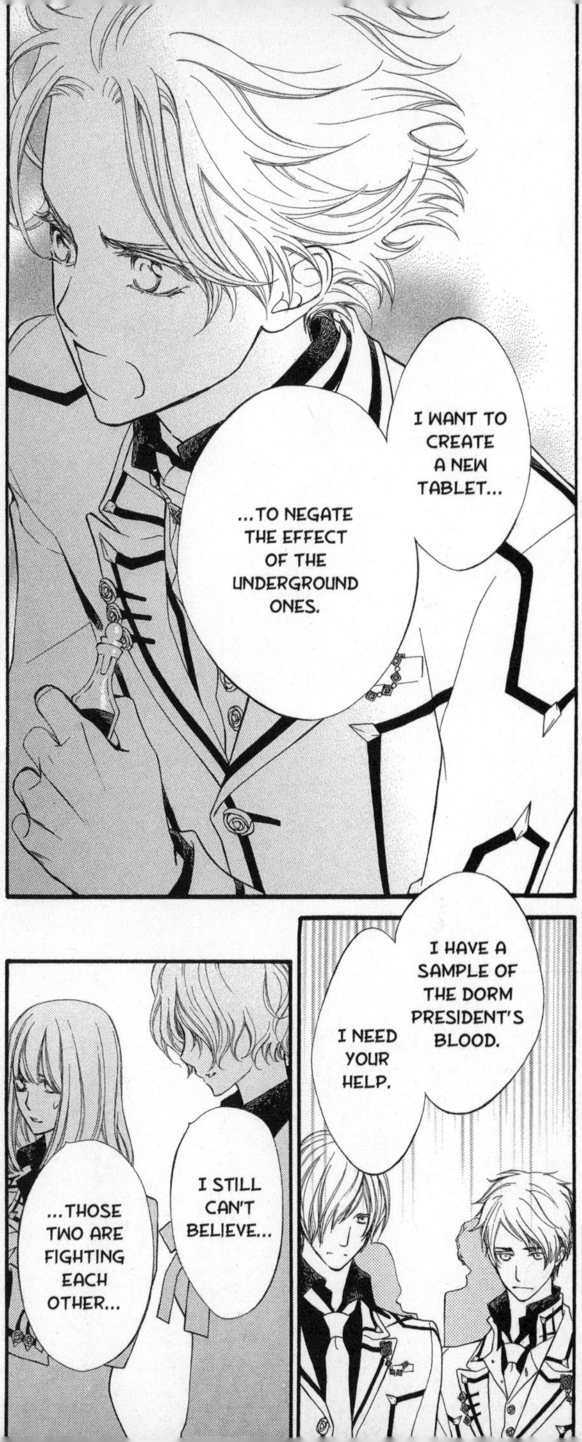
I WANT TO CREATE A NEW TABLET...
...TO NEGATE THE EFFECT OF THE UNDERGROUND ONES.
I HAVE A SAMPLE OF THE DORM PRESIDENT'S BLOOD.
I NEED YOUR HELP.
I STILL CAN'T BELIEVE...
...THOSE TWO ARE FIGHTING EACH OTHER...

I

Volume 18! Hello, Hino here!

Wow... Volume 18. This is pure coincidence, but it's been almost 18 years since I made my debut in *LaLa*. Both are 18! (laugh) Working for eighteen years as a professional mangaka has been a great experience.

I must keep my scope wide as I work on the remaining chapters so I won't have any regrets after the series ends. Otherwise I will let down all the people who have been supporting me, and all the readers who have supported this series. One more volume left until the final chapter. I must put all my effort into it!!

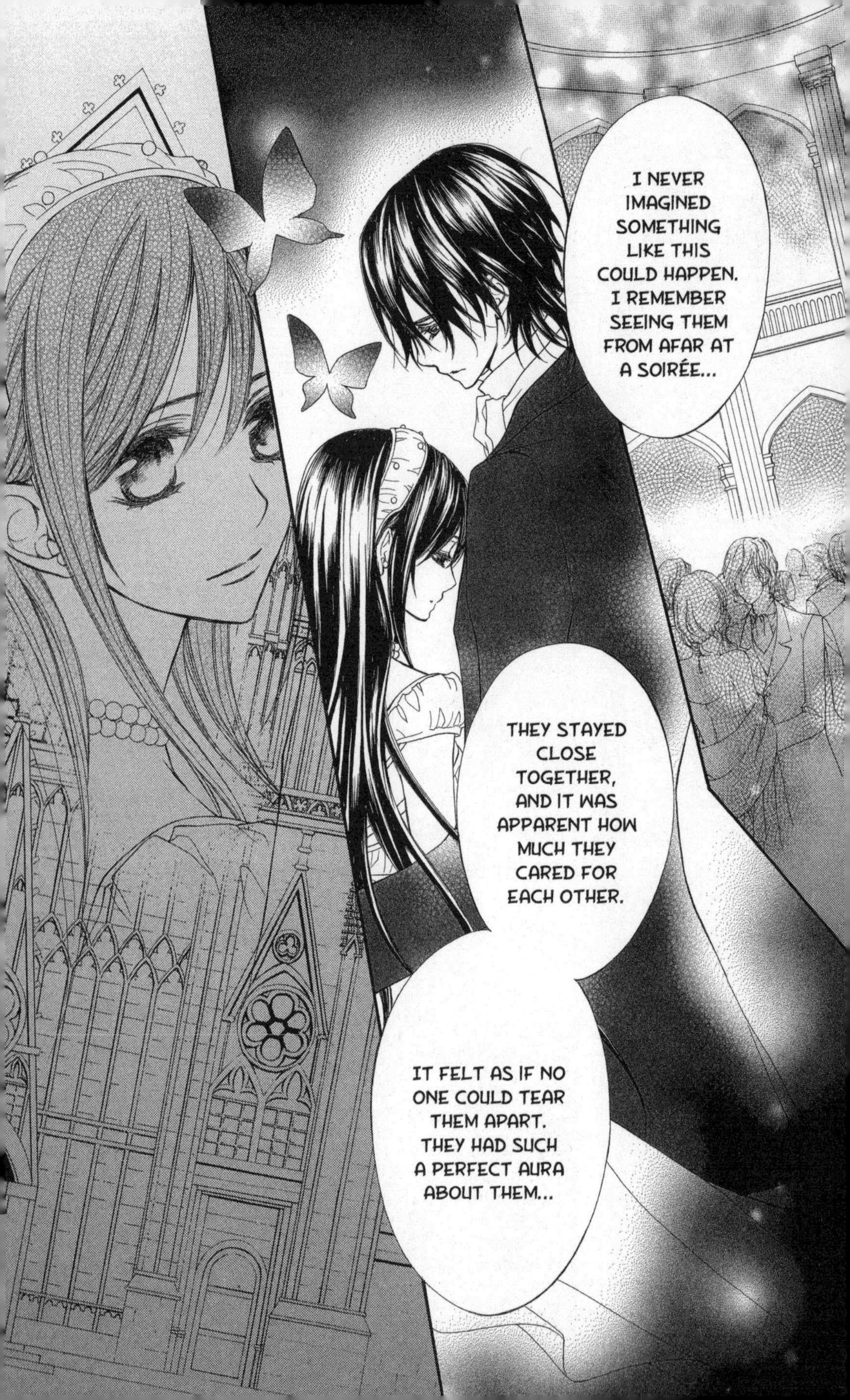
I NEVER IMAGINED SOMETHING LIKE THIS COULD HAPPEN. I REMEMBER SEEING THEM FROM AFAR AT A SOIRÉE...
THEY STAYED CLOSE TOGETHER, AND IT WAS APPARENT HOW MUCH THEY CARED FOR EACH OTHER.
IT FELT AS IF NO ONE COULD TEAR THEM APART. THEY HAD SUCH A PERFECT AURA ABOUT THEM...

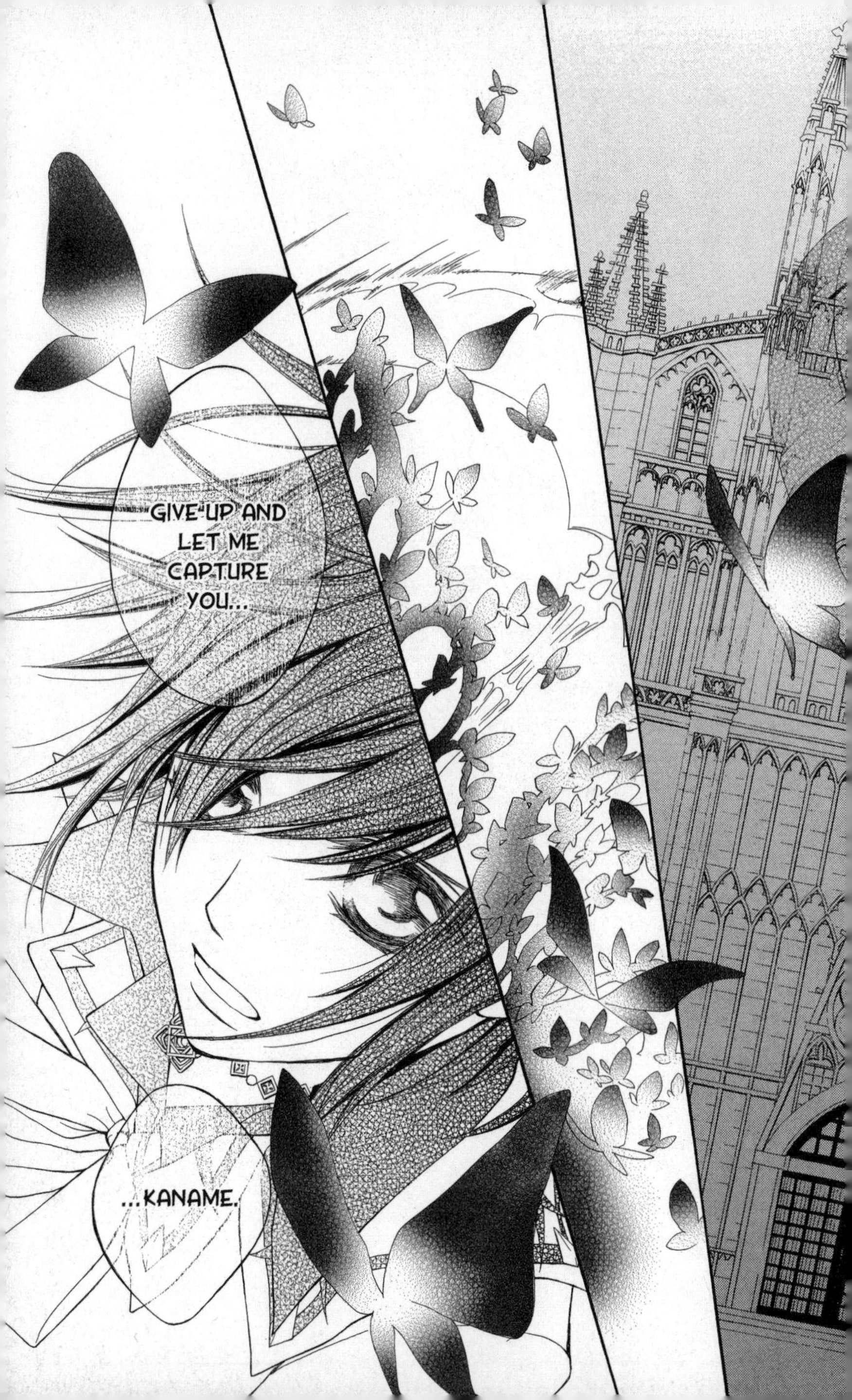
GIVE UP AND LET ME CAPTURE YOU...
...KANAME.

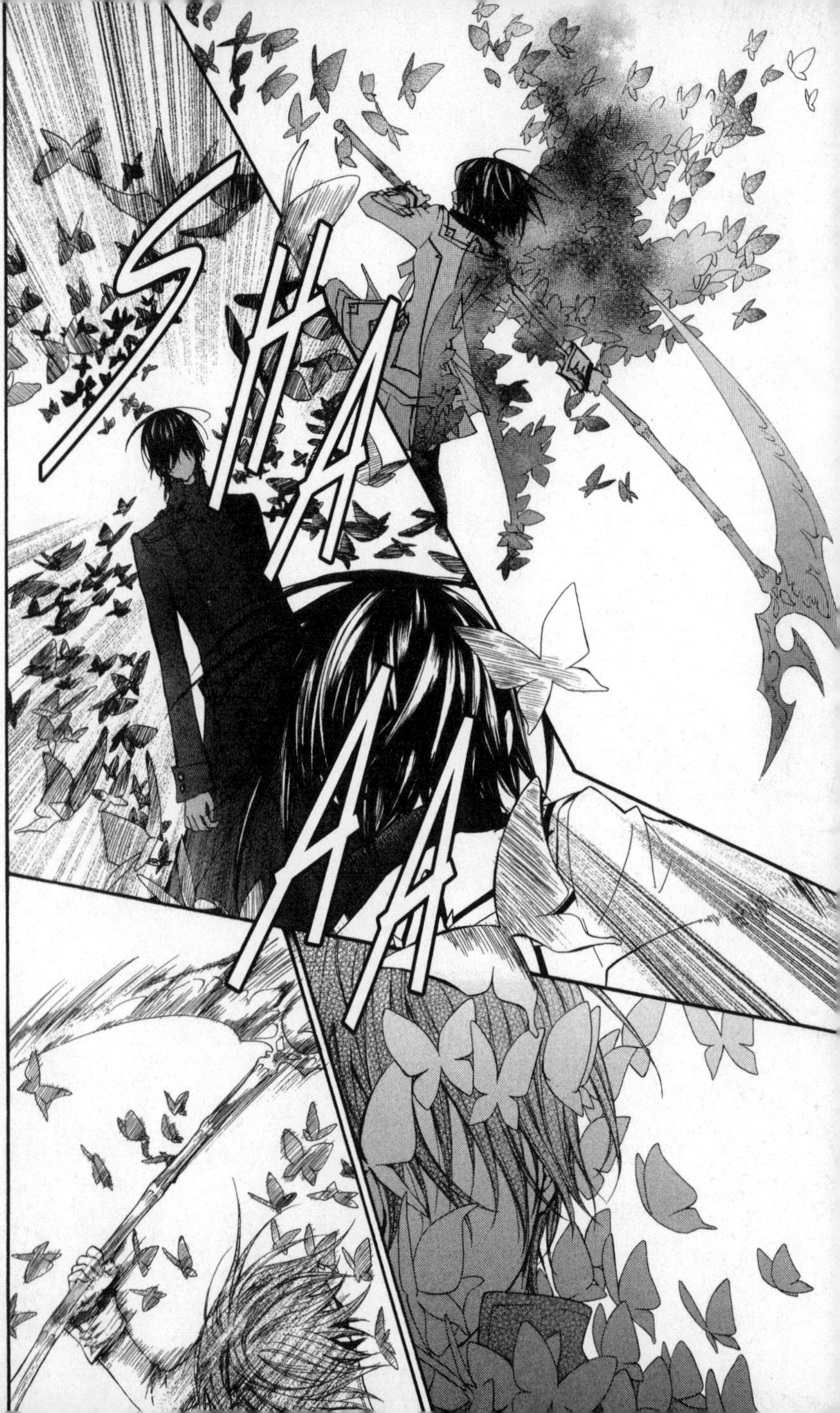
SHAAAA

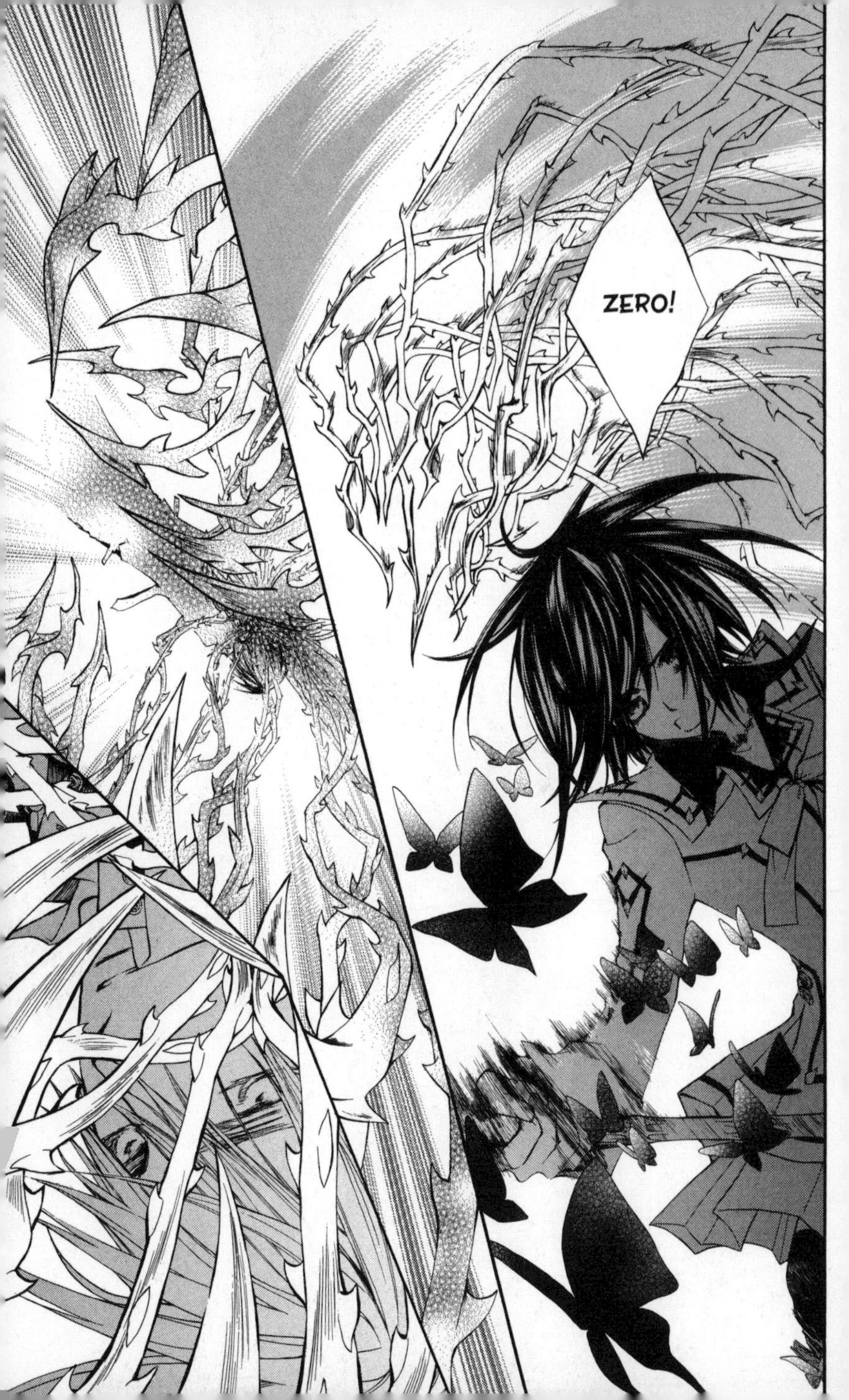
ZERO!

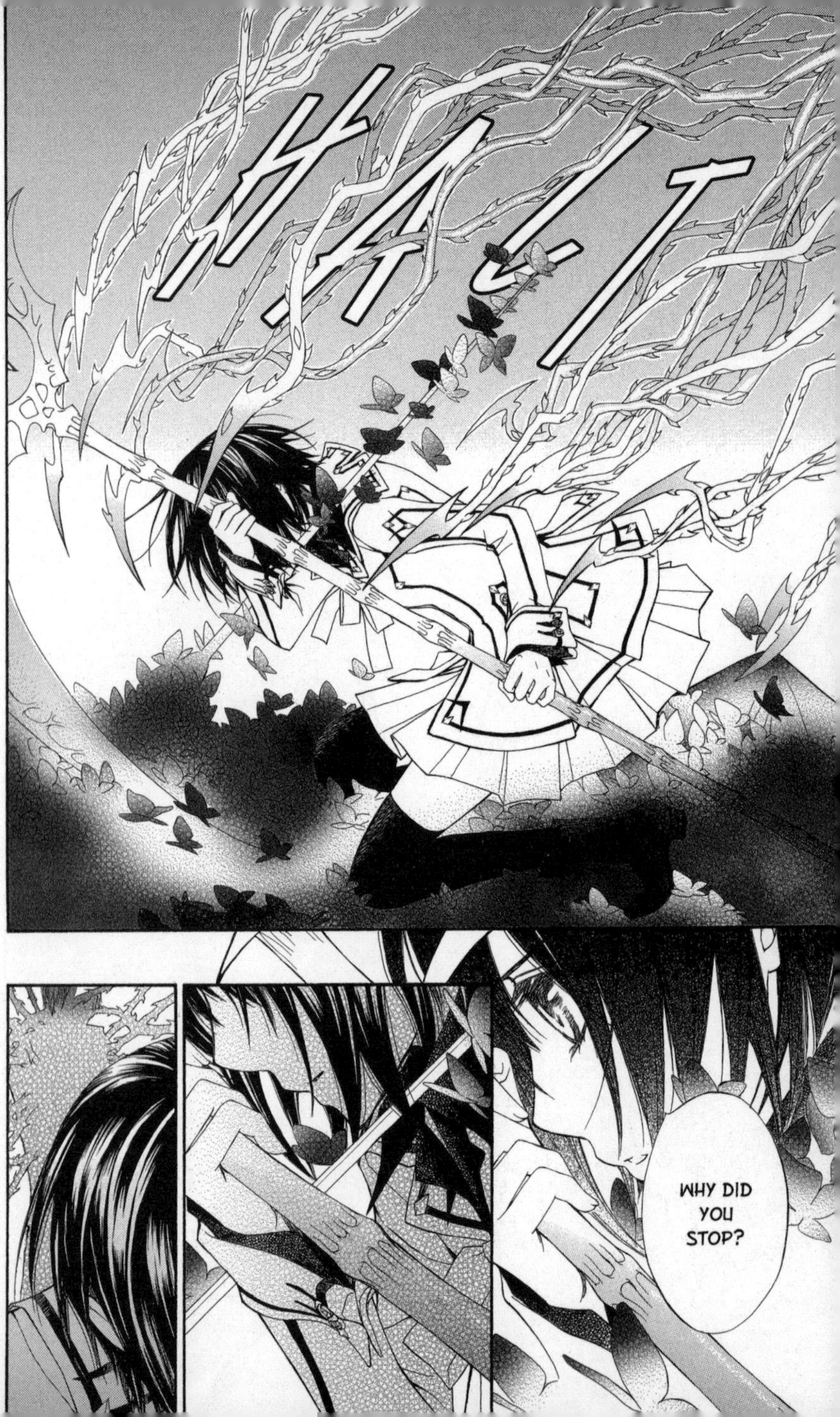
WAIT
WHY DID YOU STOP?

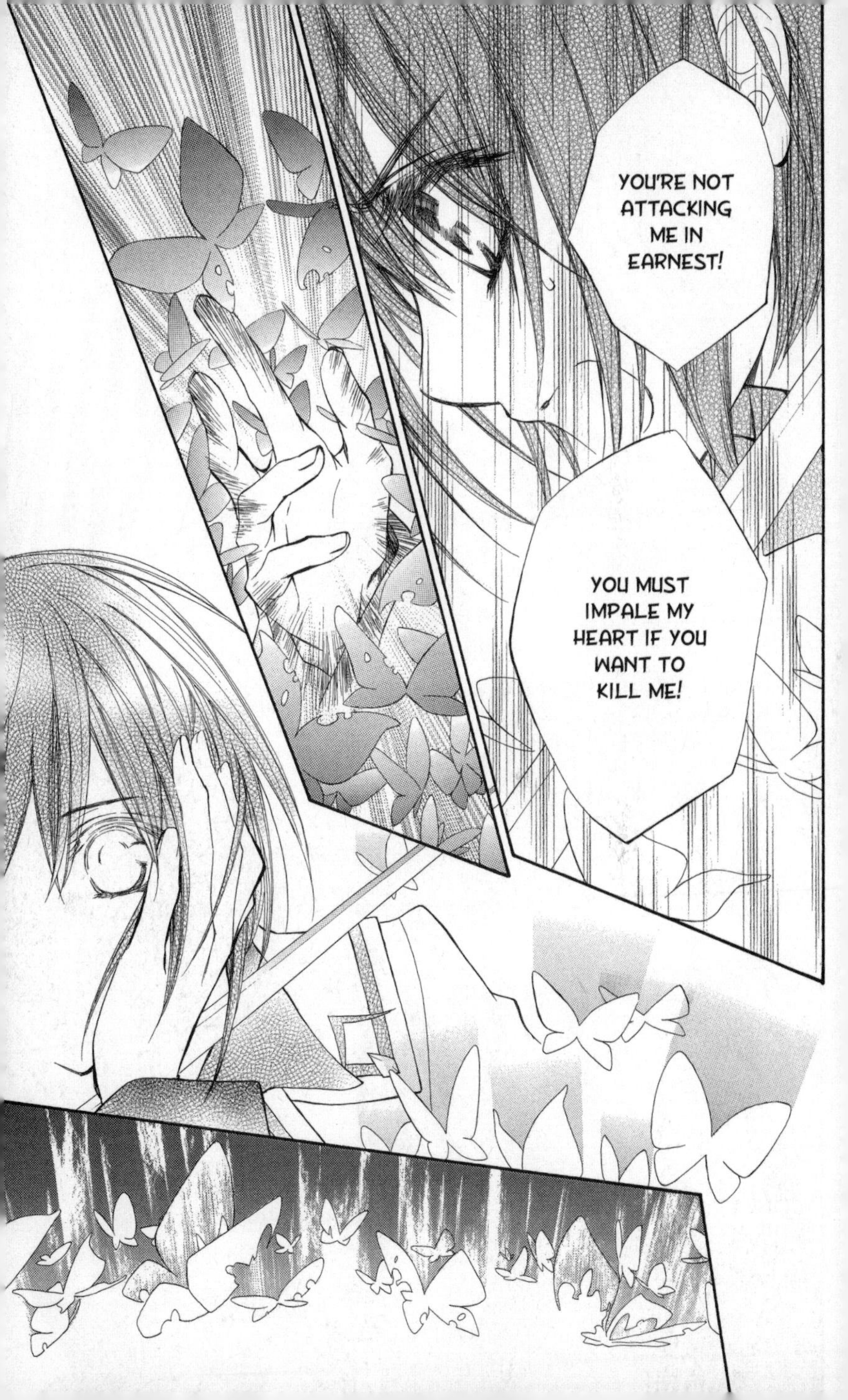
YOU'RE NOT ATTACKING ME IN EARNEST!
YOU MUST IMPALE MY HEART IF YOU WANT TO KILL ME!

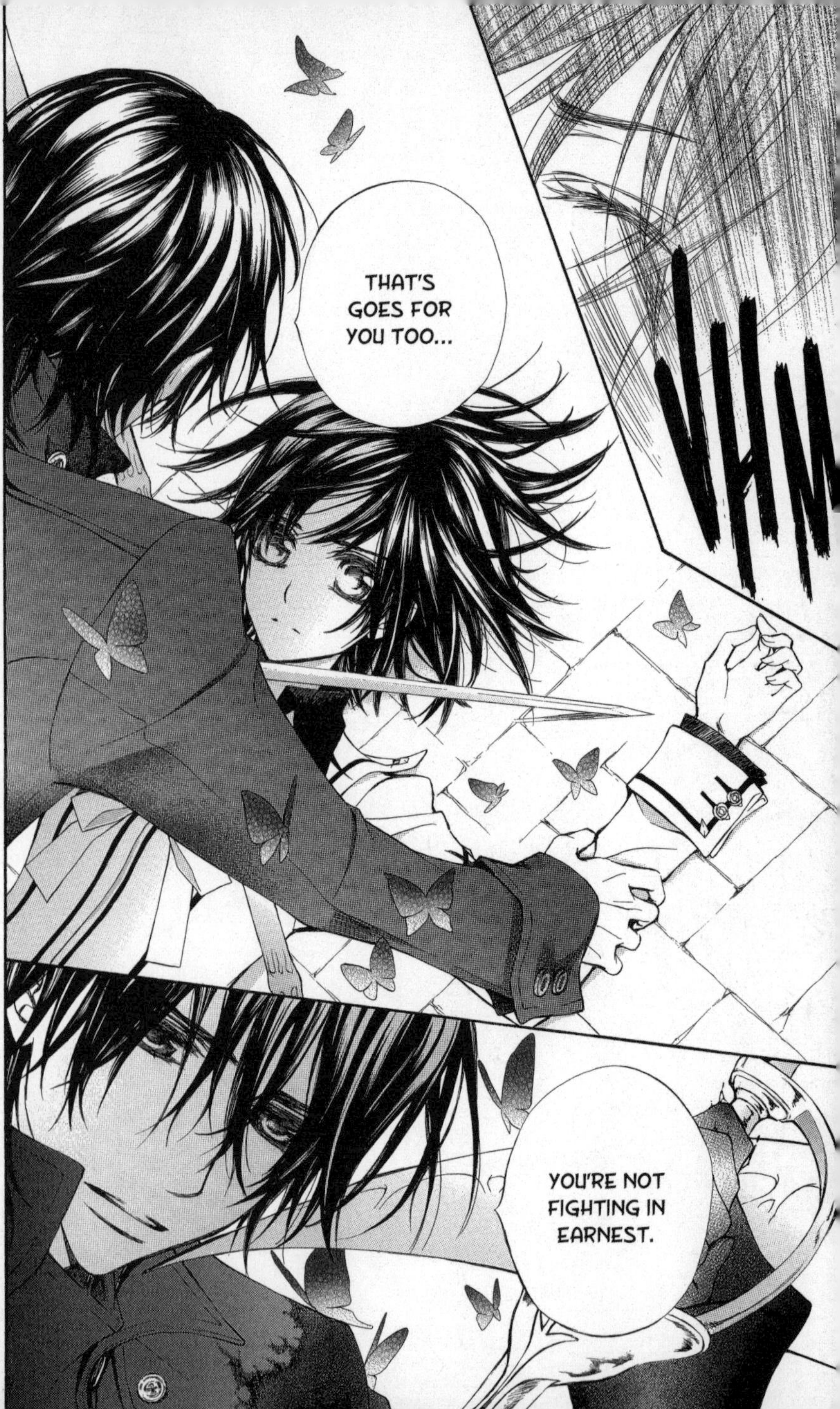
THAT'S GOES FOR YOU TOO...
VHM
YOU'RE NOT FIGHTING IN EARNEST.

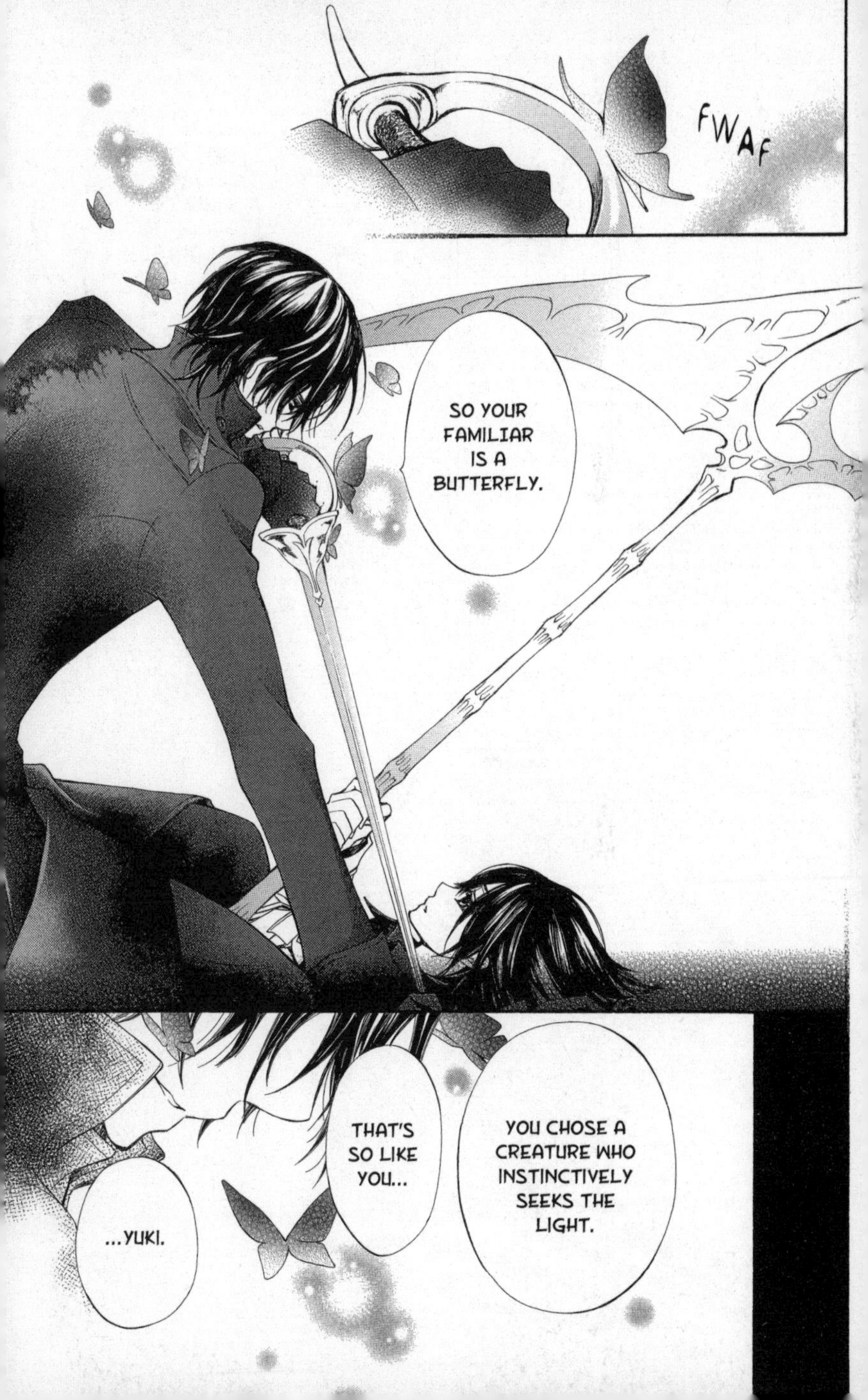
FWAF
SO YOUR FAMILIAR IS A BUTTERFLY.
YOU CHOSE A CREATURE WHO INSTINCTIVELY SEEKS THE LIGHT.
THAT'S SO LIKE YOU...
...YUKI.

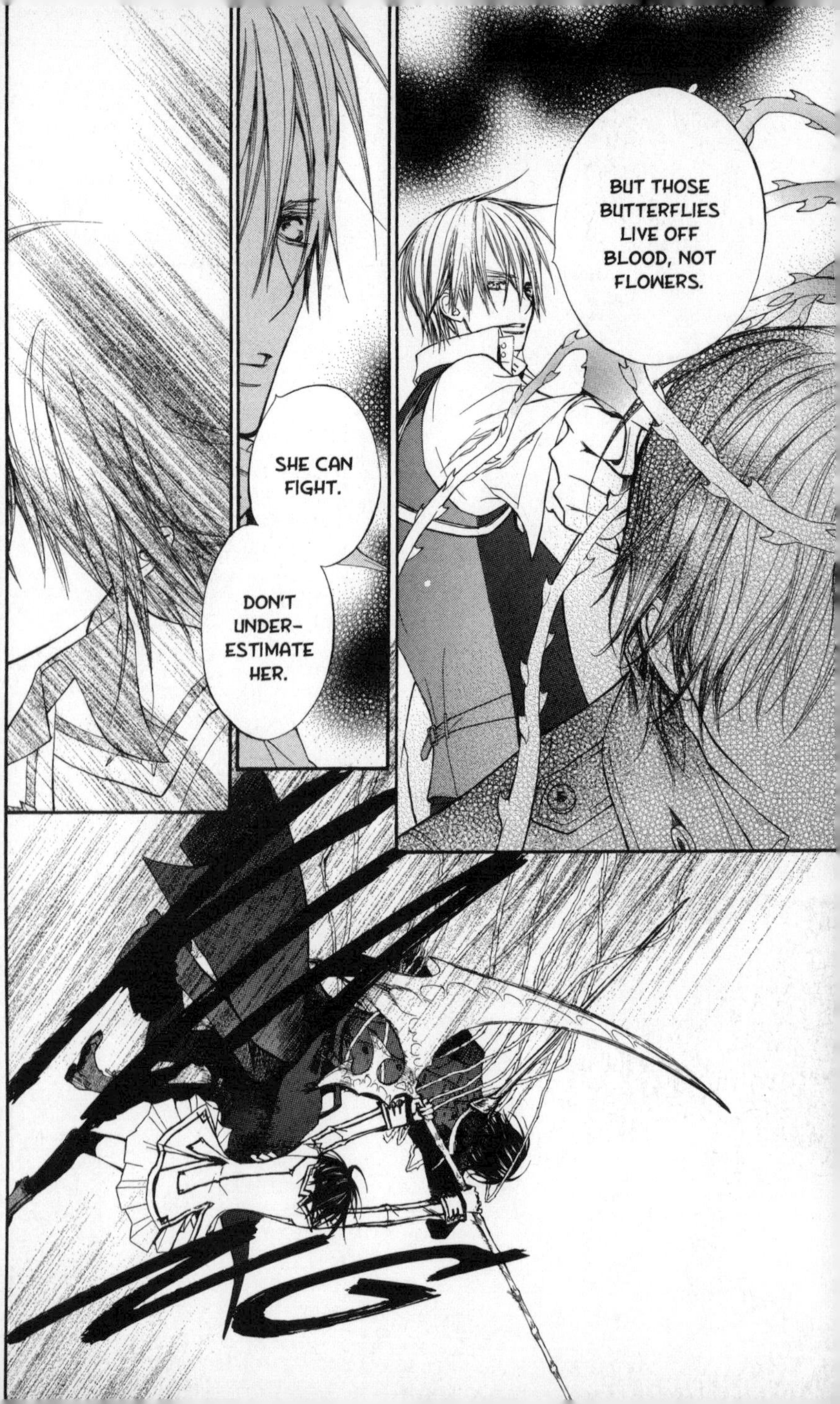
BUT THOSE BUTTERFLIES LIVE OFF BLOOD, NOT FLOWERS.
SHE CAN FIGHT.
DON'T UNDER-ESTIMATE HER.

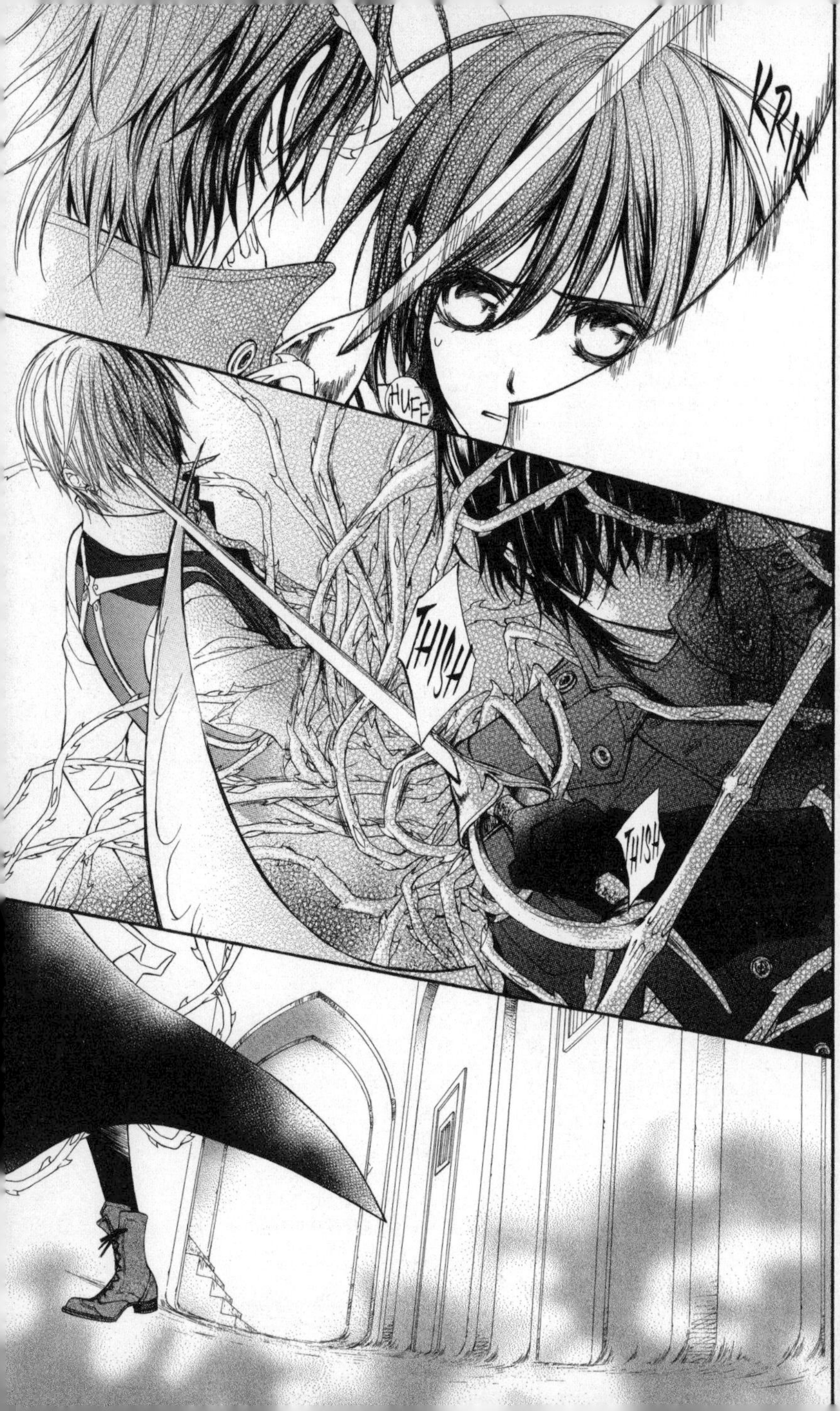
KRIK
HUFF
THISH
THISH

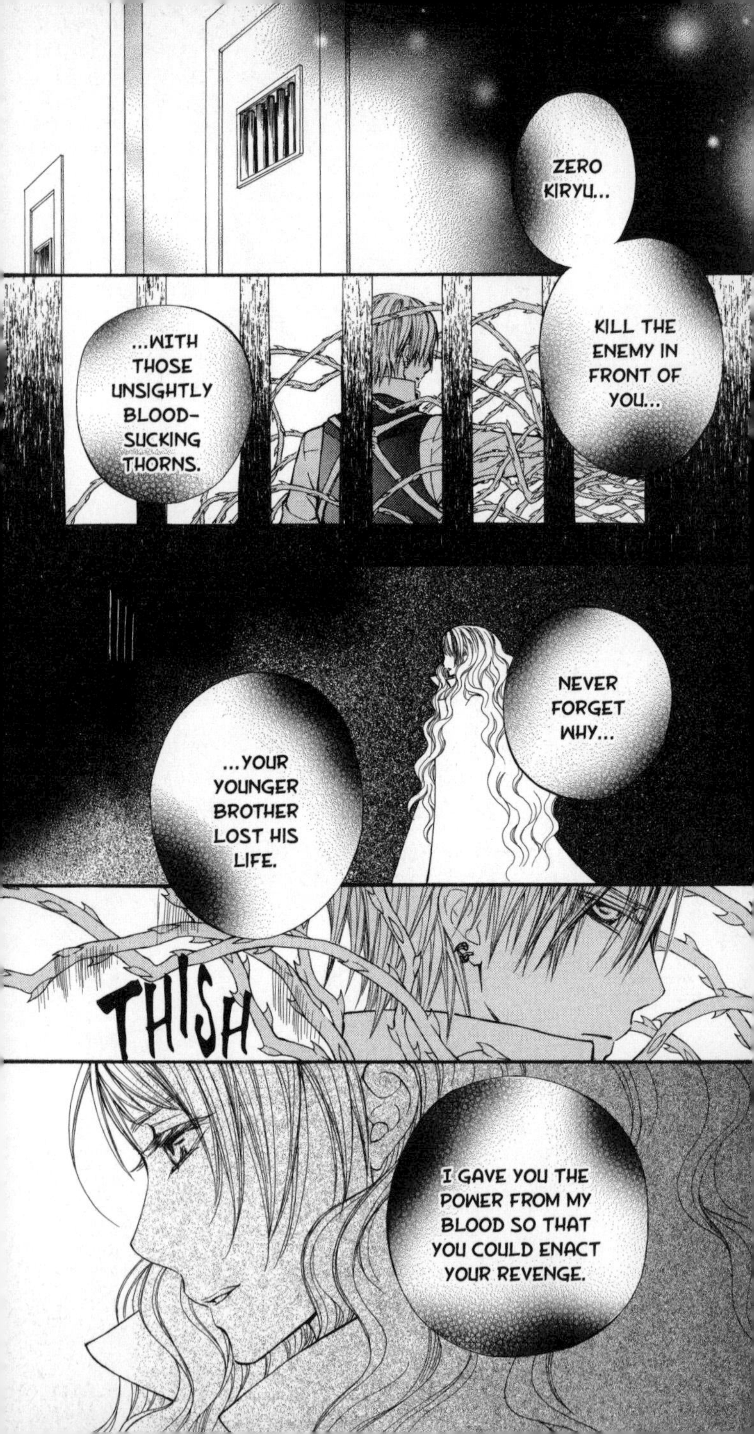
ZERO KIRYU...
KILL THE ENEMY IN FRONT OF YOU...
...WITH THOSE UNSIGHTLY BLOOD-SUCKING THORNS.
NEVER FORGET WHY...
...YOUR YOUNGER BROTHER LOST HIS LIFE.
THISH
I GAVE YOU THE POWER FROM MY BLOOD SO THAT YOU COULD ENACT YOUR REVENGE.

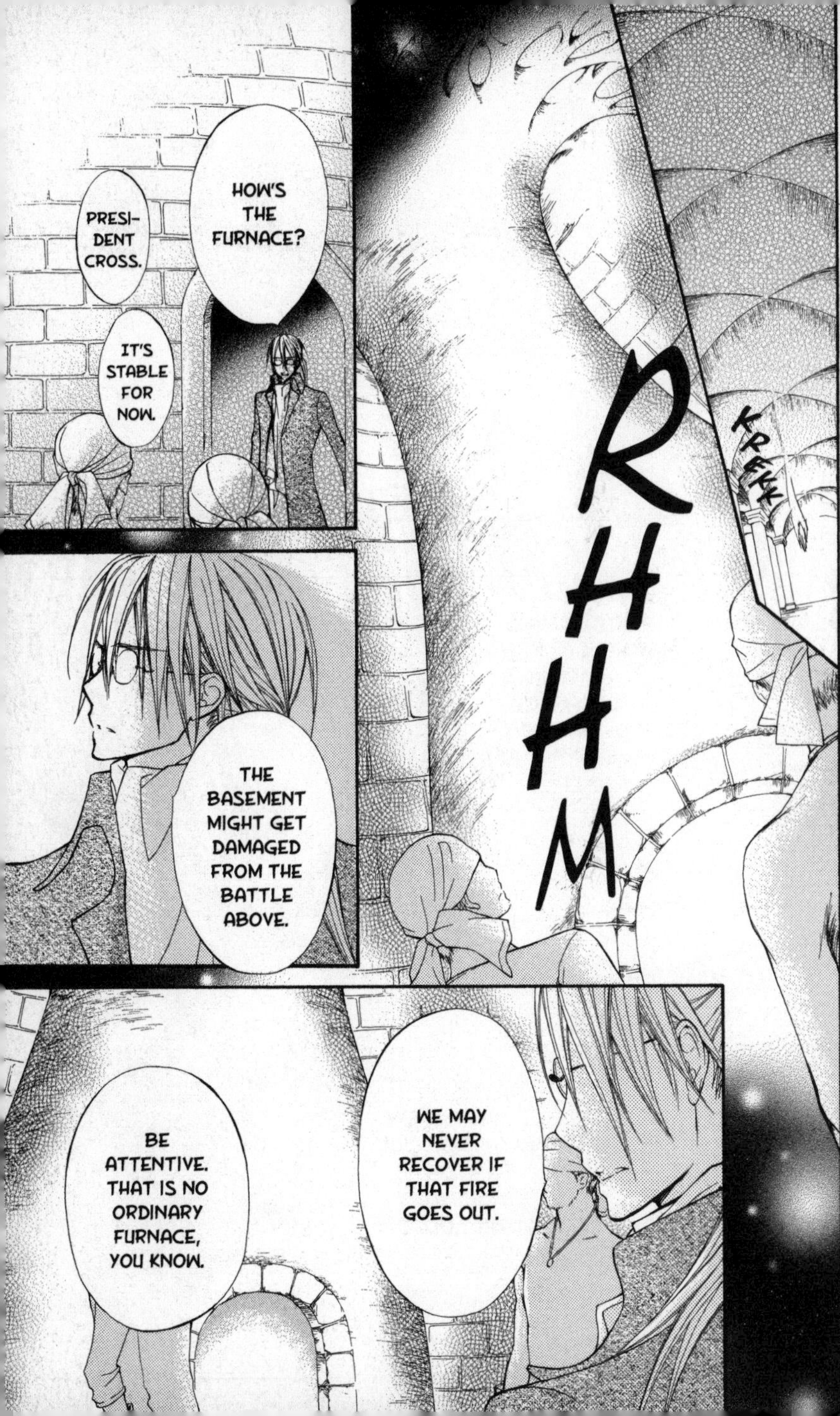
KREKK
RHHM
HOW'S THE FURNACE?
PRESI-DENT CROSS.
IT'S STABLE FOR NOW.
THE BASEMENT MIGHT GET DAMAGED FROM THE BATTLE ABOVE.
WE MAY NEVER RECOVER IF THAT FIRE GOES OUT.
BE ATTENTIVE. THAT IS NO ORDINARY FURNACE, YOU KNOW.

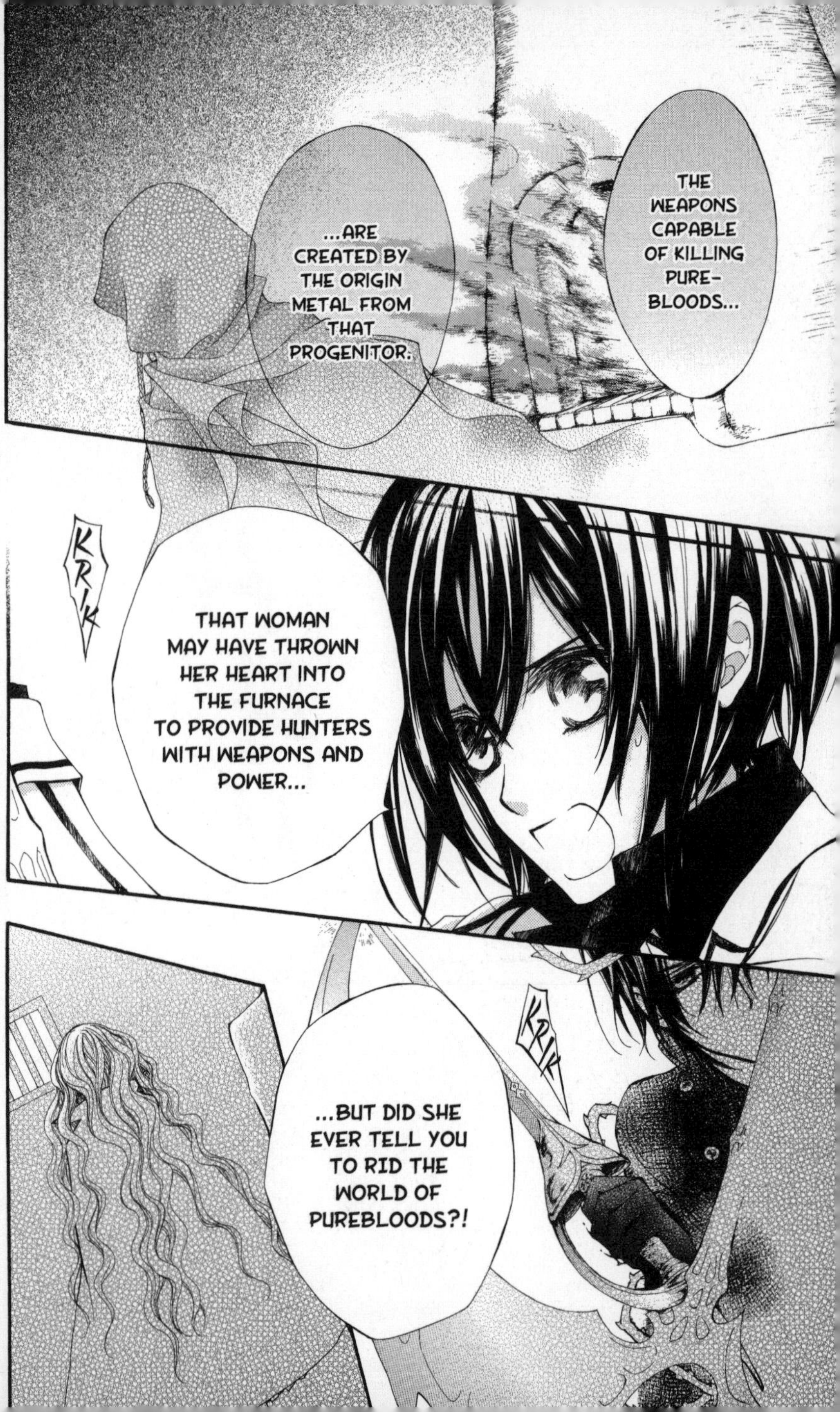
THE WEAPONS CAPABLE OF KILLING PURE-BLOODS...
...ARE CREATED BY THE ORIGIN METAL FROM THAT PROGENITOR.
THAT WOMAN MAY HAVE THROWN HER HEART INTO THE FURNACE TO PROVIDE HUNTERS WITH WEAPONS AND POWER...
KRIK
KRIK
...BUT DID SHE EVER TELL YOU TO RID THE WORLD OF PUREBLOODS?!

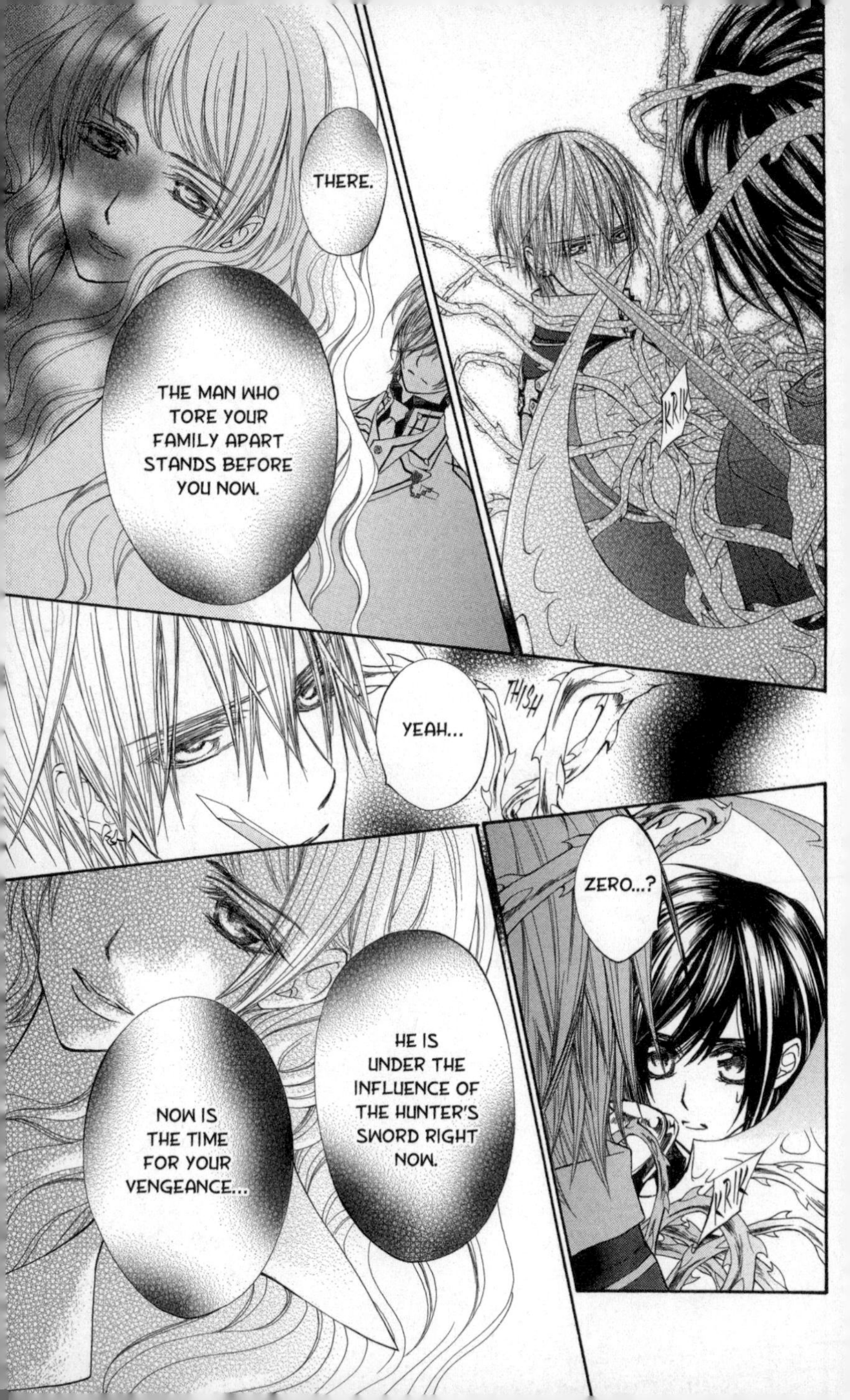
KRIK
THERE.
THE MAN WHO TORE YOUR FAMILY APART STANDS BEFORE YOU NOW.
THISH
YEAH...
ZERO...?
KRIK
HE IS UNDER THE INFLUENCE OF THE HUNTER'S SWORD RIGHT NOW.
NOW IS THE TIME FOR YOUR VENGEANCE...

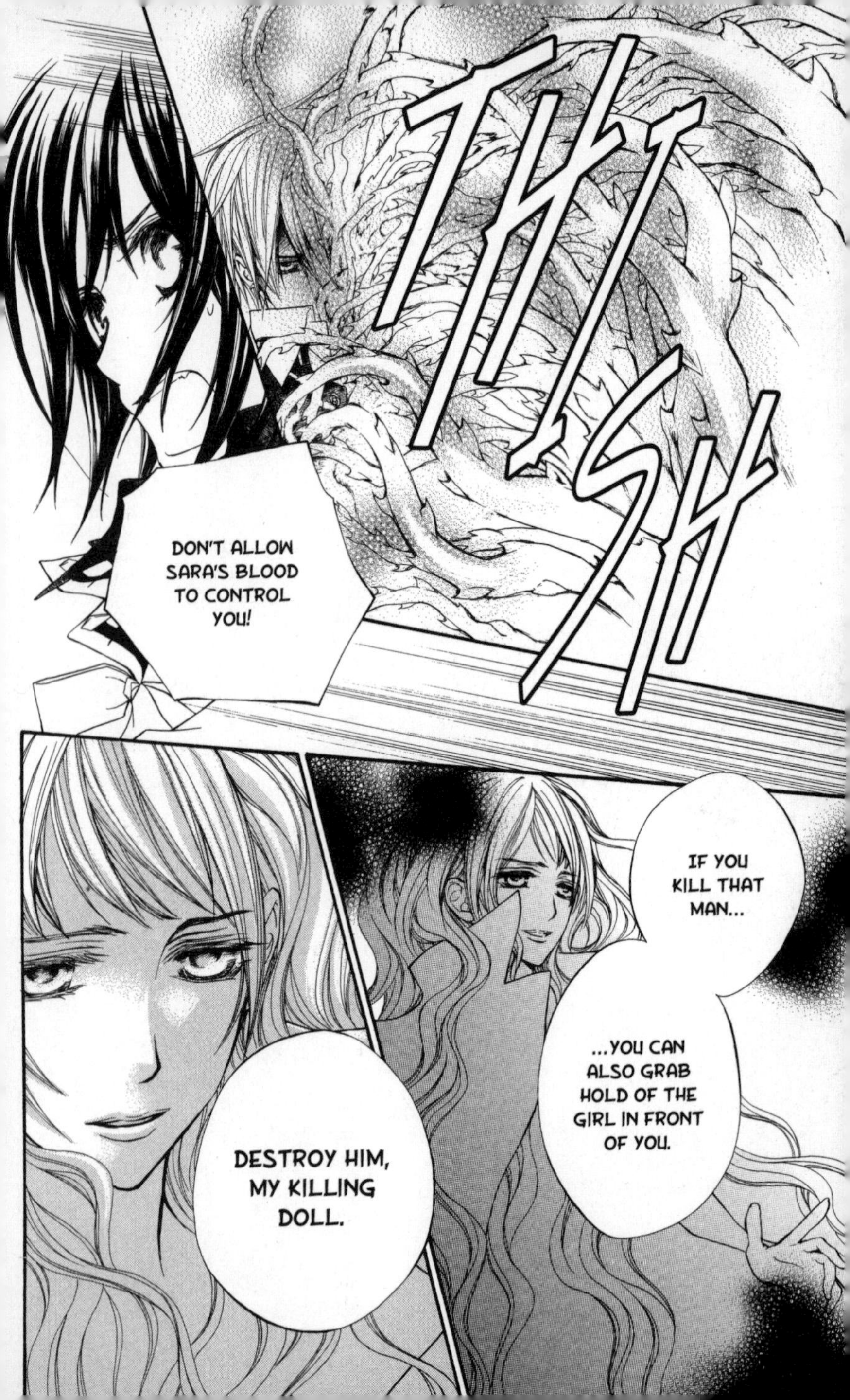
THISH
DON'T ALLOW SARA'S BLOOD TO CONTROL YOU!
IF YOU KILL THAT MAN...
...YOU CAN ALSO GRAB HOLD OF THE GIRL IN FRONT OF YOU.
DESTROY HIM, MY KILLING DOLL.

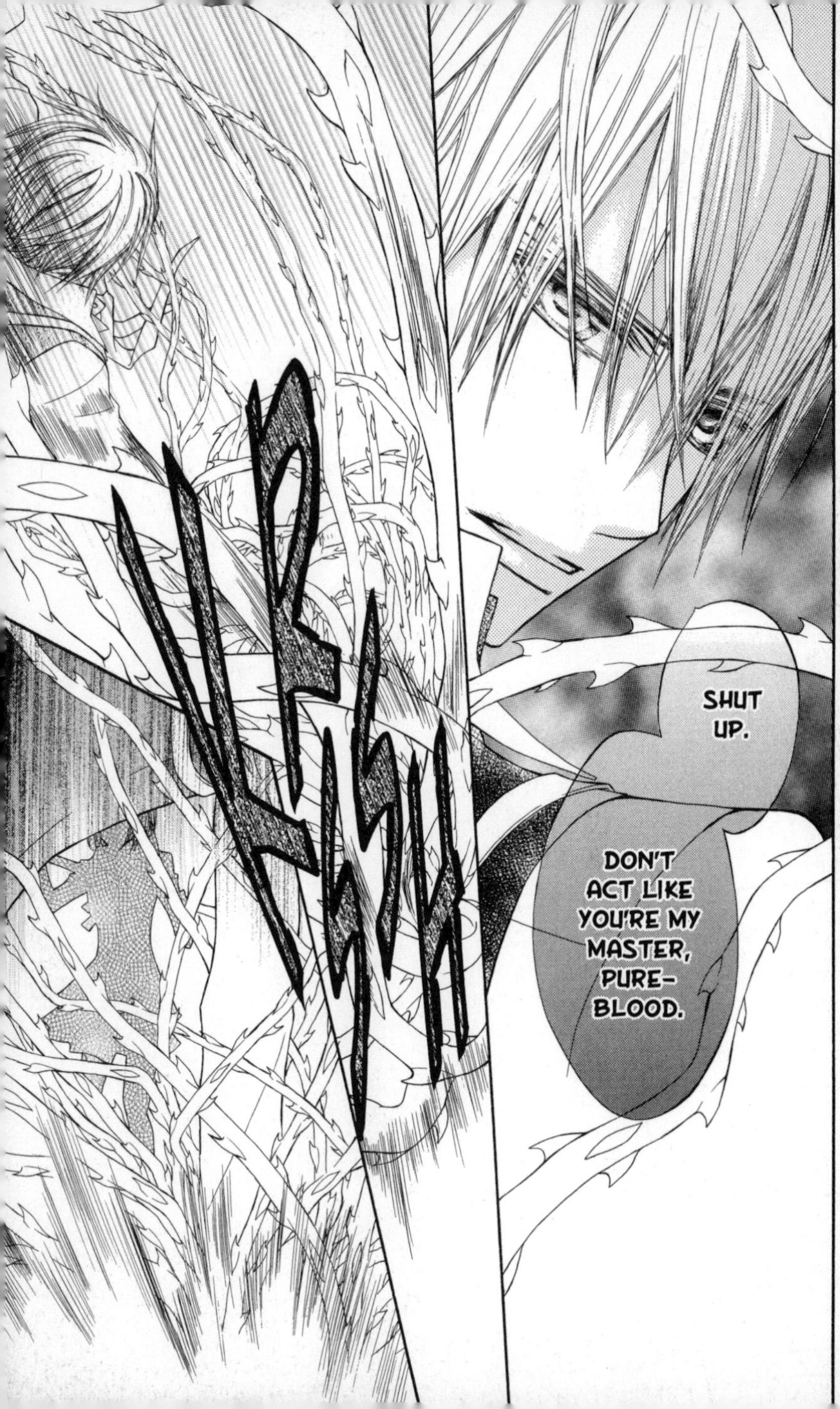
SHUT UP.
DON'T ACT LIKE YOU'RE MY MASTER, PURE-BLOOD.

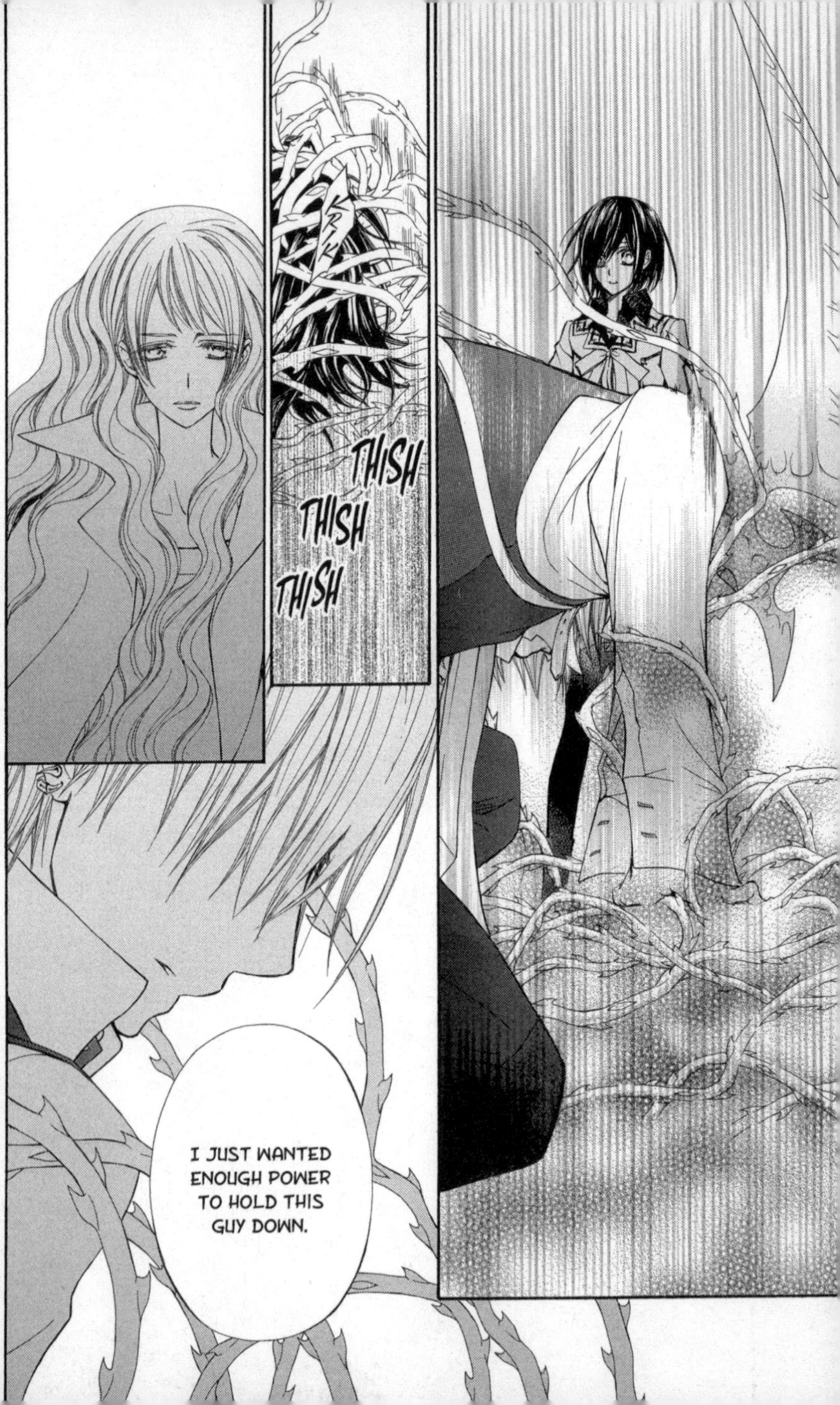
KRIK
THISH
THISH
THISH
I JUST WANTED ENOUGH POWER TO HOLD THIS GUY DOWN.

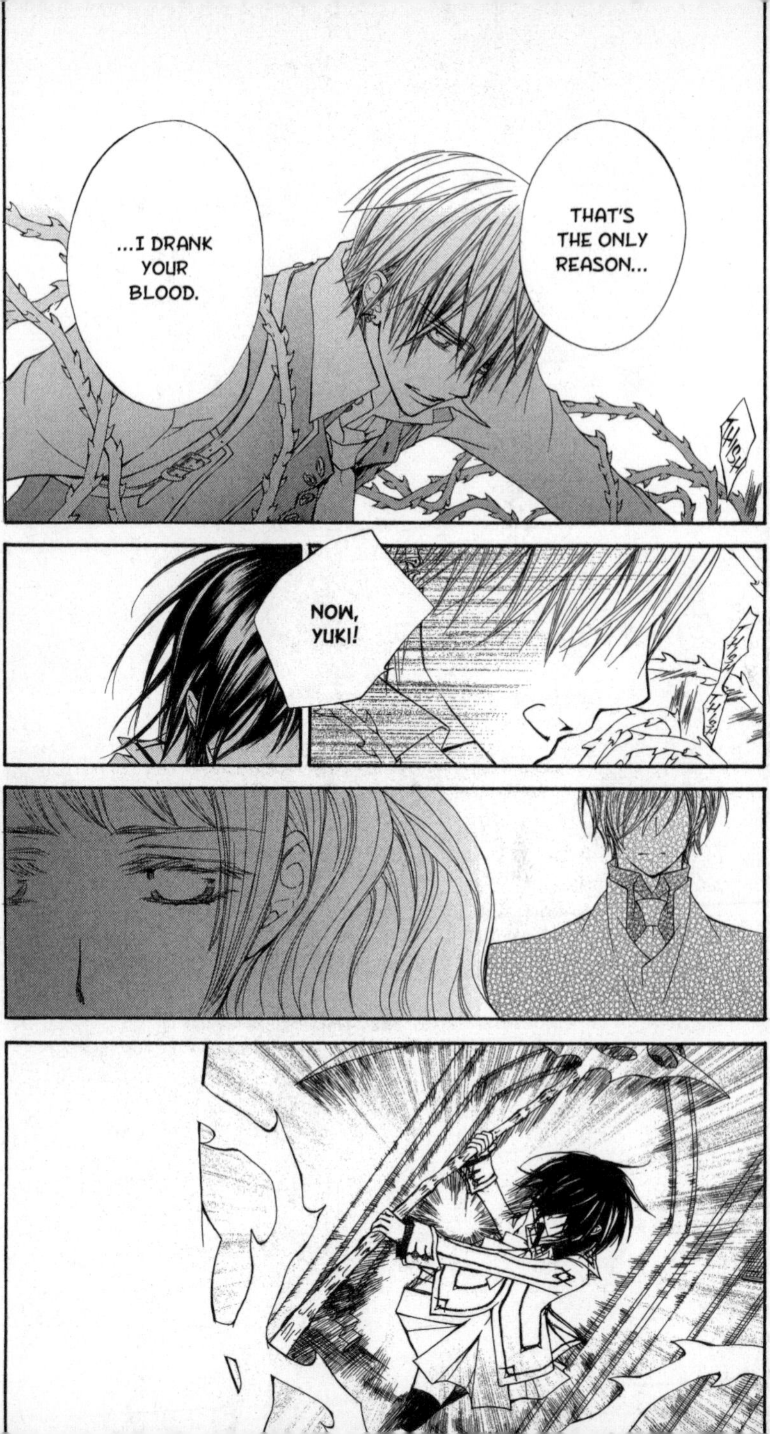
THAT'S THE ONLY REASON...
...I DRANK YOUR BLOOD.
THISH
THISH
THISH
NOW, YUKI!

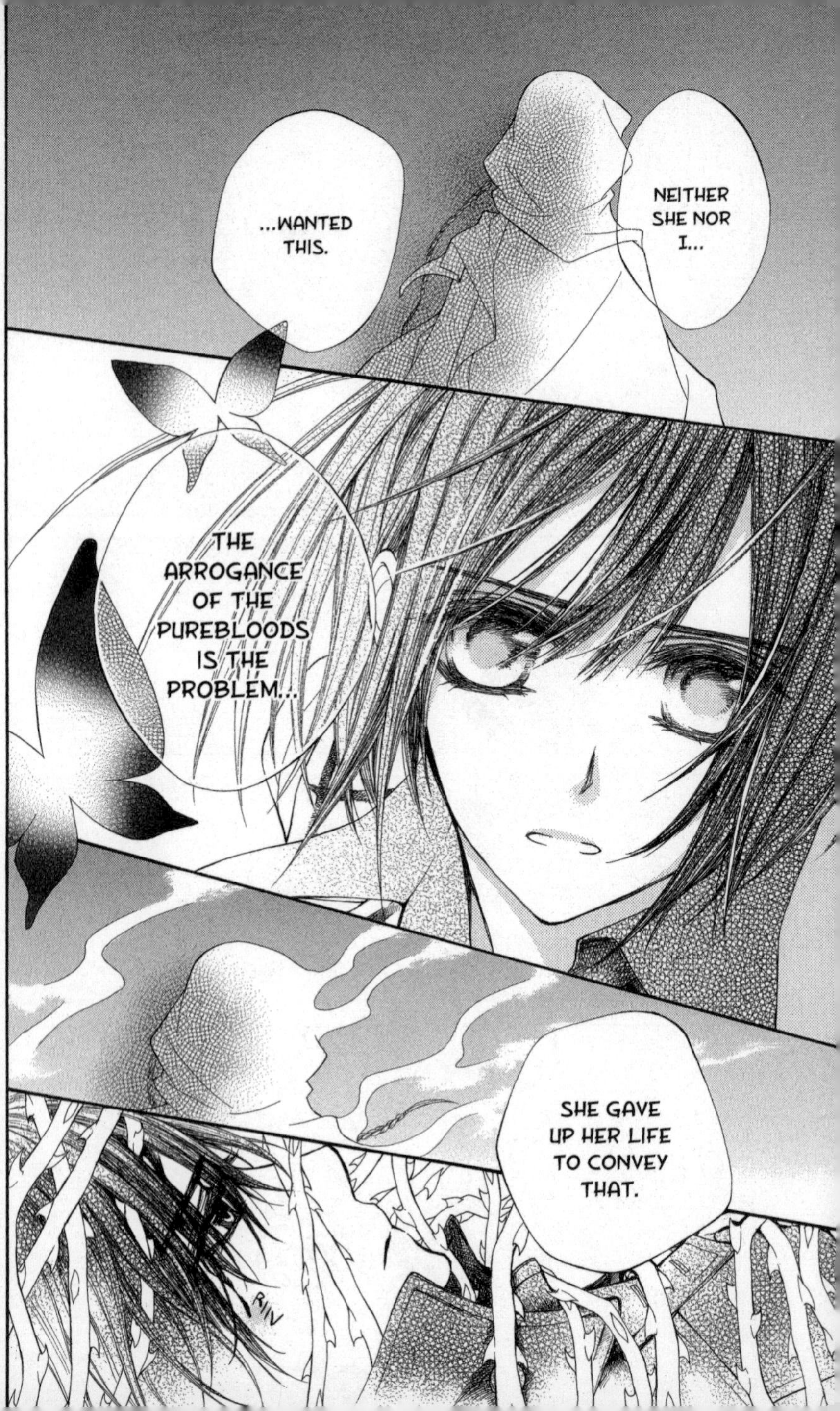
NEITHER SHE NOR I...
...WANTED THIS.
THE ARROGANCE OF THE PUREBLOODS IS THE PROBLEM...
SHE GAVE UP HER LIFE TO CONVEY THAT.

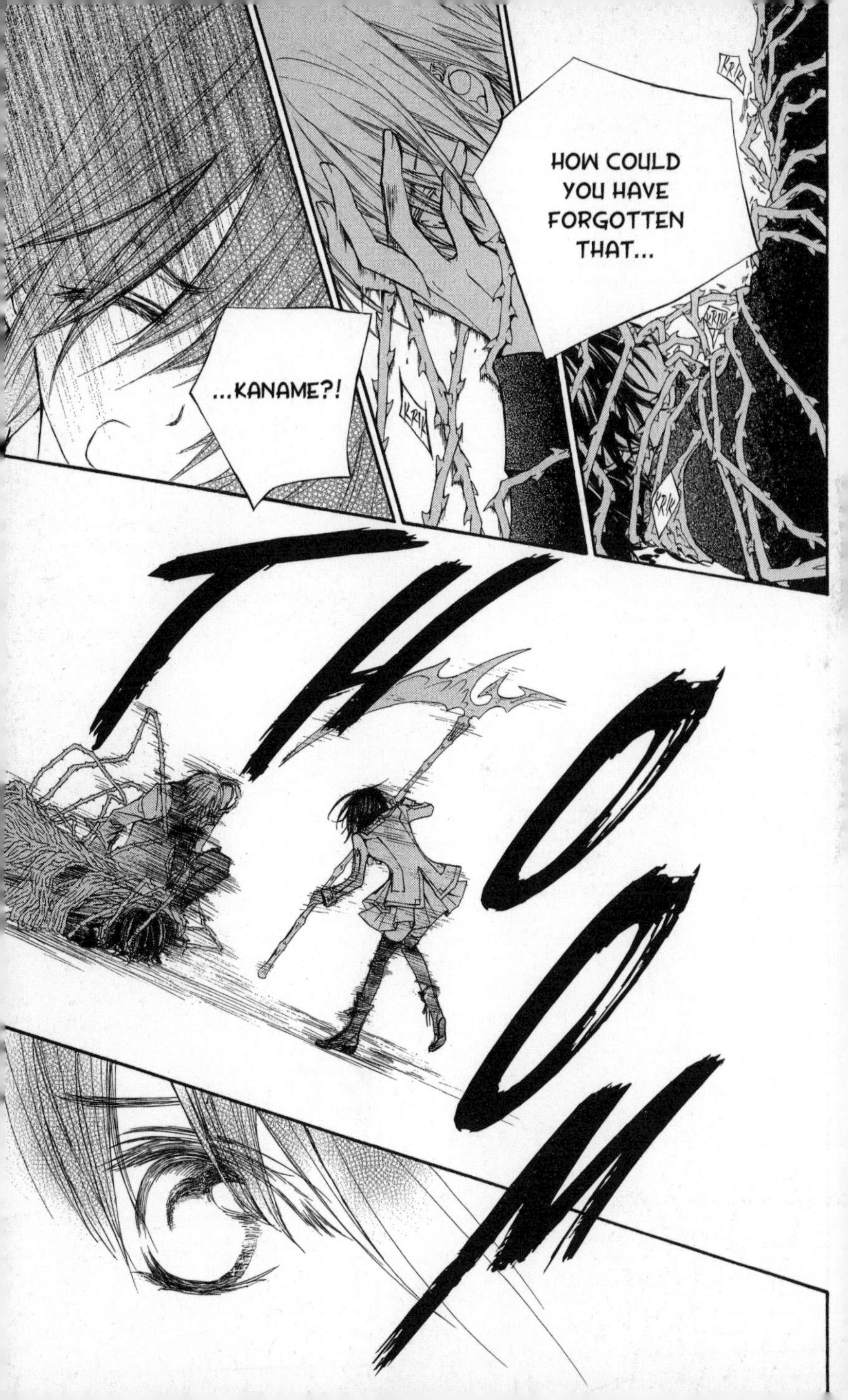
KRIK
HOW COULD YOU HAVE FORGOTTEN THAT...
KRIK
KRIK
KRIK
...KANAME?!
THOOM

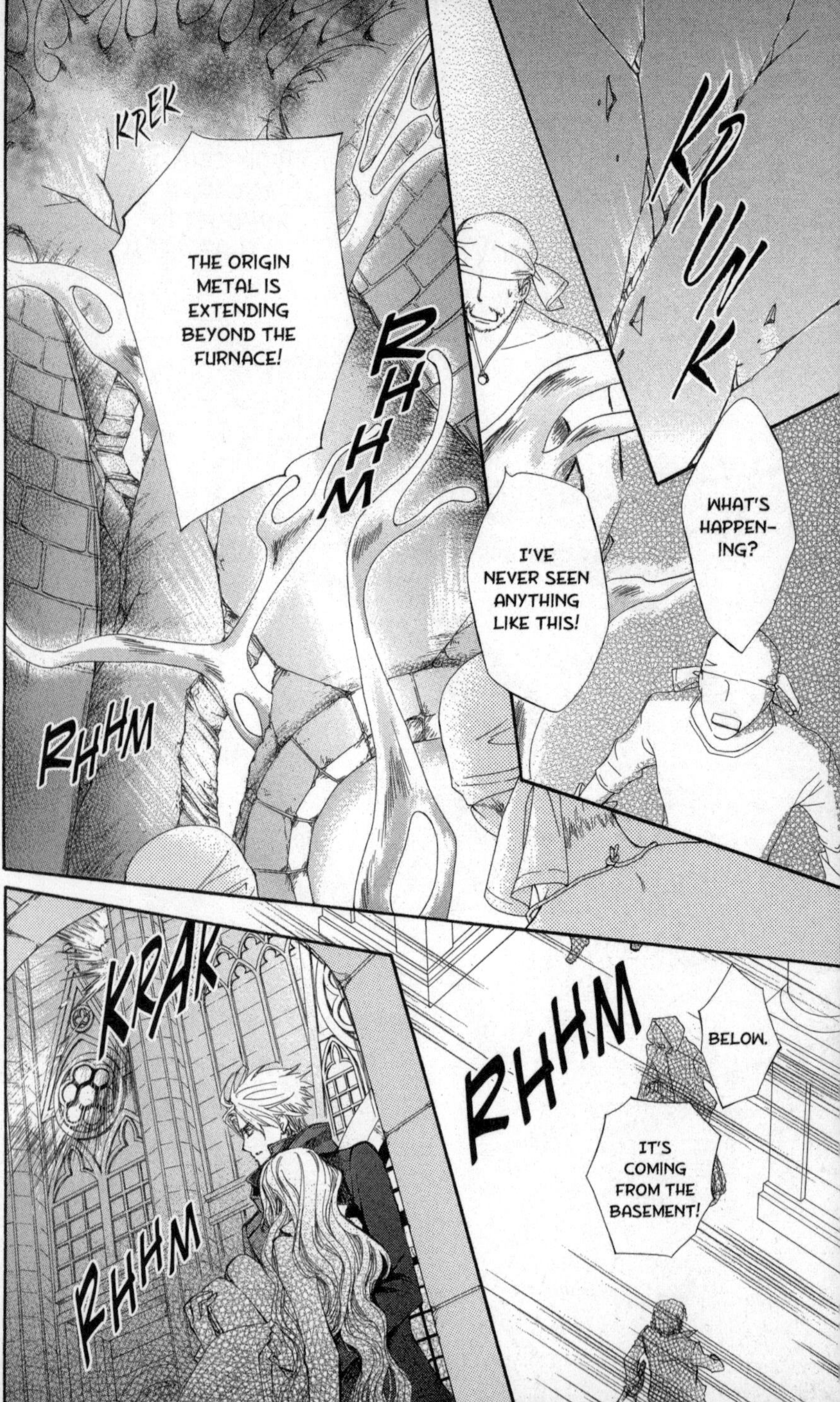
KRUNK
WHAT'S HAPPEN-ING?
I'VE NEVER SEEN ANYTHING LIKE THIS!
KREK
THE ORIGIN METAL IS EXTENDING BEYOND THE FURNACE!
RHHM
RHHM
RHHM
BELOW.
IT'S COMING FROM THE BASEMENT!
KRAK
RHHM

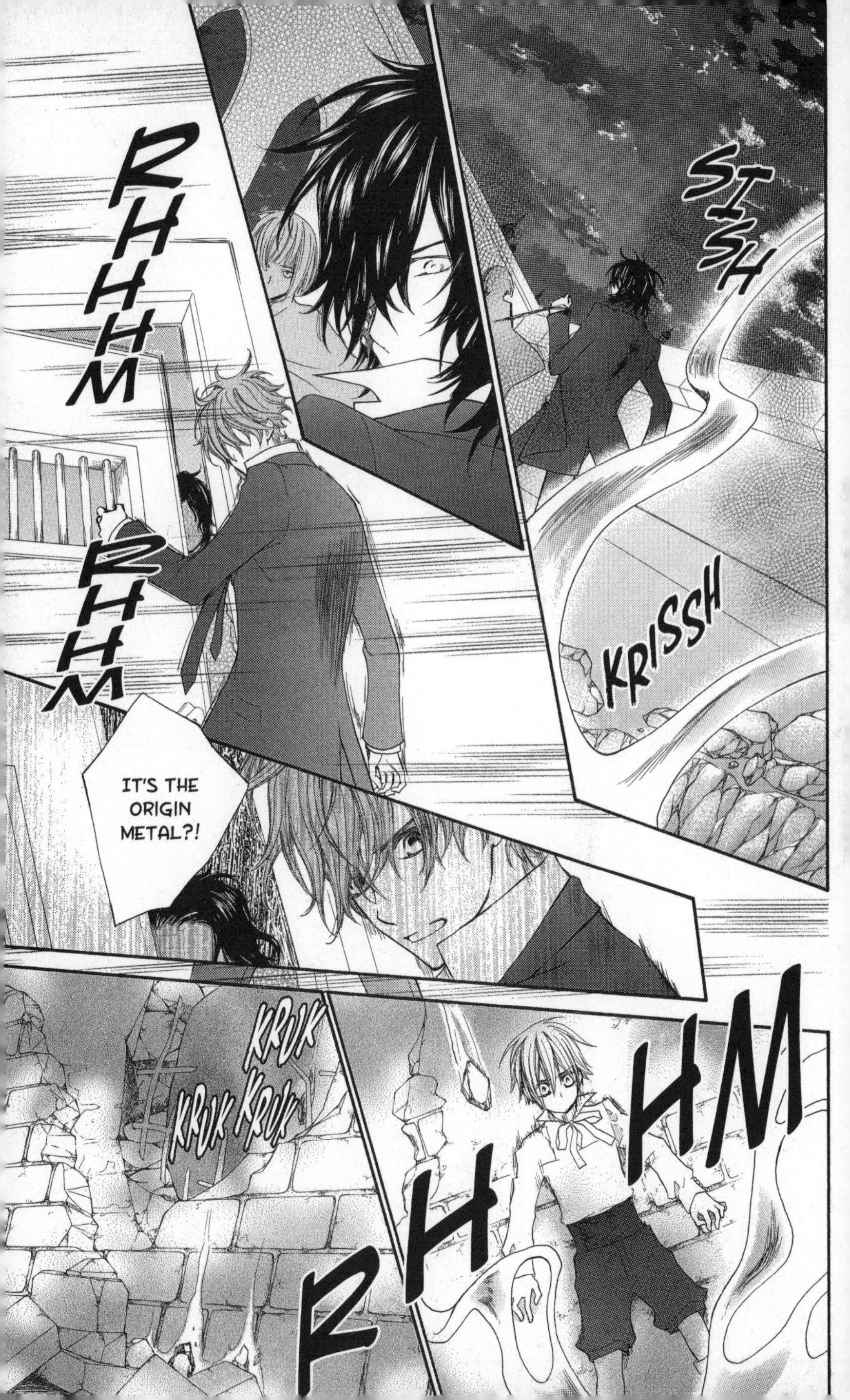
SISH
KRISSH
RHHHM
RHHM
IT'S THE ORIGIN METAL?!
RHHM
KRUK KRUK
KRUK KRUK

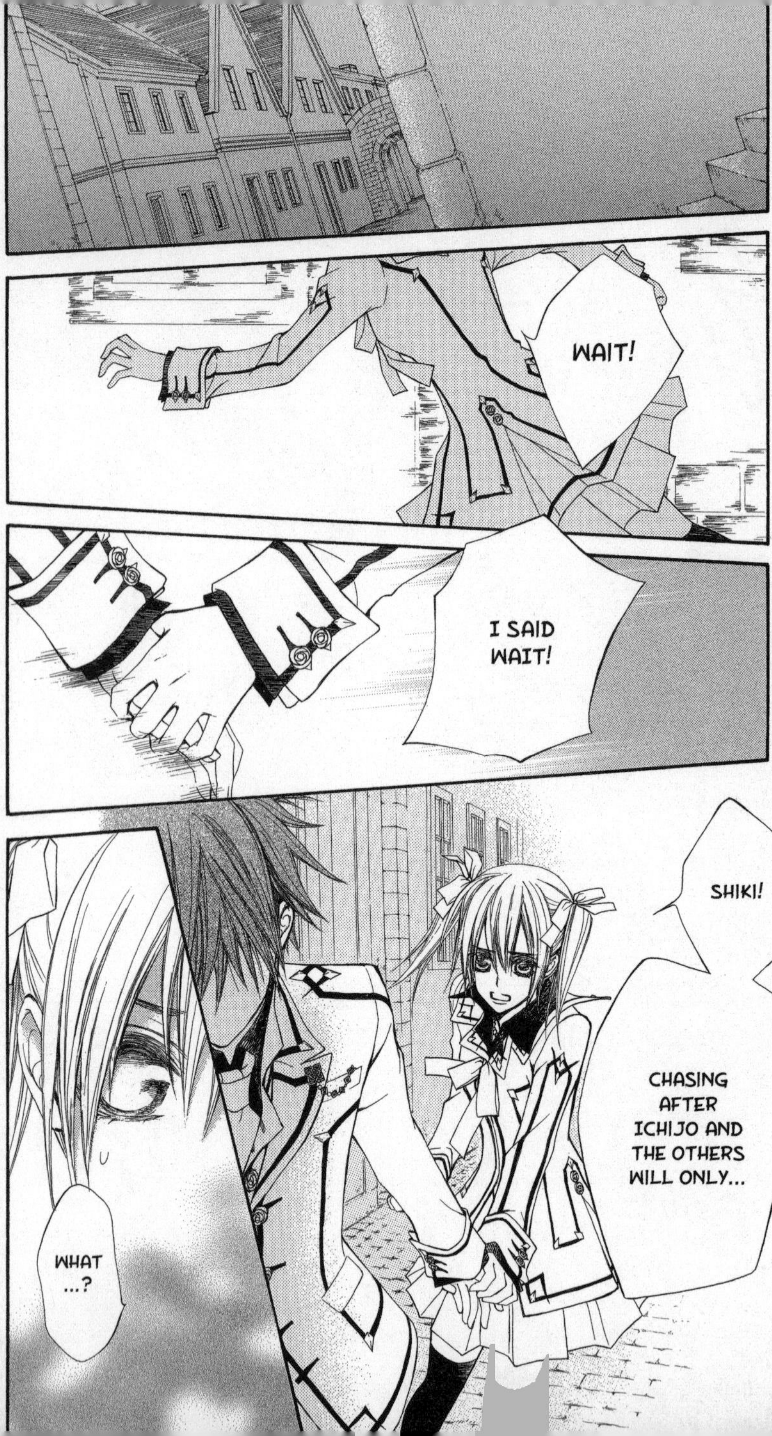
WAIT!
I SAID WAIT!
SHIKI!
CHASING AFTER ICHIJO AND THE OTHERS WILL ONLY...
WHAT ...?

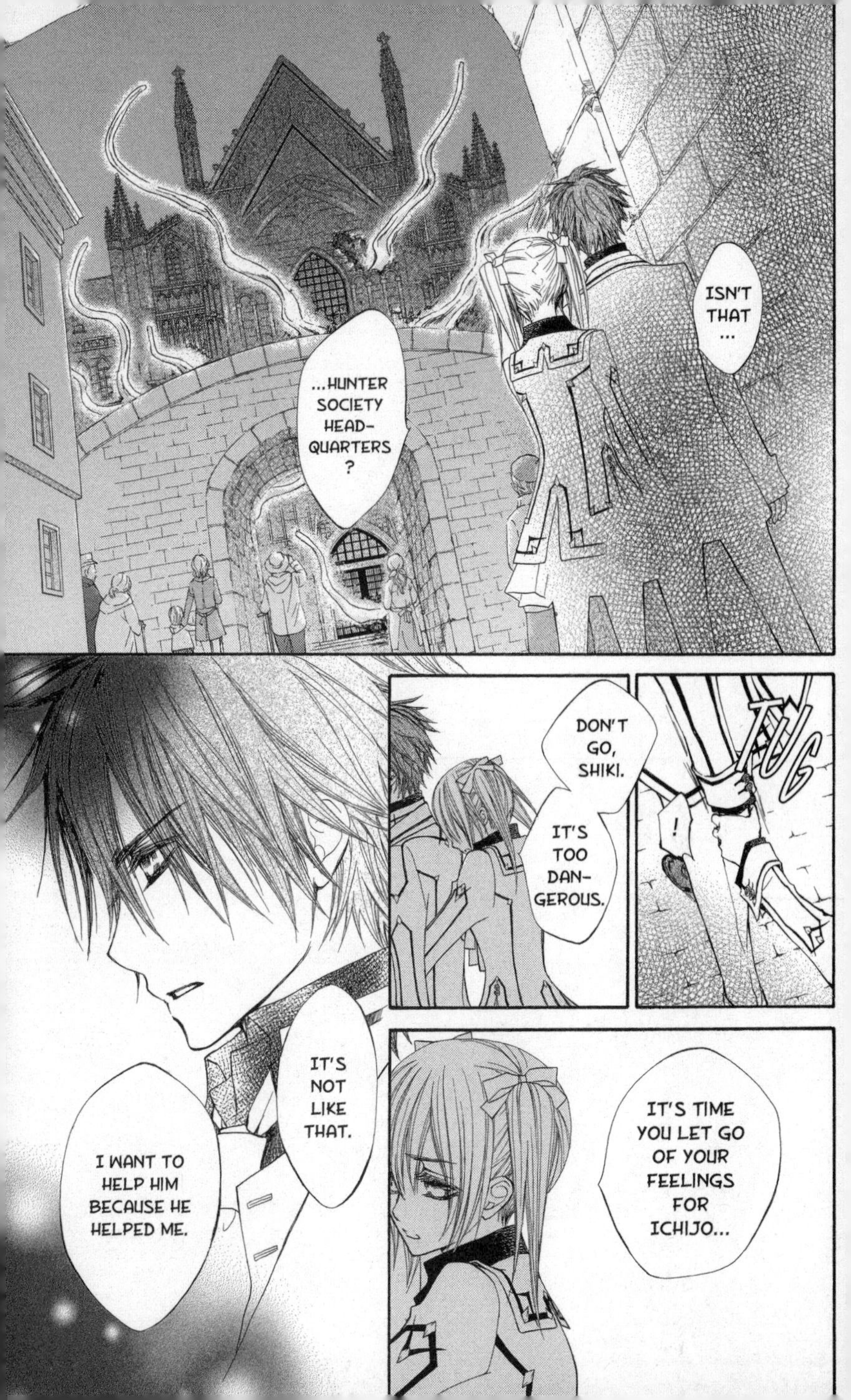
ISN'T THAT...
...HUNTER SOCIETY HEADQUARTERS?
TUG
!
DON'T GO, SHIKI.
IT'S TOO DANGEROUS.
IT'S TIME YOU LET GO OF YOUR FEELINGS FOR ICHIJO...
IT'S NOT LIKE THAT.
I WANT TO HELP HIM BECAUSE HE HELPED ME.

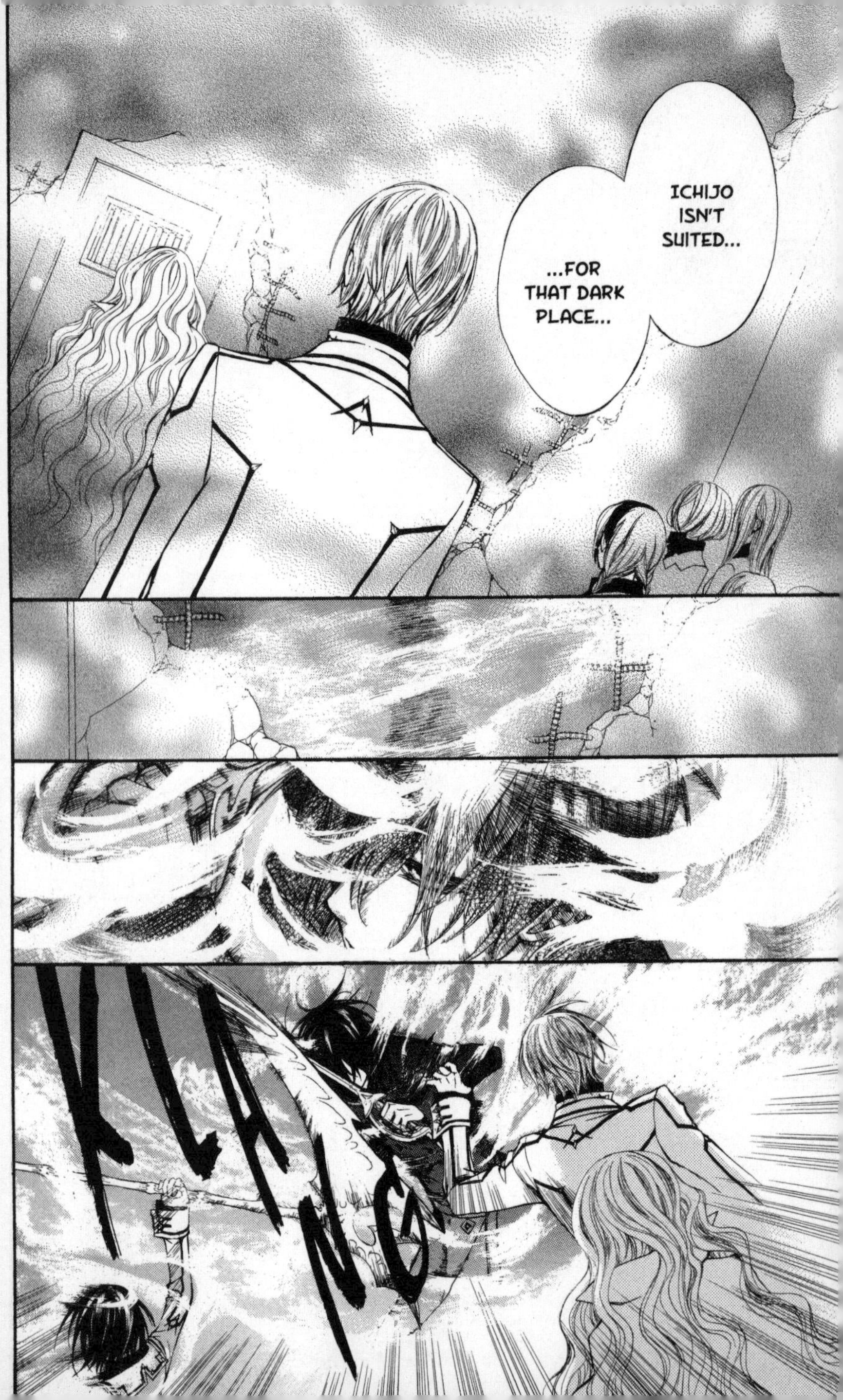
ICHIJO ISN'T SUITED...
...FOR THAT DARK PLACE...

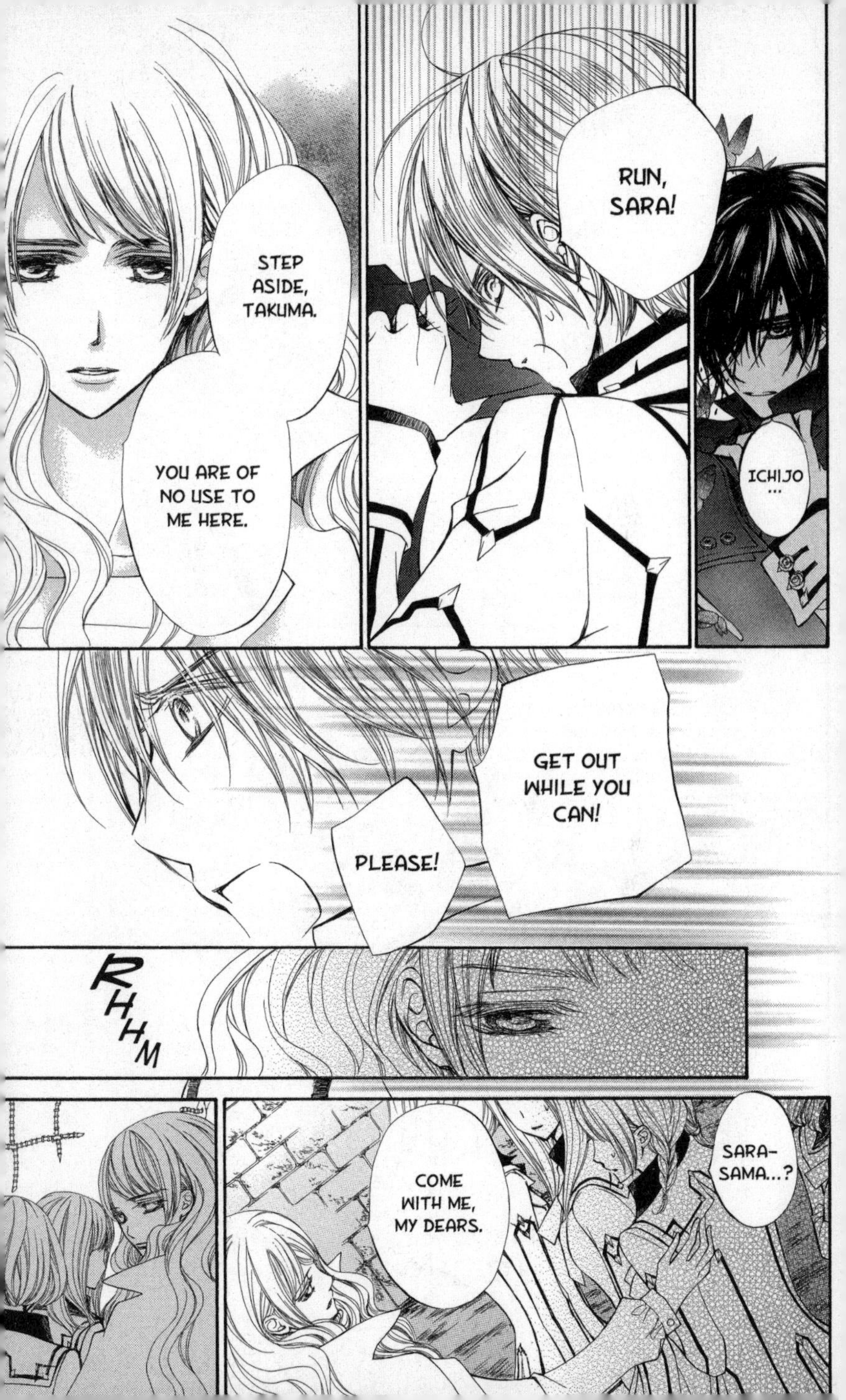
ICHIJO ...
RUN, SARA!
STEP ASIDE, TAKUMA.
YOU ARE OF NO USE TO ME HERE.
GET OUT WHILE YOU CAN!
PLEASE!
RHHM
SARA-SAMA...?
COME WITH ME, MY DEARS.

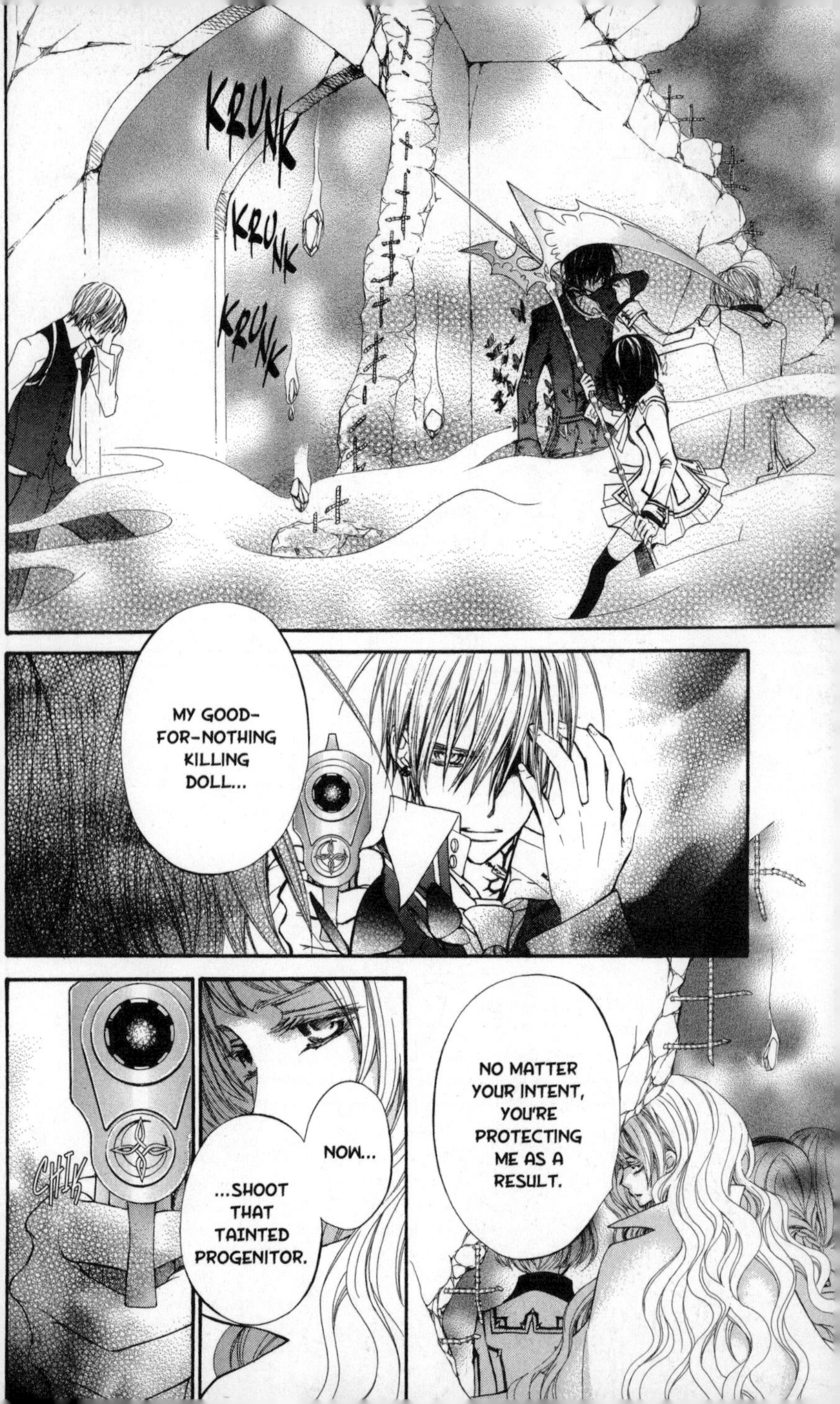
KRUNK
KRUNK
KRUNK
MY GOOD-FOR-NOTHING KILLING DOLL...
NO MATTER YOUR INTENT, YOU'RE PROTECTING ME AS A RESULT.
NOW...
...SHOOT THAT TAINTED PROGENITOR.
CHIK

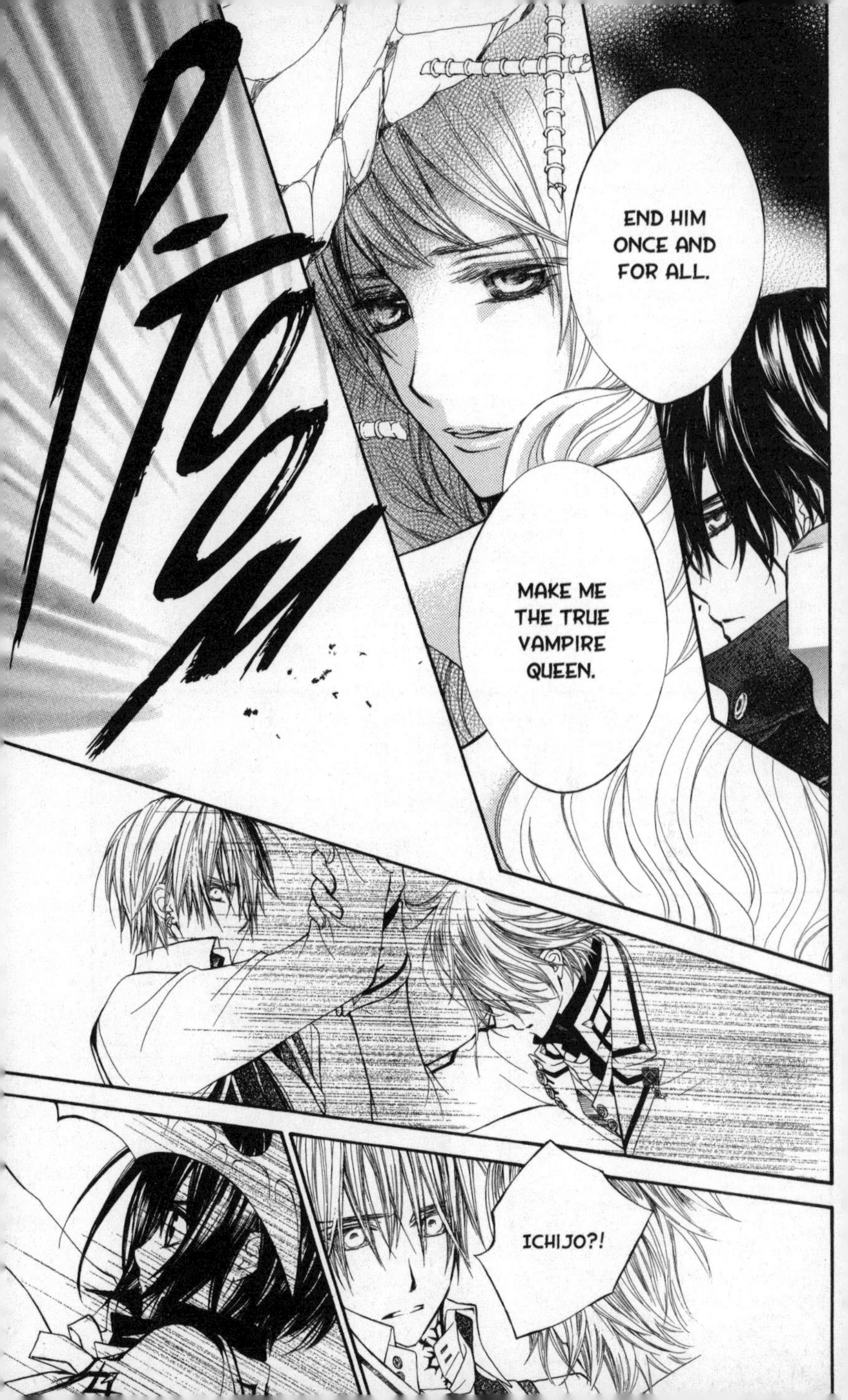
END HIM ONCE AND FOR ALL.
MAKE ME THE TRUE VAMPIRE QUEEN.
ICHIJO?!

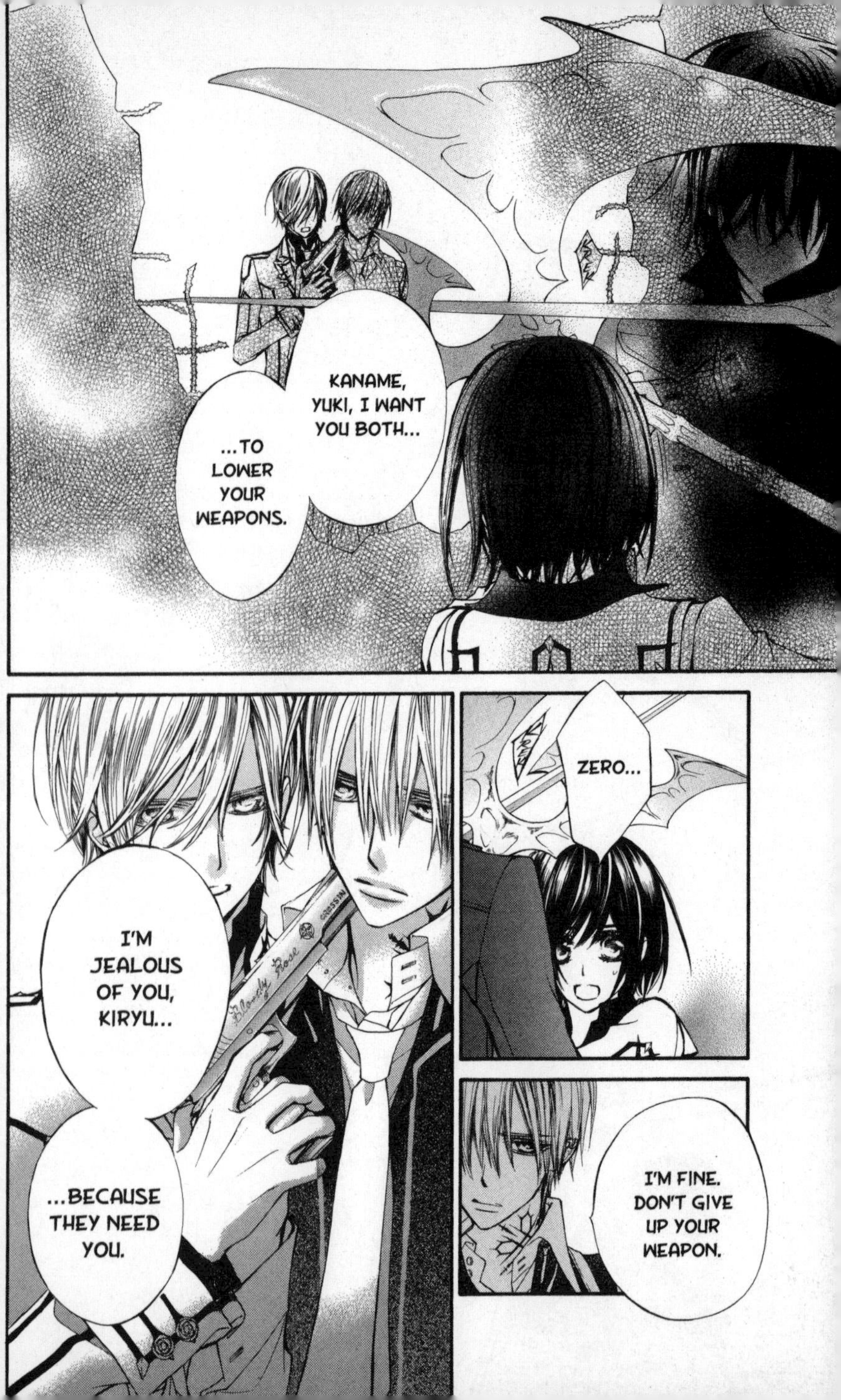
KANAME, YUKI, I WANT YOU BOTH...
...TO LOWER YOUR WEAPONS.
ZERO...
I'M FINE. DON'T GIVE UP YOUR WEAPON.
I'M JEALOUS OF YOU, KIRYU...
...BECAUSE THEY NEED YOU.

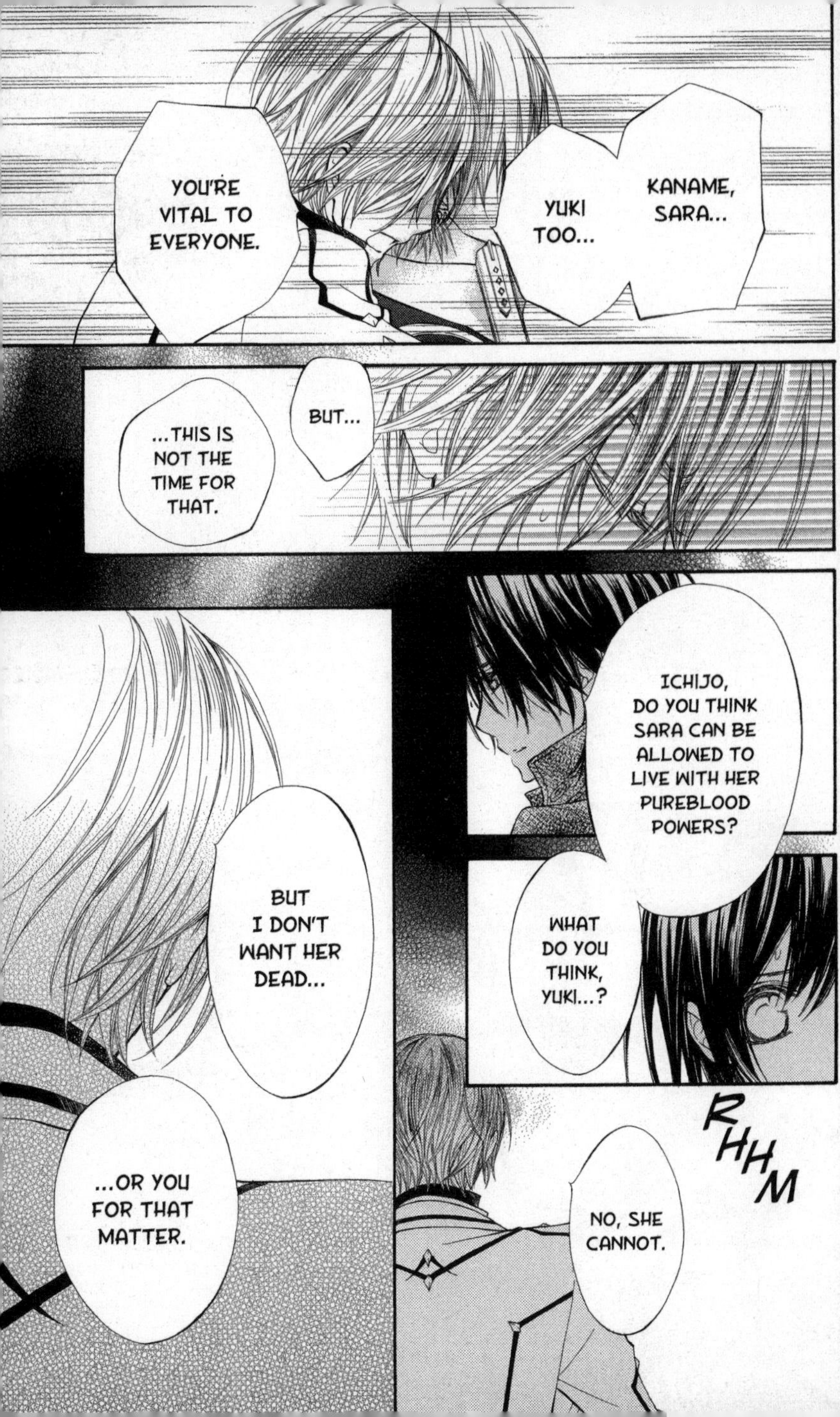
KANAME, SARA...
YUKI TOO...
YOU'RE VITAL TO EVERYONE.
BUT...
...THIS IS NOT THE TIME FOR THAT.
ICHIJO, DO YOU THINK SARA CAN BE ALLOWED TO LIVE WITH HER PUREBLOOD POWERS?
WHAT DO YOU THINK, YUKI...?
RHHM
NO, SHE CANNOT.
BUT I DON'T WANT HER DEAD...
...OR YOU FOR THAT MATTER.

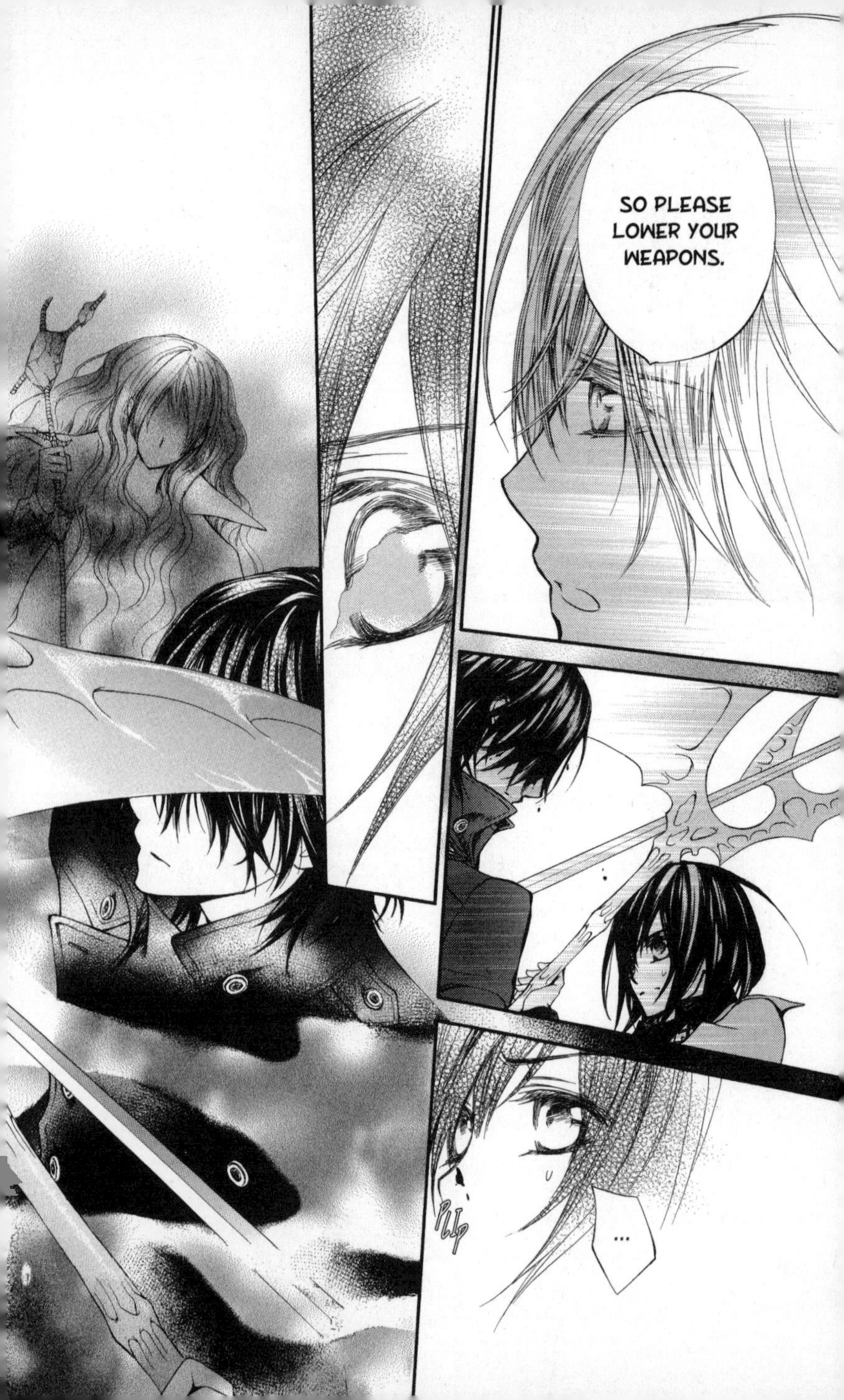
SO PLEASE LOWER YOUR WEAPONS.
PLIP
...

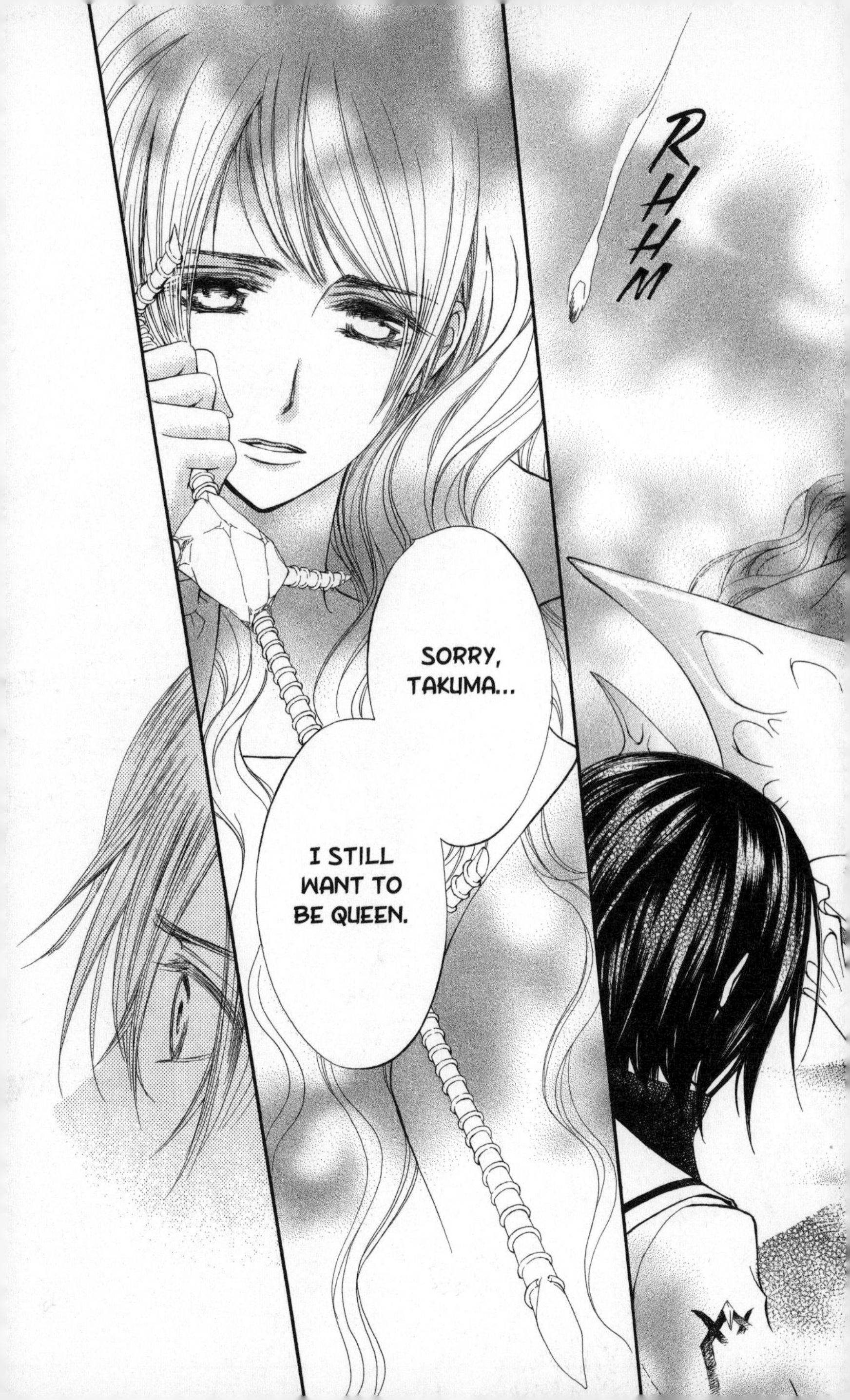
RHHM
SORRY, TAKUMA...
I STILL WANT TO BE QUEEN.

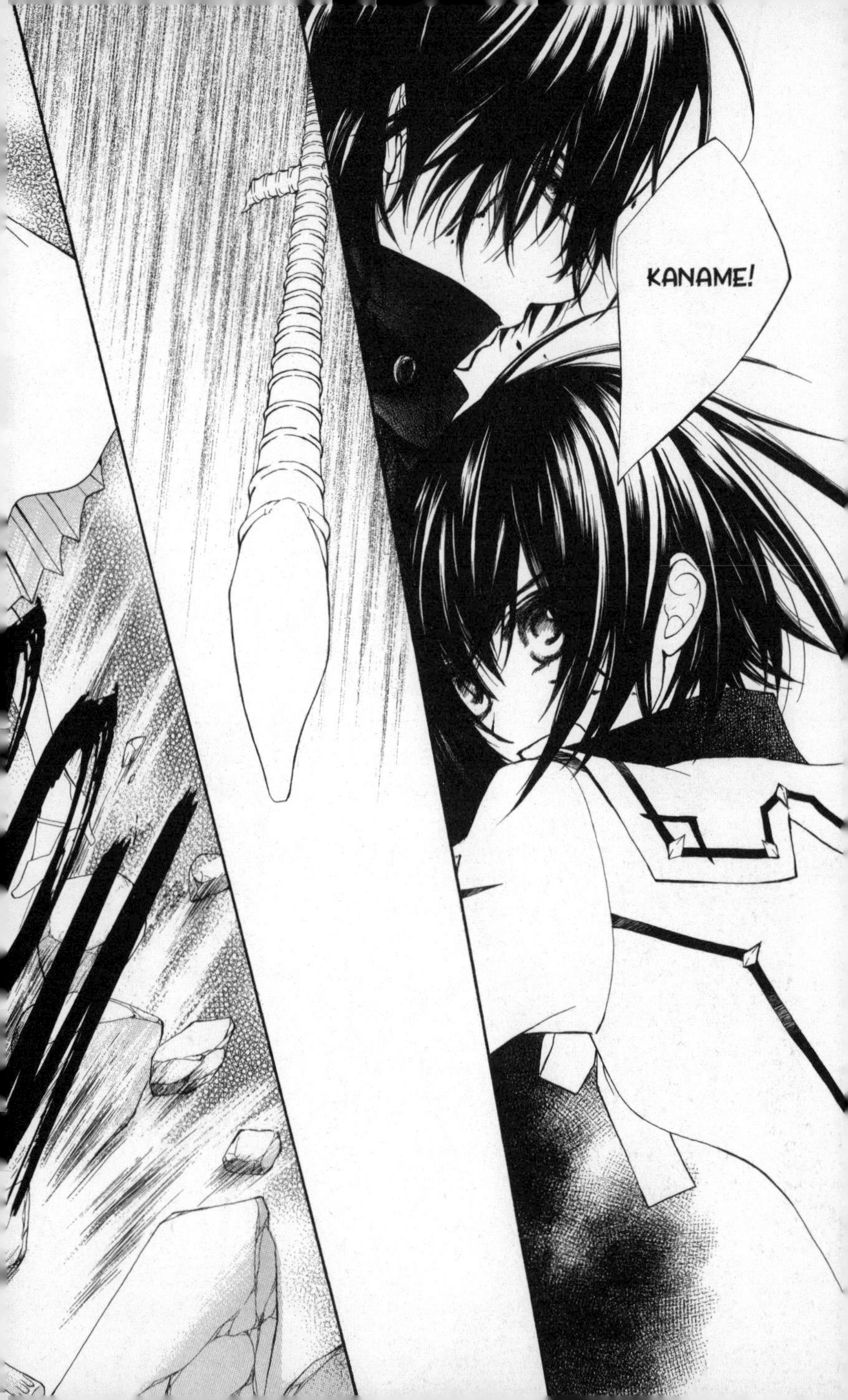
KANAME!

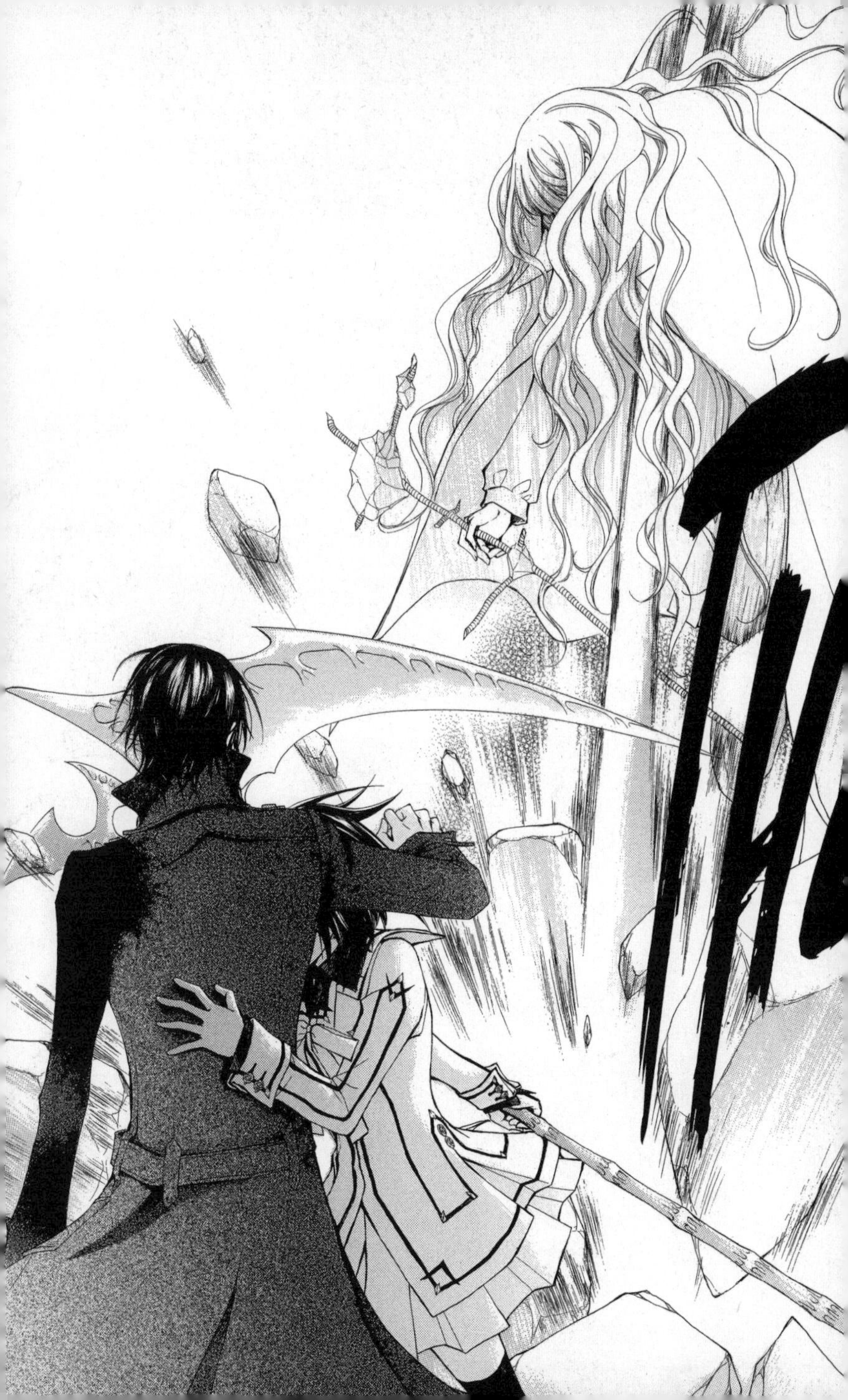
TH

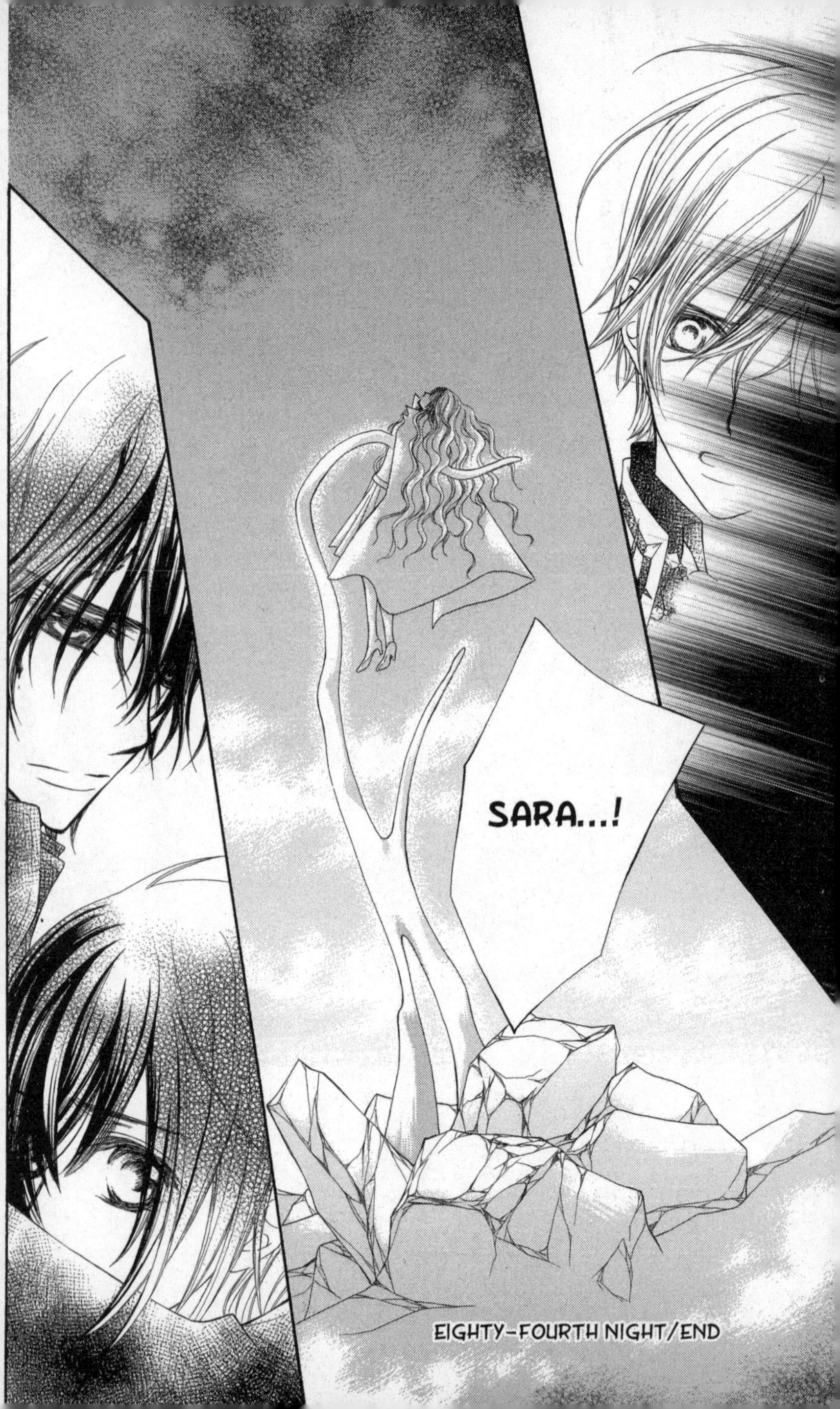
SARA...!
EIGHTY-FOURTH NIGHT/END

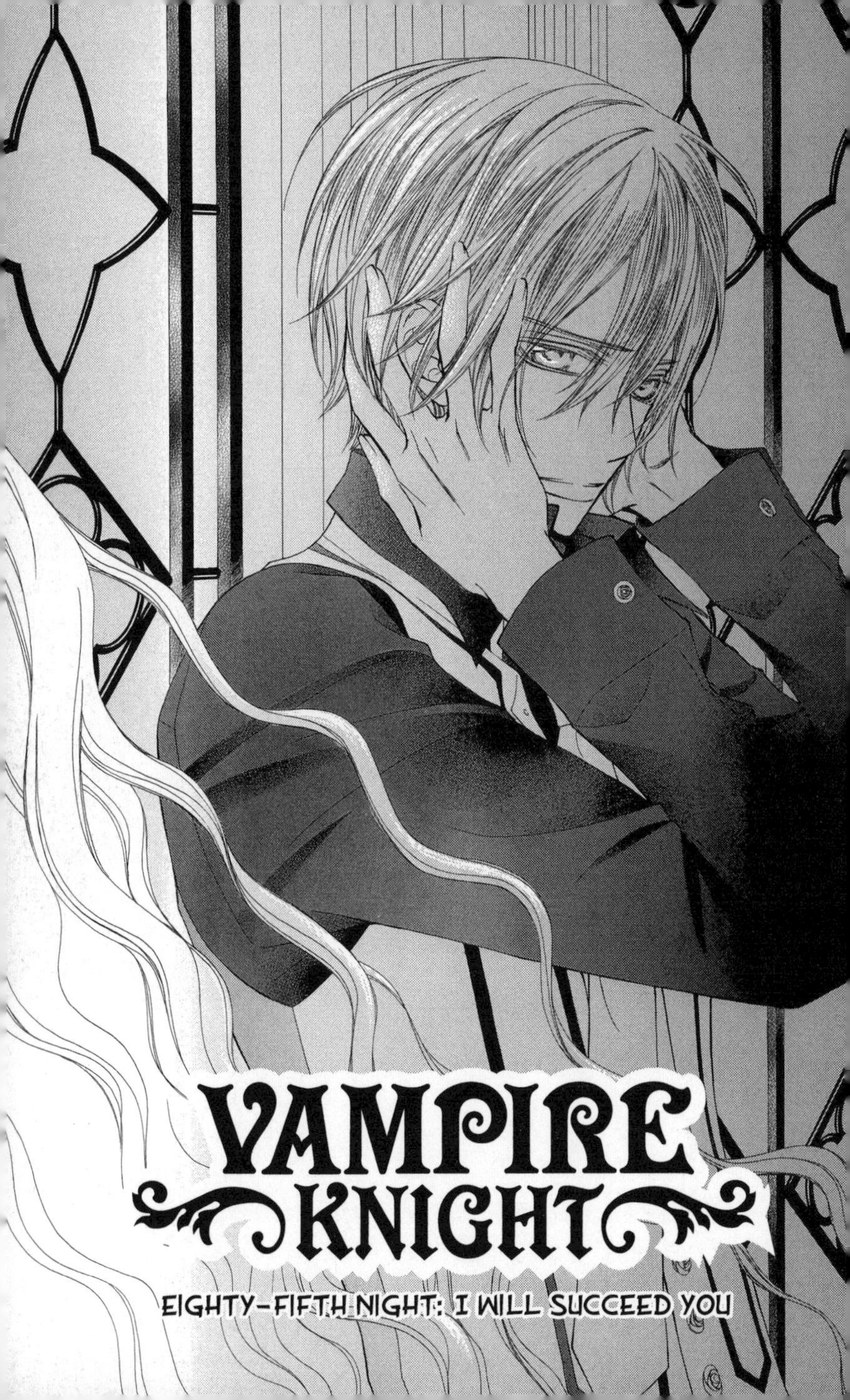
VAMPIRE KNIGHT
EIGHTY-FIFTH NIGHT: I WILL SUCCEED YOU

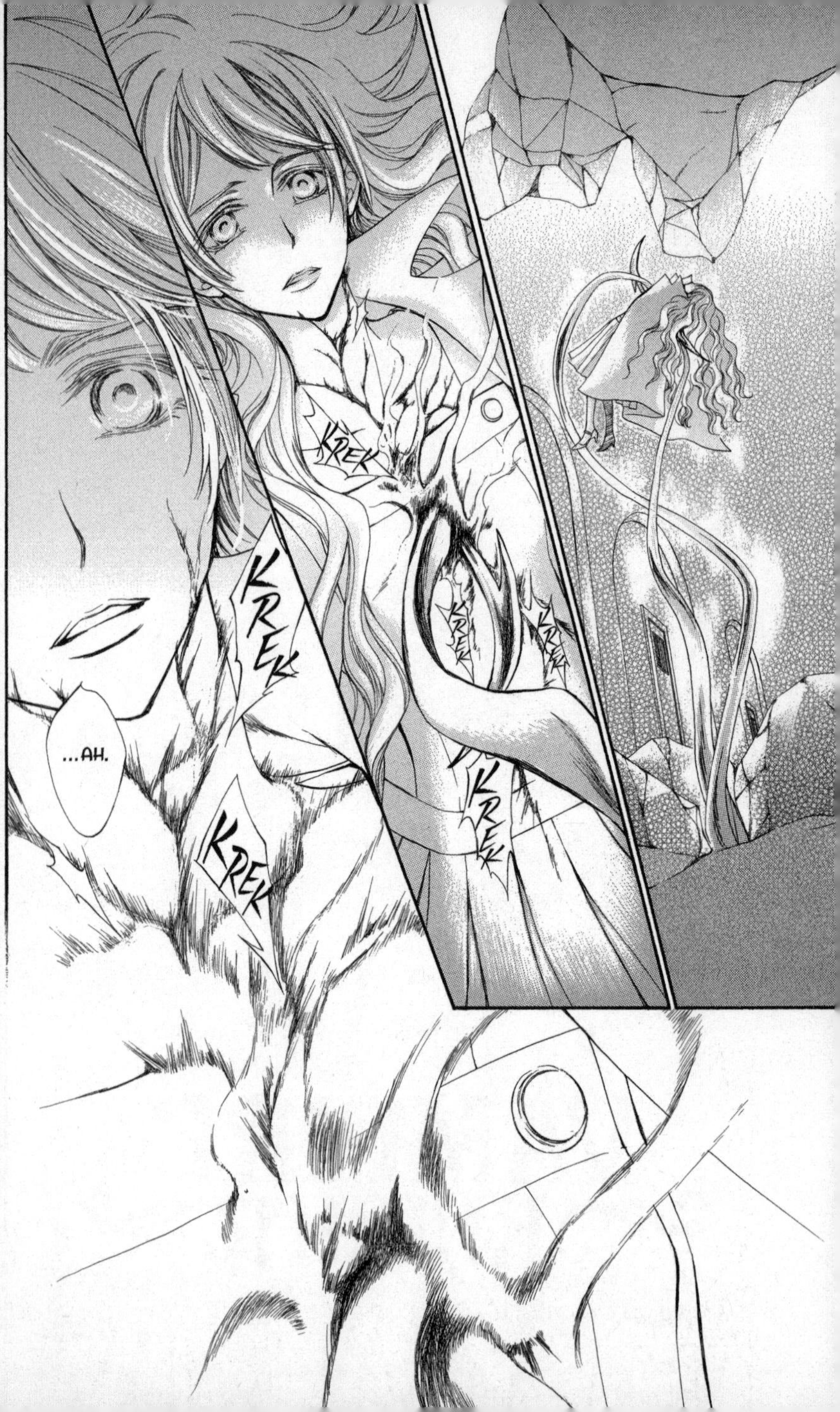
KREK
KREK
KREK
KREK
KREK
KREK
...AH.

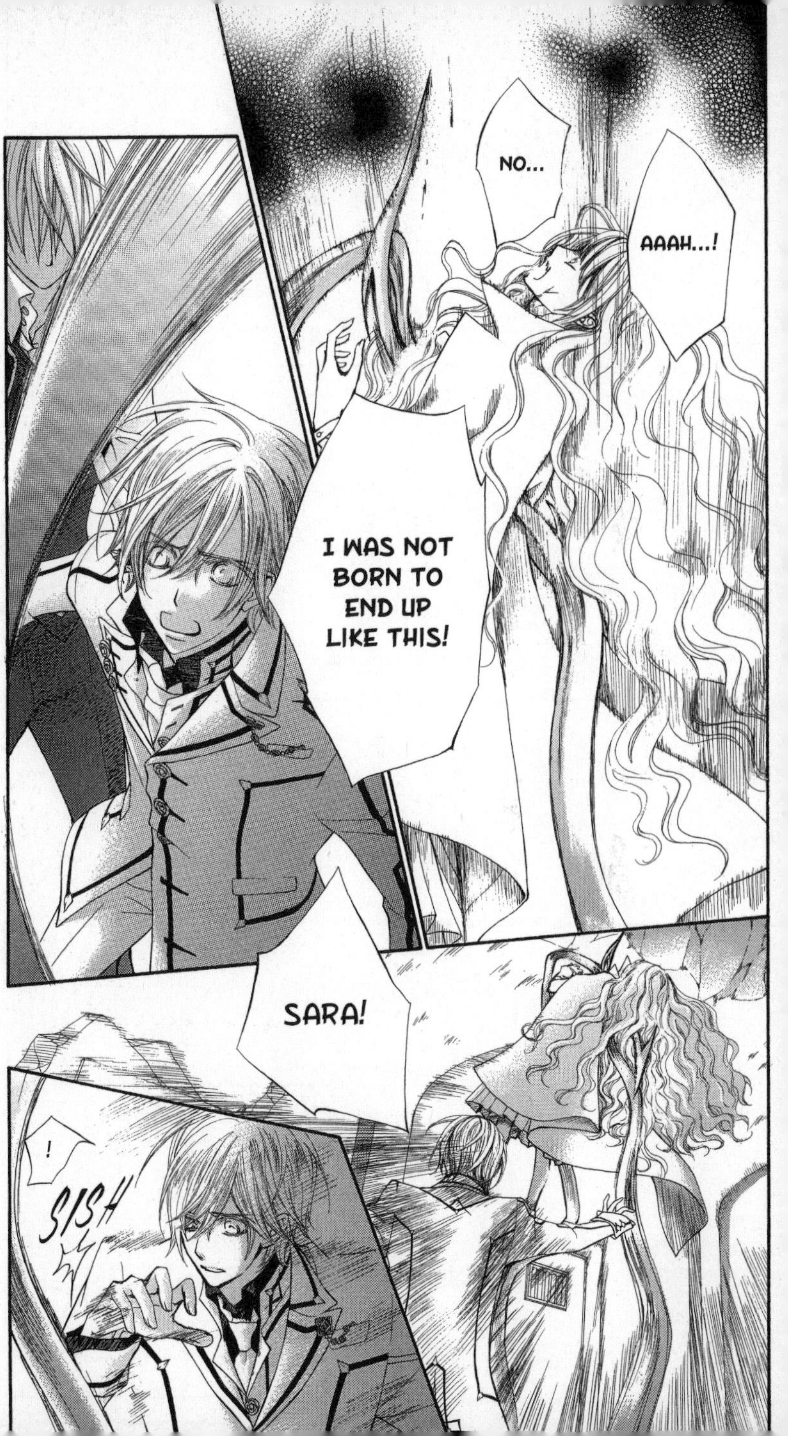
NO...
AAAH...!
I WAS NOT BORN TO END UP LIKE THIS!
SARA!
!
SISH

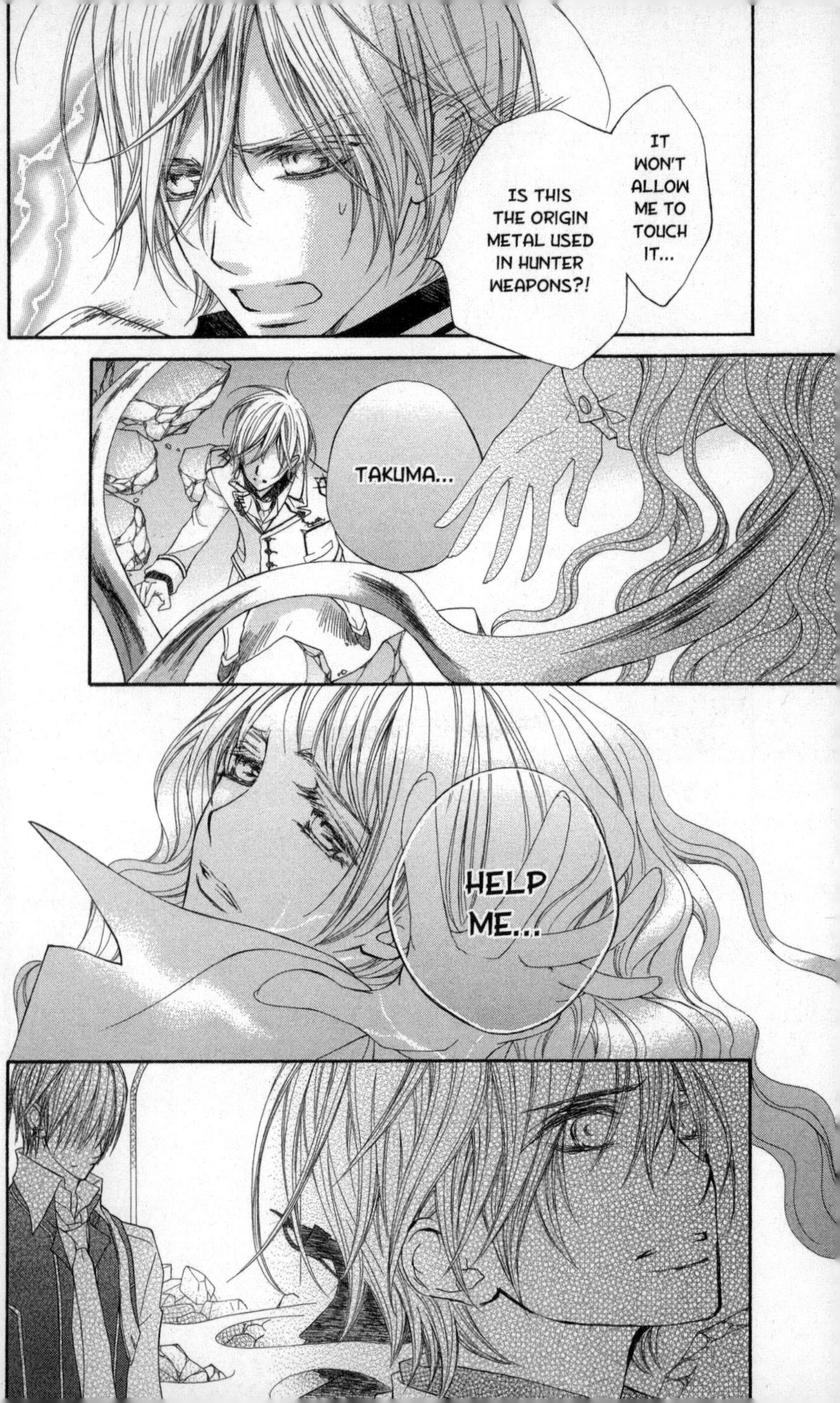
IT WON'T ALLOW ME TO TOUCH IT...
IS THIS THE ORIGIN METAL USED IN HUNTER WEAPONS?!
TAKUMA...
HELP ME...

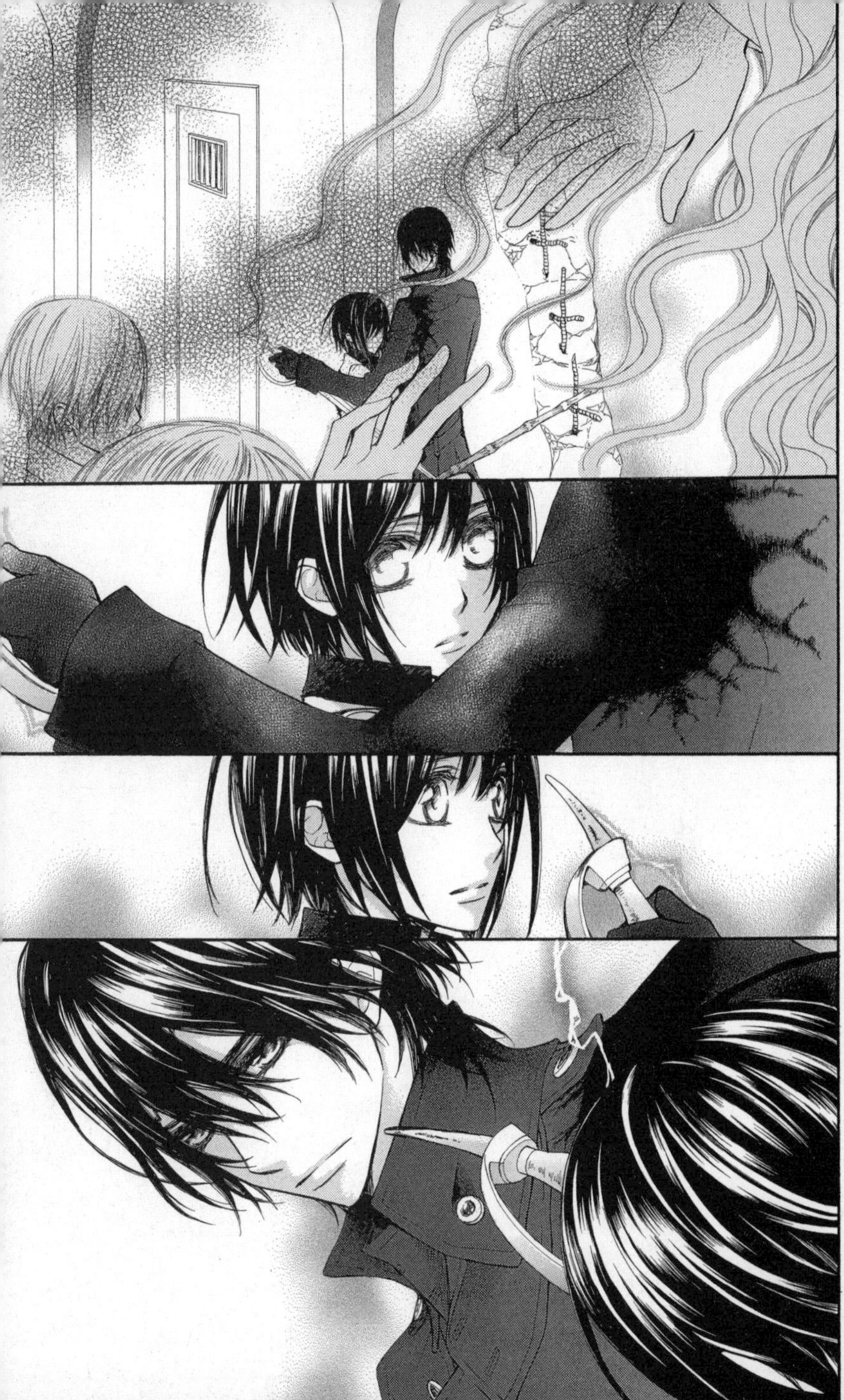

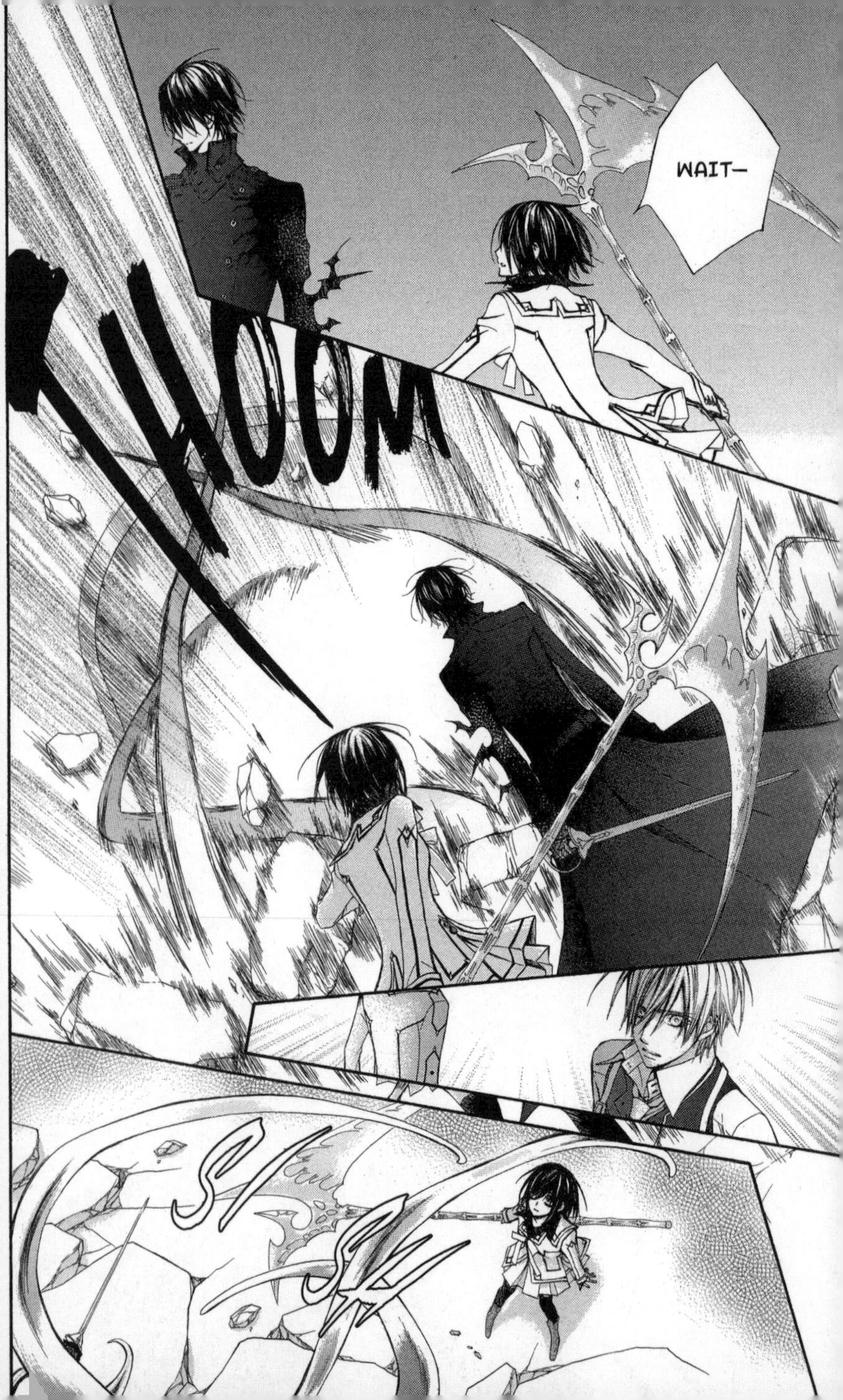
WAIT–
VHOOM
SLISH

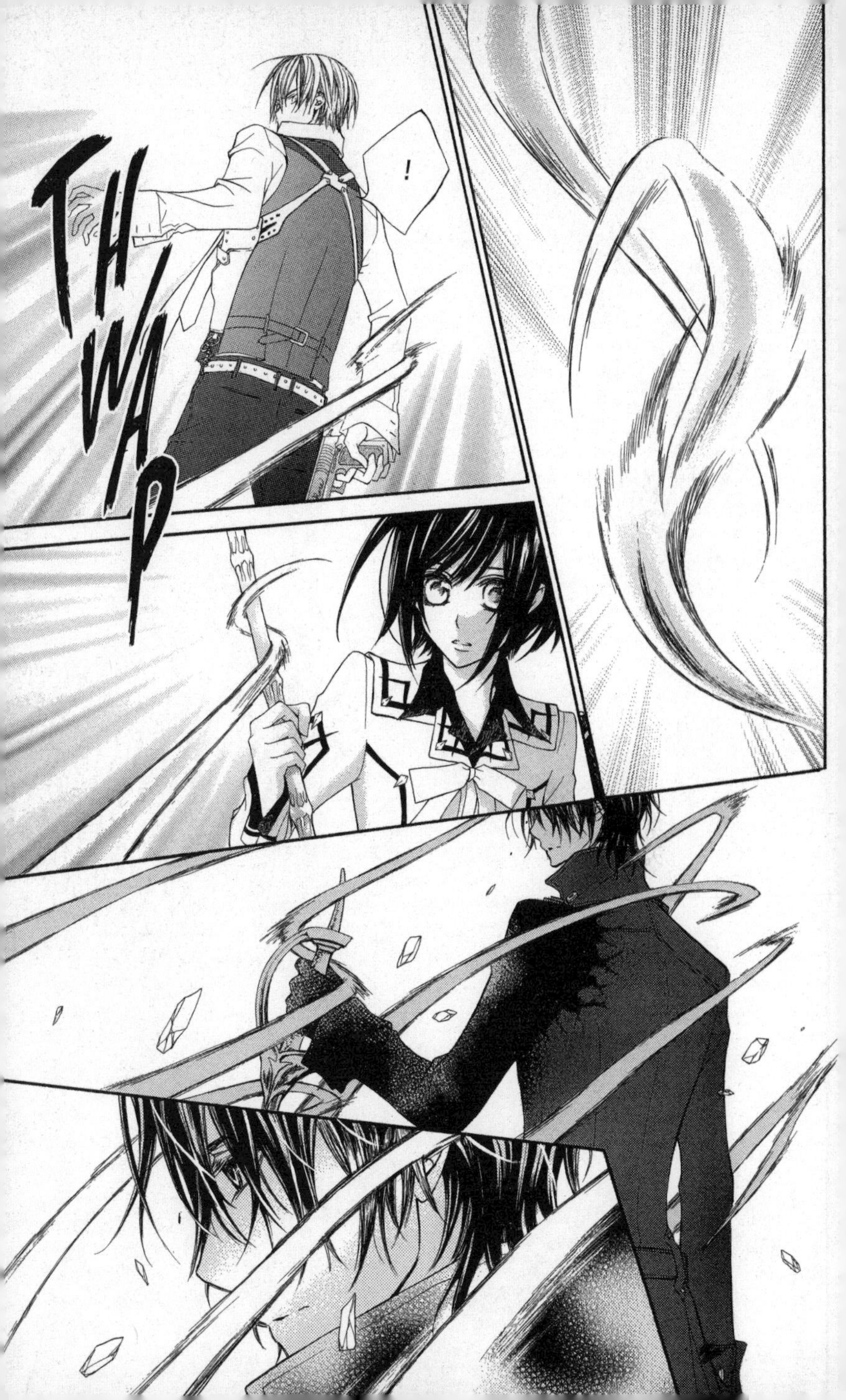

!
THWAP

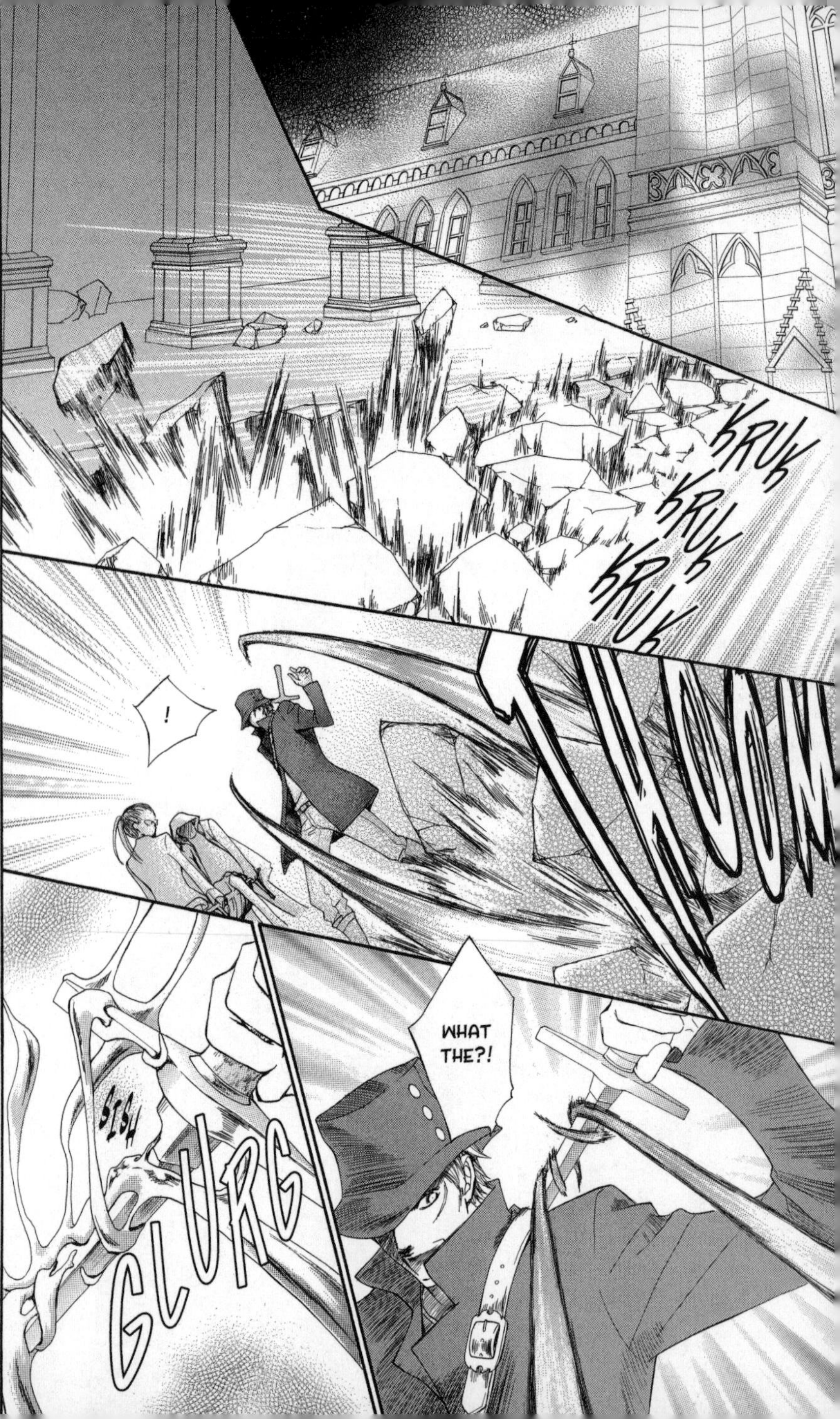
KRUK
KRUK
KRUK
!
WHOOM
WHAT THE?!
GLURG
SISH

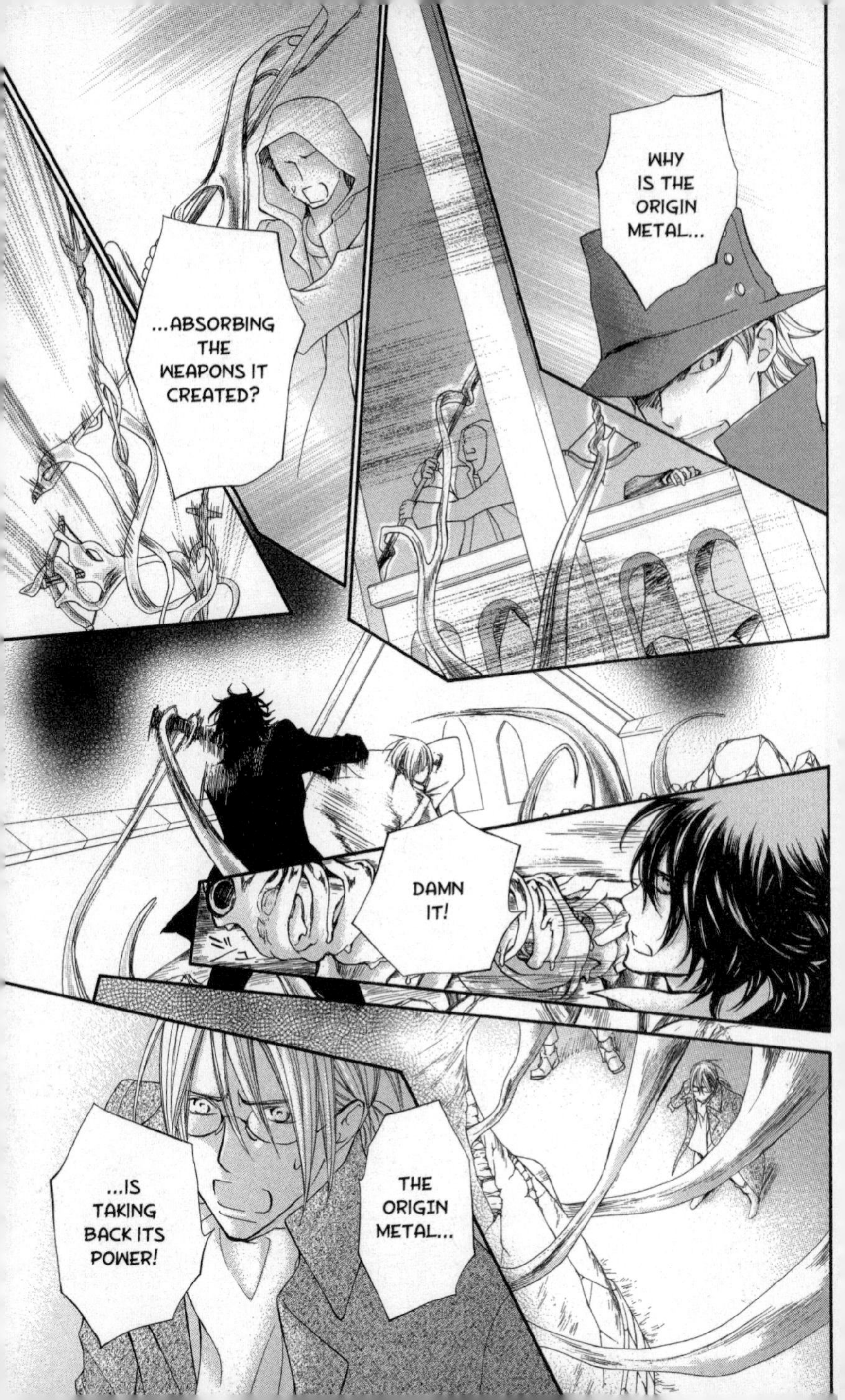
WHY IS THE ORIGIN METAL...
...ABSORBING THE WEAPONS IT CREATED?
DAMN IT!
THE ORIGIN METAL...
...IS TAKING BACK ITS POWER!

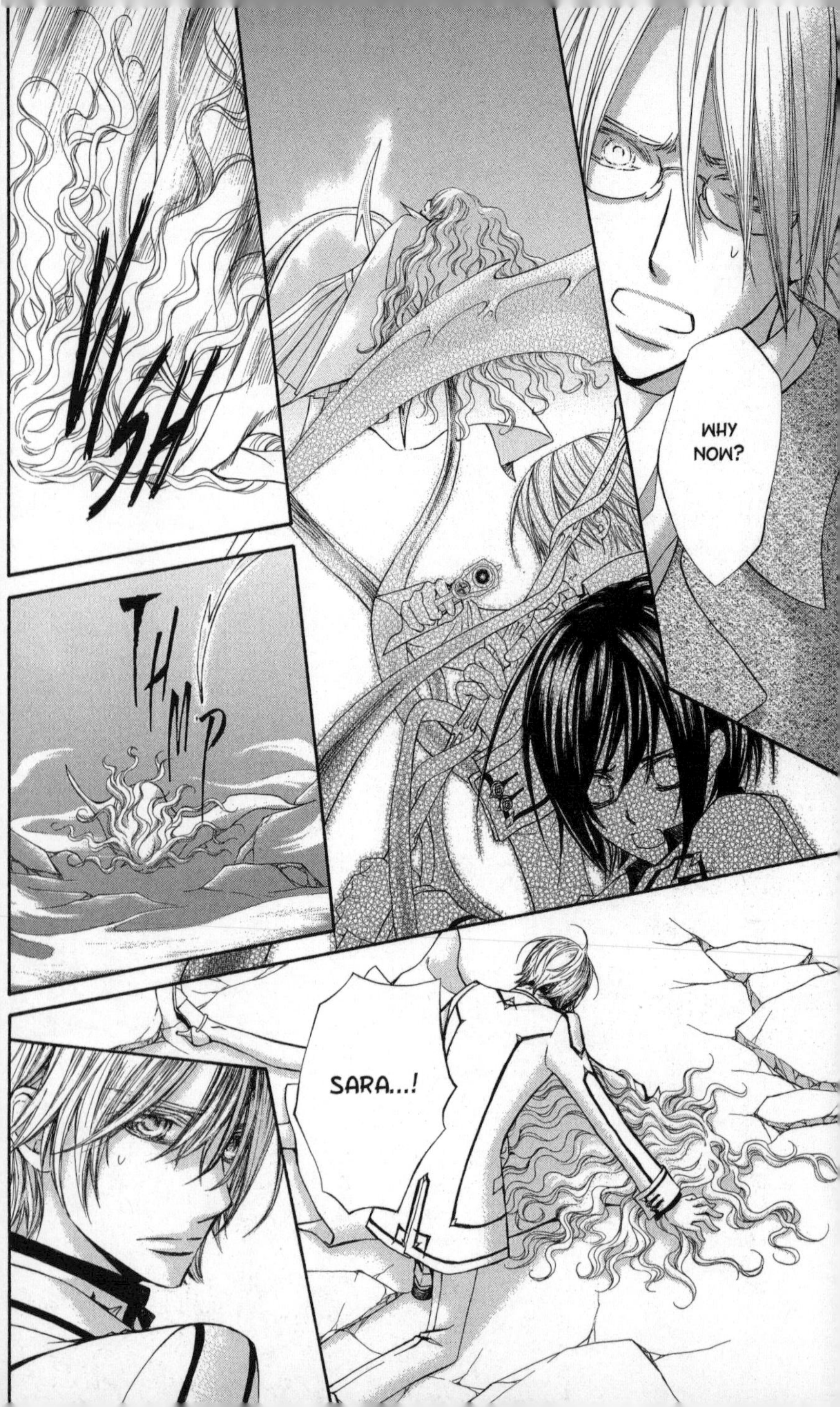
WHY NOW?
VISH
THMP
SARA...!

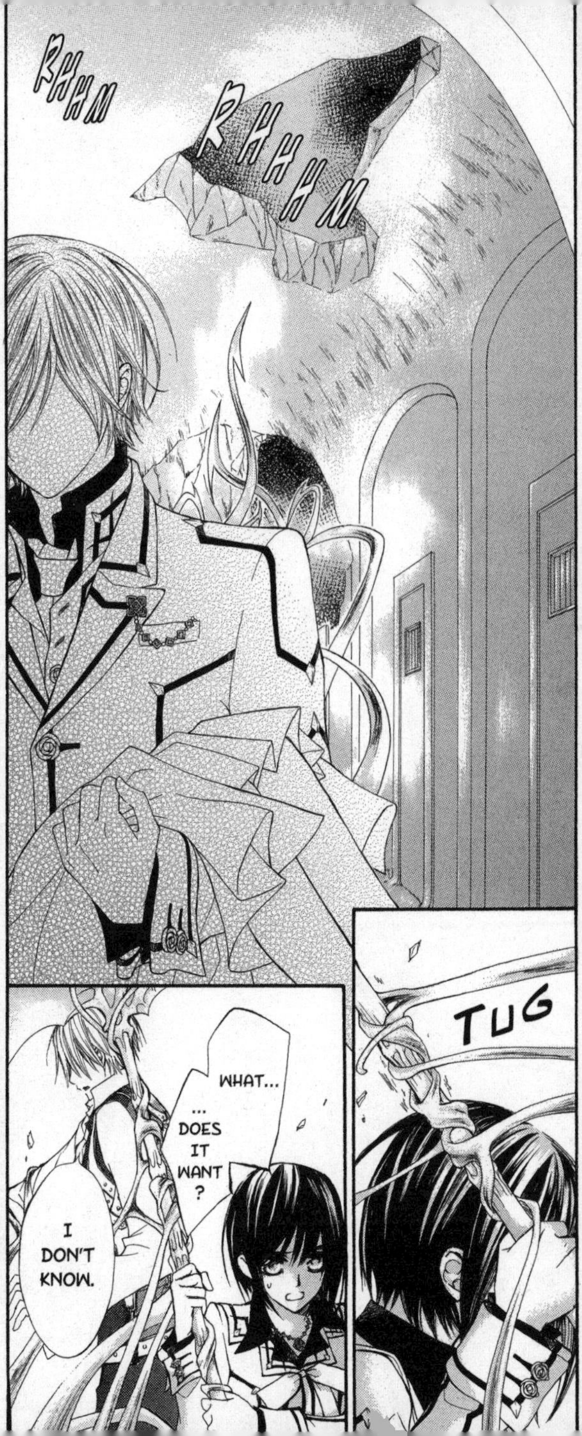
RHHM
RHHHHM
TUG
WHAT...
...DOES IT WANT?
I DON'T KNOW.

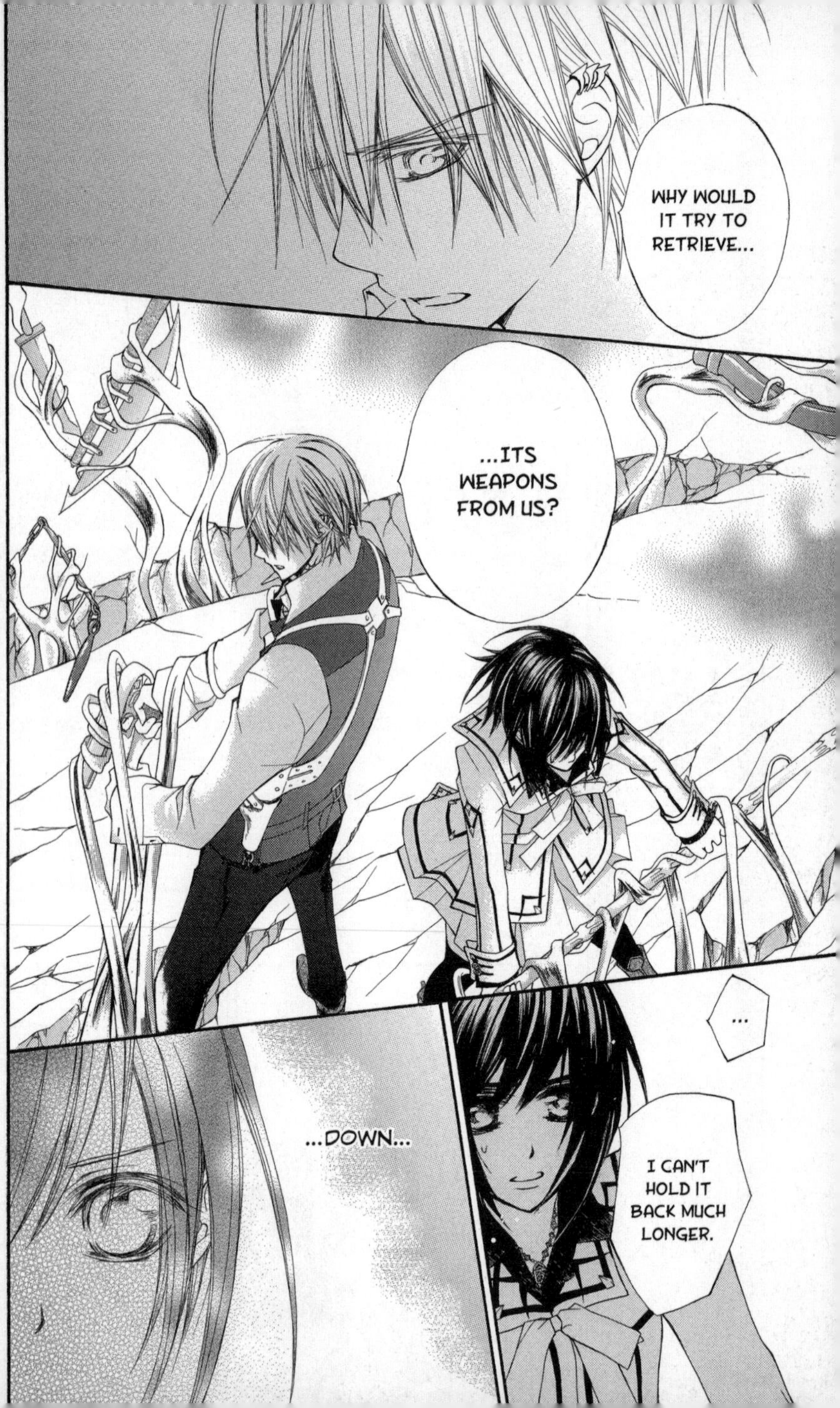
WHY WOULD IT TRY TO RETRIEVE...
...ITS WEAPONS FROM US?
...
I CAN'T HOLD IT BACK MUCH LONGER.
...DOWN...

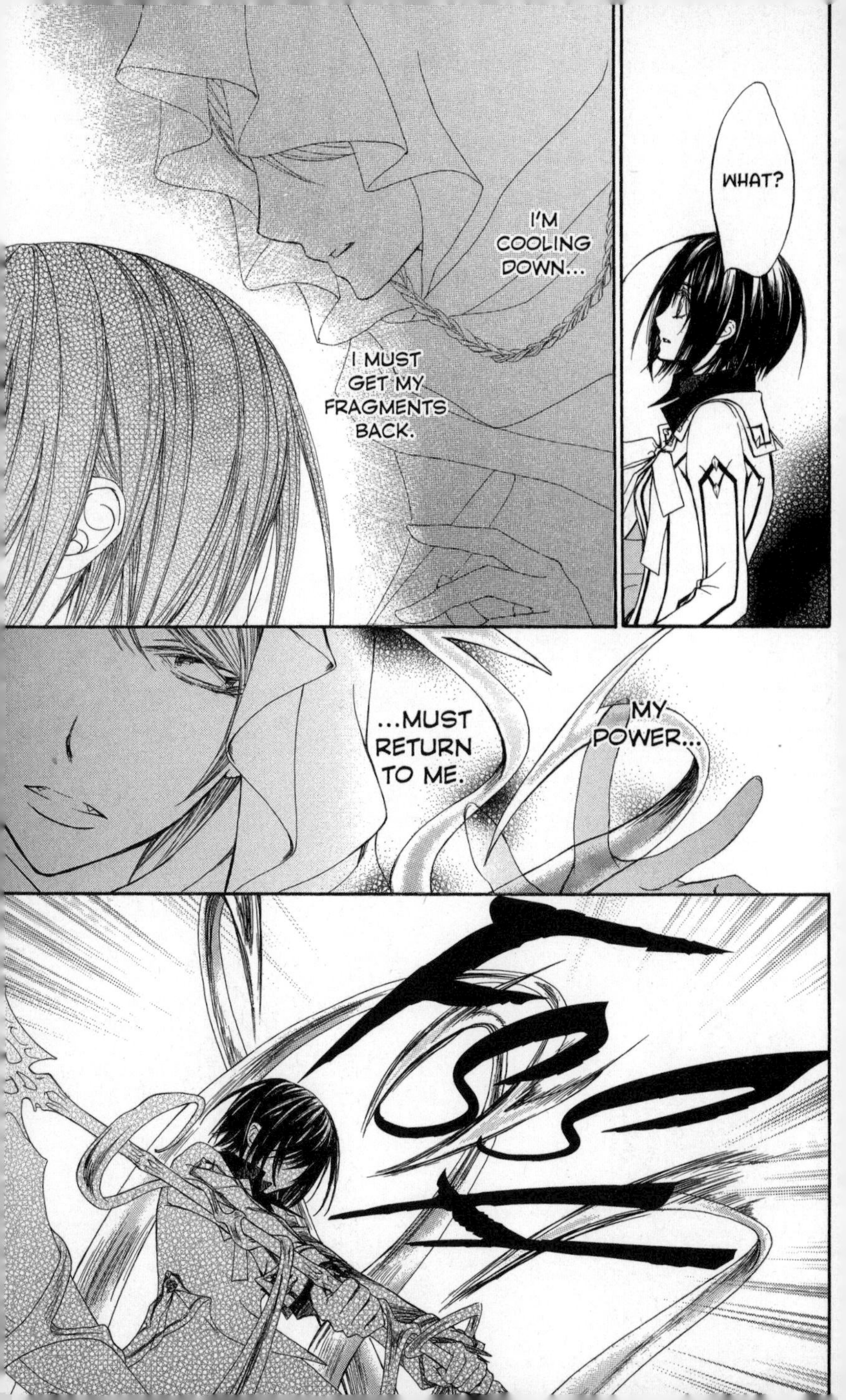
WHAT?
I'M COOLING DOWN...
I MUST GET MY FRAGMENTS BACK.
MY POWER...
...MUST RETURN TO ME.

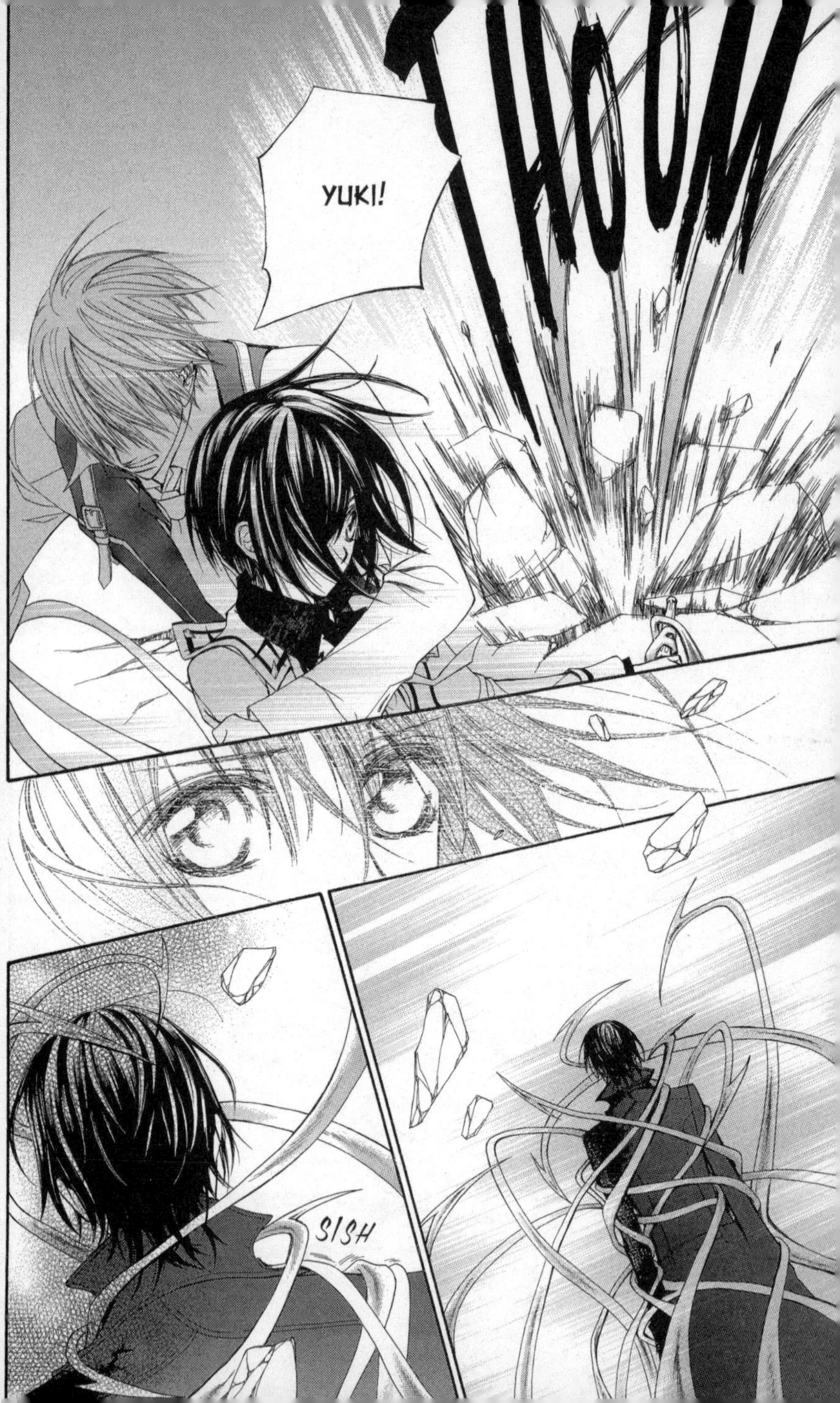
THOOM
YUKI!
SISH

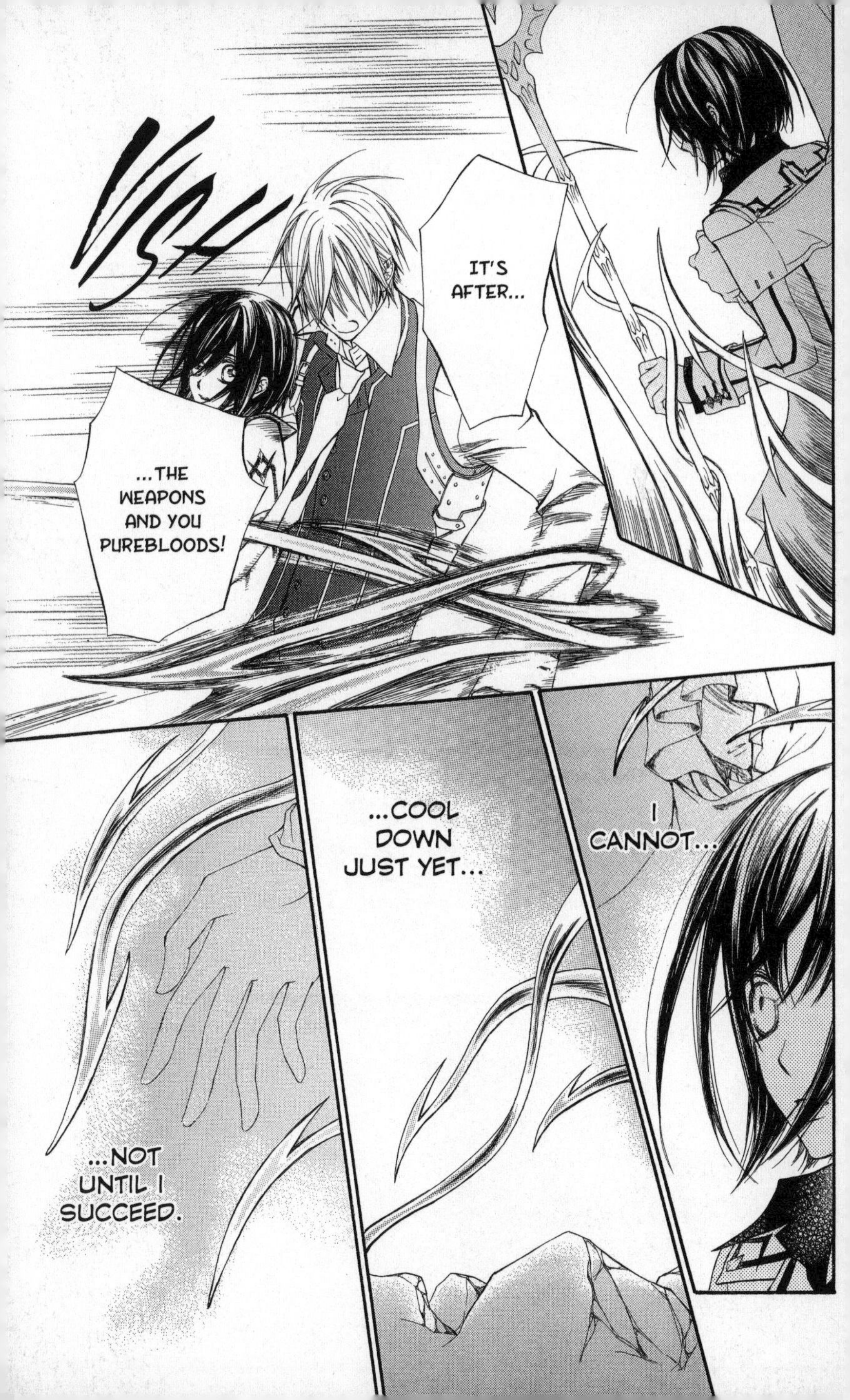
VSH
IT'S AFTER...
...THE WEAPONS AND YOU PUREBLOODS!
I CANNOT...
...COOL DOWN JUST YET...
...NOT UNTIL I SUCCEED.

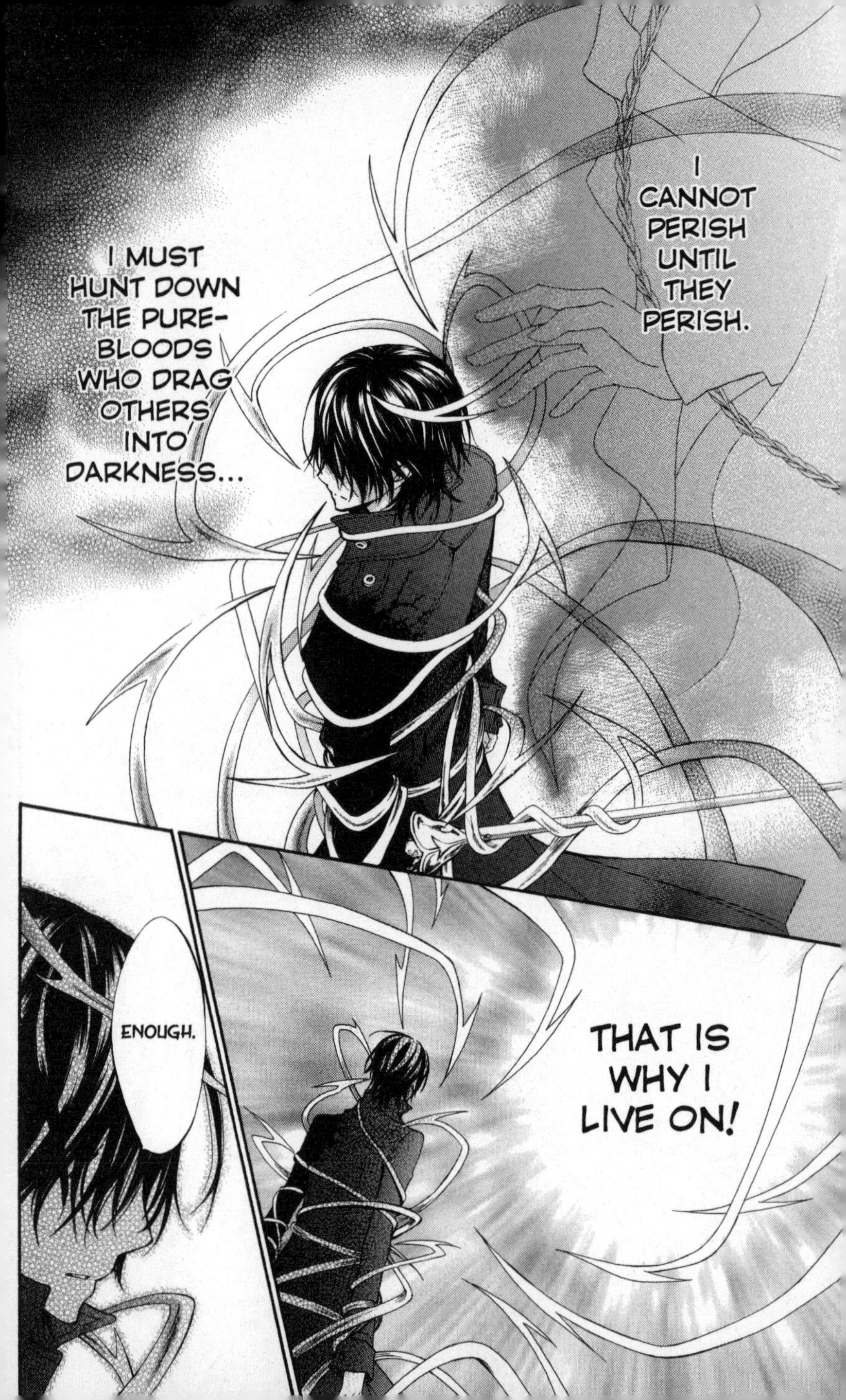
I CANNOT PERISH UNTIL THEY PERISH.
I MUST HUNT DOWN THE PUREBLOODS WHO DRAG OTHERS INTO DARKNESS...
THAT IS WHY I LIVE ON!
ENOUGH.

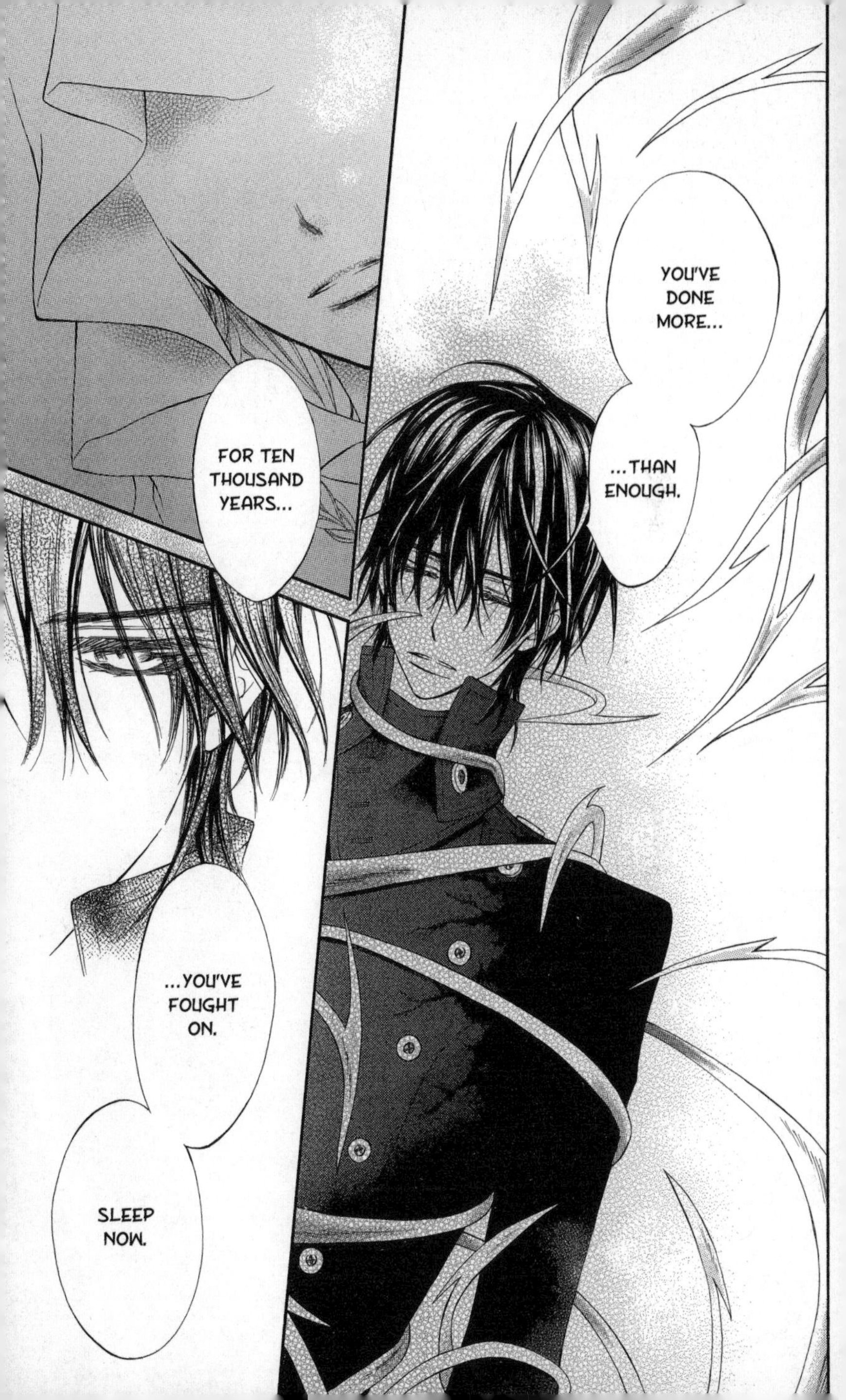
YOU'VE DONE MORE...
...THAN ENOUGH.
FOR TEN THOUSAND YEARS...
...YOU'VE FOUGHT ON.
SLEEP NOW.

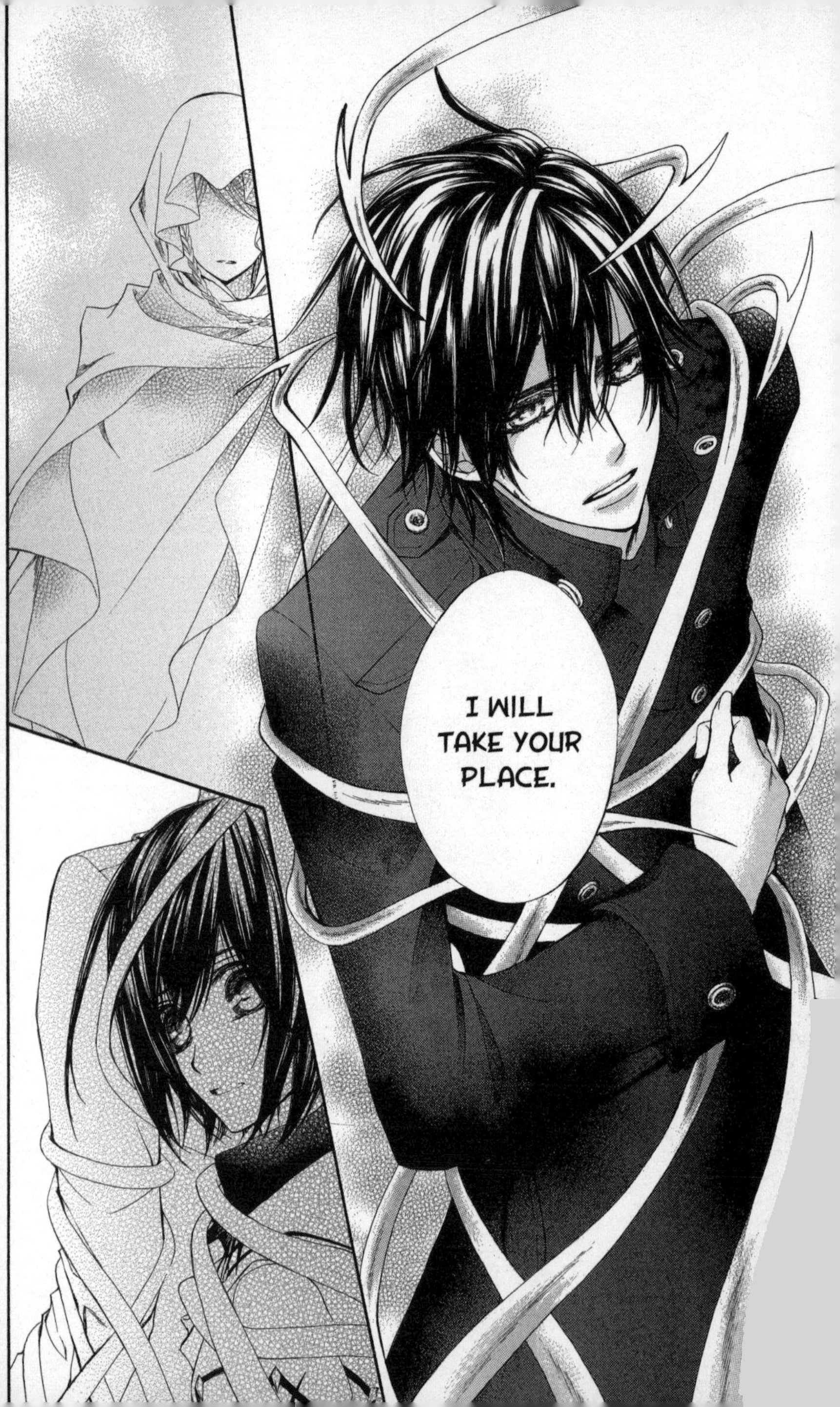
I WILL TAKE YOUR PLACE.

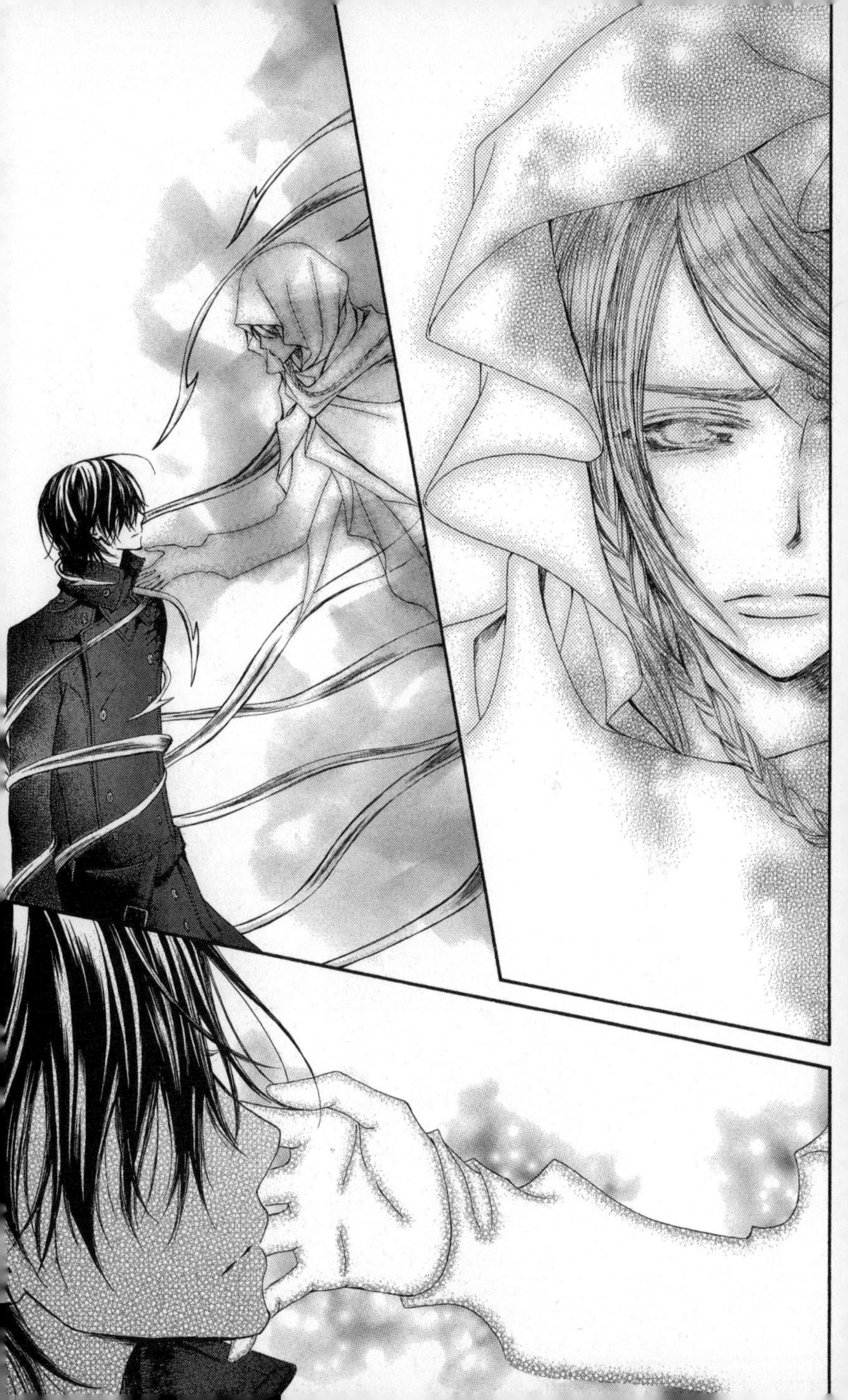

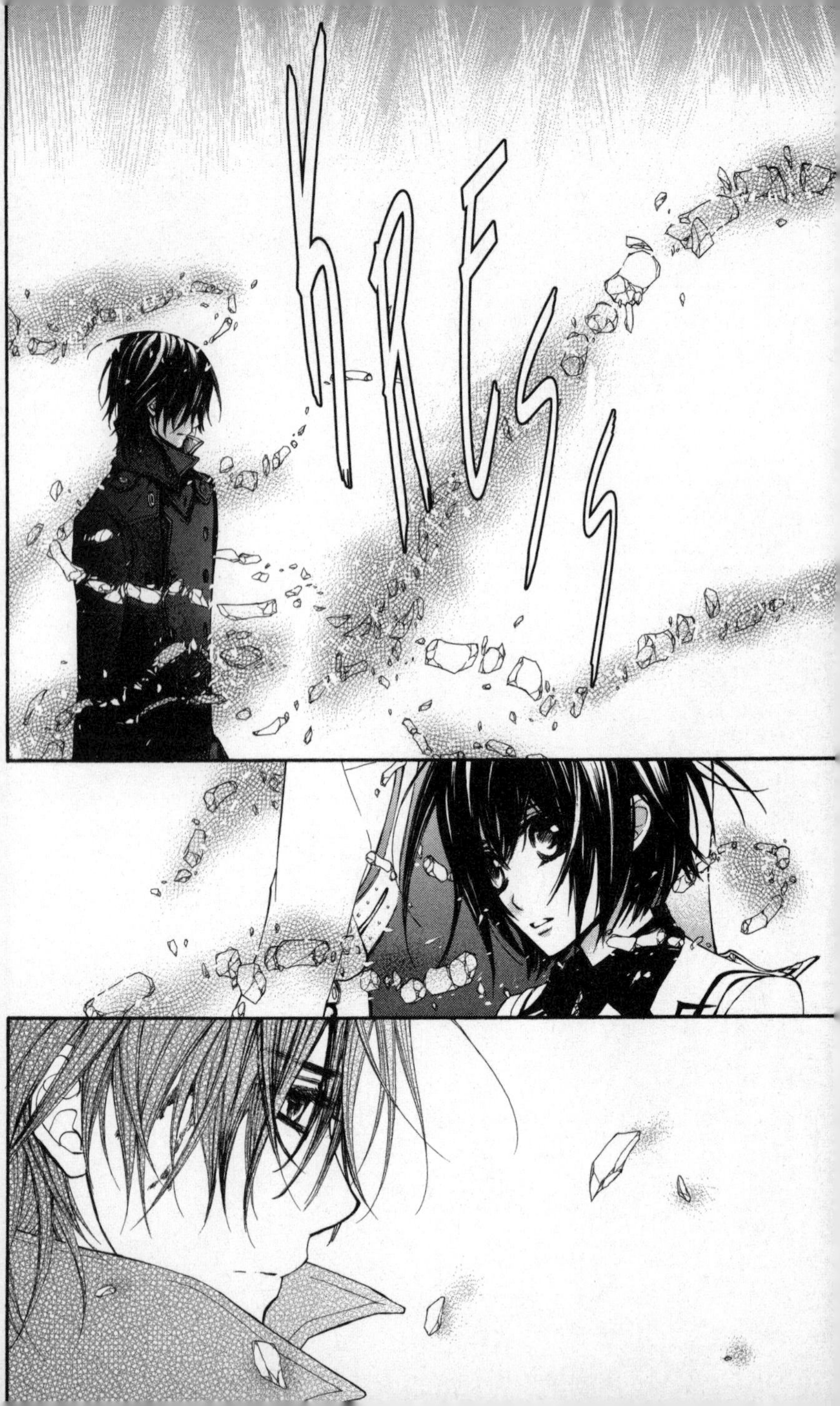
KRESS

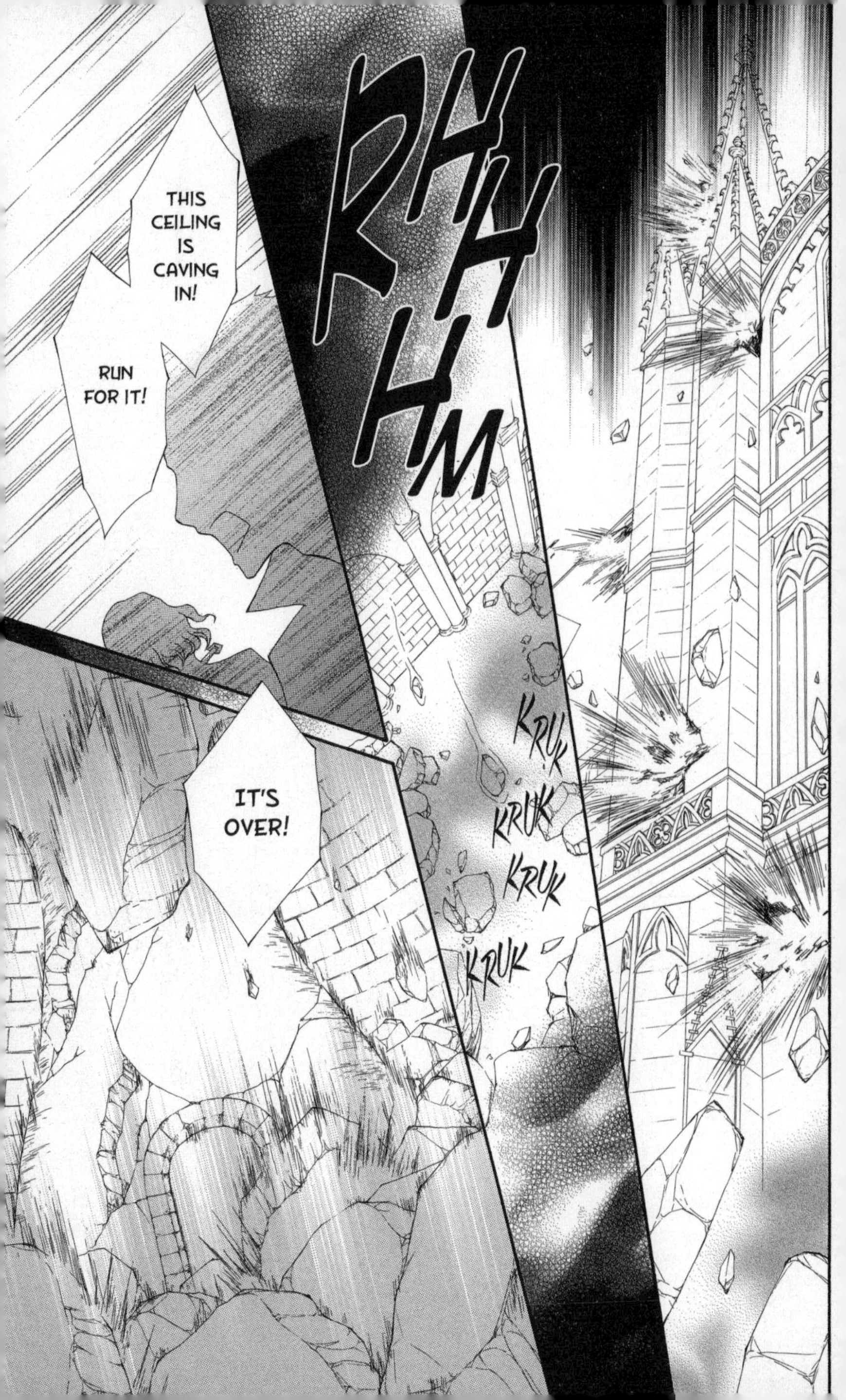
RHHM
KRUK
KRUK
KRUK
KRUK
THIS CEILING IS CAVING IN!
RUN FOR IT!
IT'S OVER!

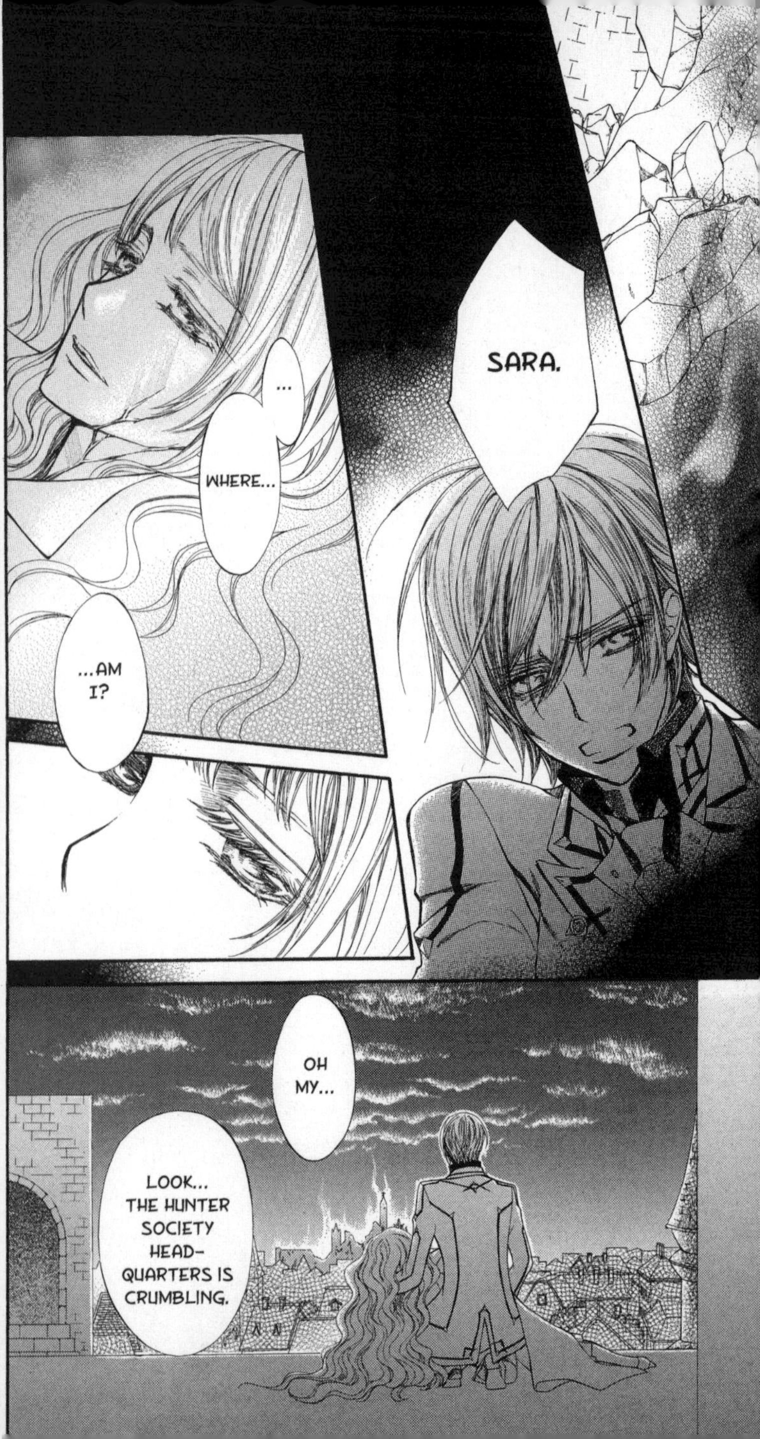
SARA.
...
WHERE...
...AM I?
OH MY...
LOOK... THE HUNTER SOCIETY HEAD-QUARTERS IS CRUMBLING.

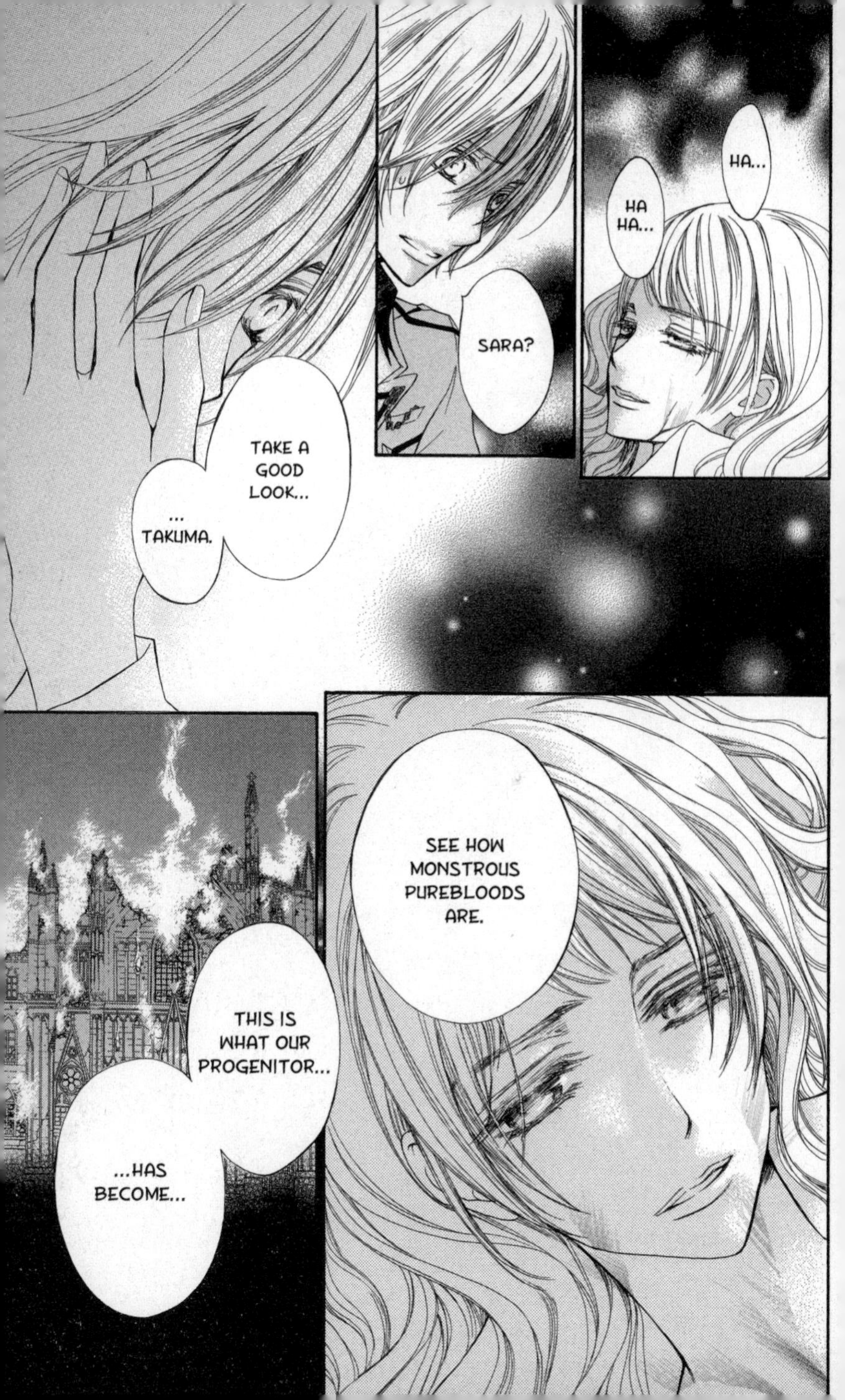
HA...
HA HA...
SARA?
TAKE A GOOD LOOK...
... TAKUMA.
SEE HOW MONSTROUS PUREBLOODS ARE.
THIS IS WHAT OUR PROGENITOR...
...HAS BECOME...

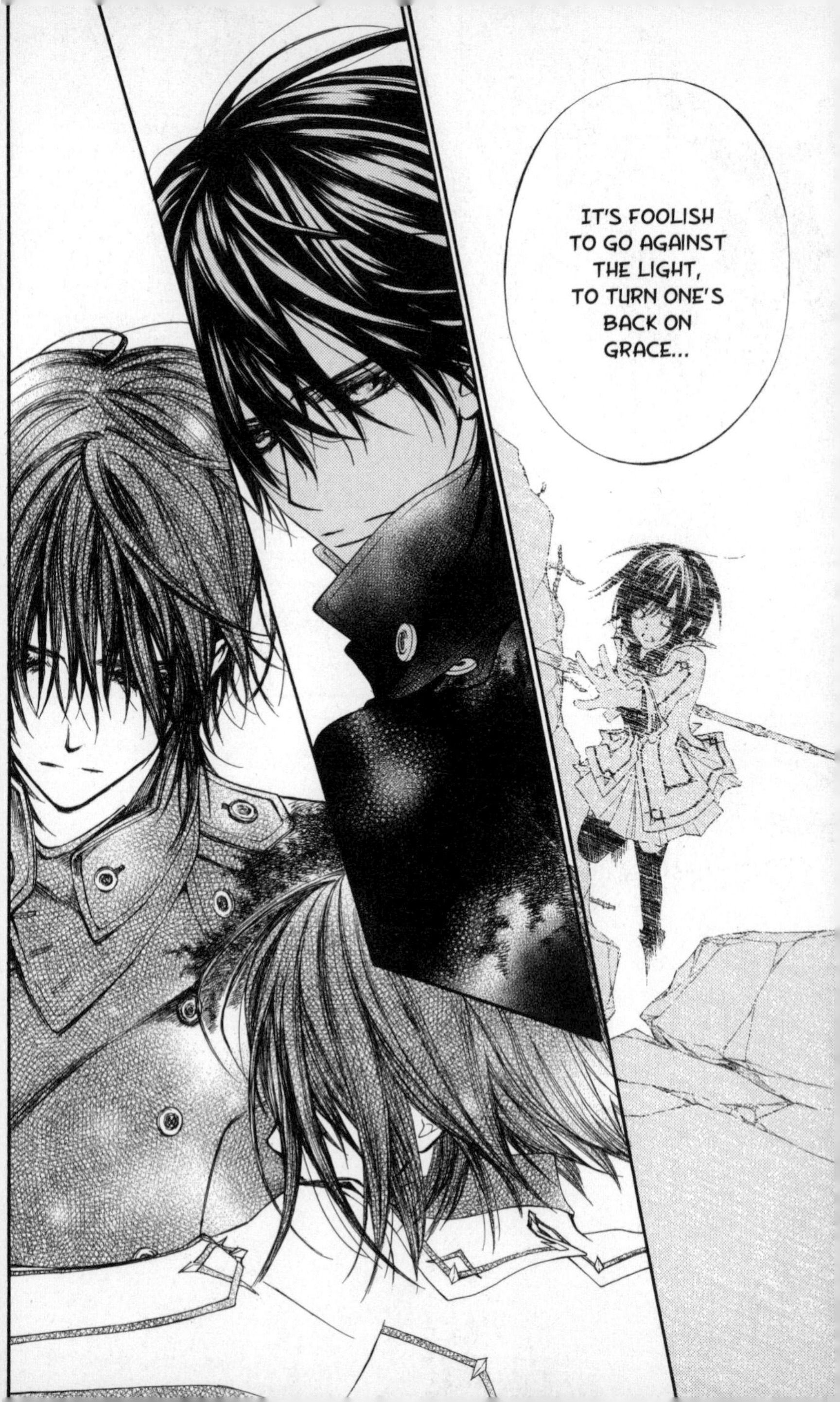
IT'S FOOLISH TO GO AGAINST THE LIGHT, TO TURN ONE'S BACK ON GRACE...

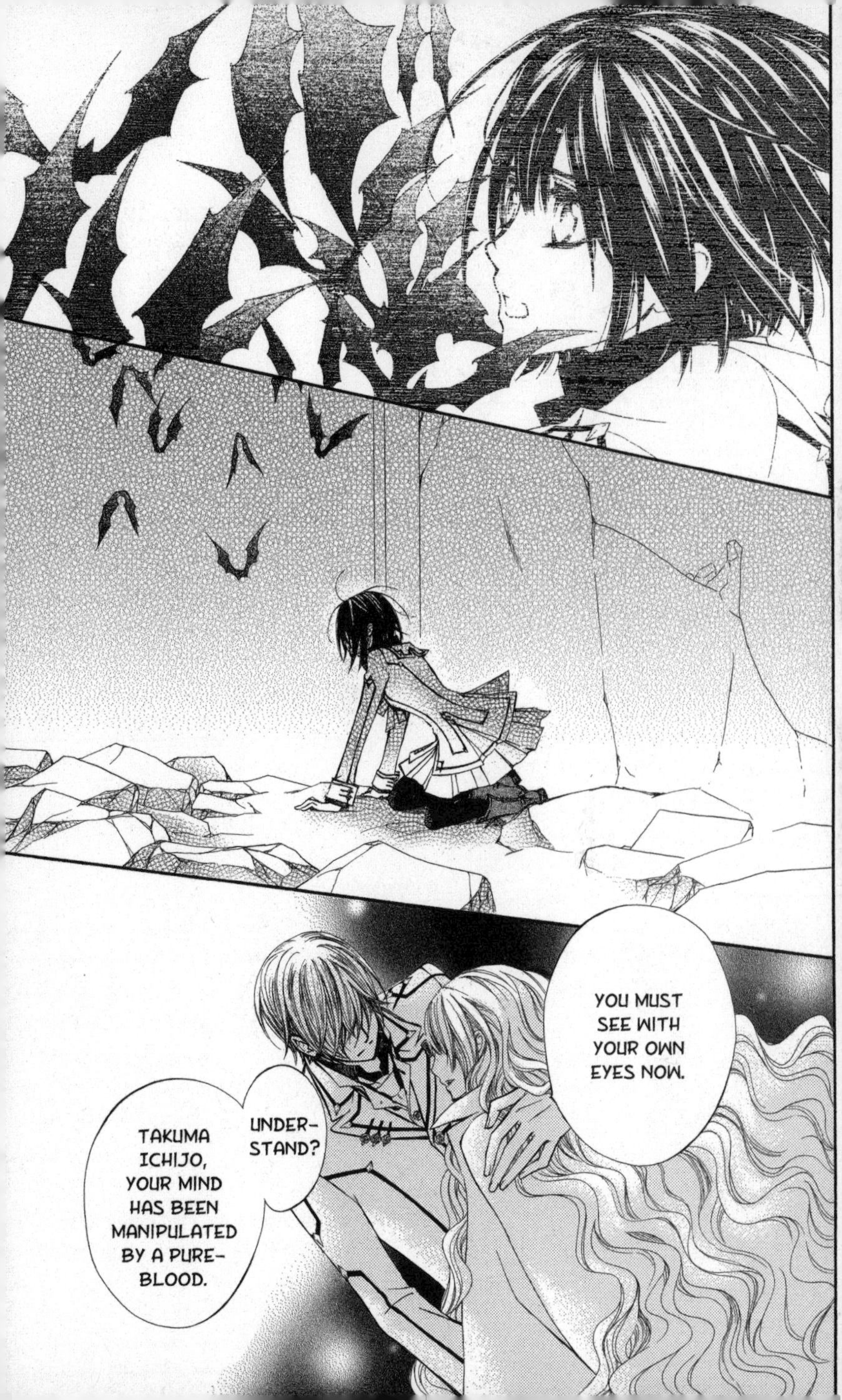
YOU MUST SEE WITH YOUR OWN EYES NOW.
UNDER-STAND?
TAKUMA ICHIJO, YOUR MIND HAS BEEN MANIPULATED BY A PURE-BLOOD.

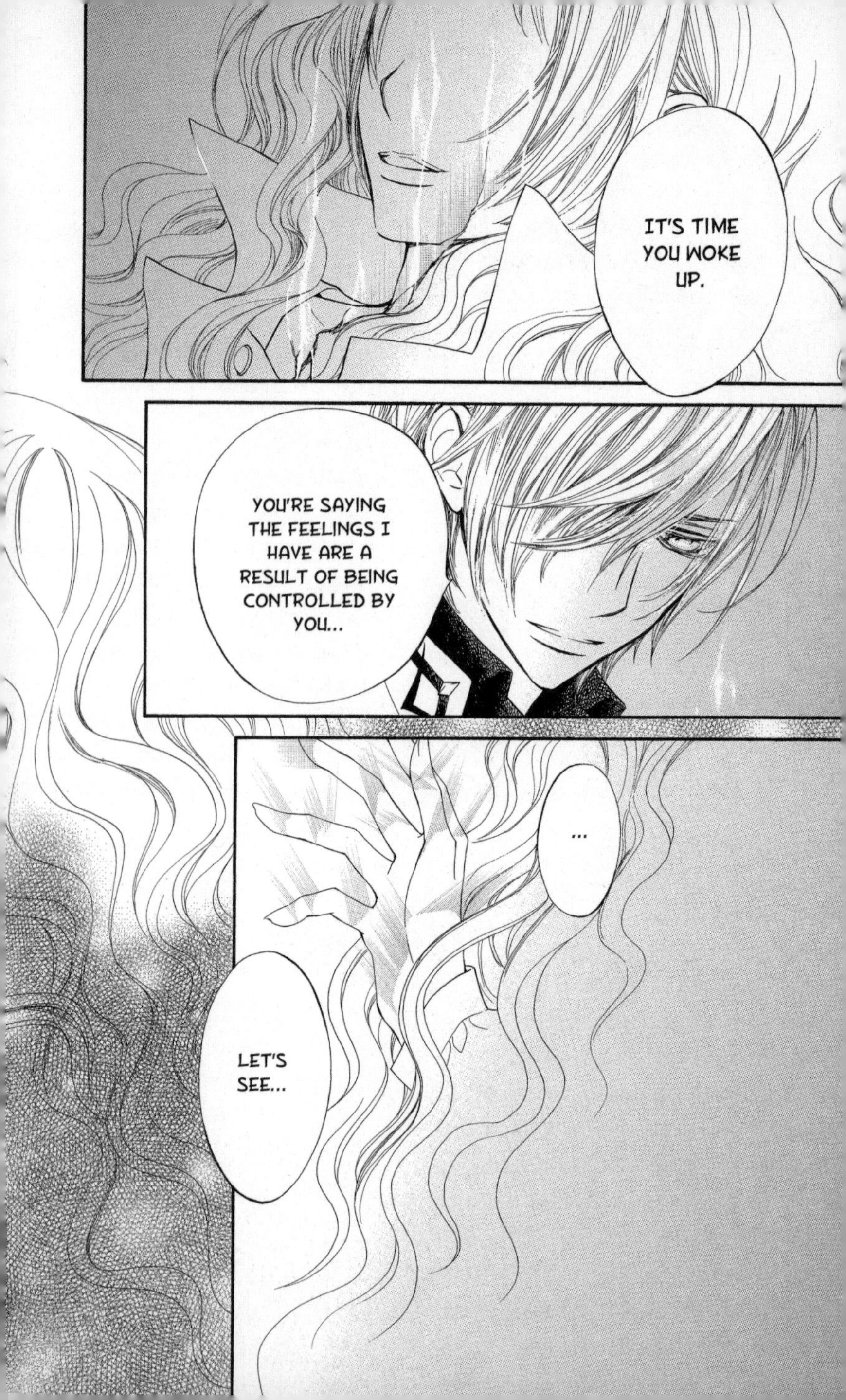
IT'S TIME YOU WOKE UP.
YOU'RE SAYING THE FEELINGS I HAVE ARE A RESULT OF BEING CONTROLLED BY YOU...
...
LET'S SEE...

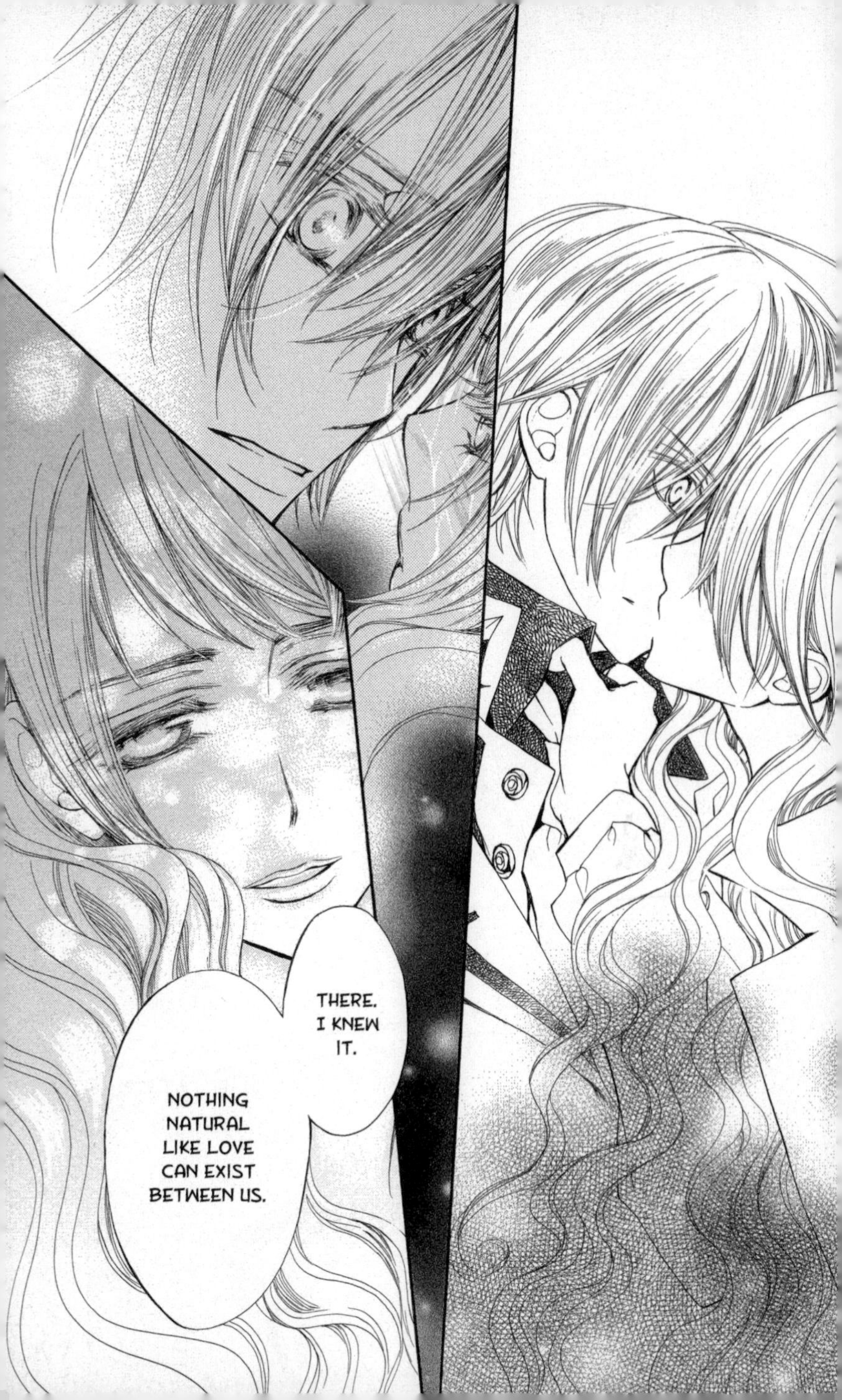
THERE. I KNEW IT.
NOTHING NATURAL LIKE LOVE CAN EXIST BETWEEN US.

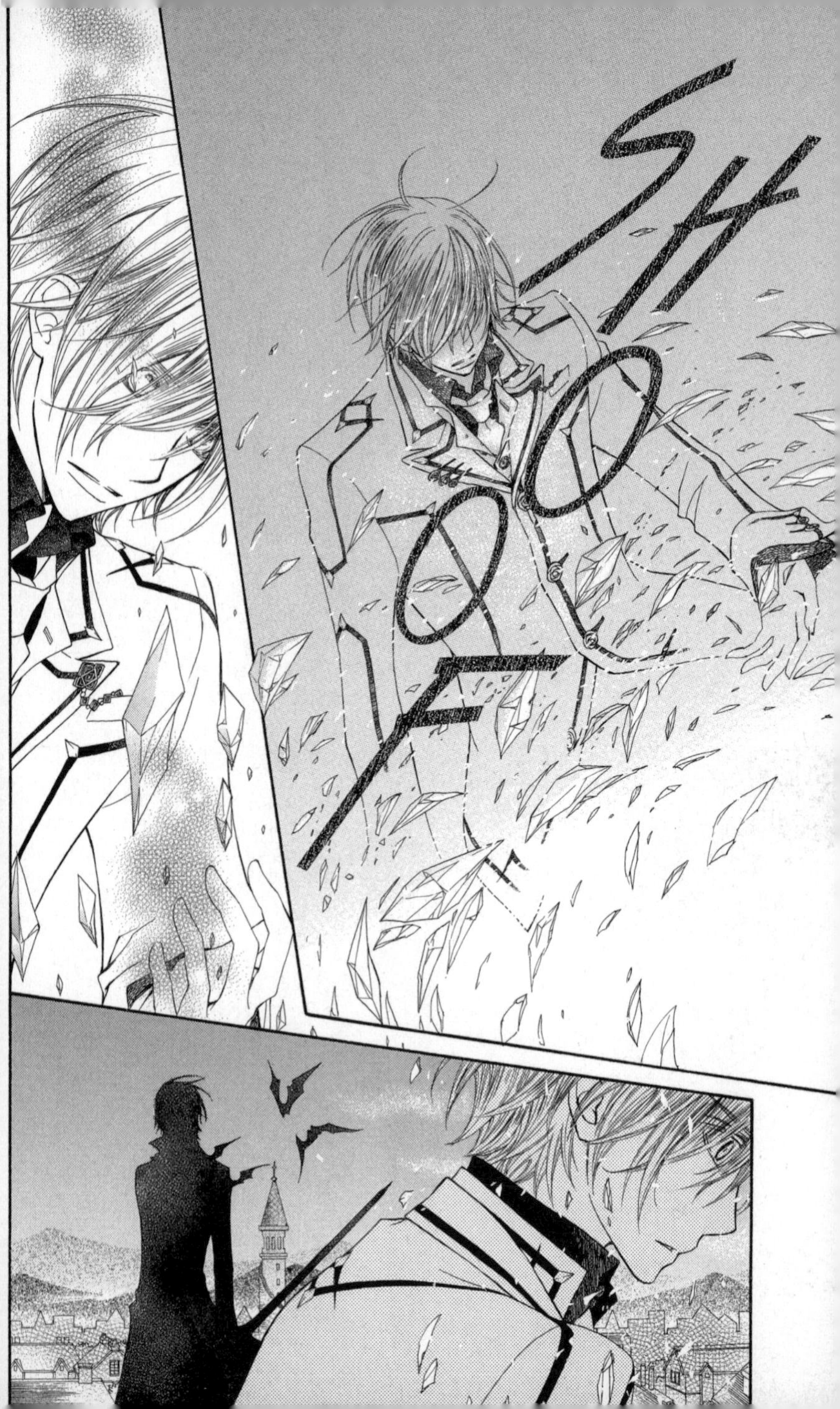
SHOOOF

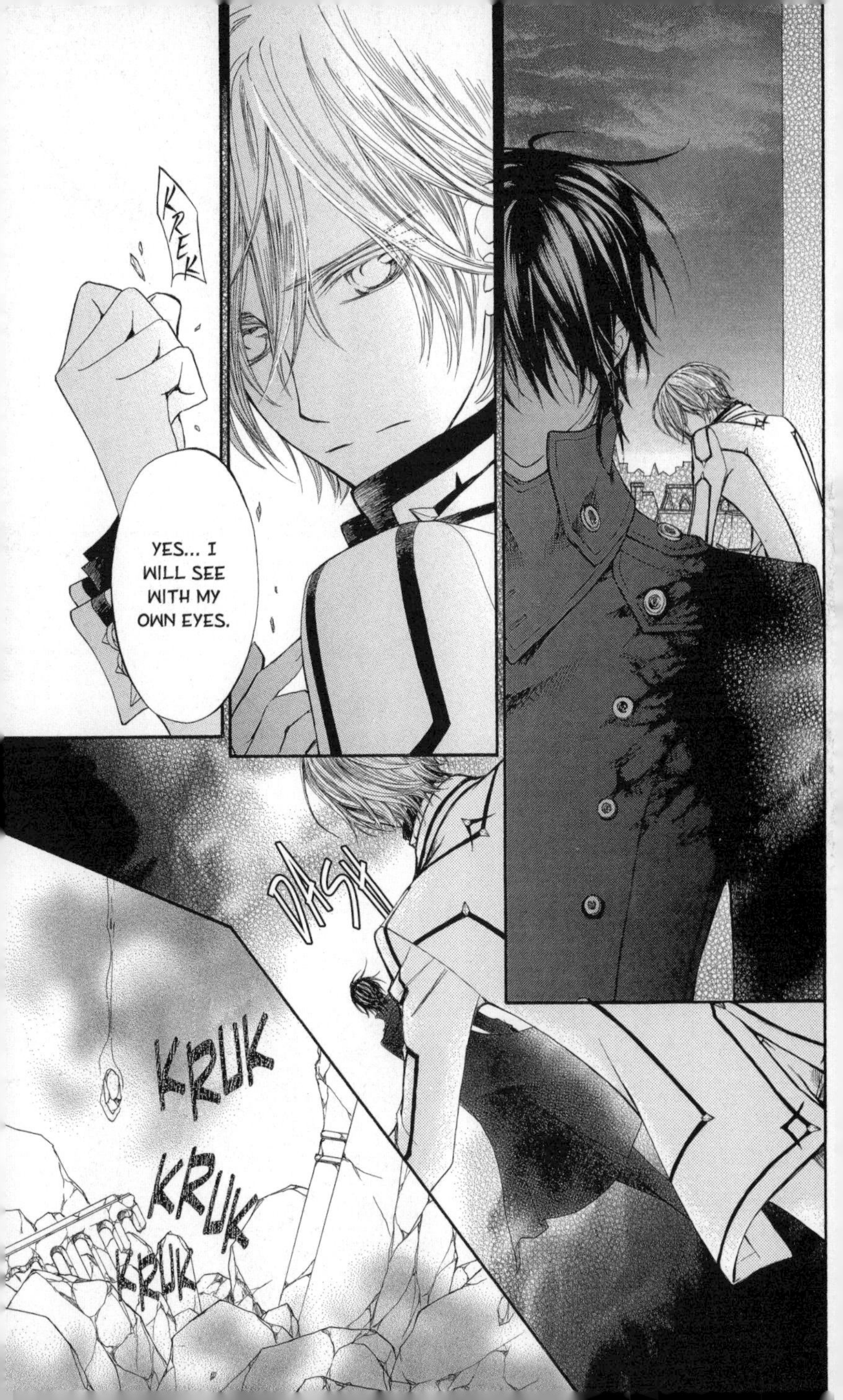
KREK
YES... I WILL SEE WITH MY OWN EYES.
DASH
KRUK
KRUK
KRUK

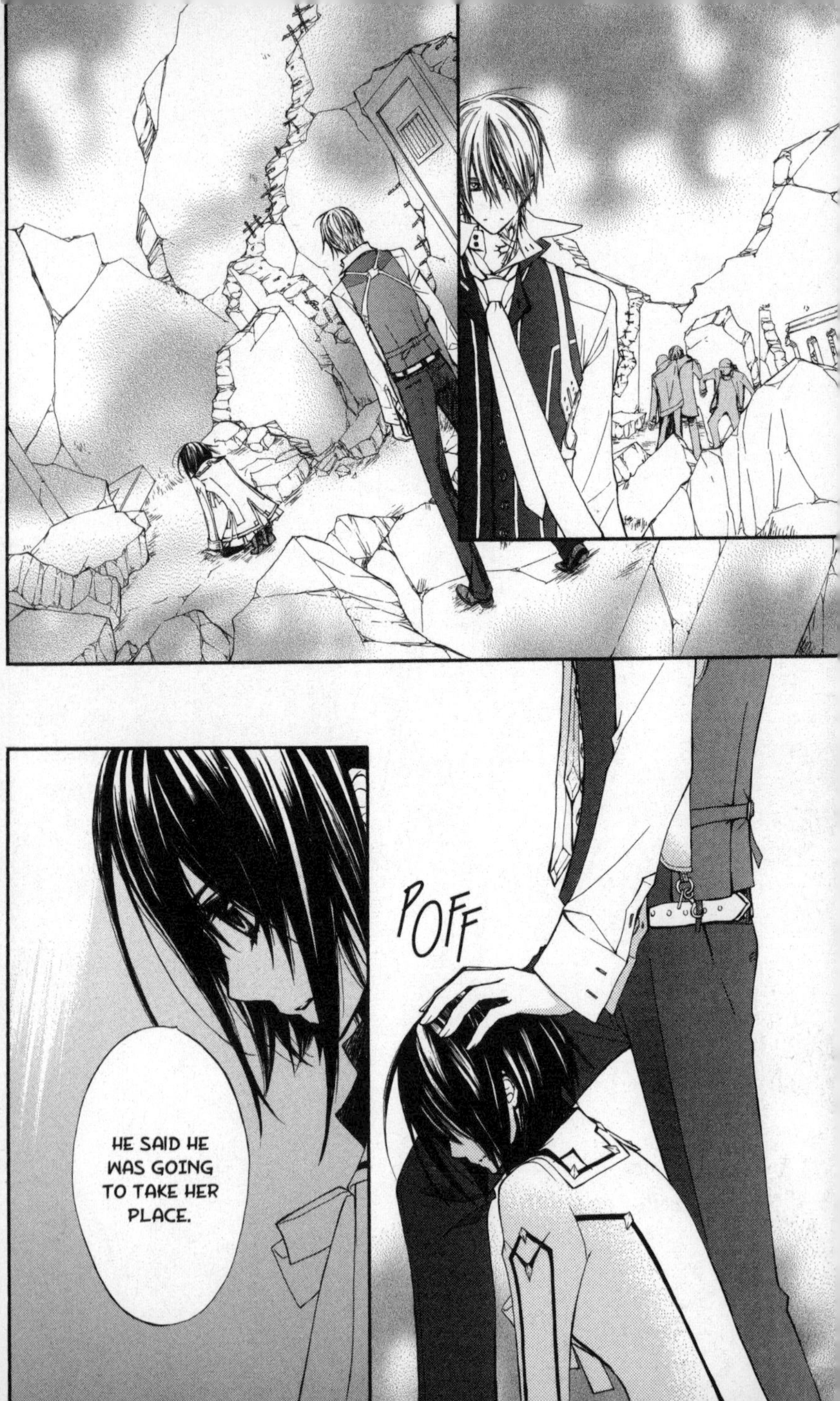
POFF
HE SAID HE WAS GOING TO TAKE HER PLACE.

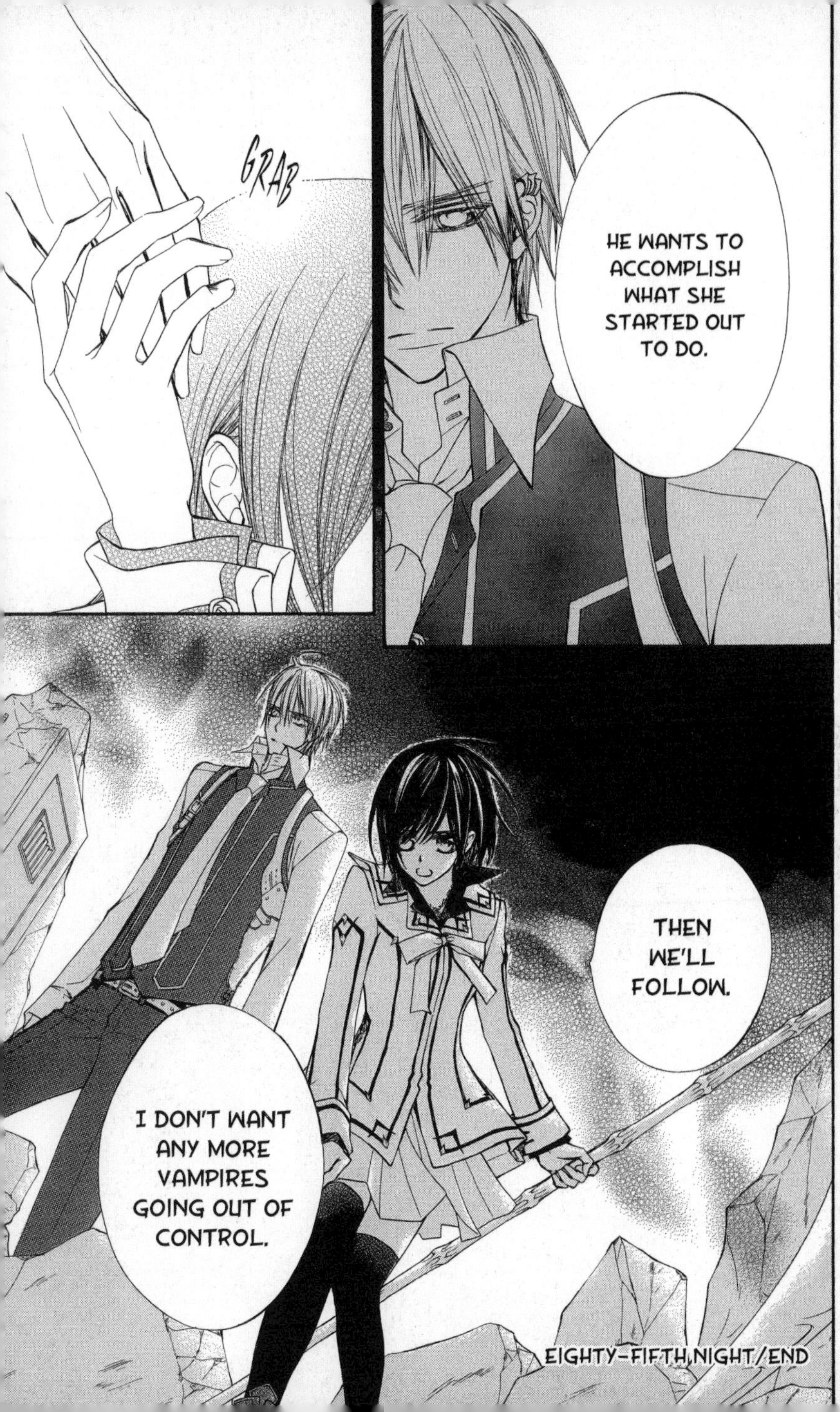
HE WANTS TO ACCOMPLISH WHAT SHE STARTED OUT TO DO.
GRAB
THEN WE'LL FOLLOW.
I DON'T WANT ANY MORE VAMPIRES GOING OUT OF CONTROL.
EIGHTY-FIFTH NIGHT/END

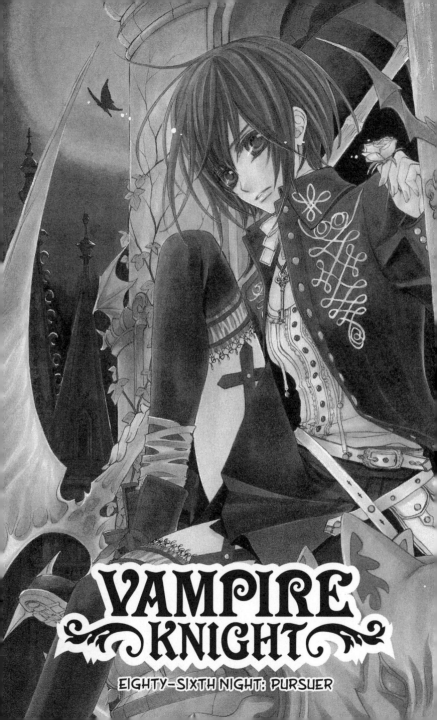

VAMPIRE KNIGHT

EIGHTY–SIXTH NIGHT: PURSUER

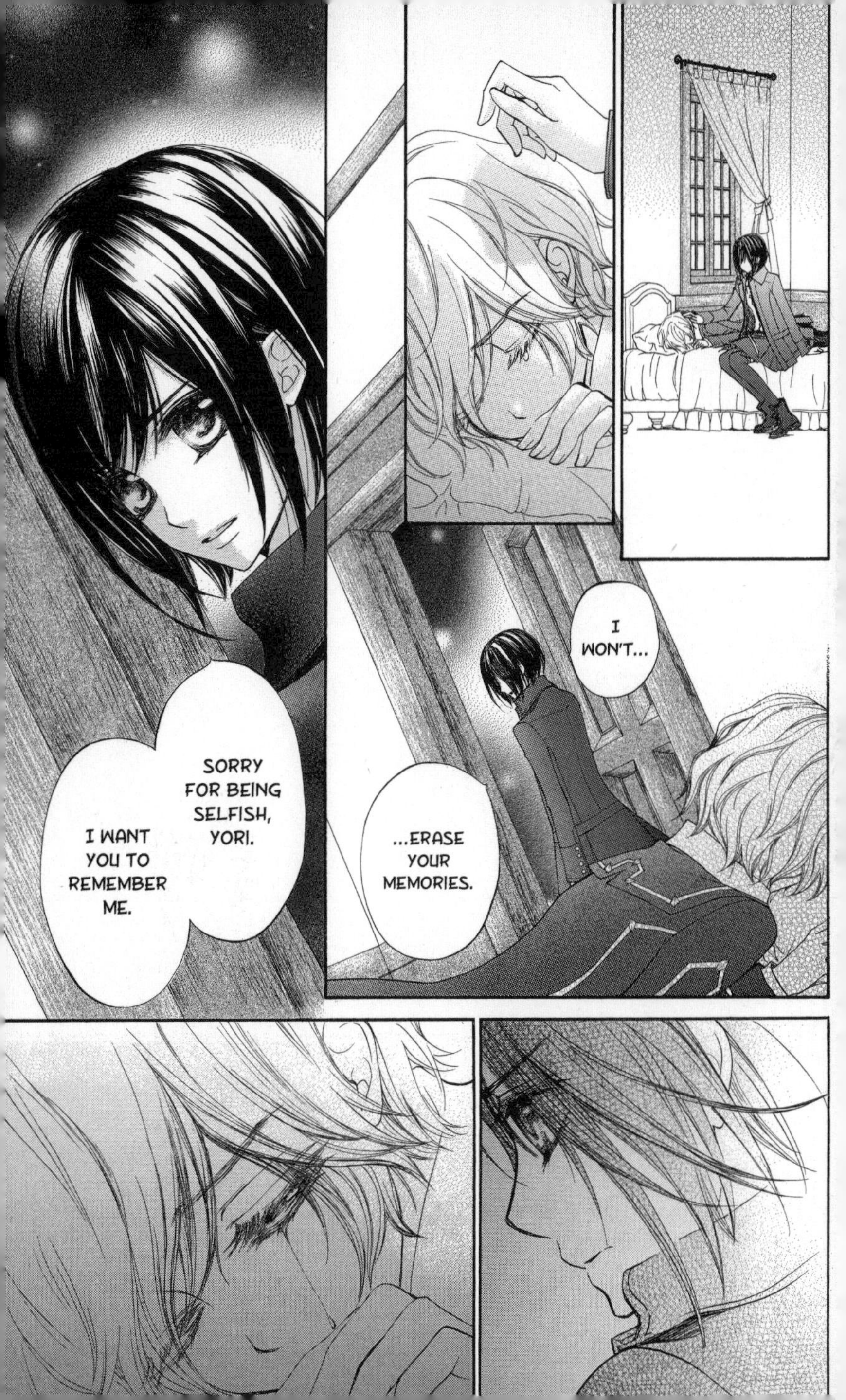
I WON'T...
...ERASE YOUR MEMORIES.
SORRY FOR BEING SELFISH, YORI.
I WANT YOU TO REMEMBER ME.

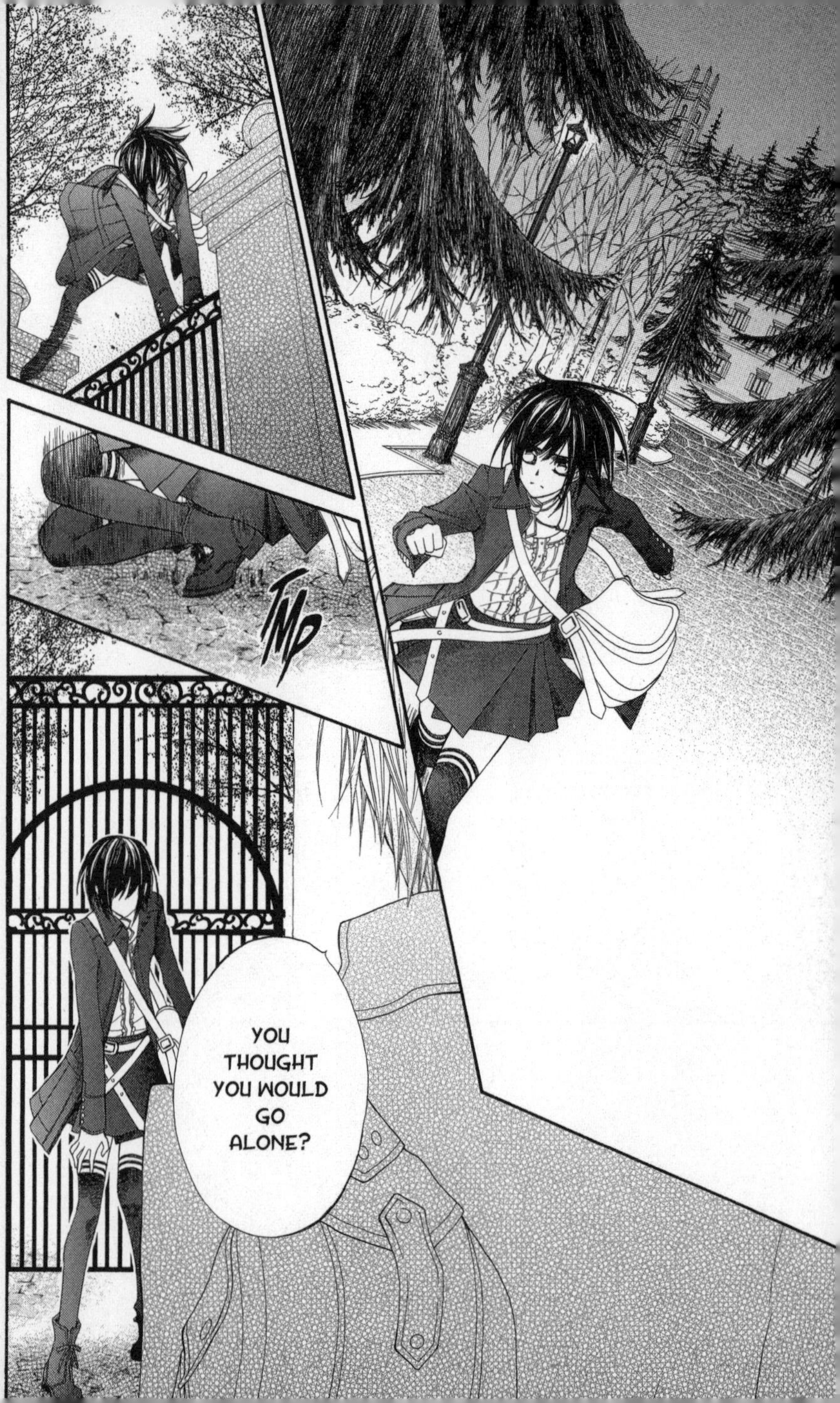
TMP
YOU THOUGHT YOU WOULD GO ALONE?

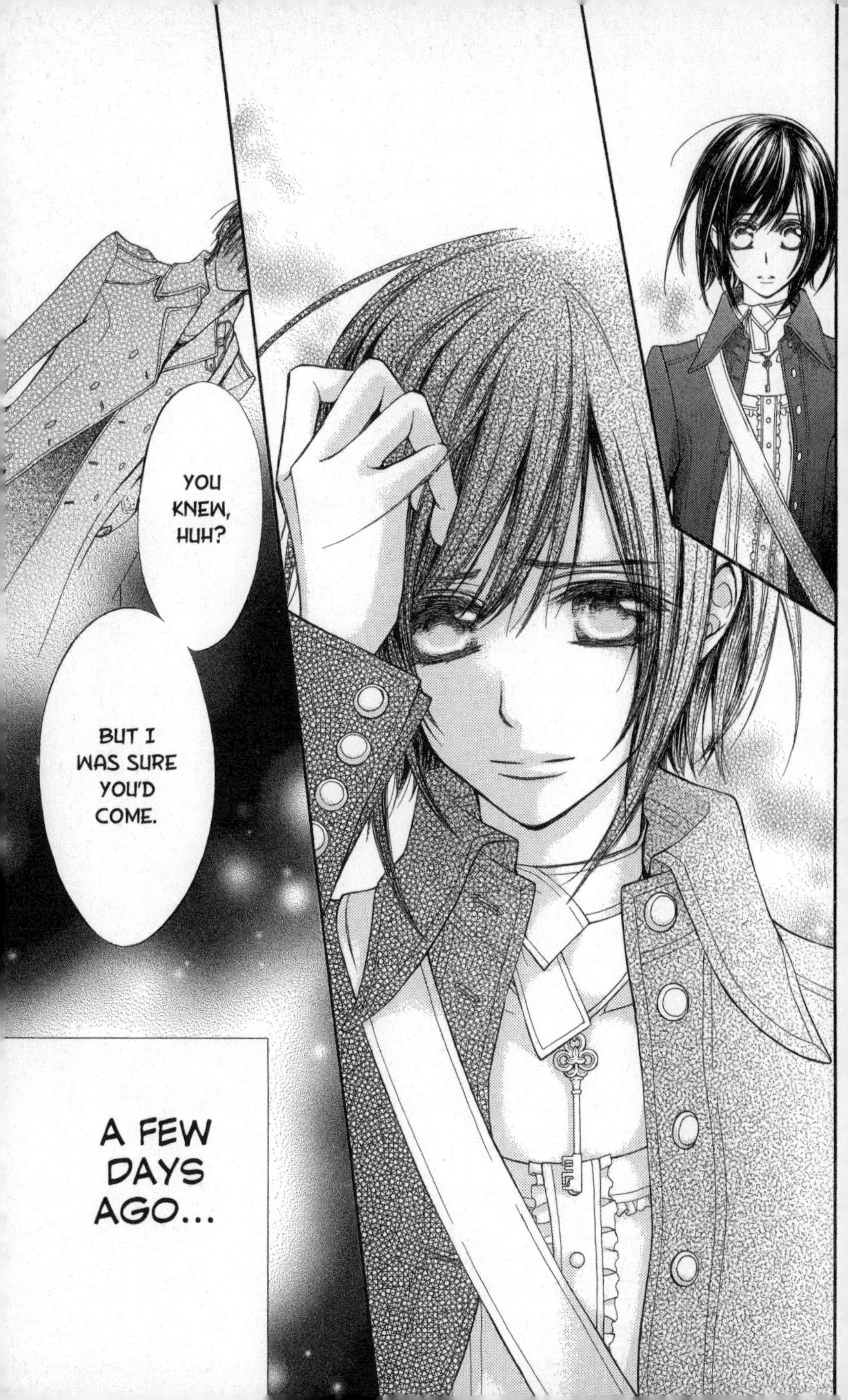
YOU KNEW, HUH?
BUT I WAS SURE YOU'D COME.
A FEW DAYS AGO...

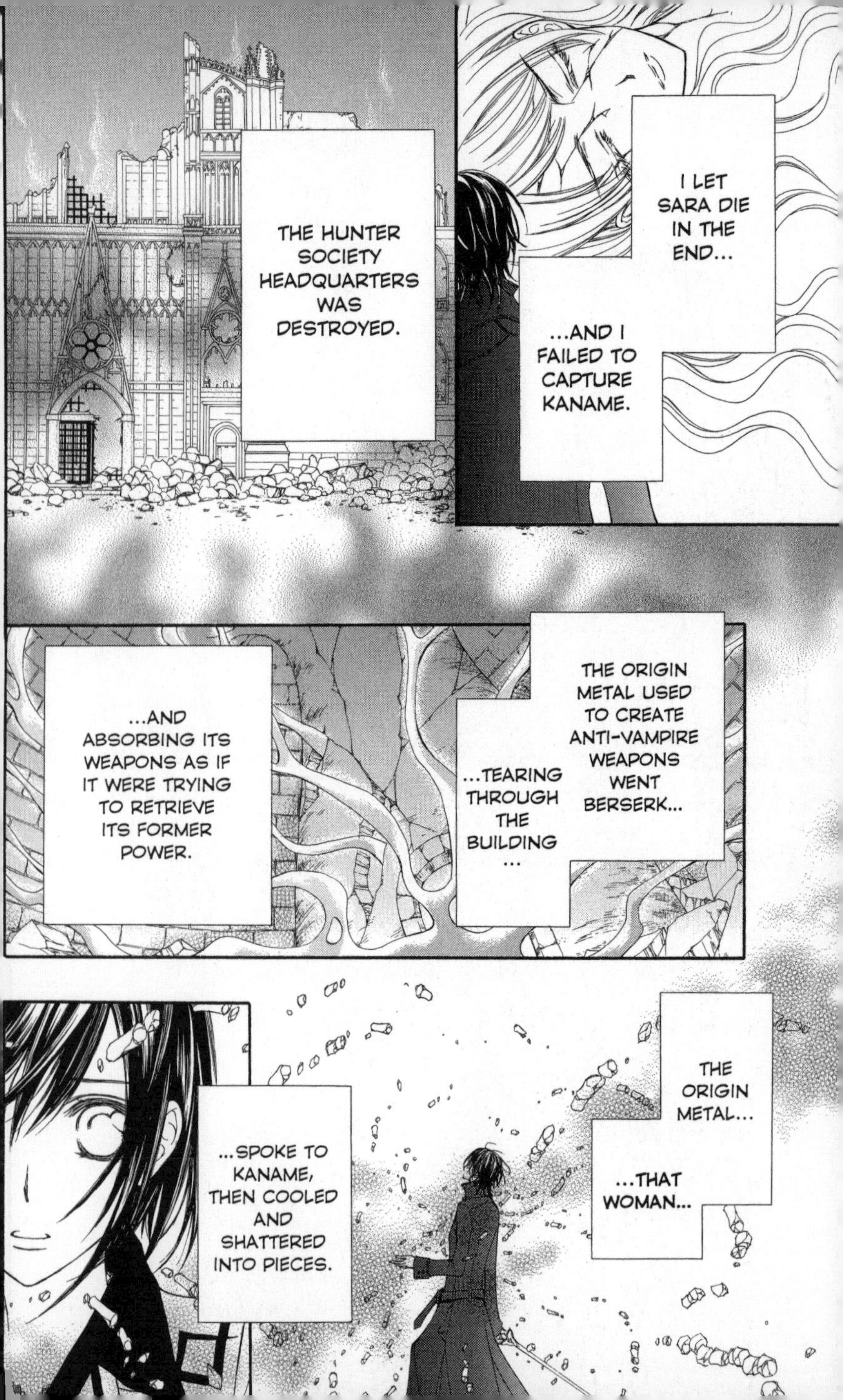
I LET SARA DIE IN THE END...
...AND I FAILED TO CAPTURE KANAME.
THE HUNTER SOCIETY HEADQUARTERS WAS DESTROYED.
THE ORIGIN METAL USED TO CREATE ANTI-VAMPIRE WEAPONS WENT BERSERK...
...TEARING THROUGH THE BUILDING...
...AND ABSORBING ITS WEAPONS AS IF IT WERE TRYING TO RETRIEVE ITS FORMER POWER.
THE ORIGIN METAL...
...THAT WOMAN...
...SPOKE TO KANAME, THEN COOLED AND SHATTERED INTO PIECES.

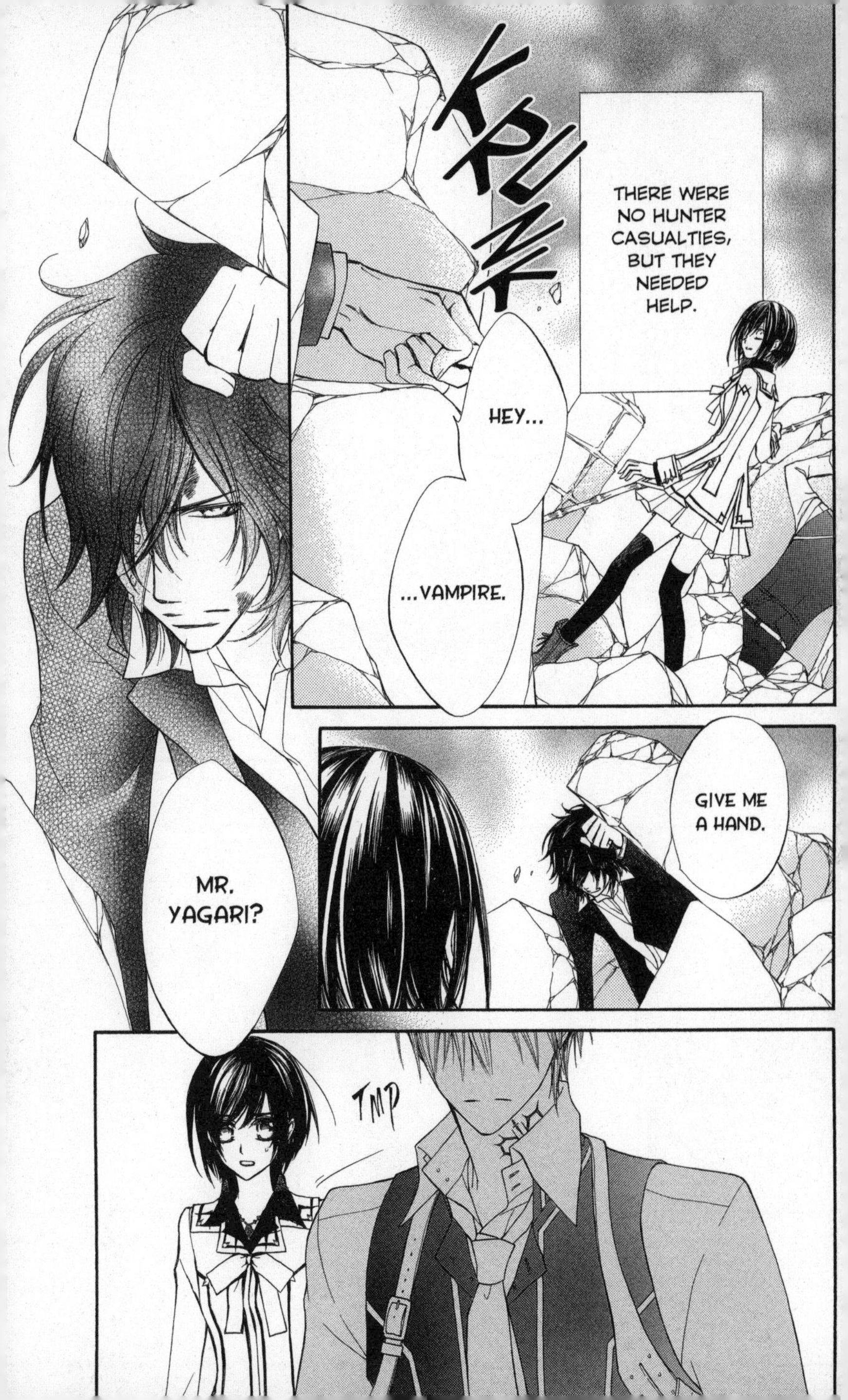
KRUNK
THERE WERE NO HUNTER CASUALTIES, BUT THEY NEEDED HELP.
HEY...
...VAMPIRE.
GIVE ME A HAND.
MR. YAGARI?
TMP

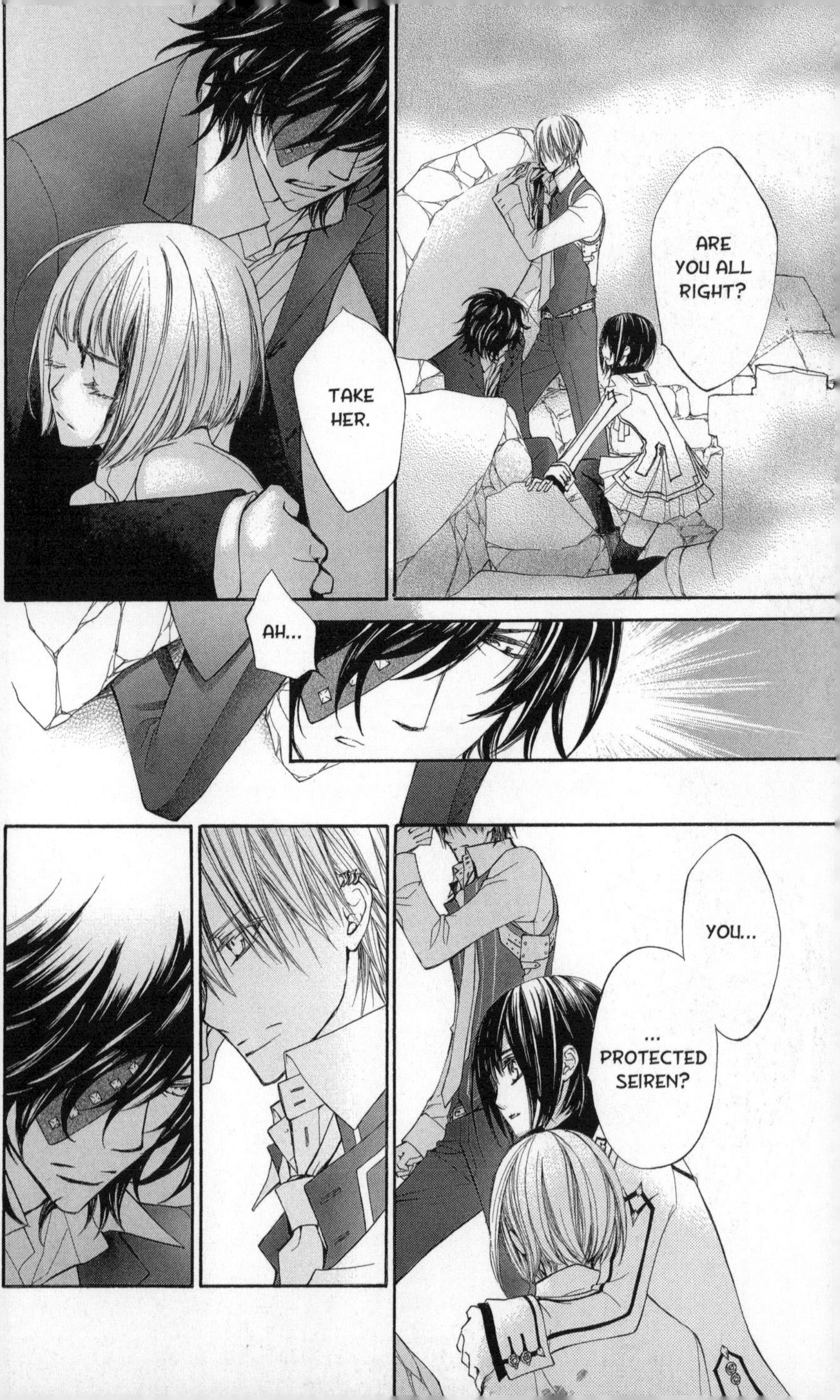
ARE YOU ALL RIGHT?
TAKE HER.
AH...
YOU...
... PROTECTED SEIREN?

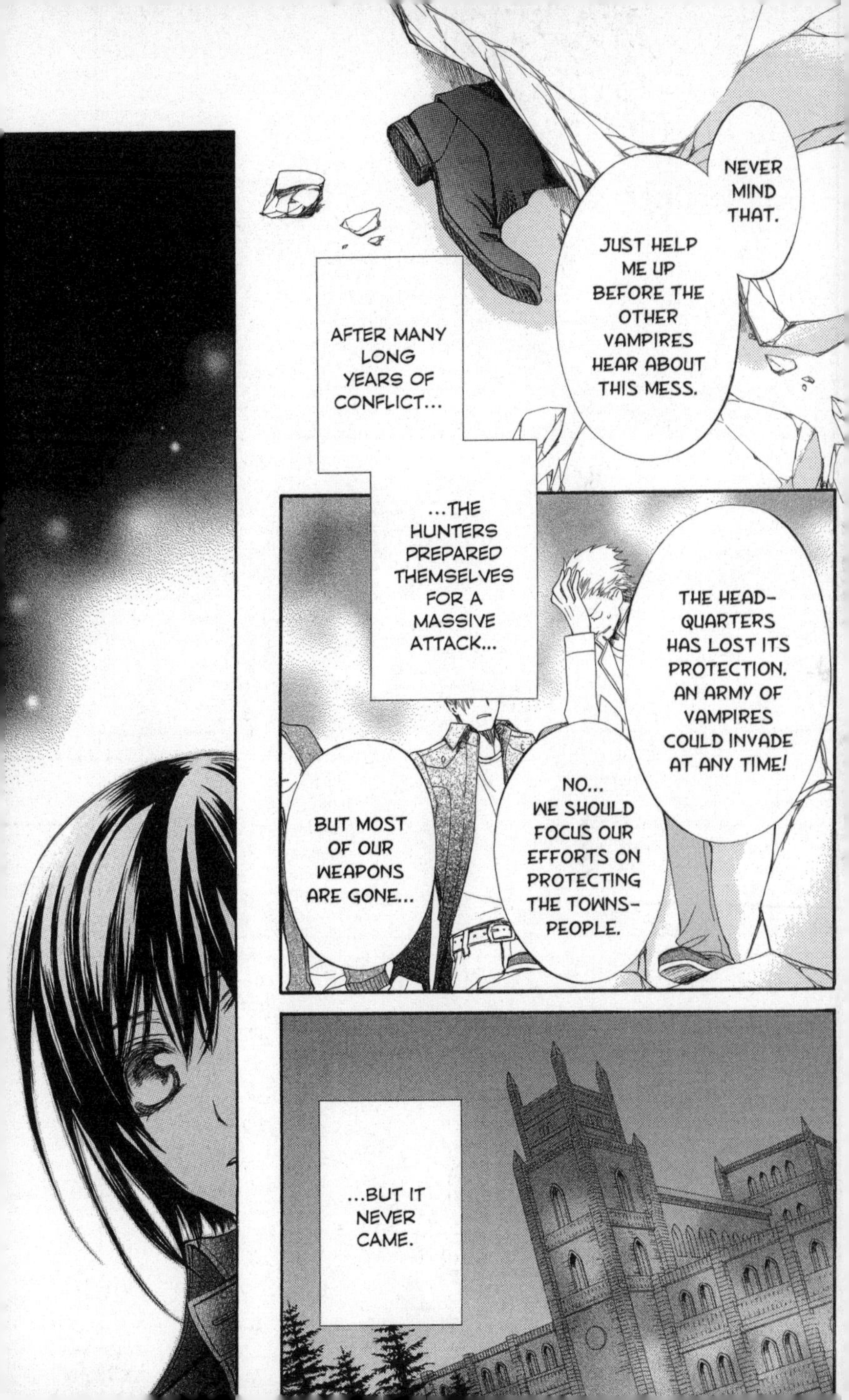
NEVER MIND THAT.
JUST HELP ME UP BEFORE THE OTHER VAMPIRES HEAR ABOUT THIS MESS.
AFTER MANY LONG YEARS OF CONFLICT...
...THE HUNTERS PREPARED THEMSELVES FOR A MASSIVE ATTACK...
THE HEAD-QUARTERS HAS LOST ITS PROTECTION. AN ARMY OF VAMPIRES COULD INVADE AT ANY TIME!
NO... WE SHOULD FOCUS OUR EFFORTS ON PROTECTING THE TOWNS-PEOPLE.
BUT MOST OF OUR WEAPONS ARE GONE...
...BUT IT NEVER CAME.

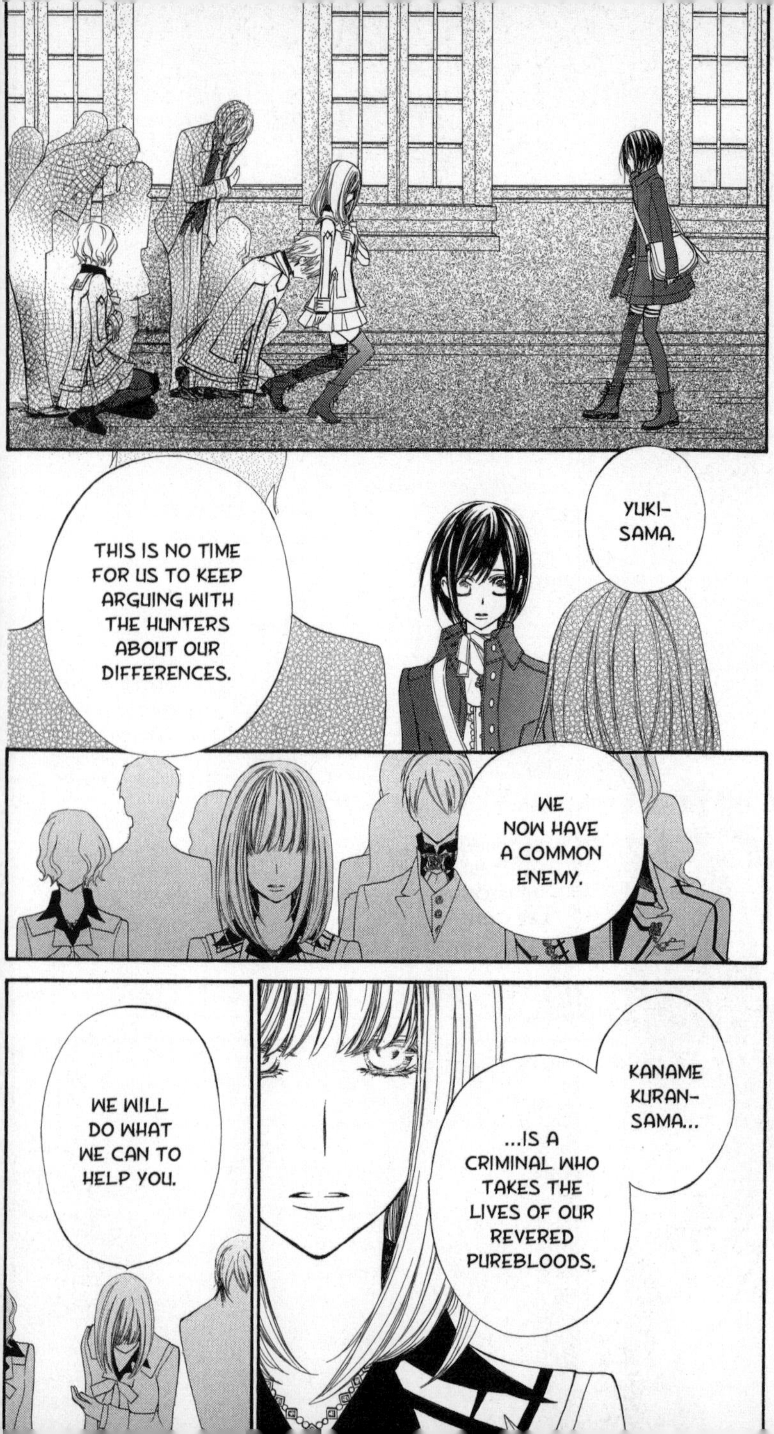
YUKI-SAMA.
THIS IS NO TIME FOR US TO KEEP ARGUING WITH THE HUNTERS ABOUT OUR DIFFERENCES.
WE NOW HAVE A COMMON ENEMY.
KANAME KURAN-SAMA...
...IS A CRIMINAL WHO TAKES THE LIVES OF OUR REVERED PUREBLOODS.
WE WILL DO WHAT WE CAN TO HELP YOU.

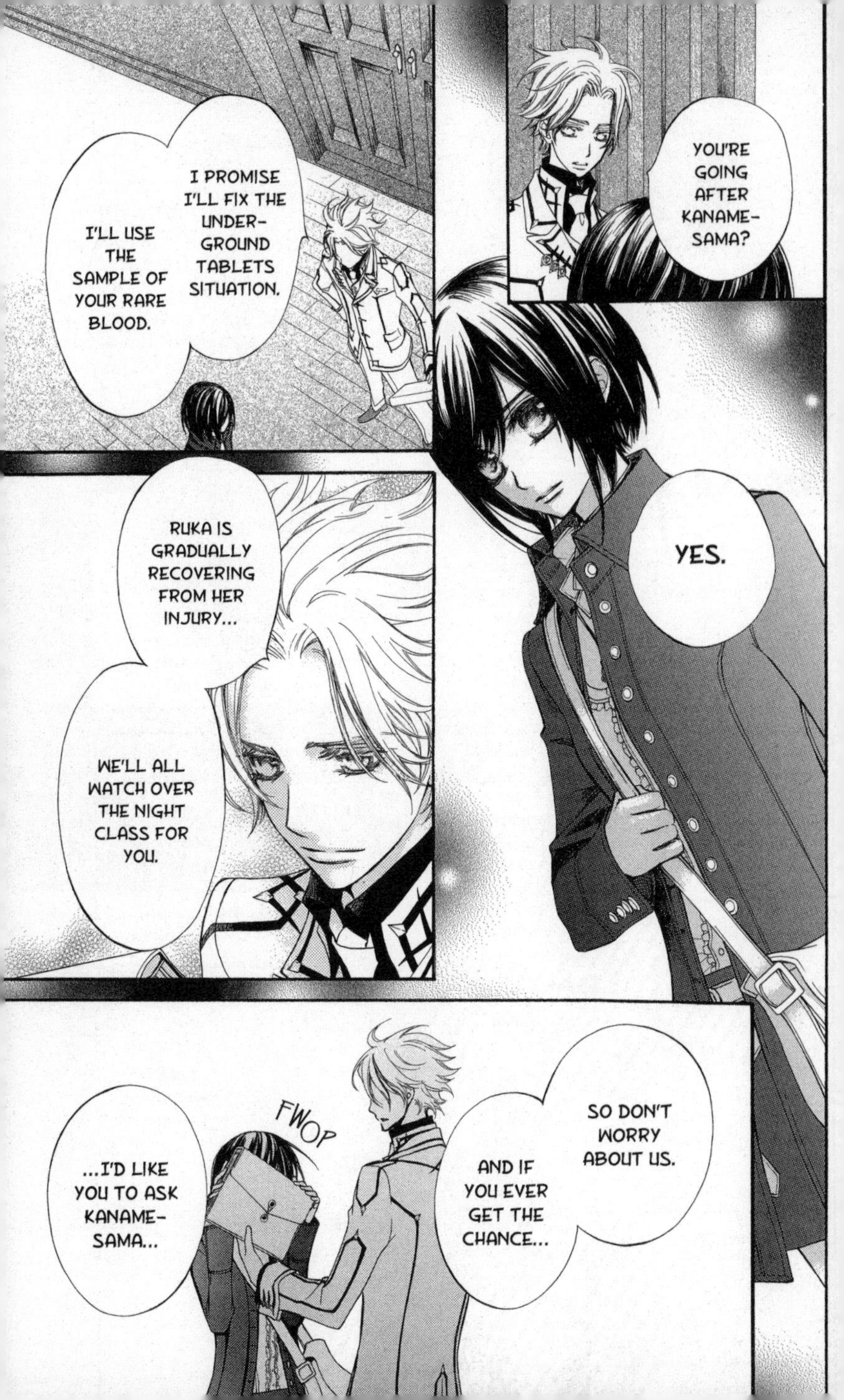
YOU'RE GOING AFTER KANAME-SAMA?
YES.
I PROMISE I'LL FIX THE UNDER-GROUND TABLETS SITUATION.
I'LL USE THE SAMPLE OF YOUR RARE BLOOD.
RUKA IS GRADUALLY RECOVERING FROM HER INJURY...
WE'LL ALL WATCH OVER THE NIGHT CLASS FOR YOU.
SO DON'T WORRY ABOUT US.
AND IF YOU EVER GET THE CHANCE...
FWOP
...I'D LIKE YOU TO ASK KANAME-SAMA...

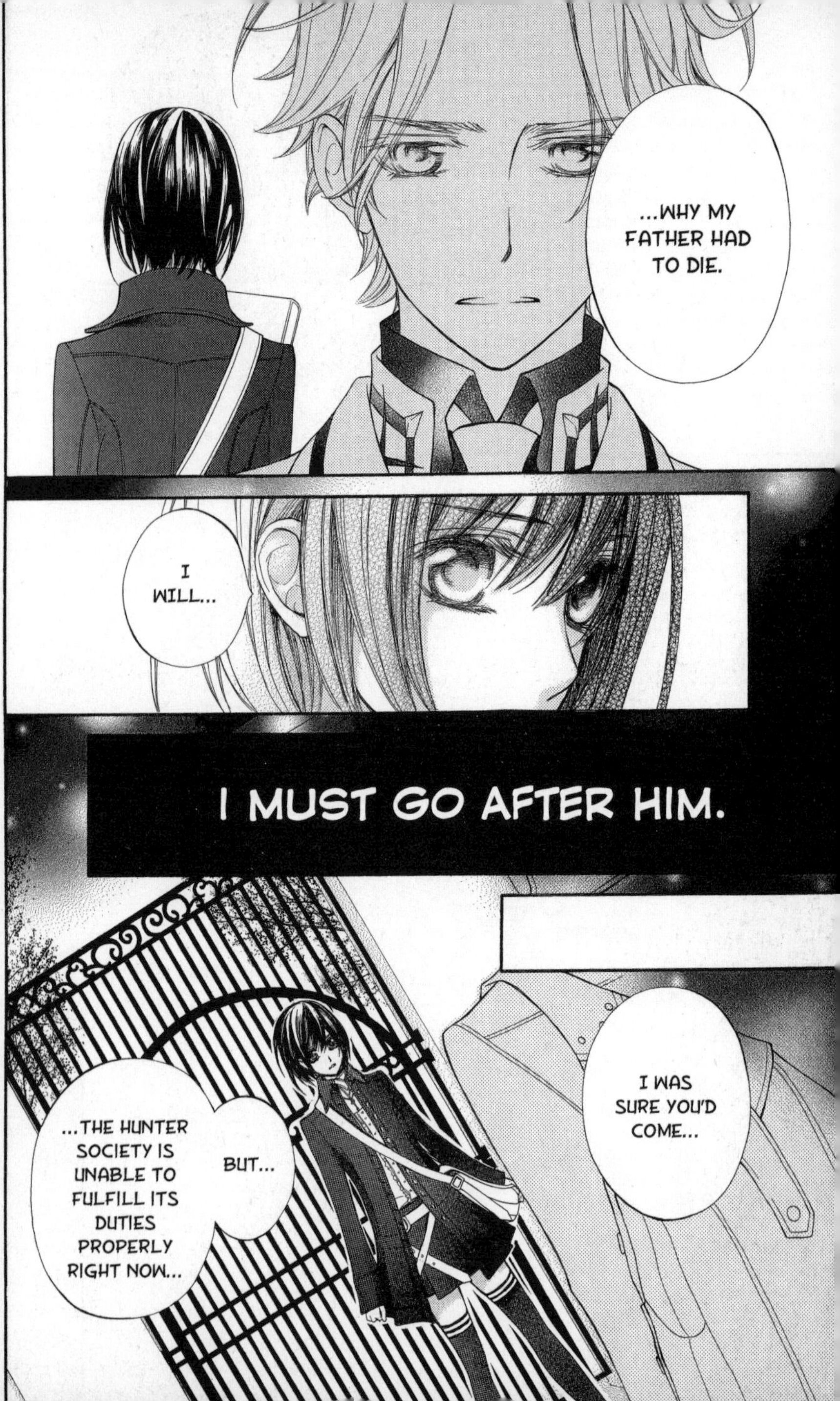
...WHY MY FATHER HAD TO DIE.
I WILL...
I MUST GO AFTER HIM.
I WAS SURE YOU'D COME...
BUT...
...THE HUNTER SOCIETY IS UNABLE TO FULFILL ITS DUTIES PROPERLY RIGHT NOW...

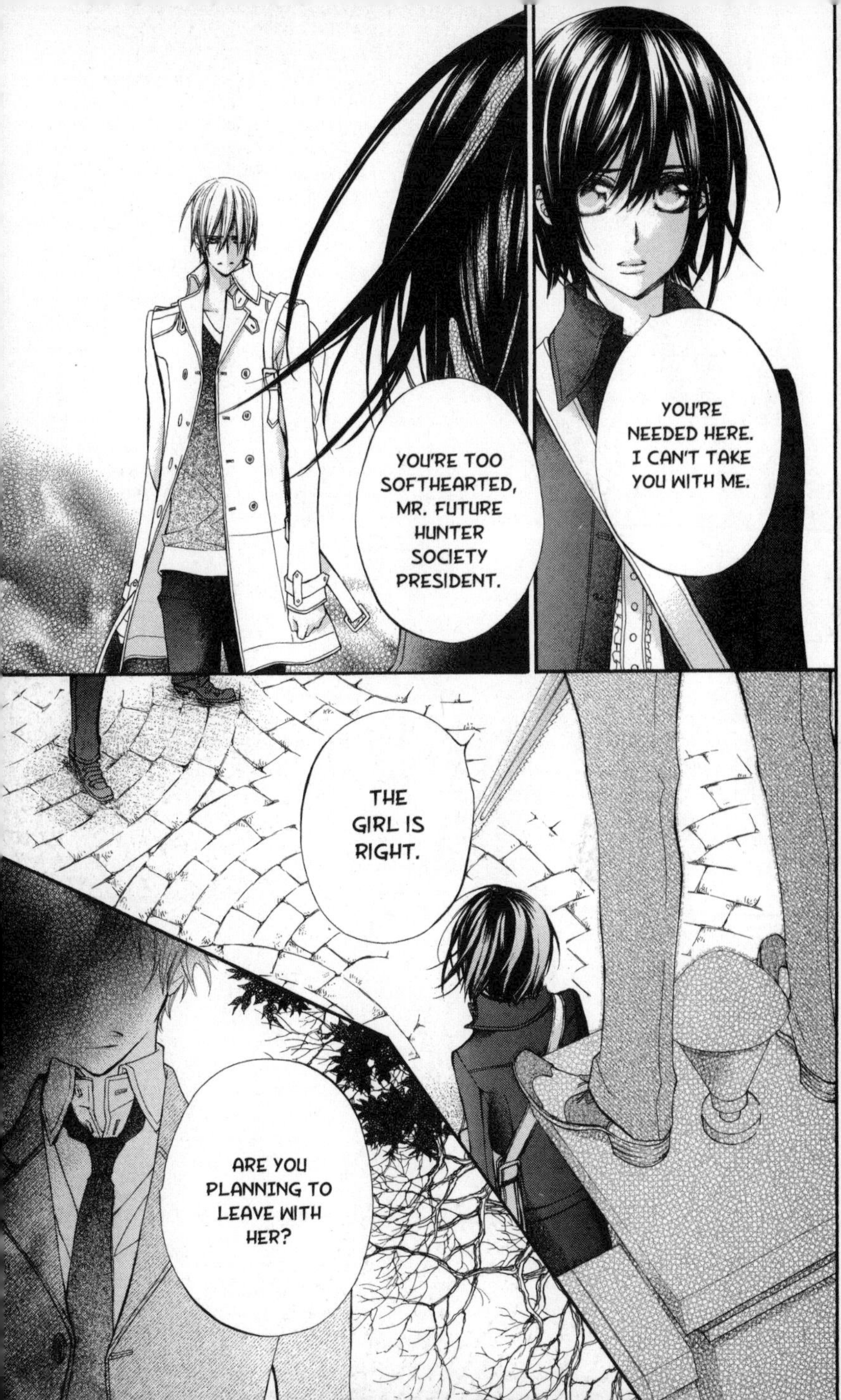
YOU'RE NEEDED HERE. I CAN'T TAKE YOU WITH ME.
YOU'RE TOO SOFTHEARTED, MR. FUTURE HUNTER SOCIETY PRESIDENT.
THE GIRL IS RIGHT.
ARE YOU PLANNING TO LEAVE WITH HER?

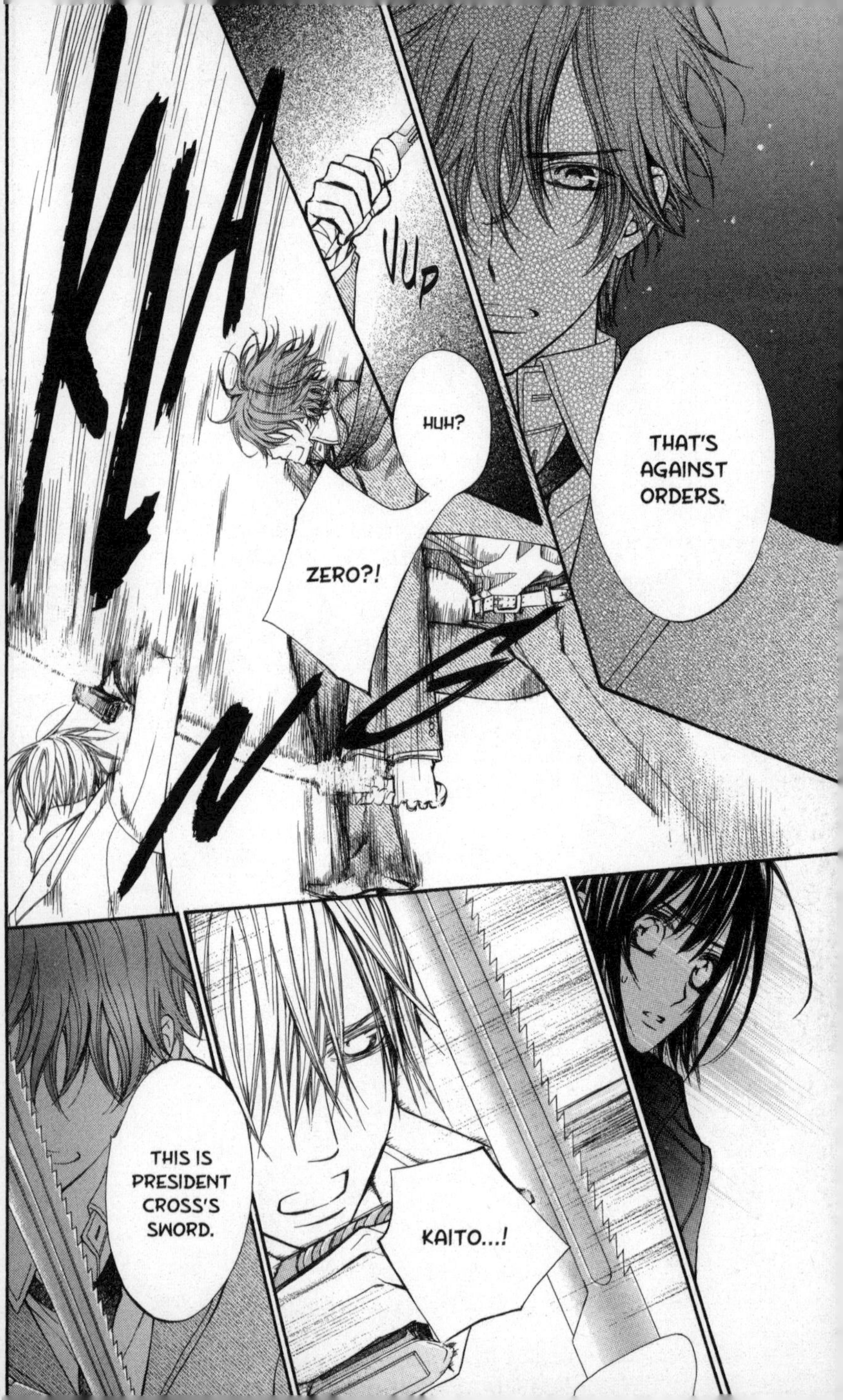
THAT'S AGAINST ORDERS.
VUP
HUH?
ZERO?!
KLANG
KAITO...!
THIS IS PRESIDENT CROSS'S SWORD.

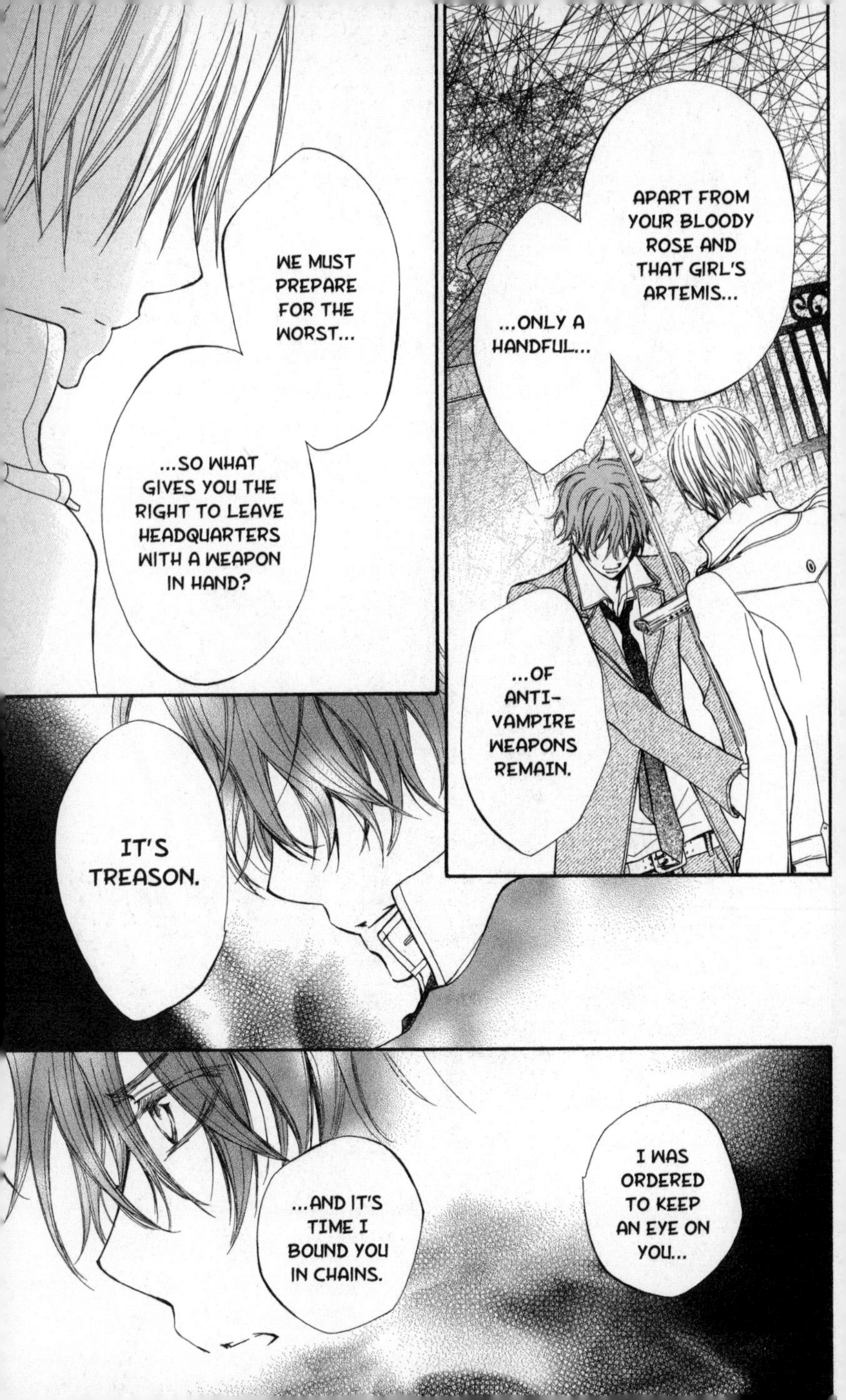
APART FROM YOUR BLOODY ROSE AND THAT GIRL'S ARTEMIS...
...ONLY A HANDFUL...
...OF ANTI-VAMPIRE WEAPONS REMAIN.
WE MUST PREPARE FOR THE WORST...
...SO WHAT GIVES YOU THE RIGHT TO LEAVE HEADQUARTERS WITH A WEAPON IN HAND?
IT'S TREASON.
I WAS ORDERED TO KEEP AN EYE ON YOU...
...AND IT'S TIME I BOUND YOU IN CHAINS.

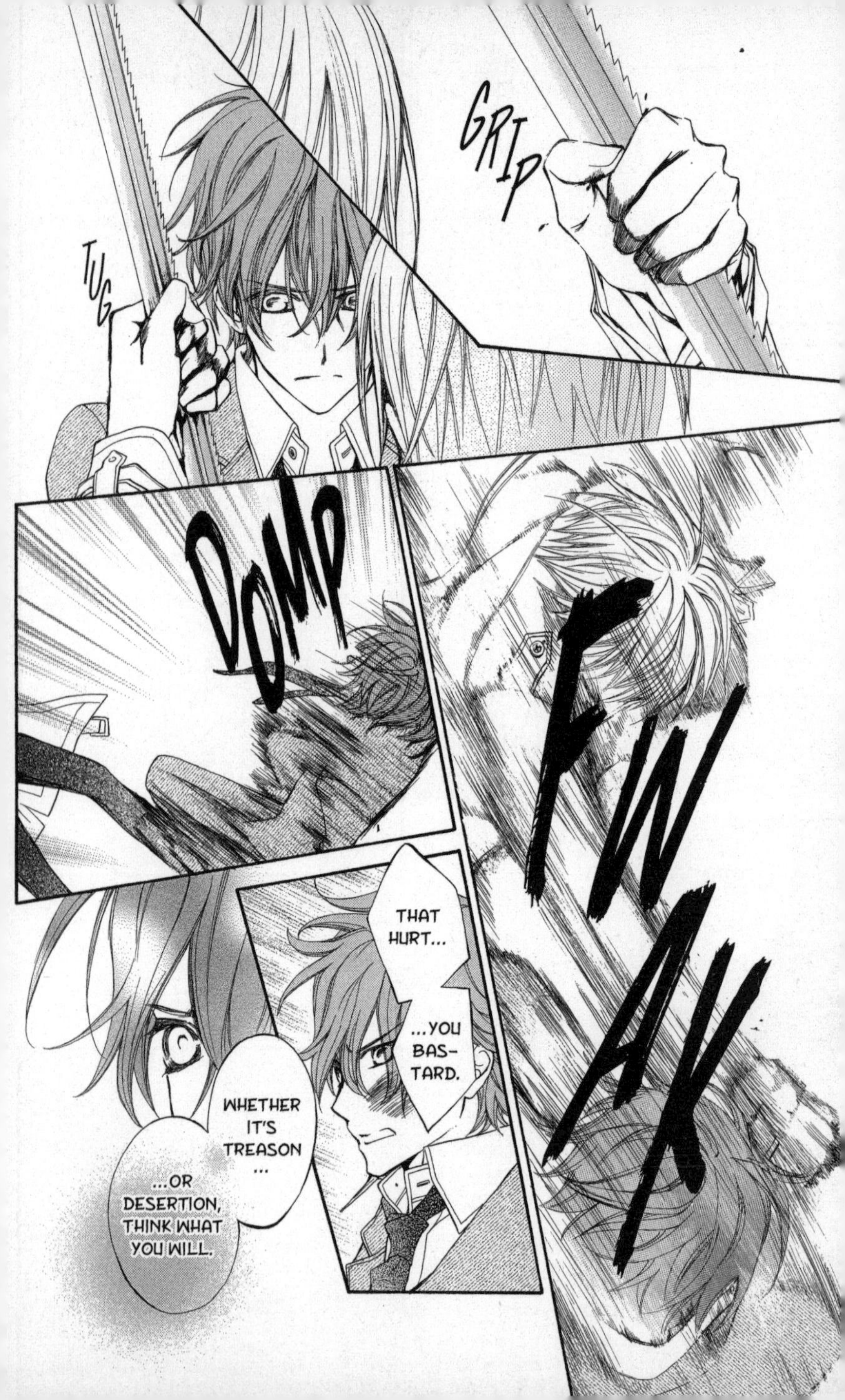
GRIP
TUG
FWAK
DOMP
THAT HURT...
...YOU BAS-TARD.
WHETHER IT'S TREASON ...
...OR DESERTION, THINK WHAT YOU WILL.

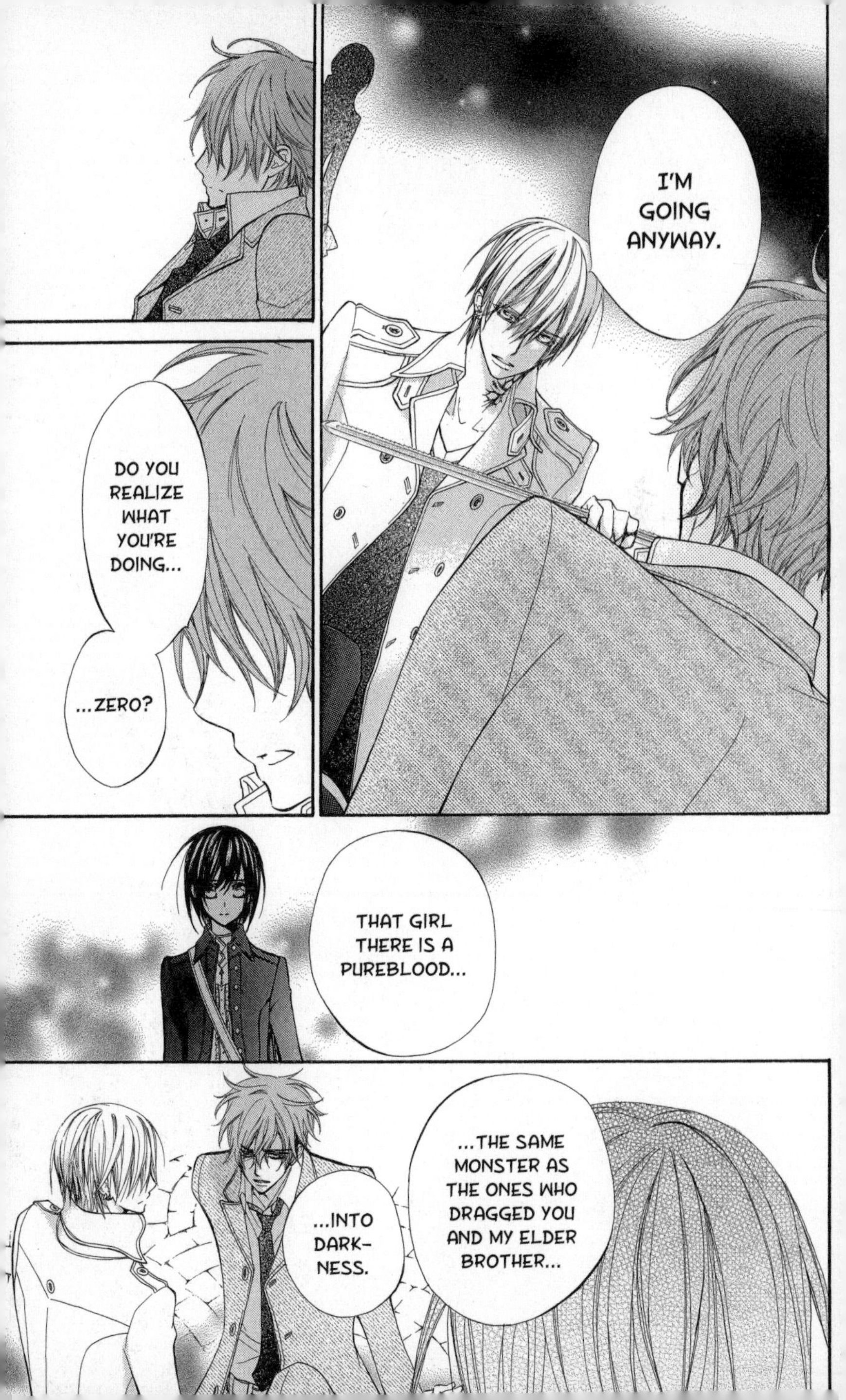
I'M GOING ANYWAY.
DO YOU REALIZE WHAT YOU'RE DOING...
...ZERO?
THAT GIRL THERE IS A PUREBLOOD...
...THE SAME MONSTER AS THE ONES WHO DRAGGED YOU AND MY ELDER BROTHER...
...INTO DARK-NESS.

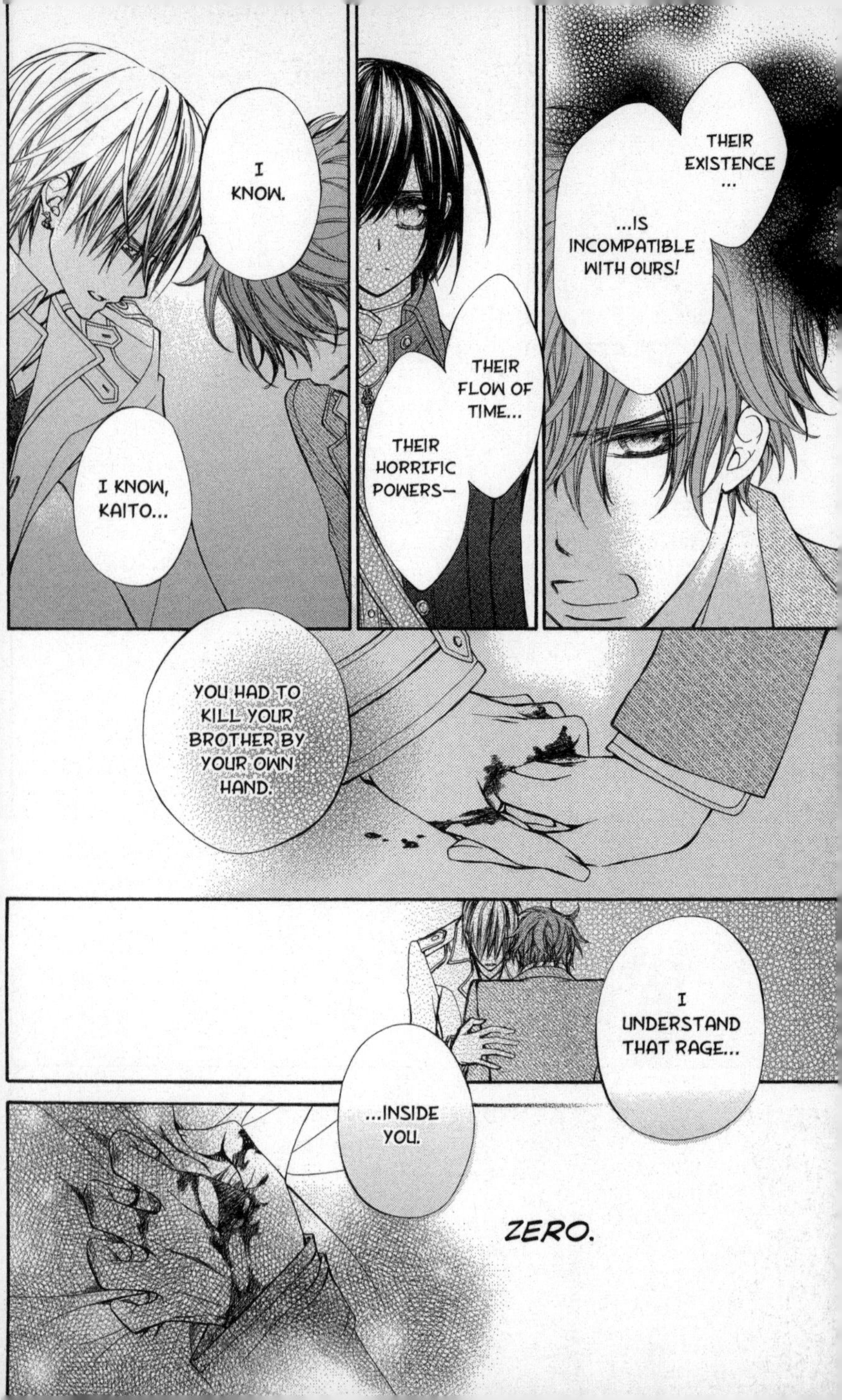
THEIR EXISTENCE ...
...IS INCOMPATIBLE WITH OURS!
THEIR FLOW OF TIME...
THEIR HORRIFIC POWERS—
I KNOW.
I KNOW, KAITO...
YOU HAD TO KILL YOUR BROTHER BY YOUR OWN HAND.
I UNDERSTAND THAT RAGE...
...INSIDE YOU.
ZERO.

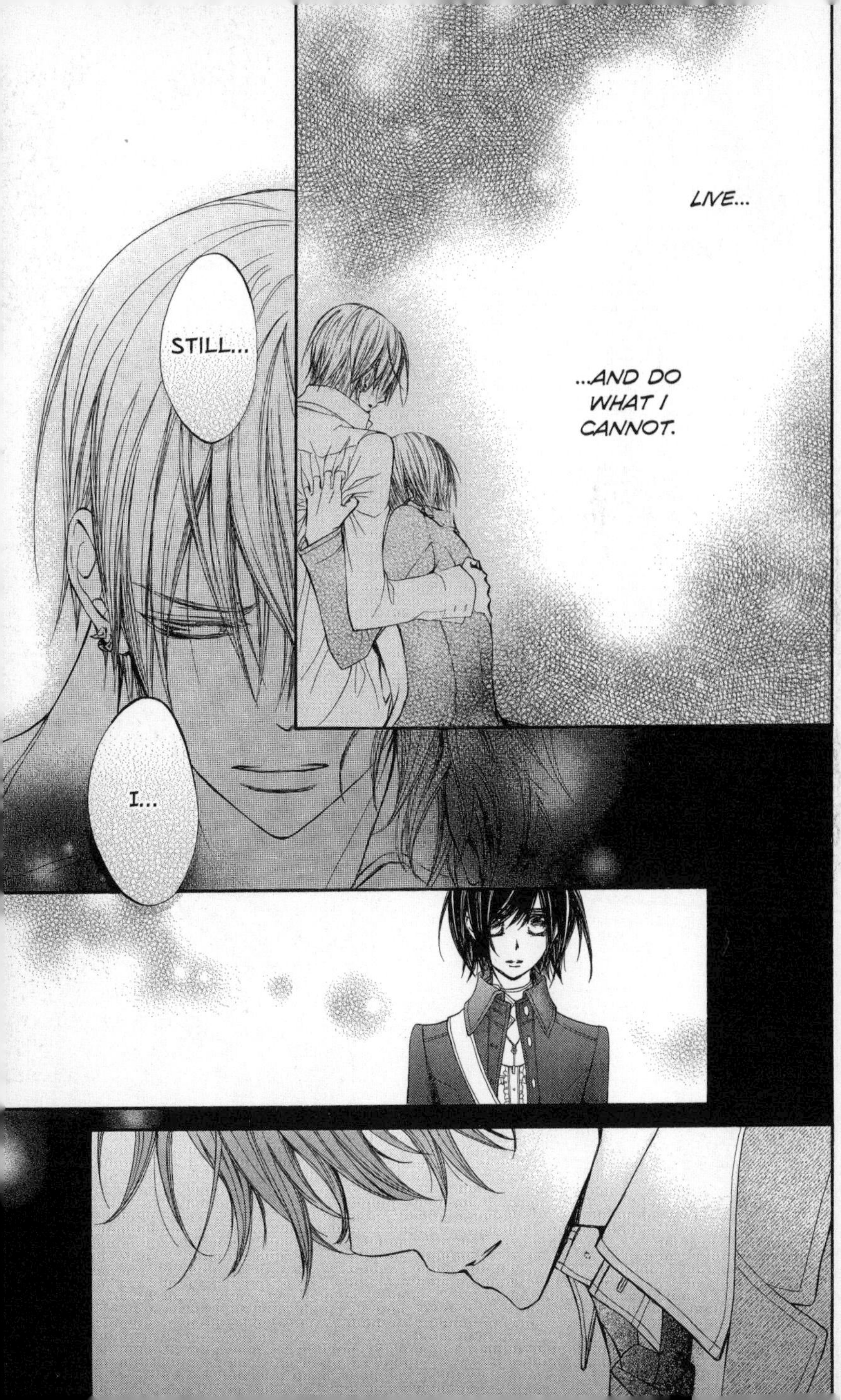
LIVE...
...AND DO WHAT I CANNOT.
STILL...
I...

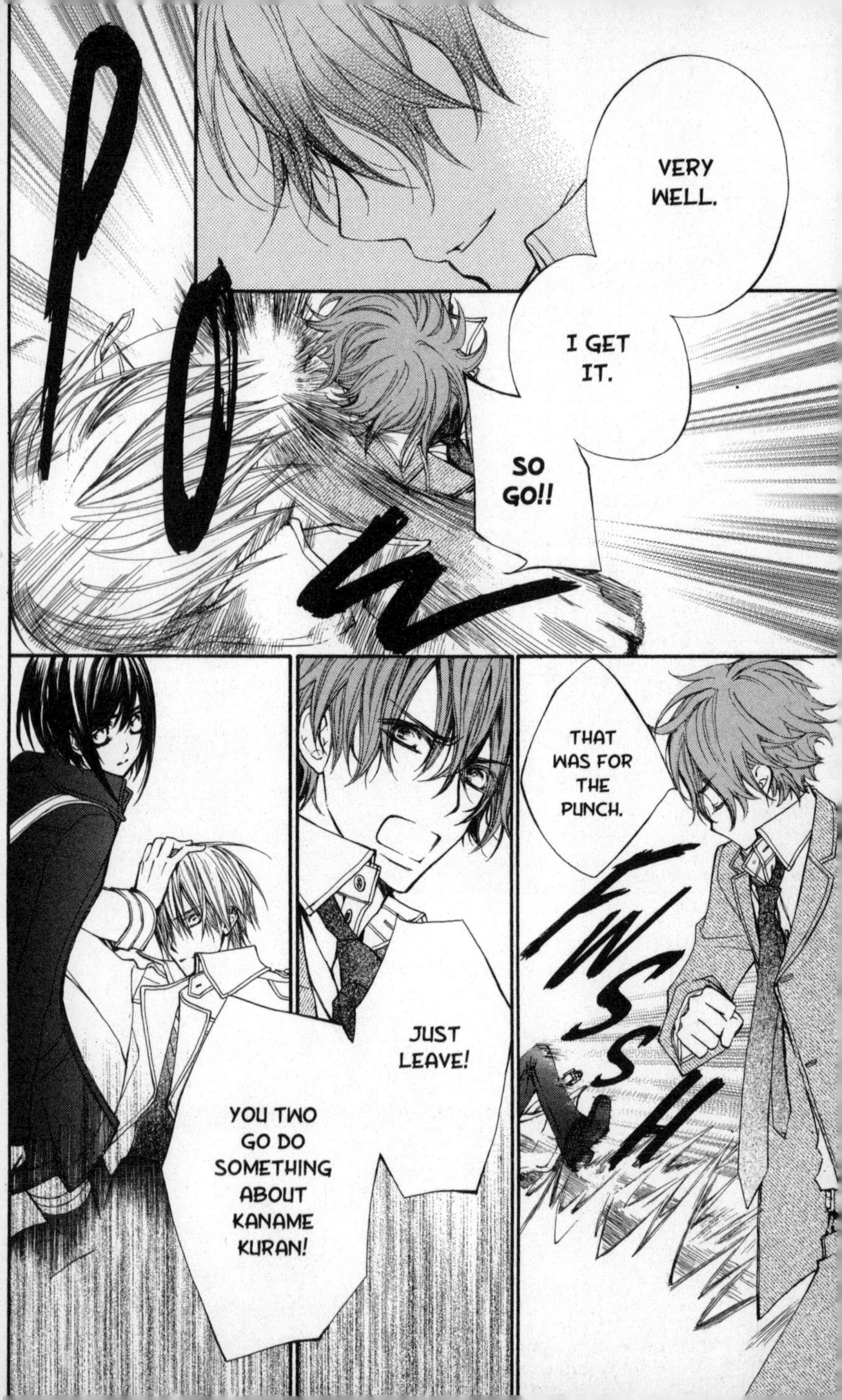
VERY WELL.
I GET IT.
SO GO!!
POW
THAT WAS FOR THE PUNCH.
FWSSH
JUST LEAVE!
YOU TWO GO DO SOMETHING ABOUT KANAME KURAN!

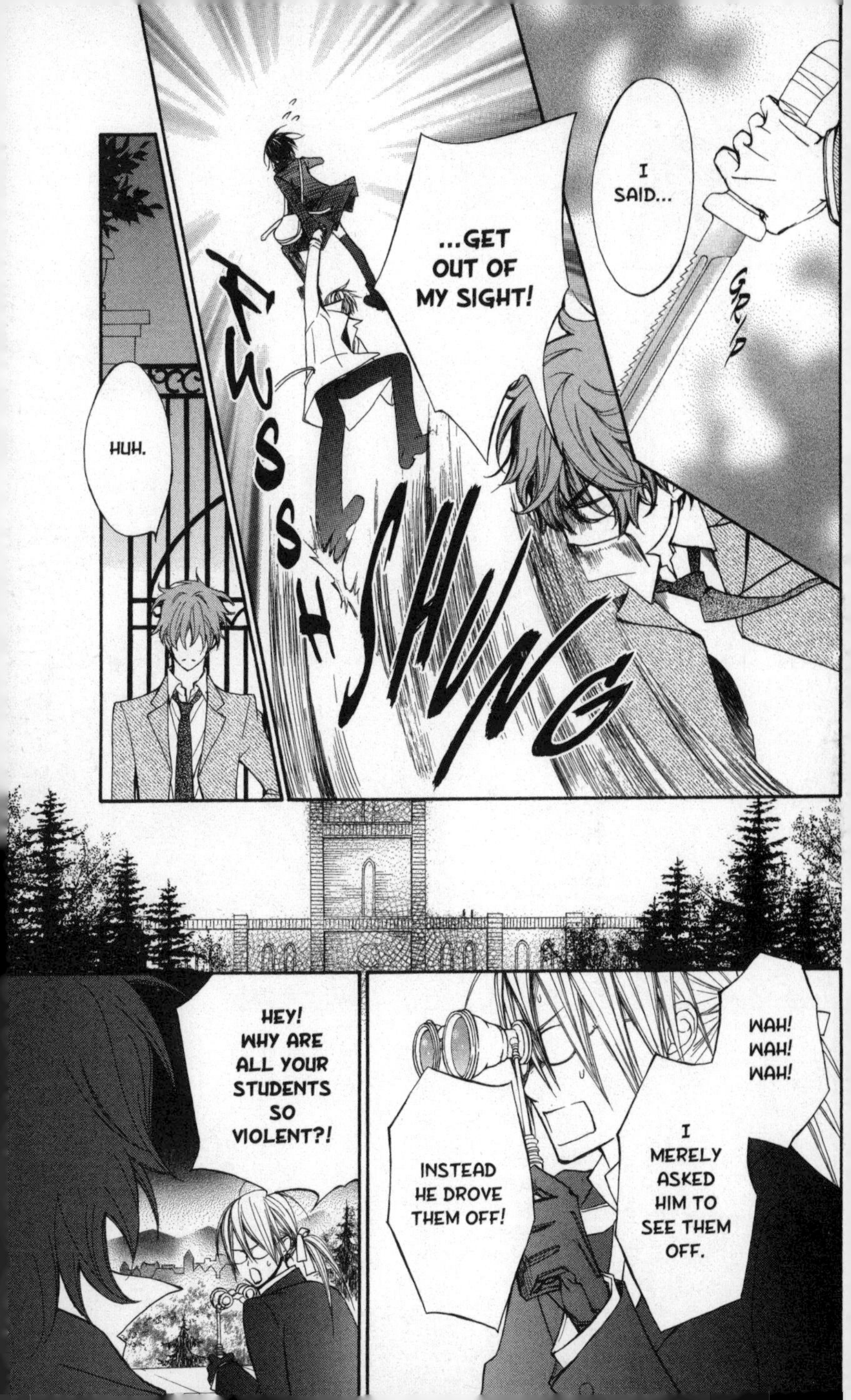
I SAID...
GRIP
...GET OUT OF MY SIGHT!
FWSSH
SHUNG
HUH.
WAH! WAH! WAH!
I MERELY ASKED HIM TO SEE THEM OFF.
INSTEAD HE DROVE THEM OFF!
HEY! WHY ARE ALL YOUR STUDENTS SO VIOLENT?!

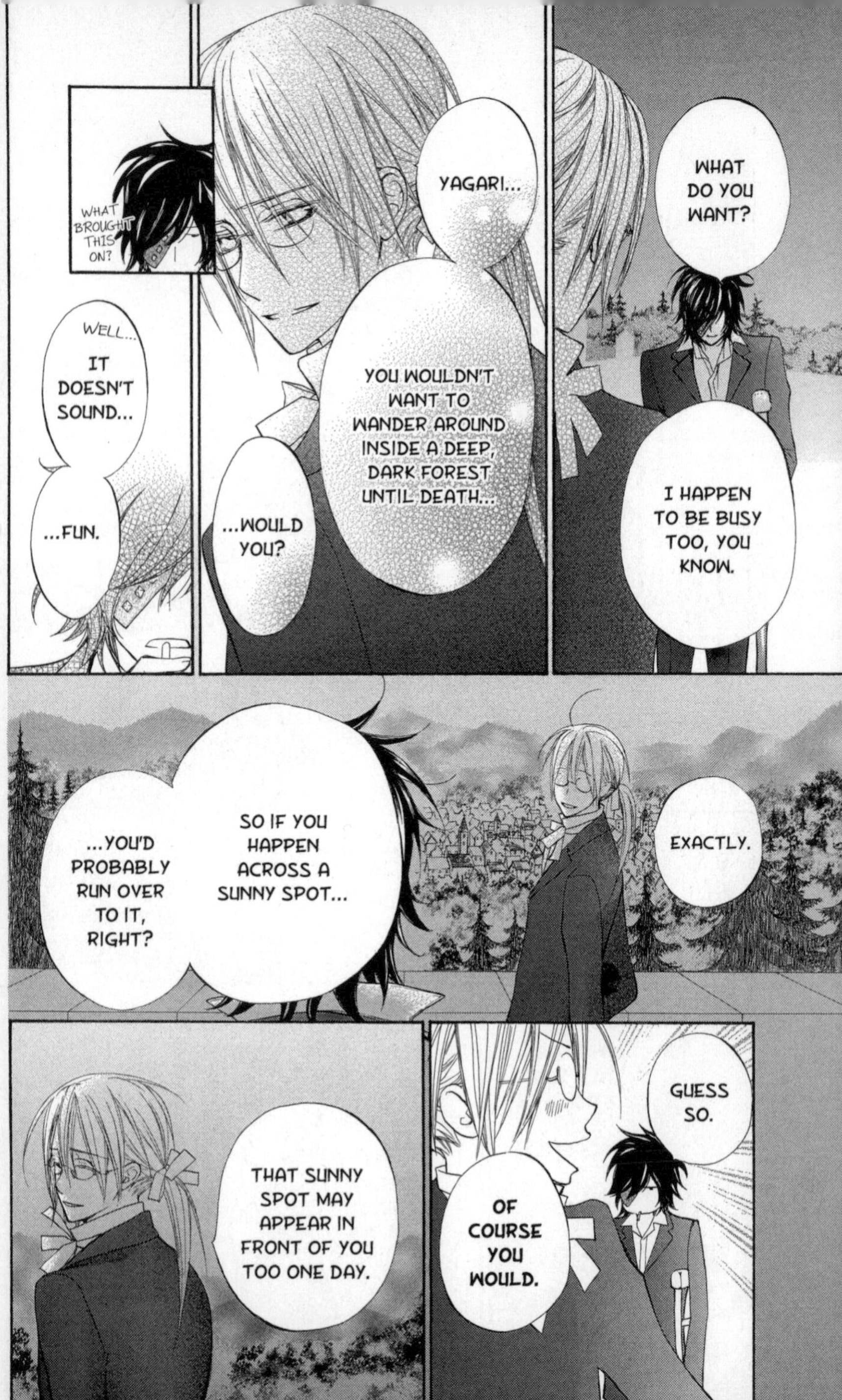
WHAT DO YOU WANT?
I HAPPEN TO BE BUSY TOO, YOU KNOW.
YAGARI...
YOU WOULDN'T WANT TO WANDER AROUND INSIDE A DEEP, DARK FOREST UNTIL DEATH...
...WOULD YOU?
WHAT BROUGHT THIS ON?
WELL... IT DOESN'T SOUND...
...FUN.
EXACTLY.
SO IF YOU HAPPEN ACROSS A SUNNY SPOT...
...YOU'D PROBABLY RUN OVER TO IT, RIGHT?
GUESS SO.
OF COURSE YOU WOULD.
THAT SUNNY SPOT MAY APPEAR IN FRONT OF YOU TOO ONE DAY.

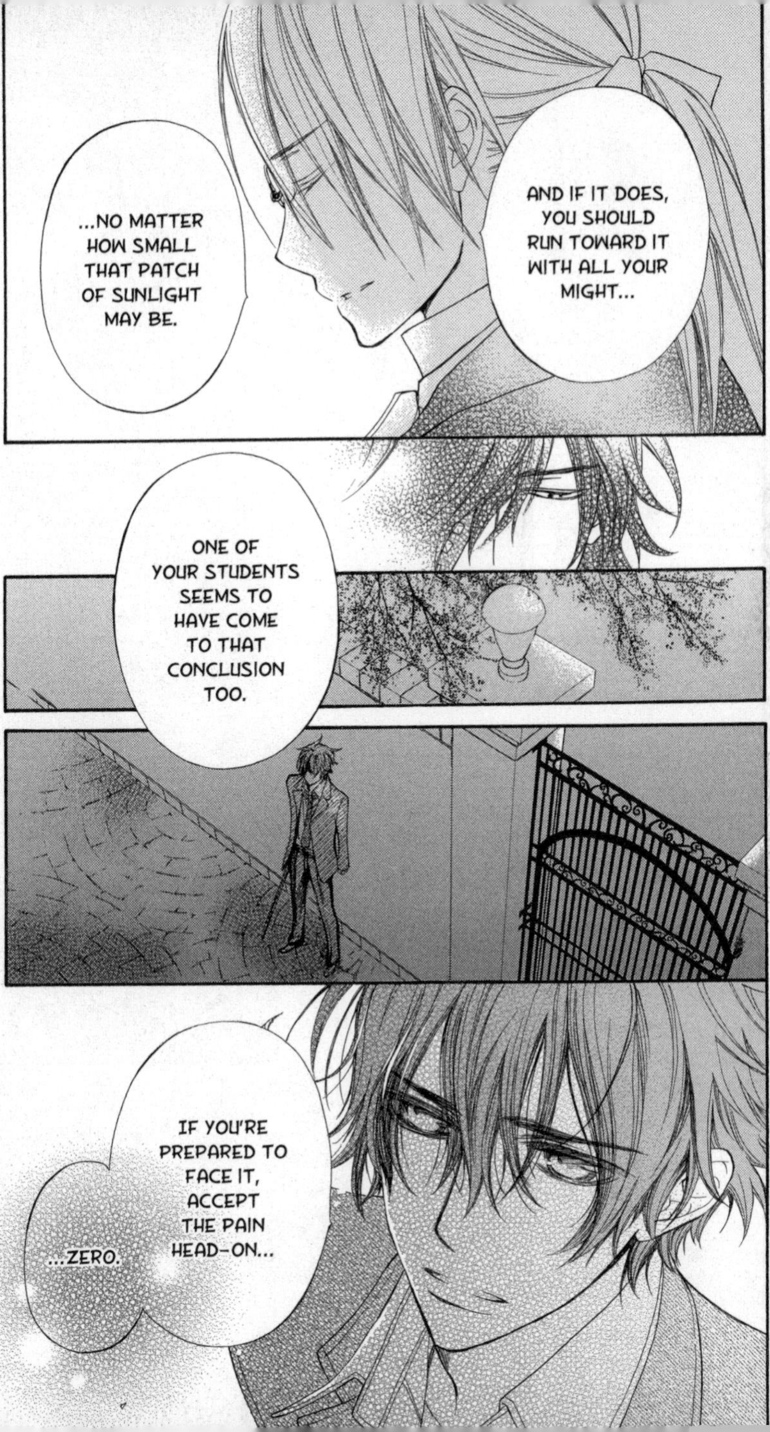
AND IF IT DOES, YOU SHOULD RUN TOWARD IT WITH ALL YOUR MIGHT...
...NO MATTER HOW SMALL THAT PATCH OF SUNLIGHT MAY BE.
ONE OF YOUR STUDENTS SEEMS TO HAVE COME TO THAT CONCLUSION TOO.
IF YOU'RE PREPARED TO FACE IT, ACCEPT THE PAIN HEAD-ON...
...ZERO.

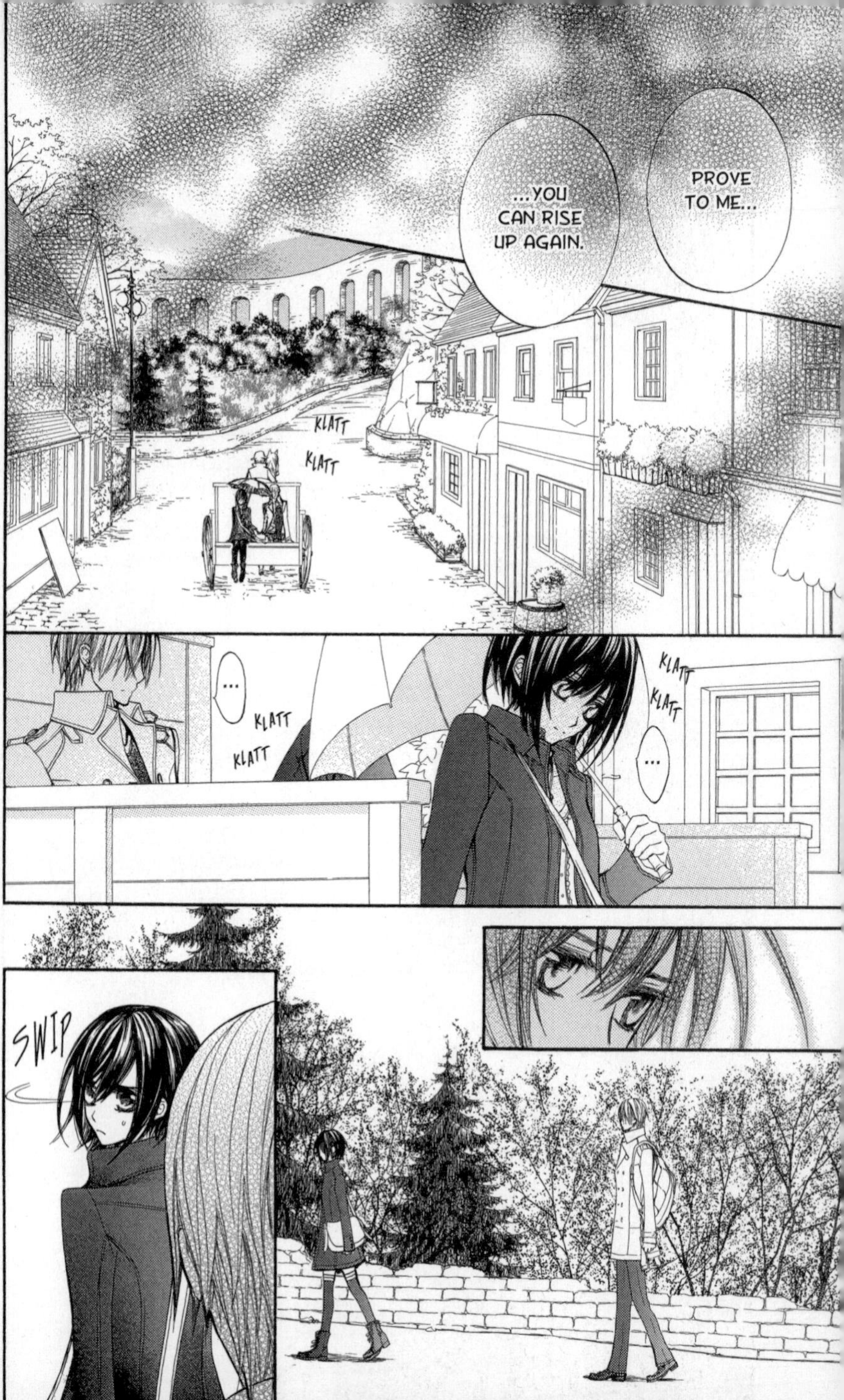
PROVE TO ME...
...YOU CAN RISE UP AGAIN.
KLATT
KLATT
KLATT
KLATT
...
...
KLATT
KLATT
SWIP

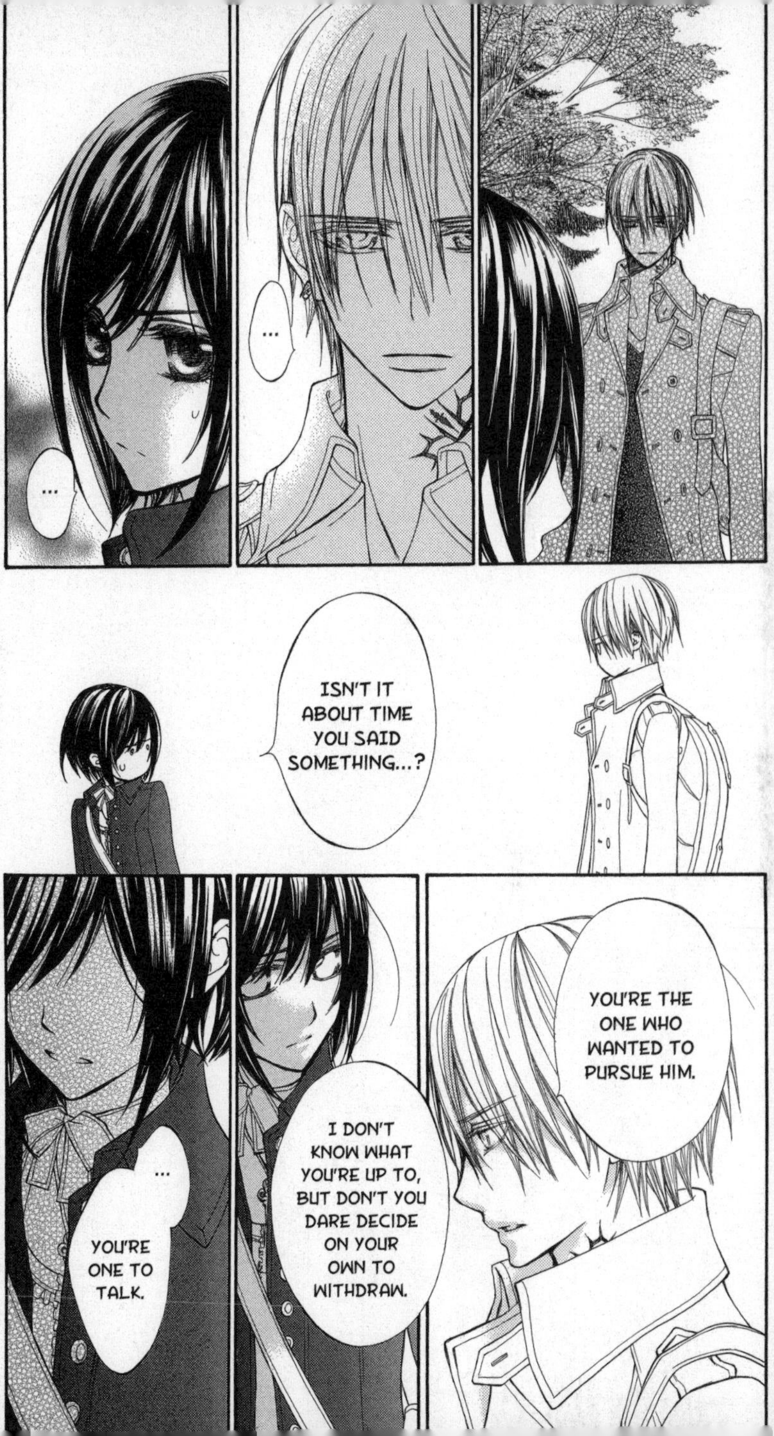
...
...
ISN'T IT ABOUT TIME YOU SAID SOMETHING...?
YOU'RE THE ONE WHO WANTED TO PURSUE HIM.
I DON'T KNOW WHAT YOU'RE UP TO, BUT DON'T YOU DARE DECIDE ON YOUR OWN TO WITHDRAW.
...
YOU'RE ONE TO TALK.

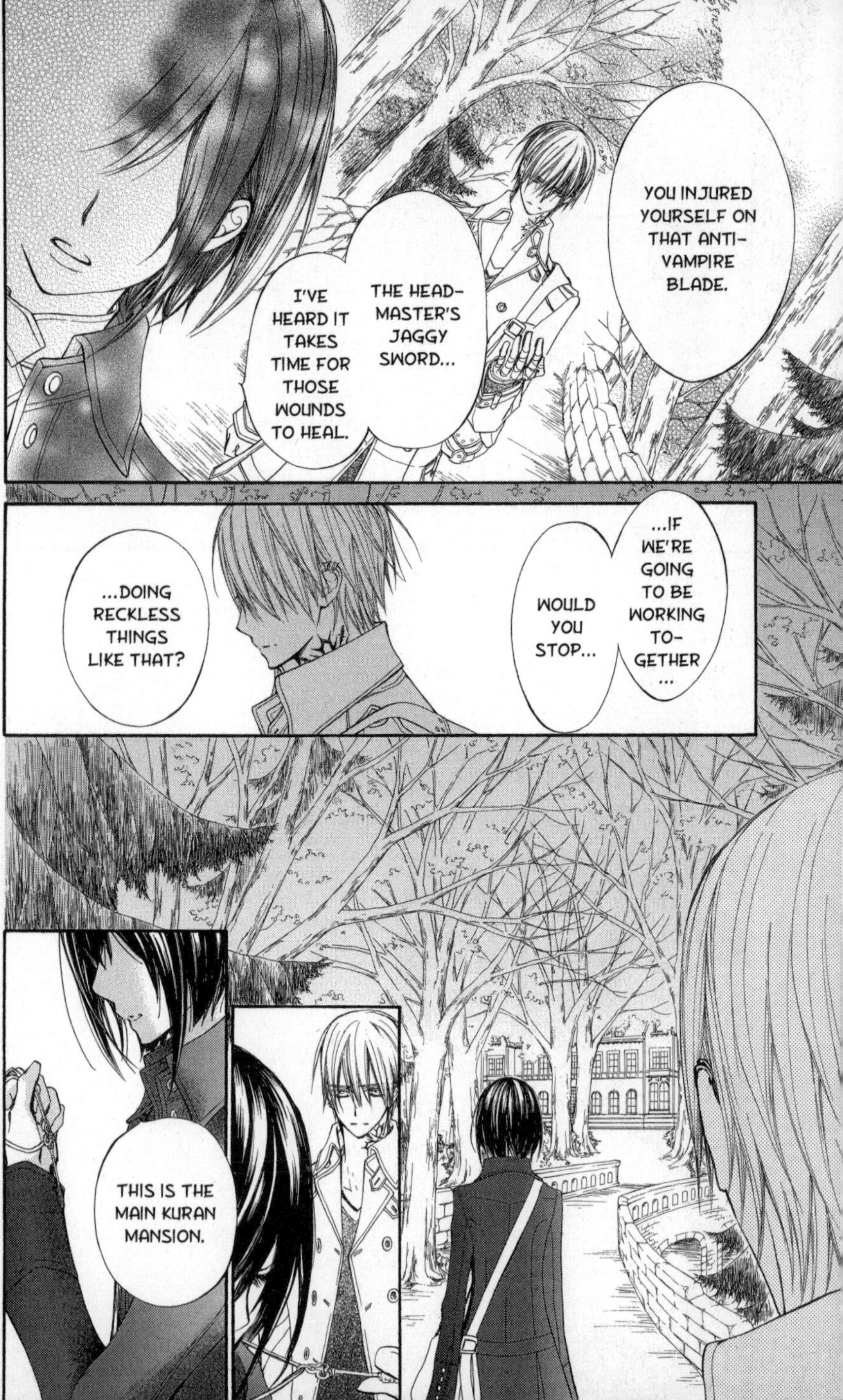
YOU INJURED YOURSELF ON THAT ANTI-VAMPIRE BLADE.
THE HEAD-MASTER'S JAGGY SWORD...
I'VE HEARD IT TAKES TIME FOR THOSE WOUNDS TO HEAL.
...IF WE'RE GOING TO BE WORKING TO-GETHER...
WOULD YOU STOP...
...DOING RECKLESS THINGS LIKE THAT?
THIS IS THE MAIN KURAN MANSION.

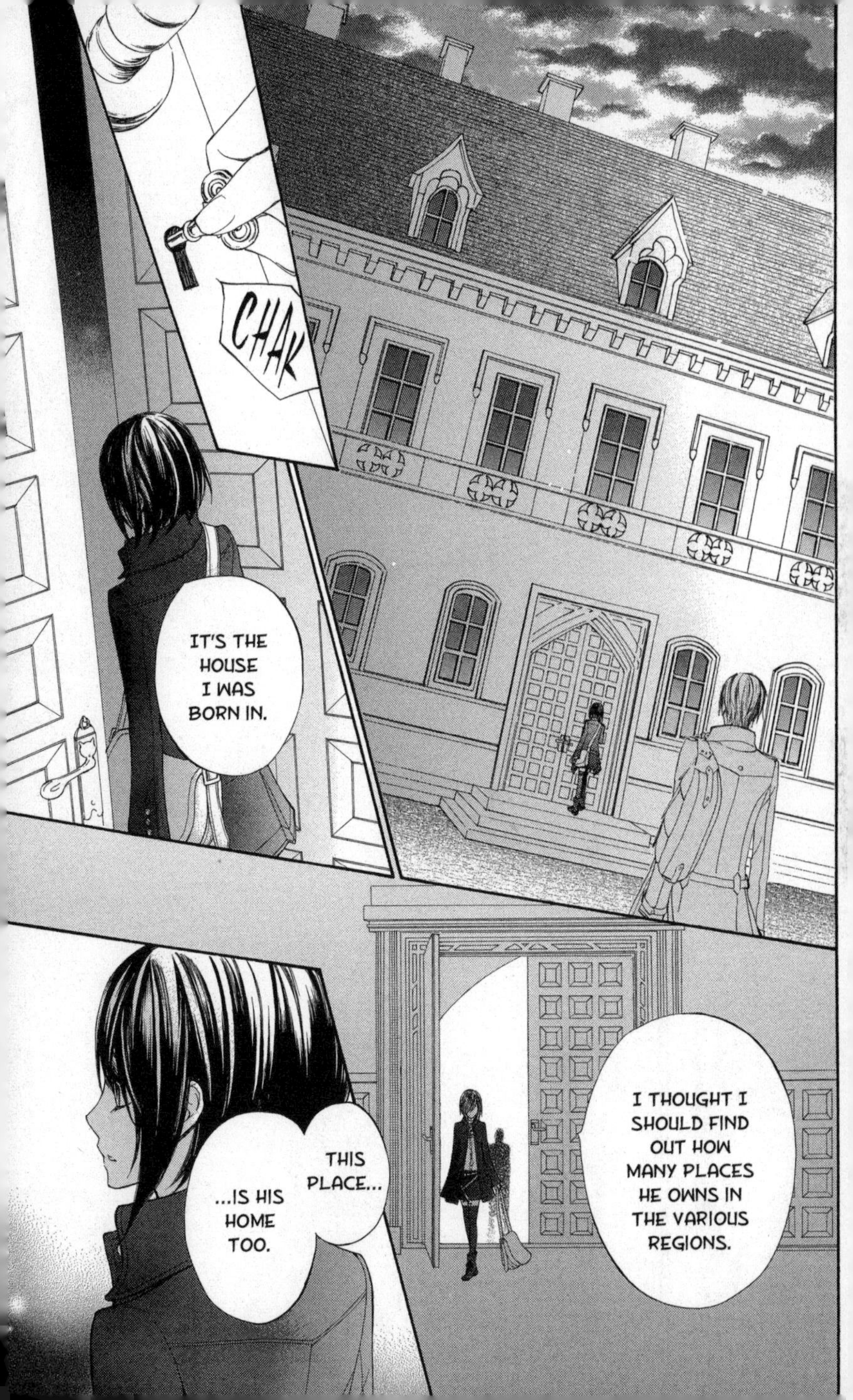
CHAK
IT'S THE HOUSE I WAS BORN IN.
I THOUGHT I SHOULD FIND OUT HOW MANY PLACES HE OWNS IN THE VARIOUS REGIONS.
THIS PLACE...
...IS HIS HOME TOO.

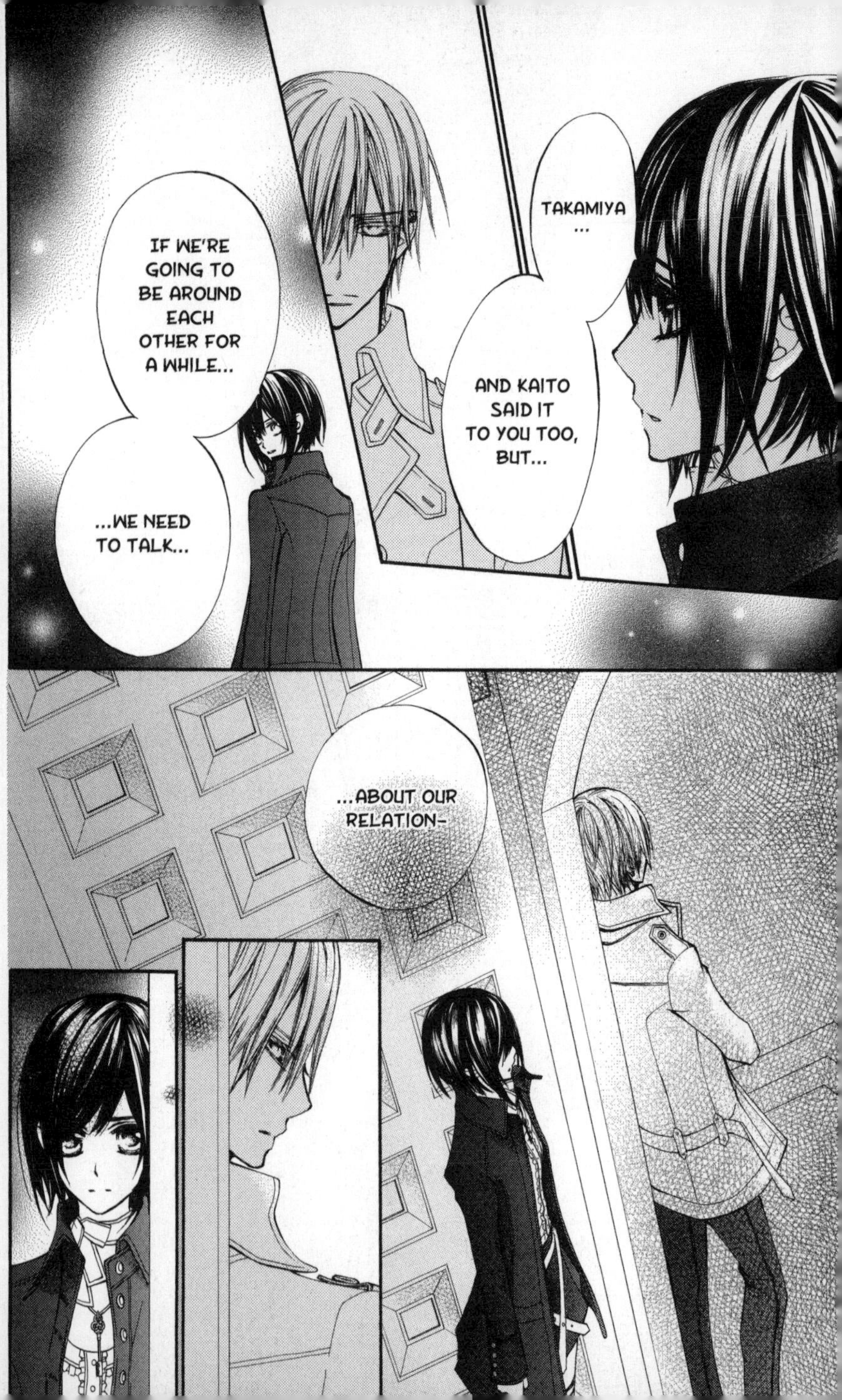
TAKAMIYA ...
AND KAITO SAID IT TO YOU TOO, BUT...
IF WE'RE GOING TO BE AROUND EACH OTHER FOR A WHILE...
...WE NEED TO TALK...
...ABOUT OUR RELATION-

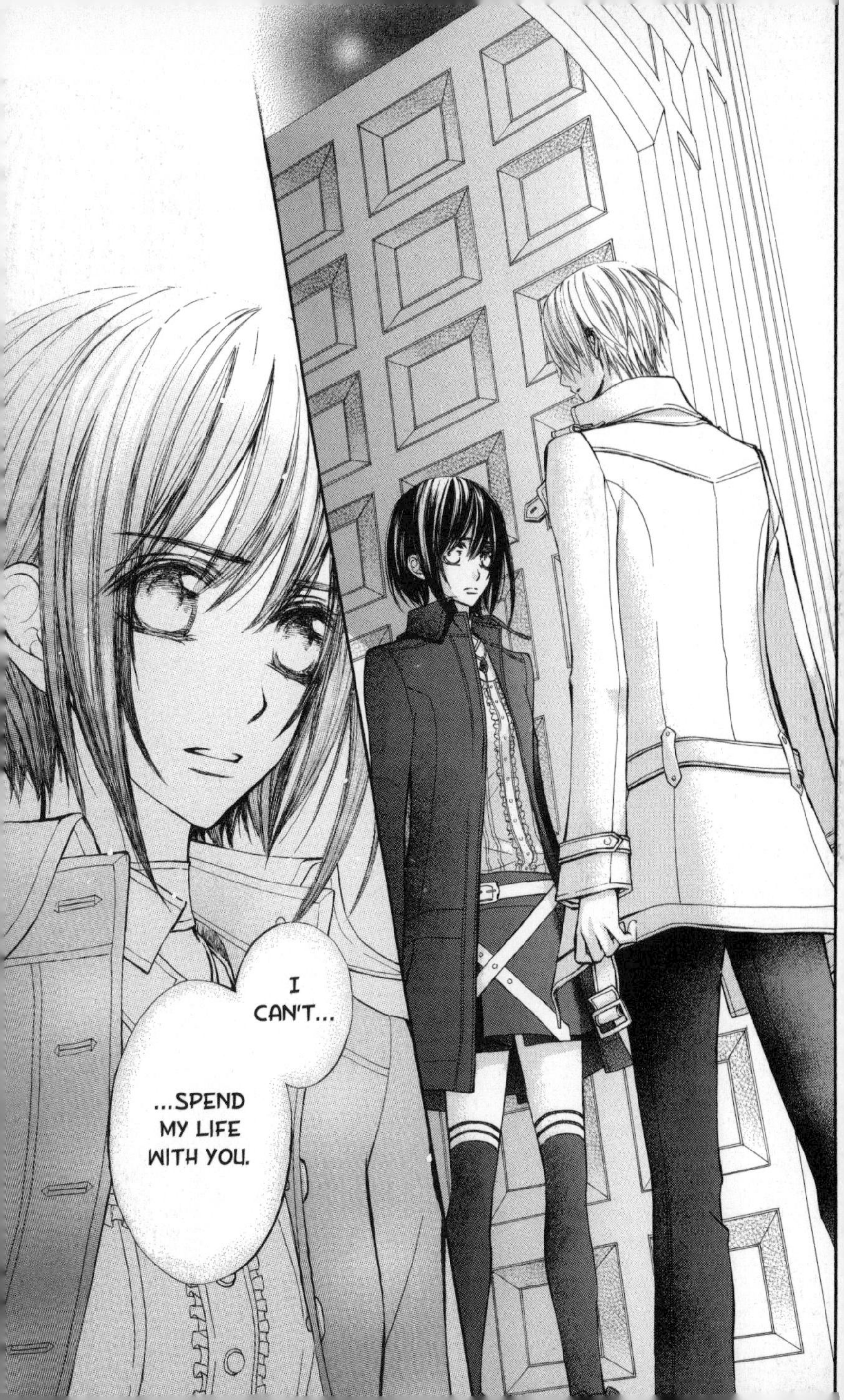
I CAN'T...
...SPEND MY LIFE WITH YOU.

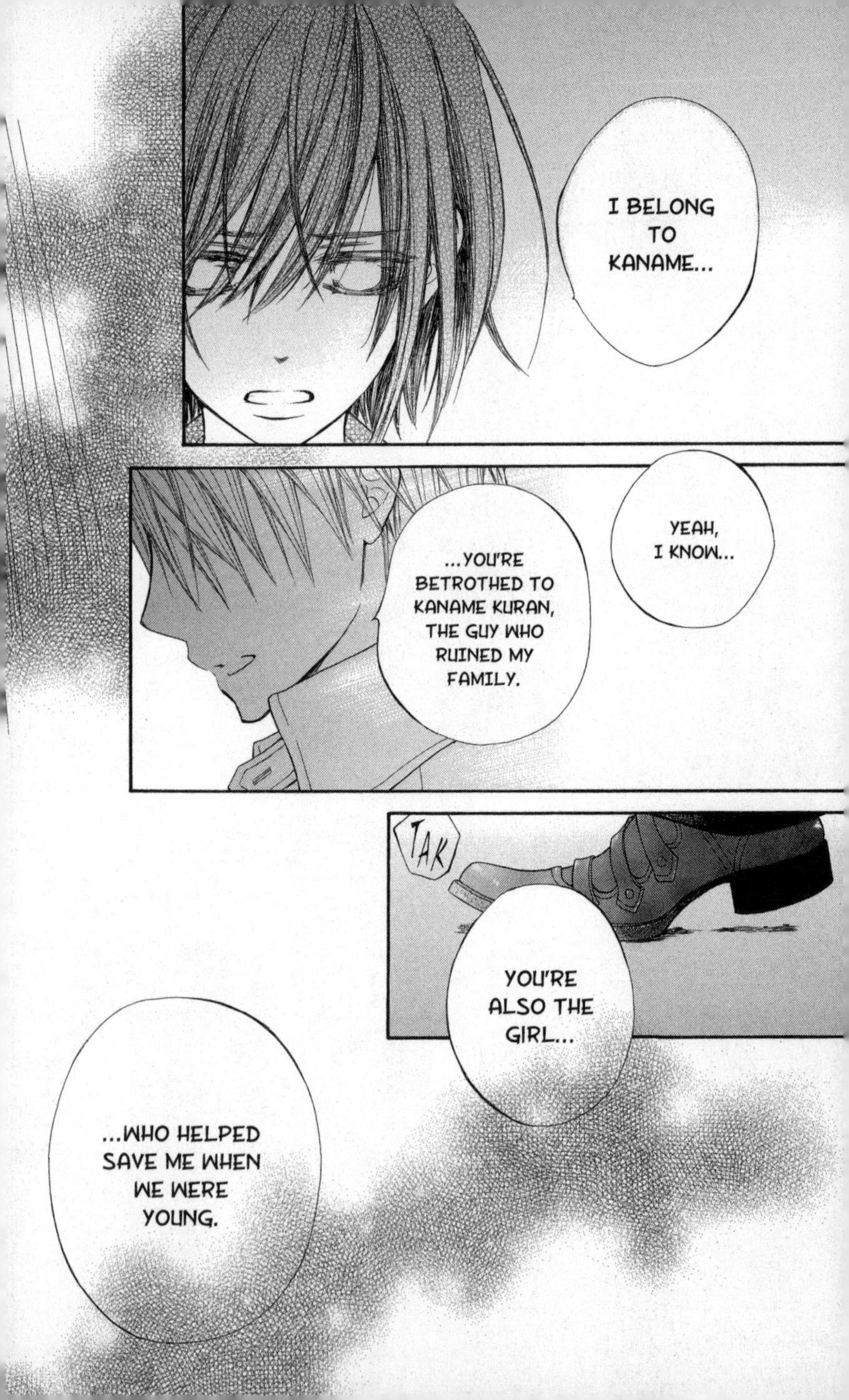
I BELONG TO KANAME...
YEAH, I KNOW...
...YOU'RE BETROTHED TO KANAME KURAN, THE GUY WHO RUINED MY FAMILY.
TAK
YOU'RE ALSO THE GIRL...
...WHO HELPED SAVE ME WHEN WE WERE YOUNG.

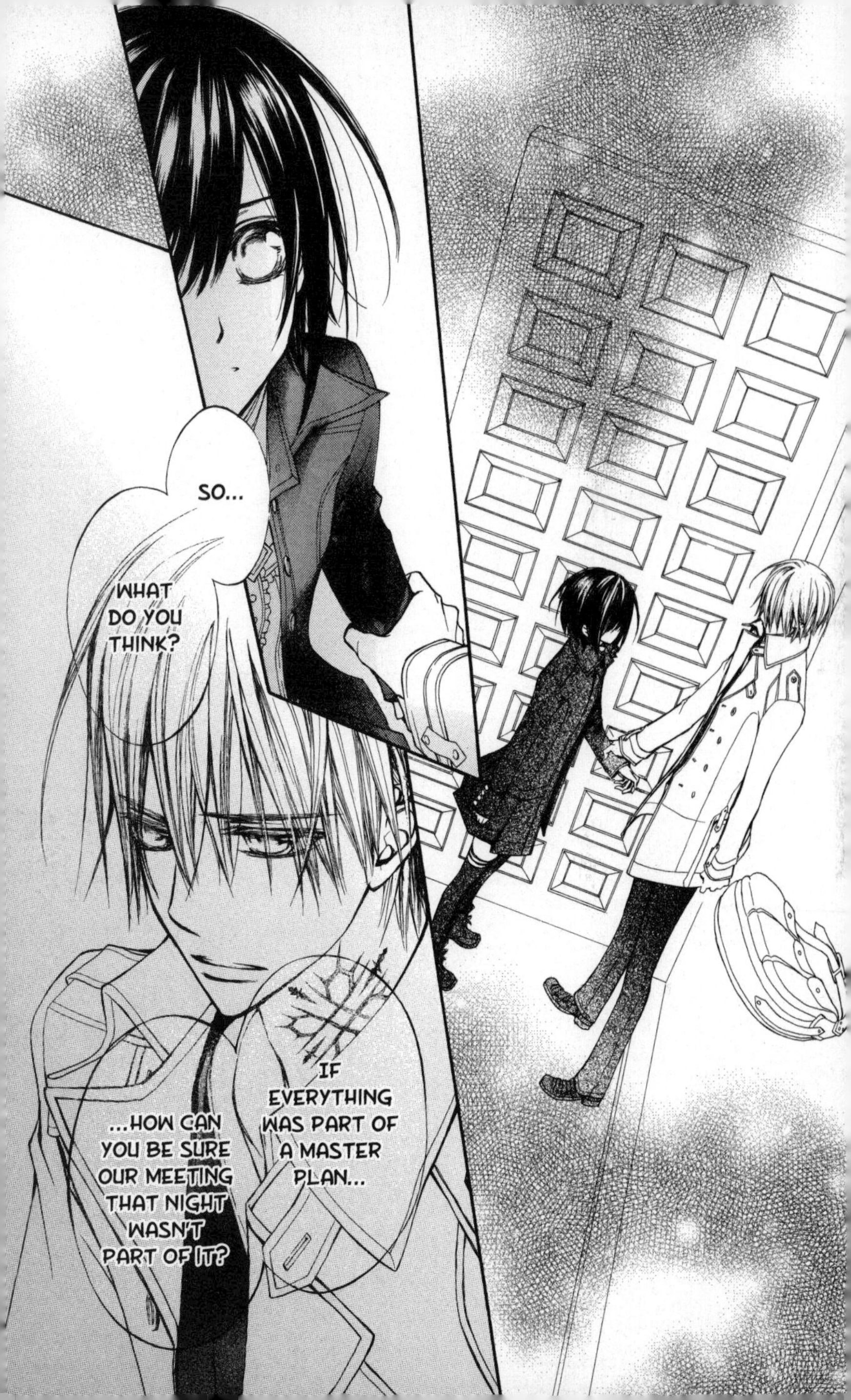
SO...
WHAT DO YOU THINK?
IF EVERYTHING WAS PART OF A MASTER PLAN...
...HOW CAN YOU BE SURE OUR MEETING THAT NIGHT WASN'T PART OF IT?

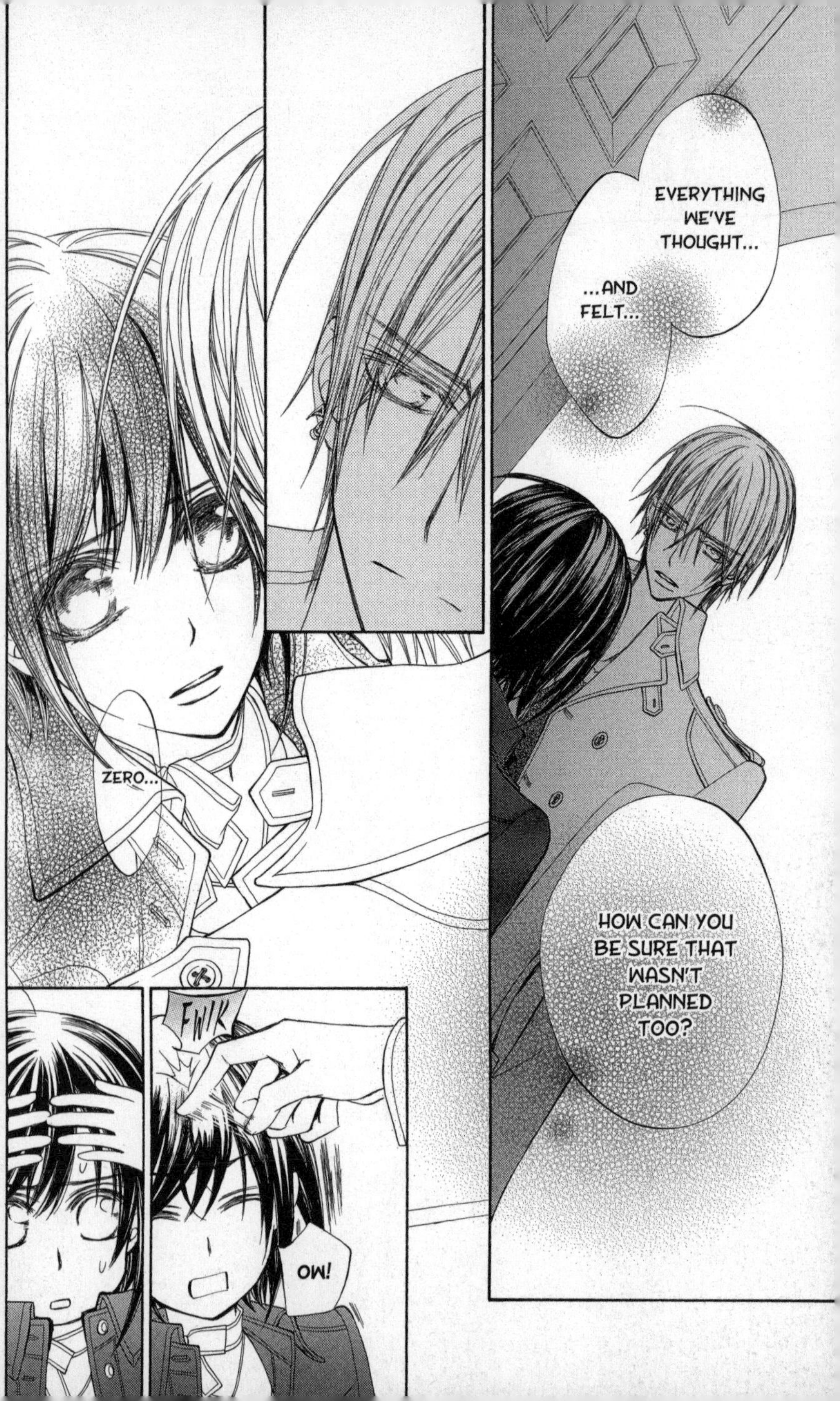
EVERYTHING WE'VE THOUGHT...
...AND FELT...
HOW CAN YOU BE SURE THAT WASN'T PLANNED TOO?
ZERO...
FWIK
OW!

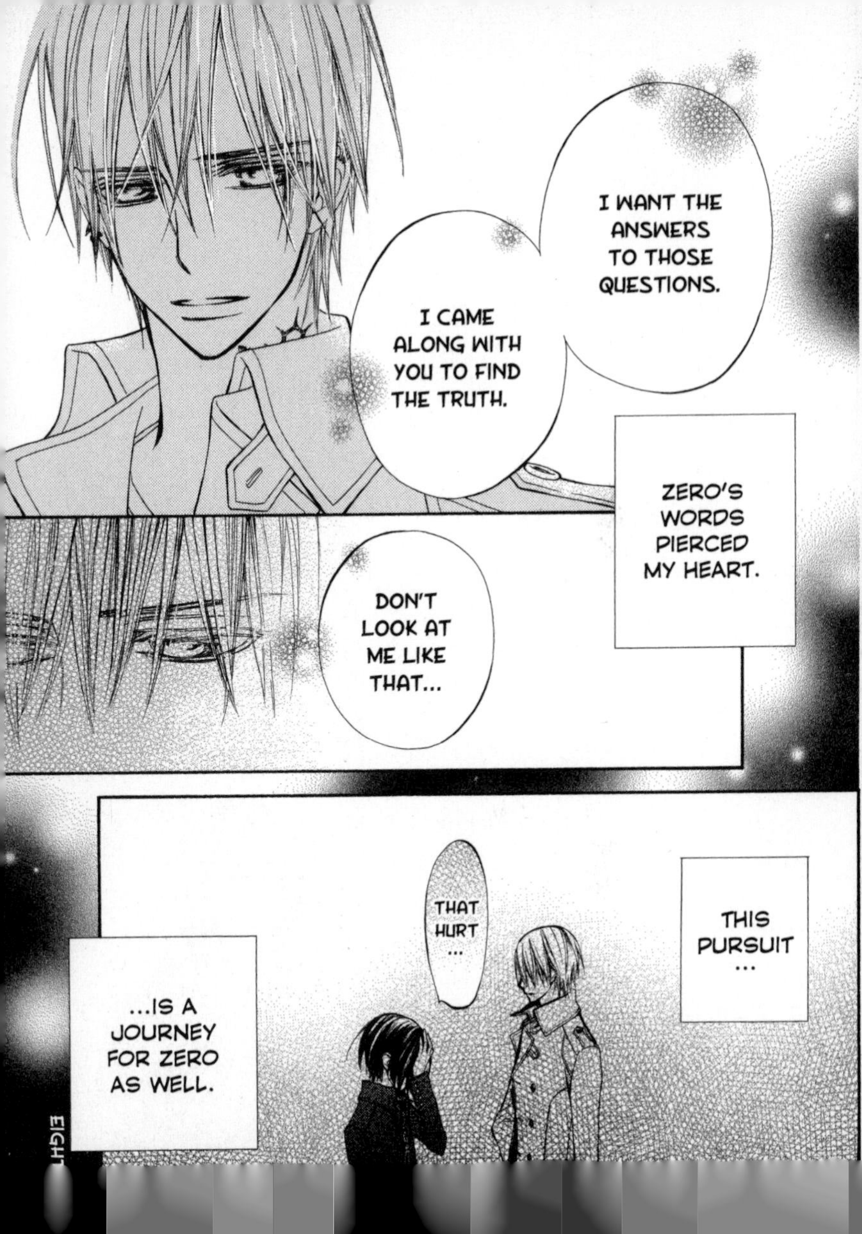
I WANT THE ANSWERS TO THOSE QUESTIONS.
I CAME ALONG WITH YOU TO FIND THE TRUTH.
ZERO'S WORDS PIERCED MY HEART.
DON'T LOOK AT ME LIKE THAT...
THIS PURSUIT...
THAT HURT...
...IS A JOURNEY FOR ZERO AS WELL.

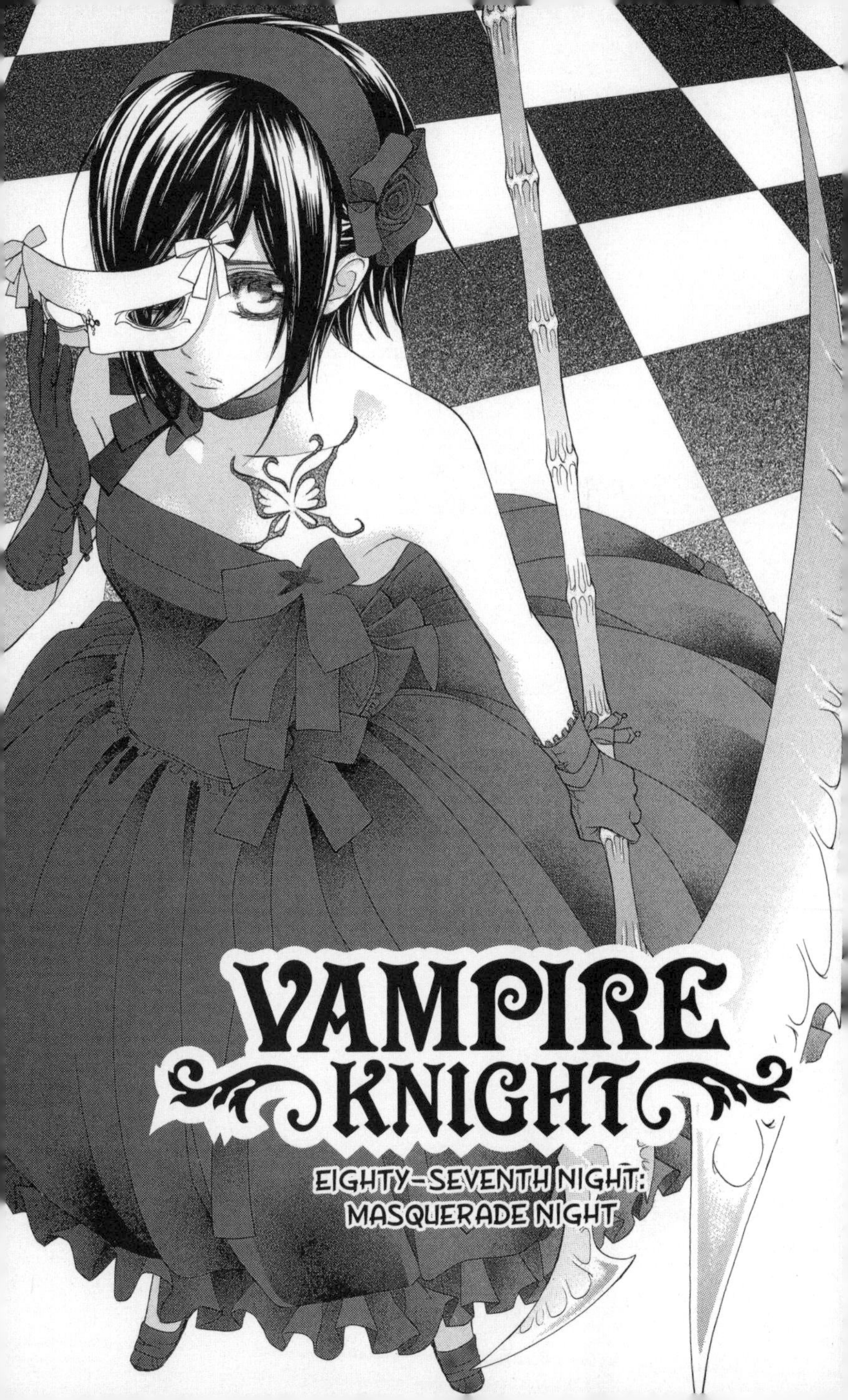
VAMPIRE KNIGHT
EIGHTY-SEVENTH NIGHT: MASQUERADE NIGHT

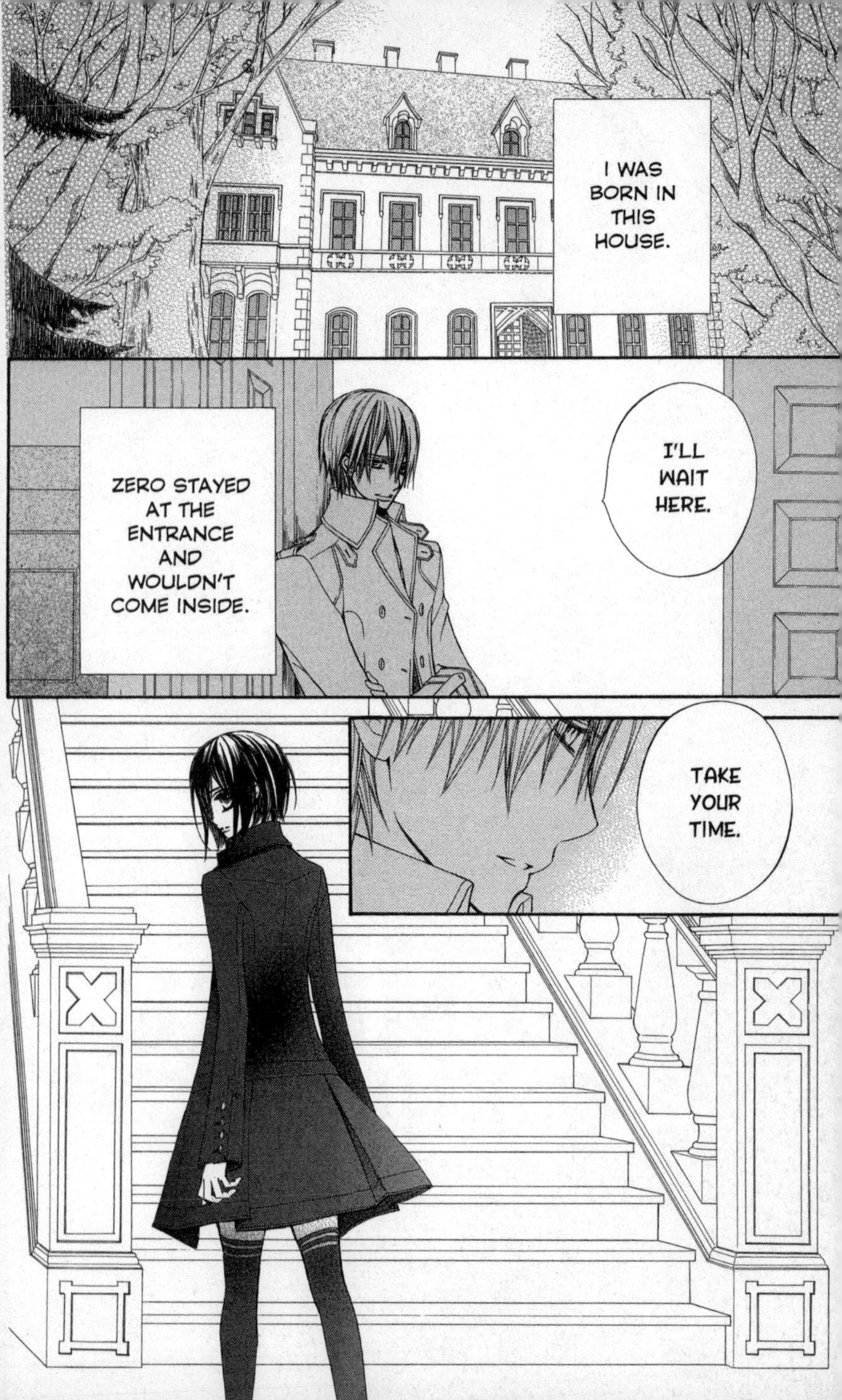
I WAS BORN IN THIS HOUSE.
I'LL WAIT HERE.
ZERO STAYED AT THE ENTRANCE AND WOULDN'T COME INSIDE.
TAKE YOUR TIME.

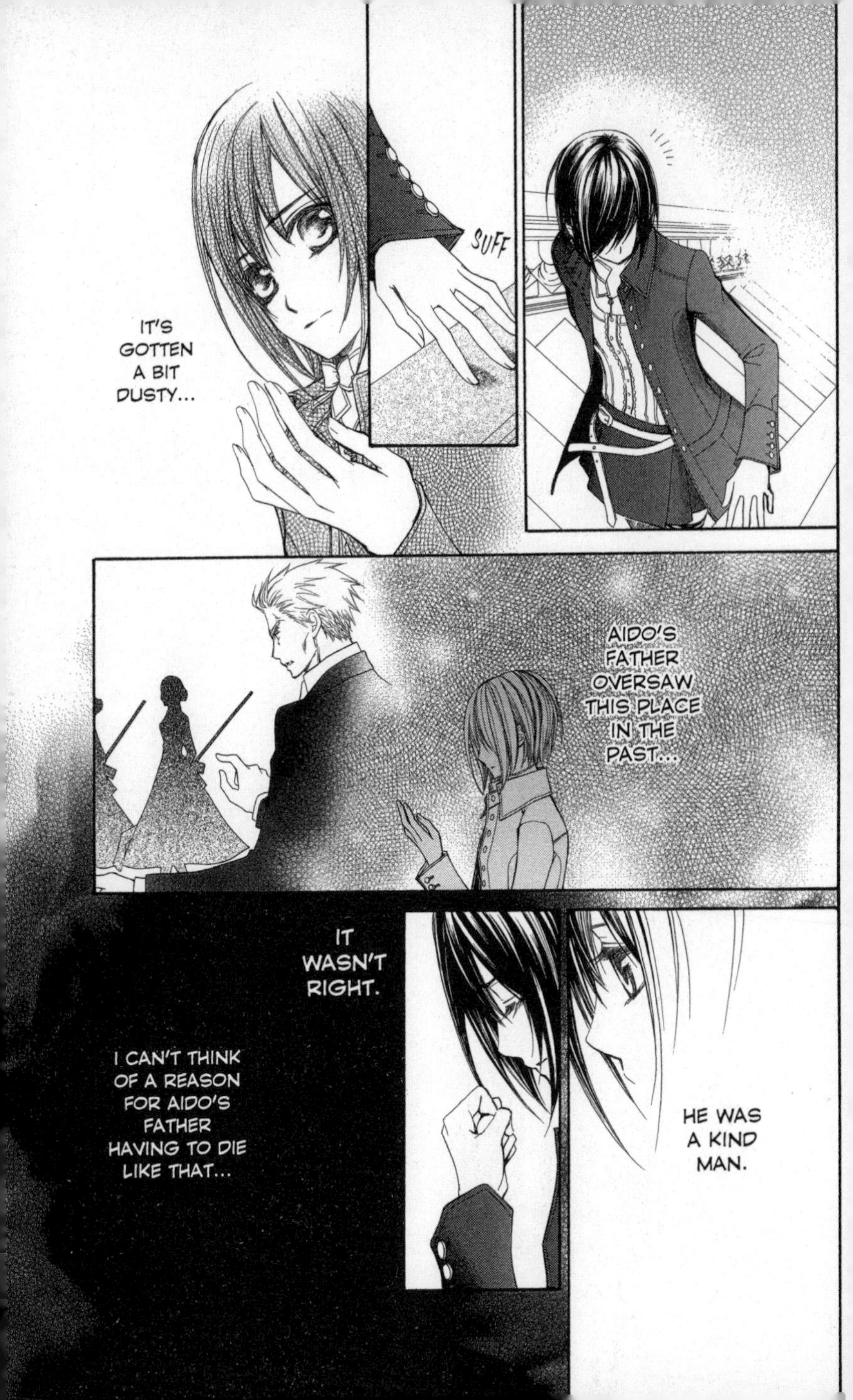
SUFF
IT'S GOTTEN A BIT DUSTY...
AIDO'S FATHER OVERSAW THIS PLACE IN THE PAST...
HE WAS A KIND MAN.
IT WASN'T RIGHT.
I CAN'T THINK OF A REASON FOR AIDO'S FATHER HAVING TO DIE LIKE THAT...

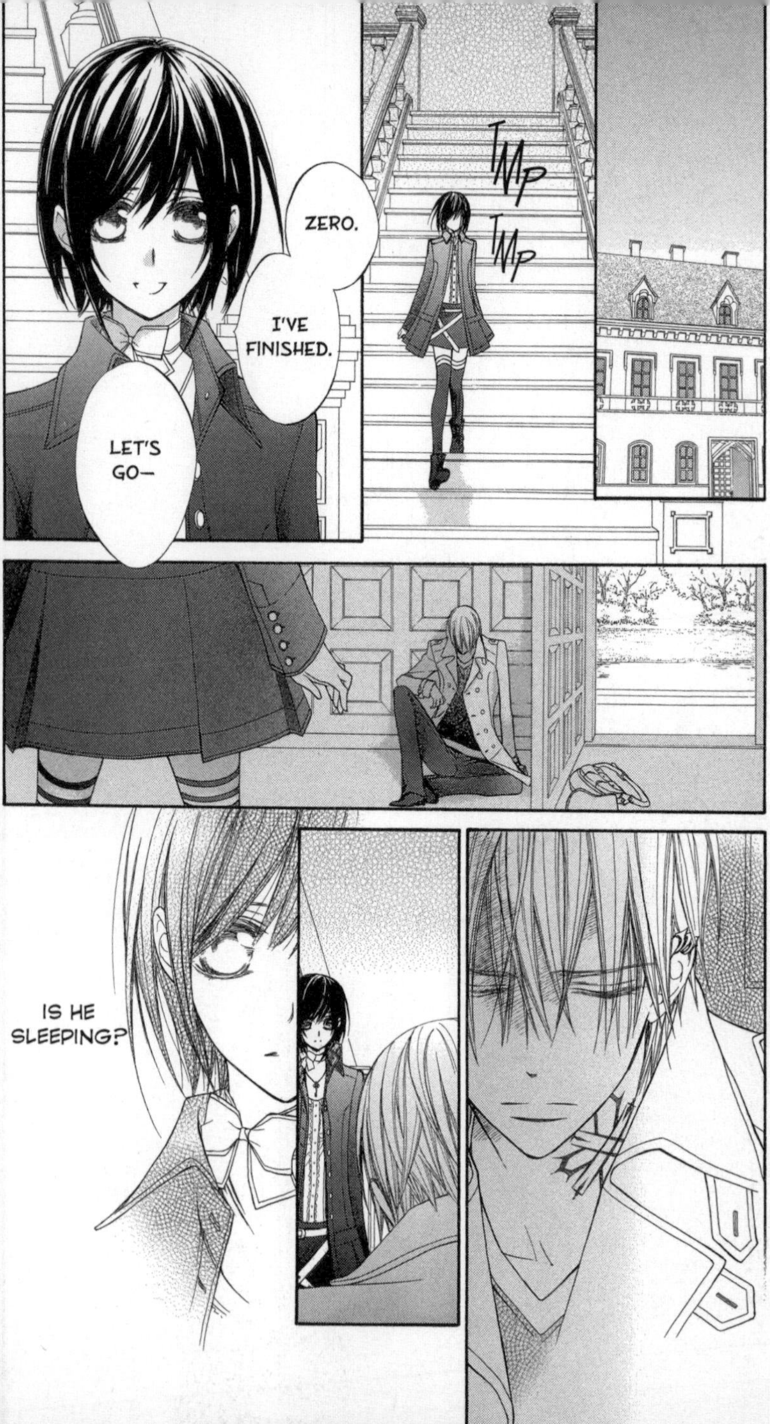
TMP
TMP
ZERO.
I'VE FINISHED.
LET'S GO—
IS HE SLEEPING?

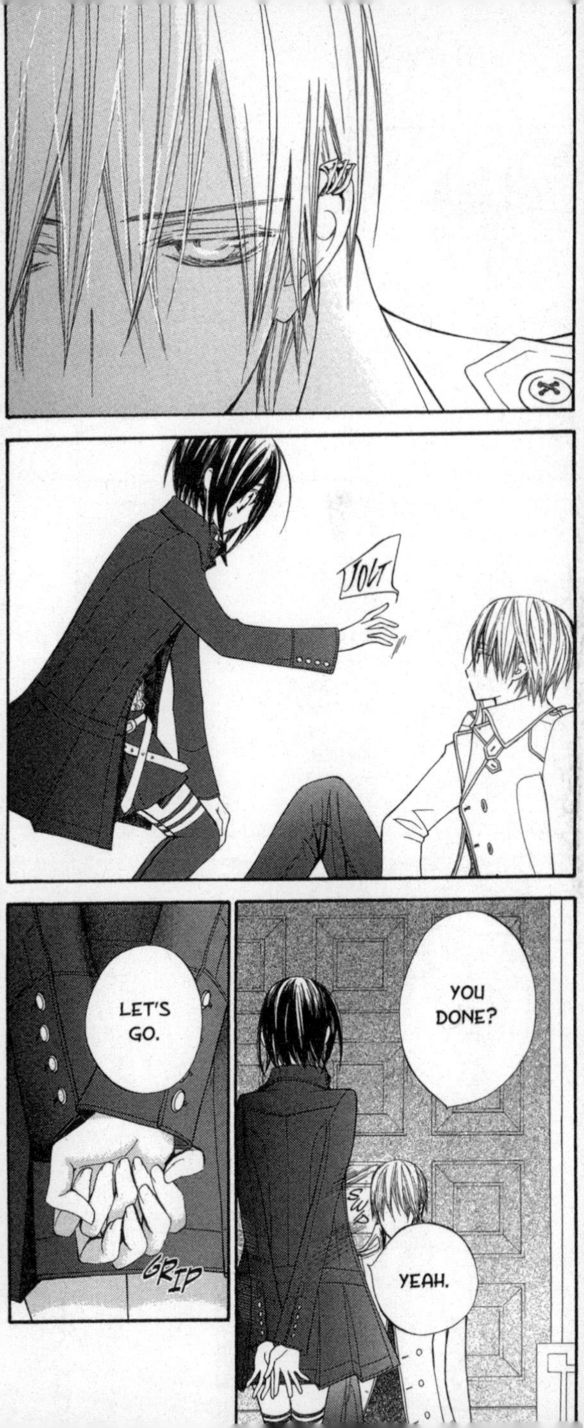
JOLT
YOU DONE?
SWP
YEAH.
LET'S GO.
GRIP

II

This manga would not have had so many characters or have run for so long without the assistance of my editor. I probably never would have thought about setting it in a school either. I don't think it would be exaggerating to say that I have had as many regrets as the number of characters in this series. I couldn't guide the characters in the right direction, and I wasn't able to make good use of my editor's great advice... But the characters are all still very dear to me. But being the person I am, I often make the wrong choice. My editor would take a look at my awful storyboards with very strict eyes and try to polish it into something that could be published. It was a tough job, and I am very grateful to my editor for giving me the opportunity to nurture numerous characters whom readers love and I too care deeply for. And I am grateful to all the readers from the bottom of my heart too...

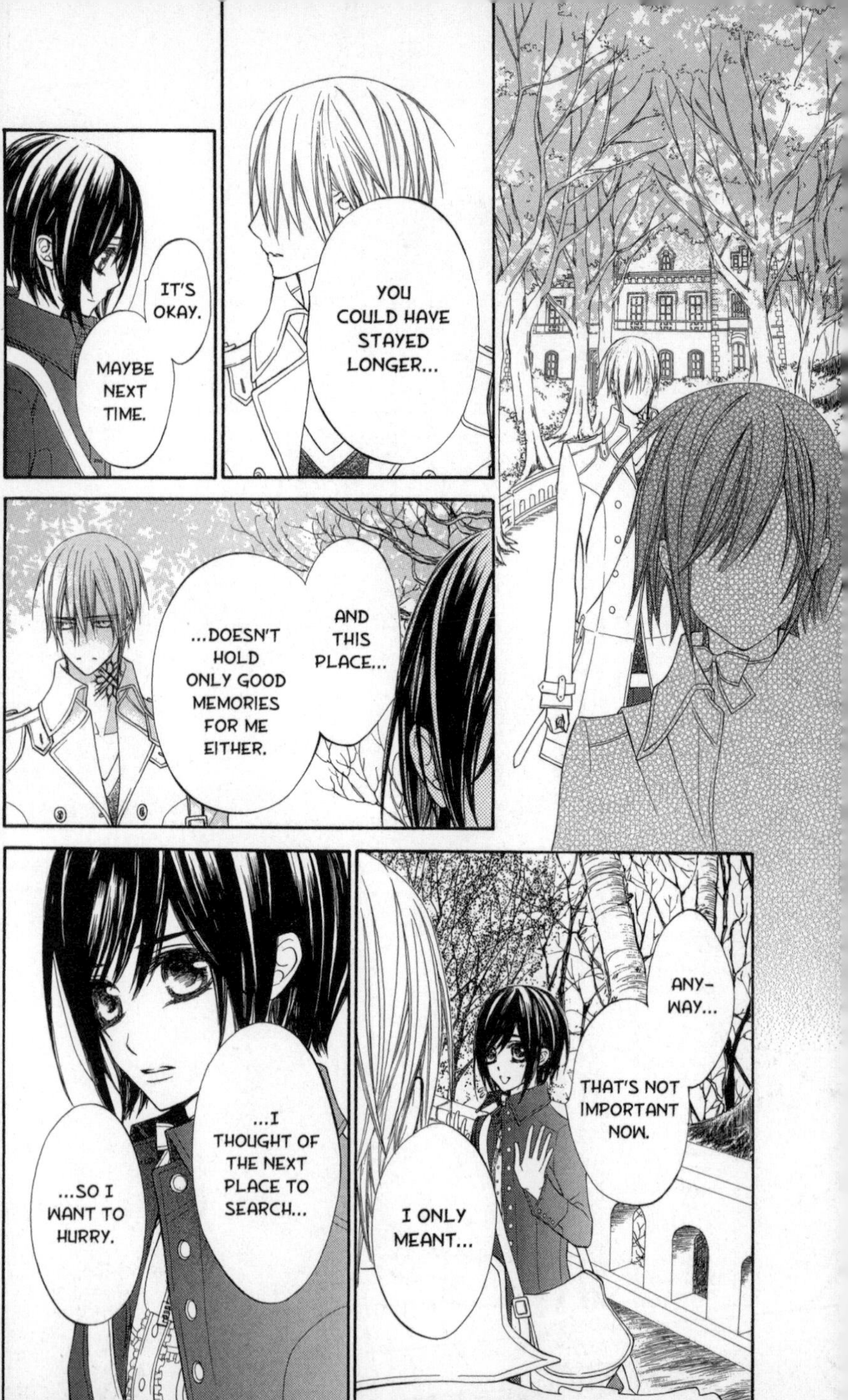
YOU COULD HAVE STAYED LONGER...
IT'S OKAY.
MAYBE NEXT TIME.
AND THIS PLACE...
...DOESN'T HOLD ONLY GOOD MEMORIES FOR ME EITHER.
ANY-WAY...
THAT'S NOT IMPORTANT NOW.
I ONLY MEANT...
...I THOUGHT OF THE NEXT PLACE TO SEARCH...
...SO I WANT TO HURRY.

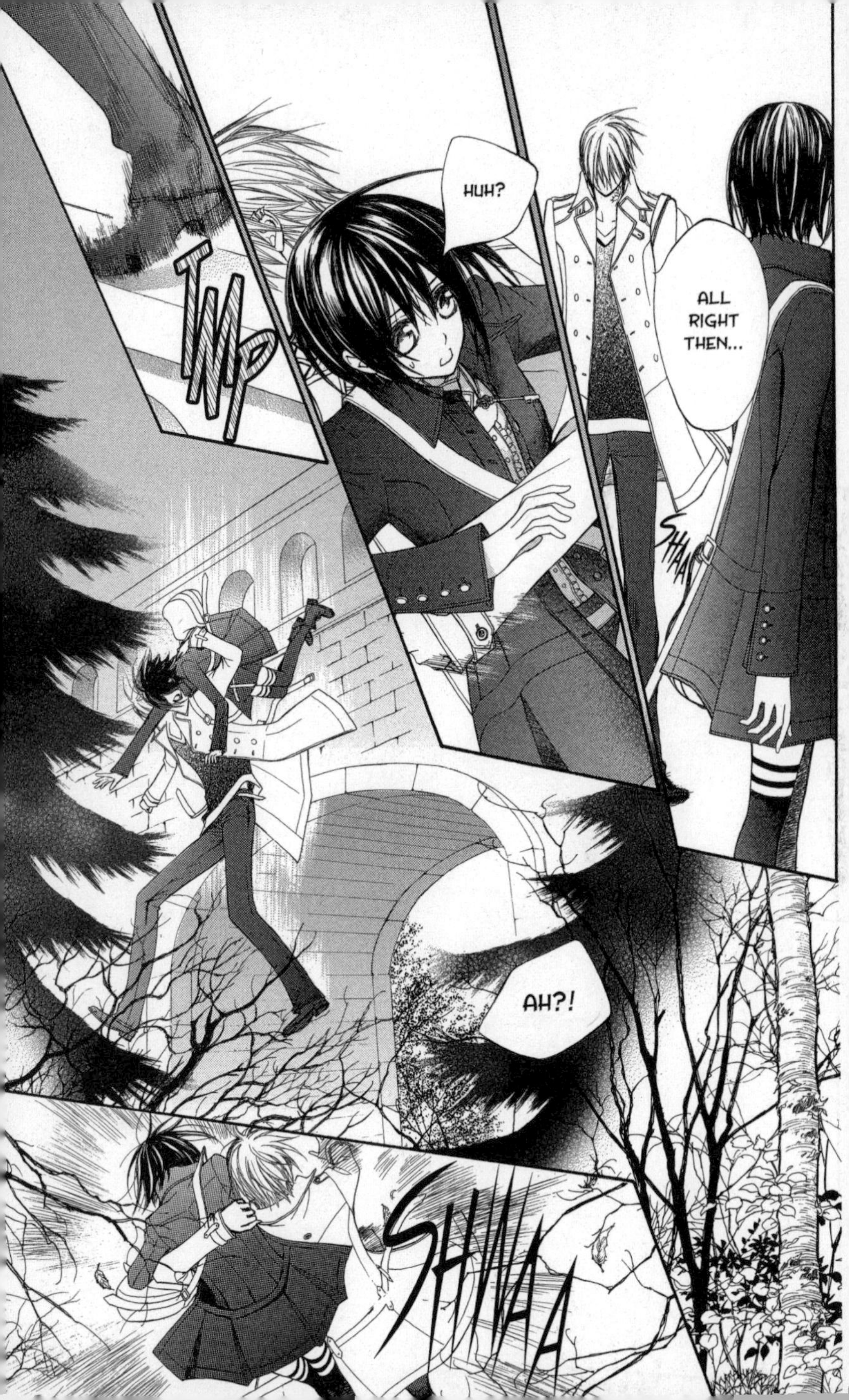
ALL RIGHT THEN...
SHAA
HUH?
TMP
AH?!
SHWAA

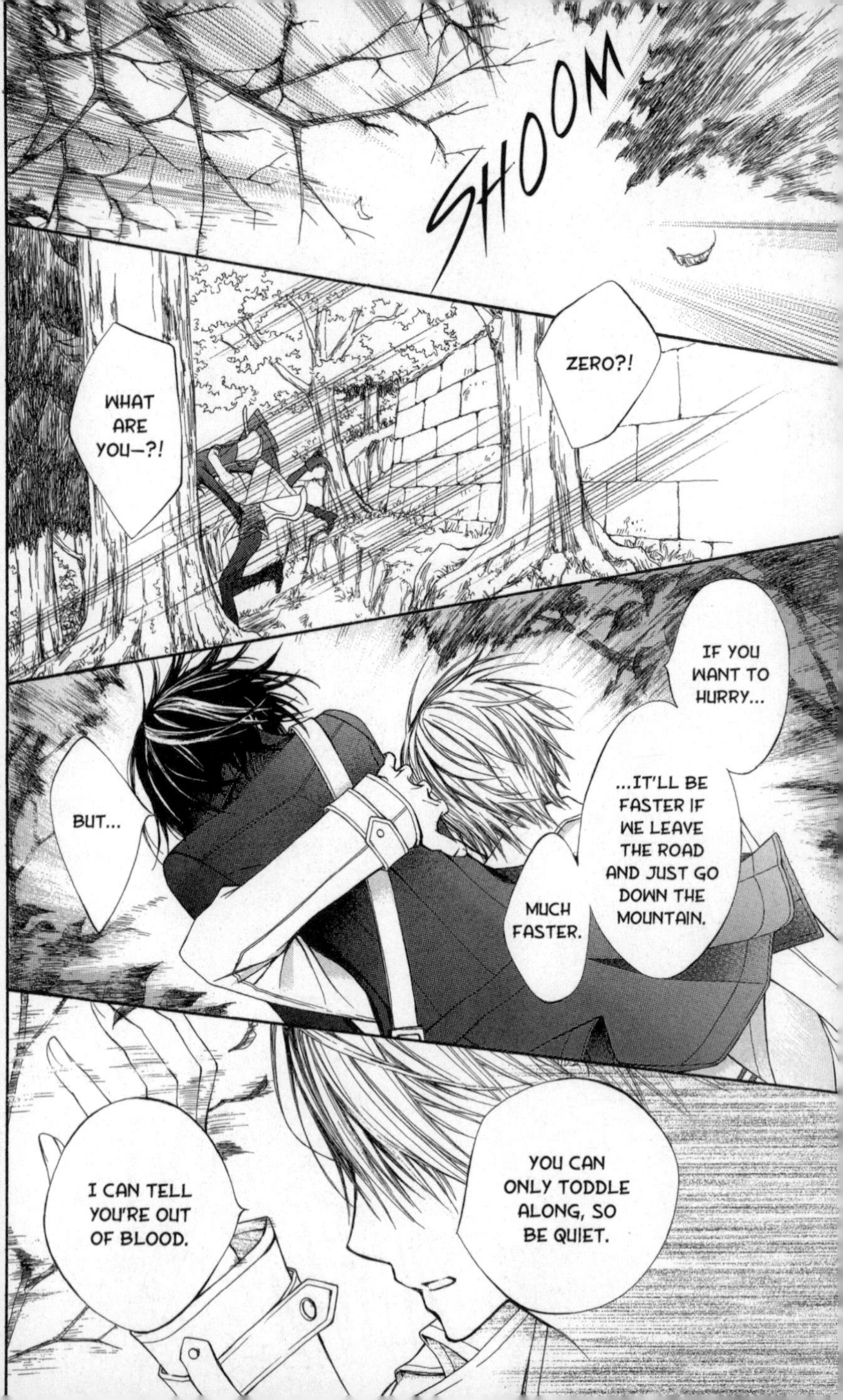
SHOOM
ZERO?!
WHAT ARE YOU—?!
IF YOU WANT TO HURRY...
...IT'LL BE FASTER IF WE LEAVE THE ROAD AND JUST GO DOWN THE MOUNTAIN.
MUCH FASTER.
BUT...
YOU CAN ONLY TODDLE ALONG, SO BE QUIET.
I CAN TELL YOU'RE OUT OF BLOOD.

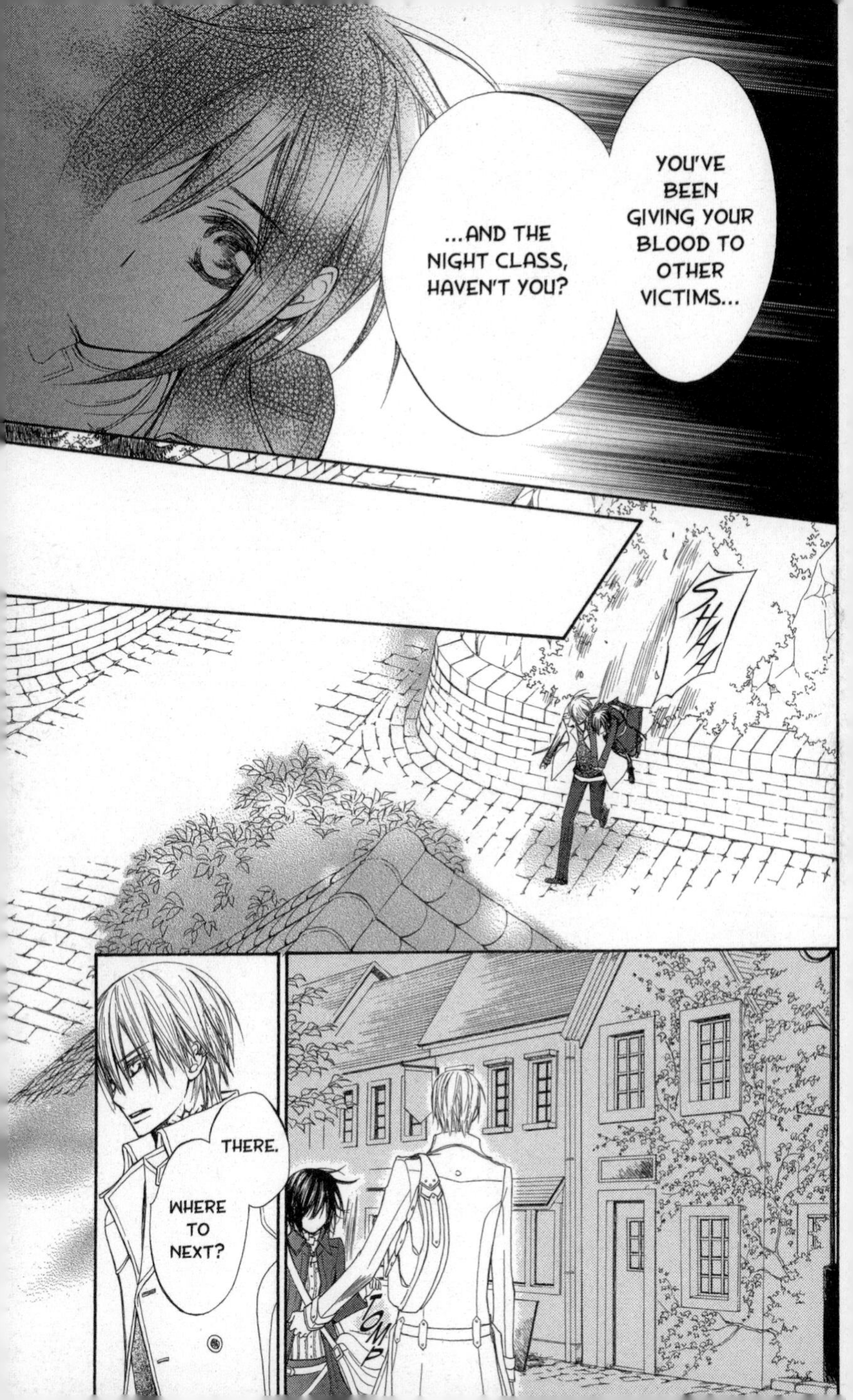
YOU'VE BEEN GIVING YOUR BLOOD TO OTHER VICTIMS...
...AND THE NIGHT CLASS, HAVEN'T YOU?
SHAA
TOMP
THERE.
WHERE TO NEXT?

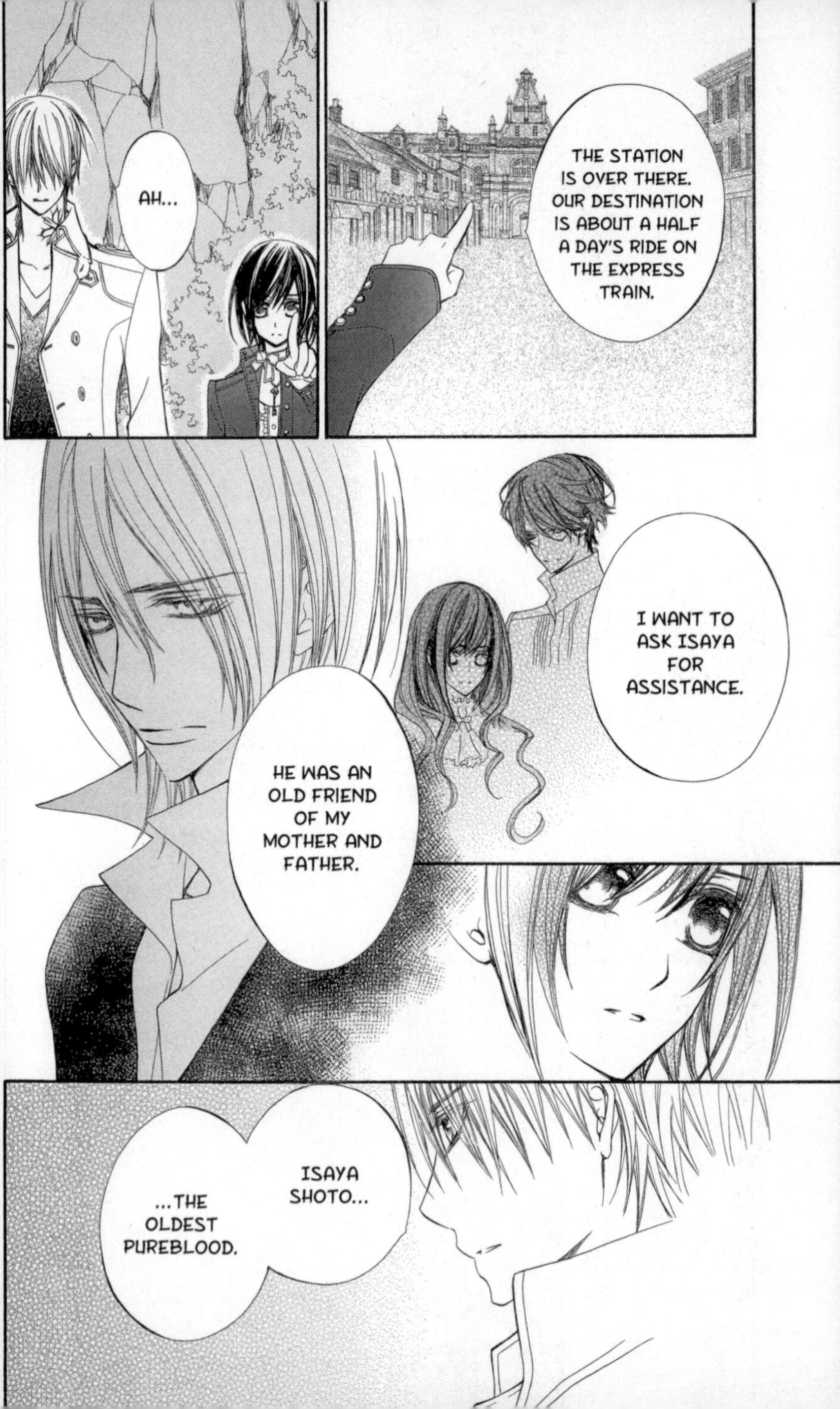
THE STATION IS OVER THERE. OUR DESTINATION IS ABOUT A HALF A DAY'S RIDE ON THE EXPRESS TRAIN.
AH...
I WANT TO ASK ISAYA FOR ASSISTANCE.
HE WAS AN OLD FRIEND OF MY MOTHER AND FATHER.
ISAYA SHOTO...
...THE OLDEST PUREBLOOD.

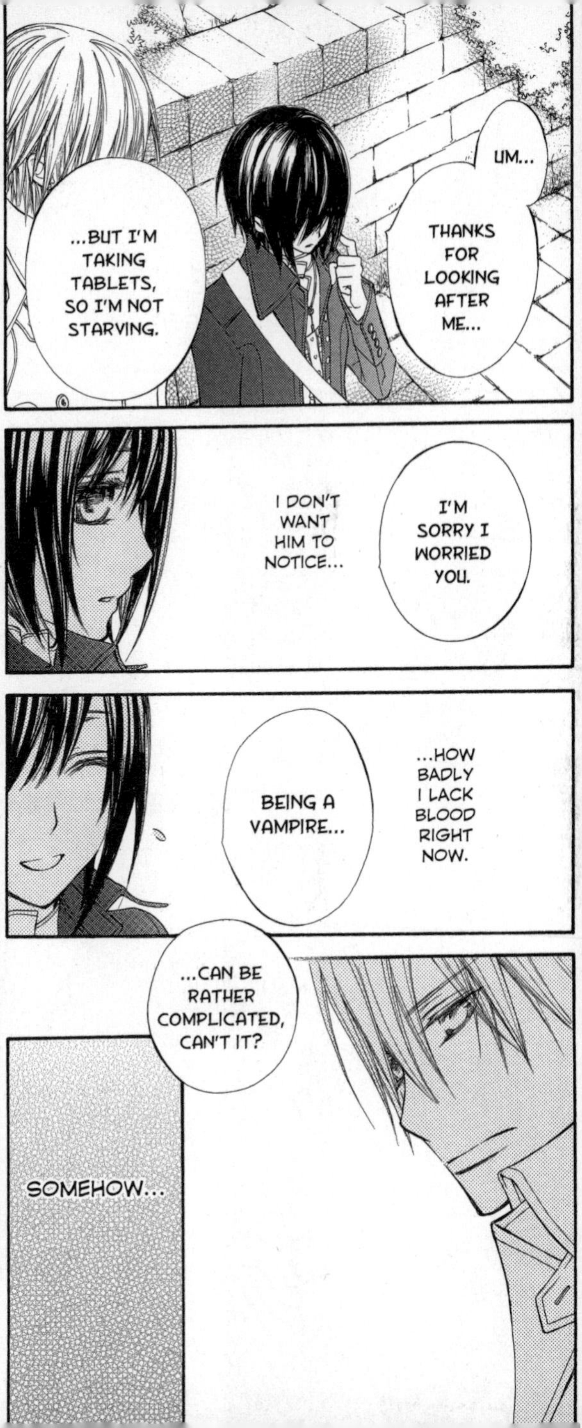
UM...
THANKS FOR LOOKING AFTER ME...
...BUT I'M TAKING TABLETS, SO I'M NOT STARVING.
I'M SORRY I WORRIED YOU.
I DON'T WANT HIM TO NOTICE...
...HOW BADLY I LACK BLOOD RIGHT NOW.
BEING A VAMPIRE...
...CAN BE RATHER COMPLICATED, CAN'T IT?
SOMEHOW...

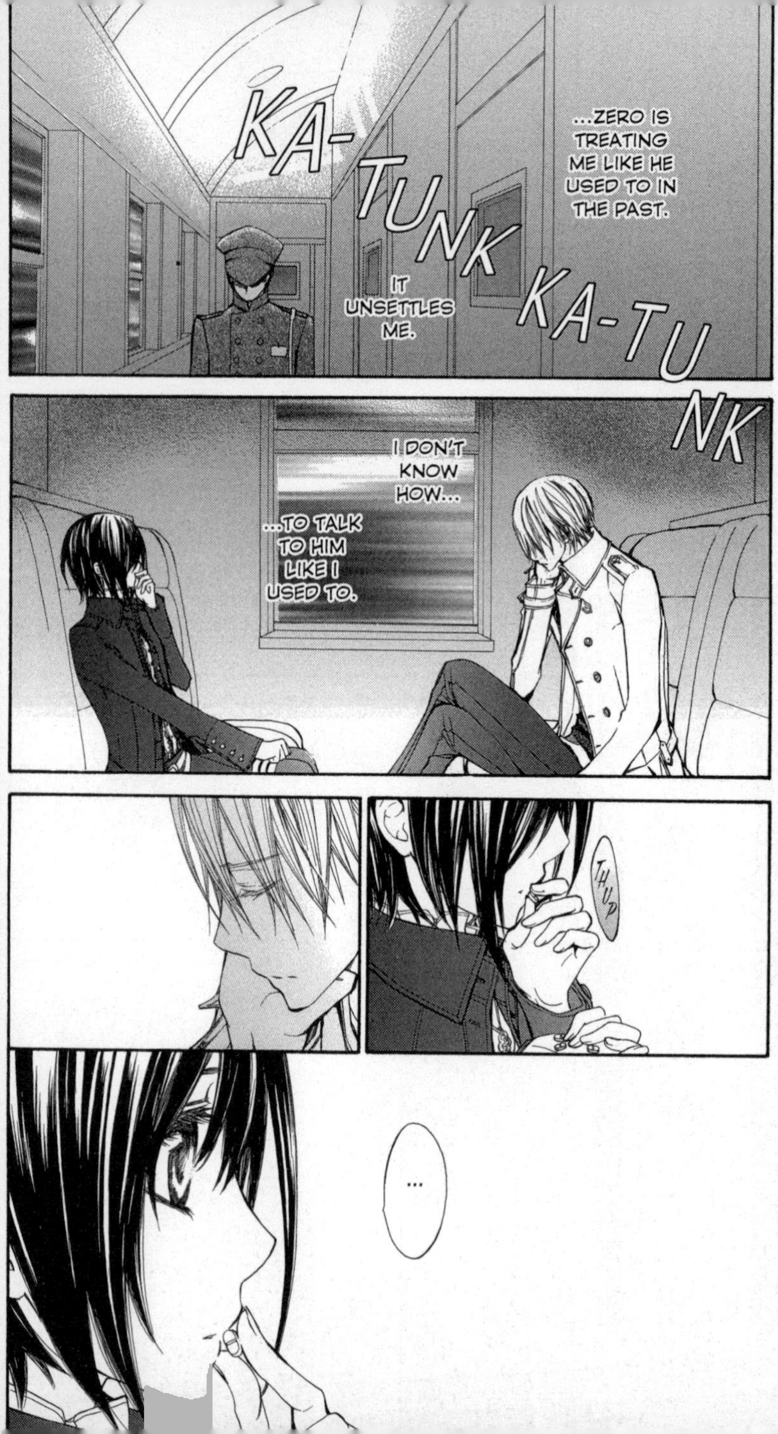
KA-TUNK
...ZERO IS TREATING ME LIKE HE USED TO IN THE PAST.
IT UNSETTLES ME.
KA-TUNK
I DON'T KNOW HOW...
...TO TALK TO HIM LIKE I USED TO.
THUP
...

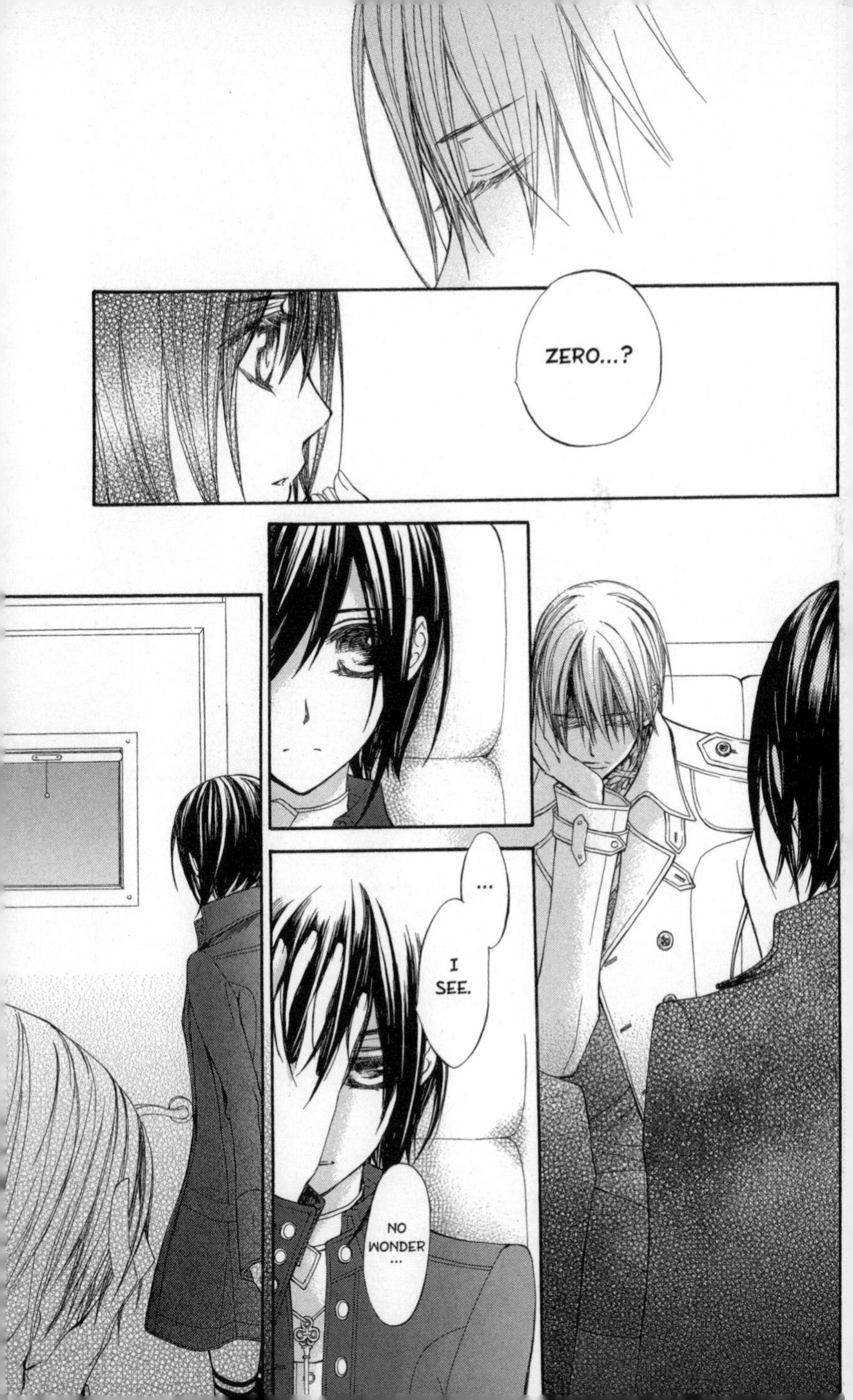
ZERO...?
...
I SEE.
NO WONDER ...

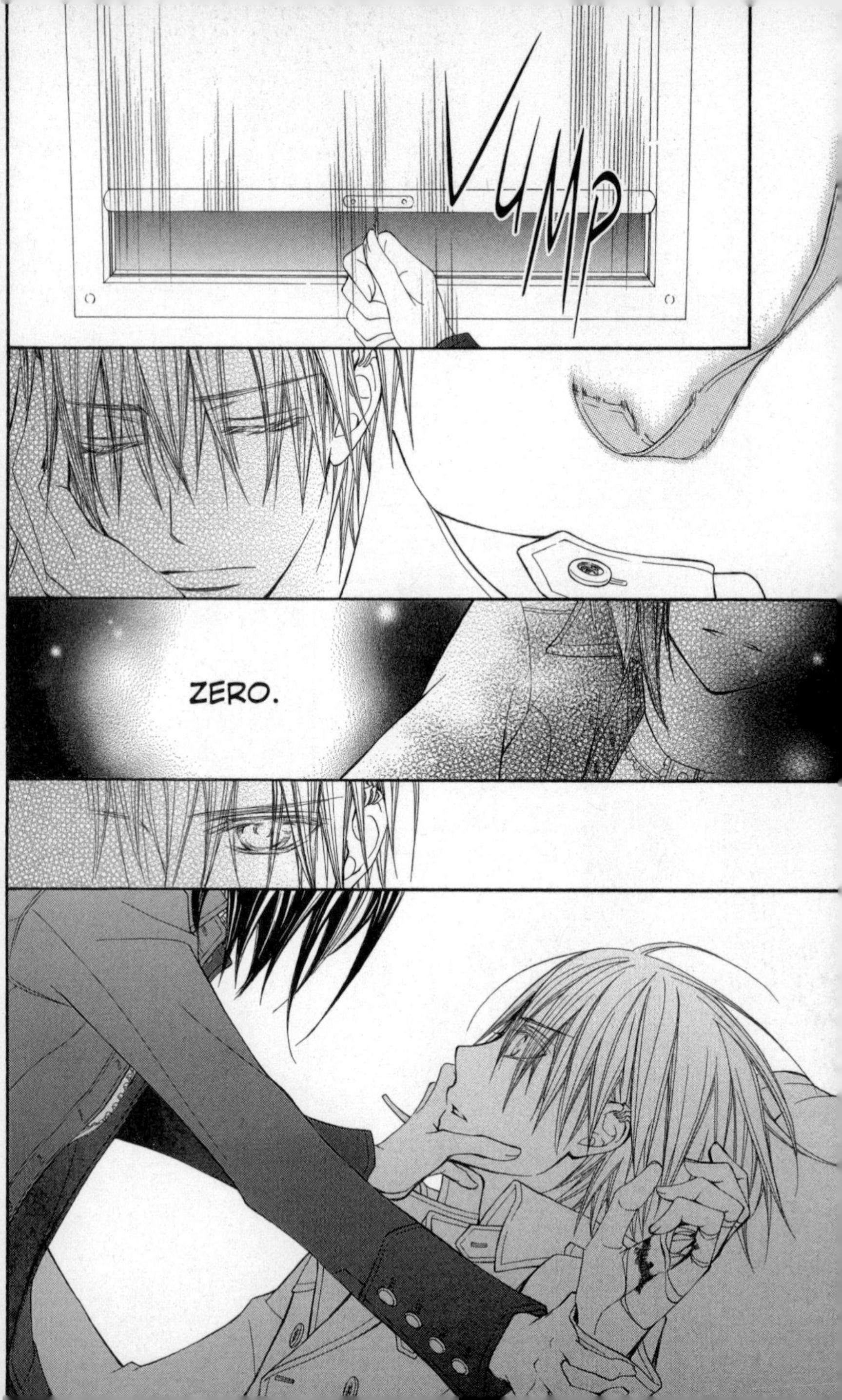
VUMP
ZERO.

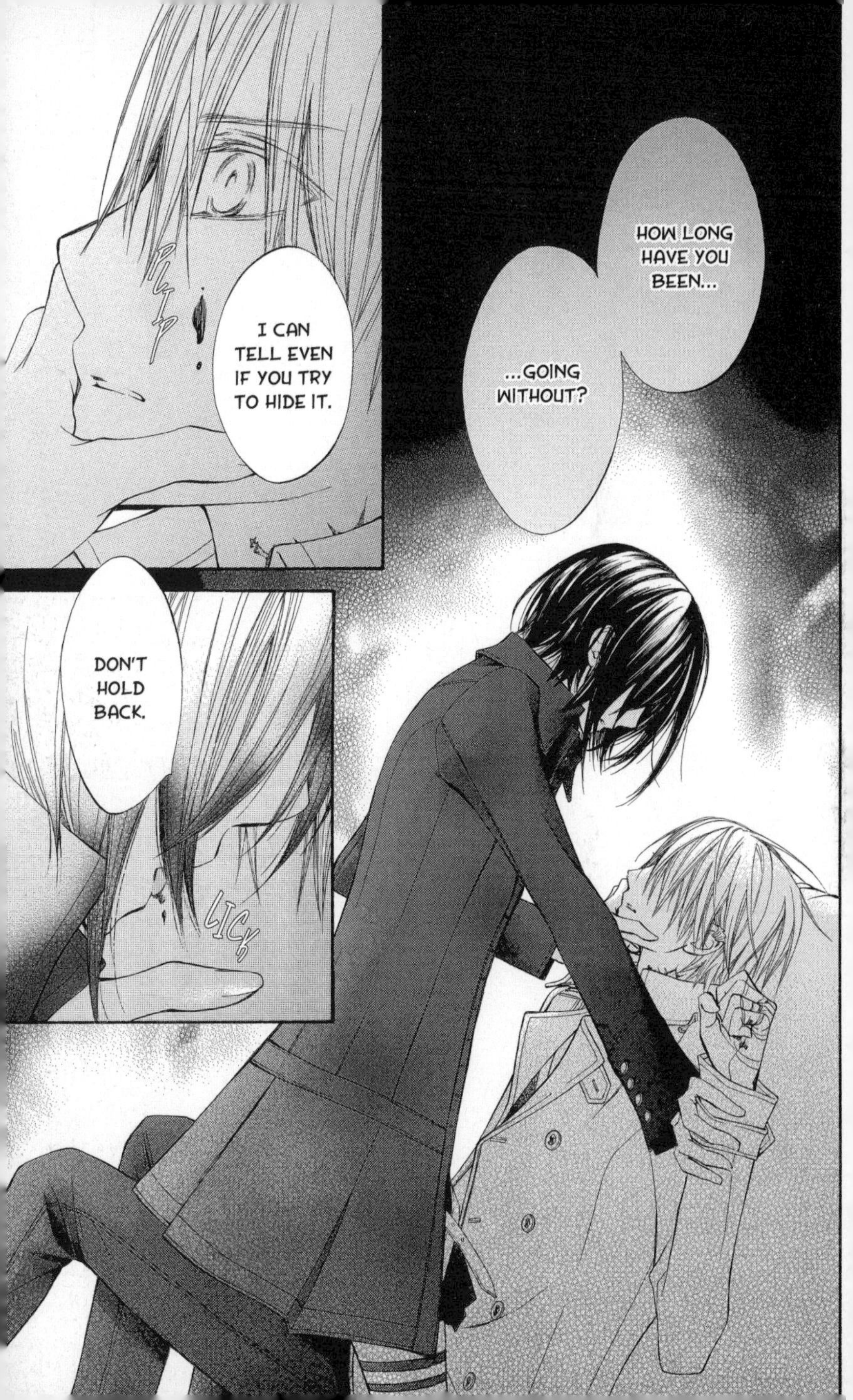
HOW LONG HAVE YOU BEEN...
...GOING WITHOUT?
PLIP
I CAN TELL EVEN IF YOU TRY TO HIDE IT.
DON'T HOLD BACK.
LICK

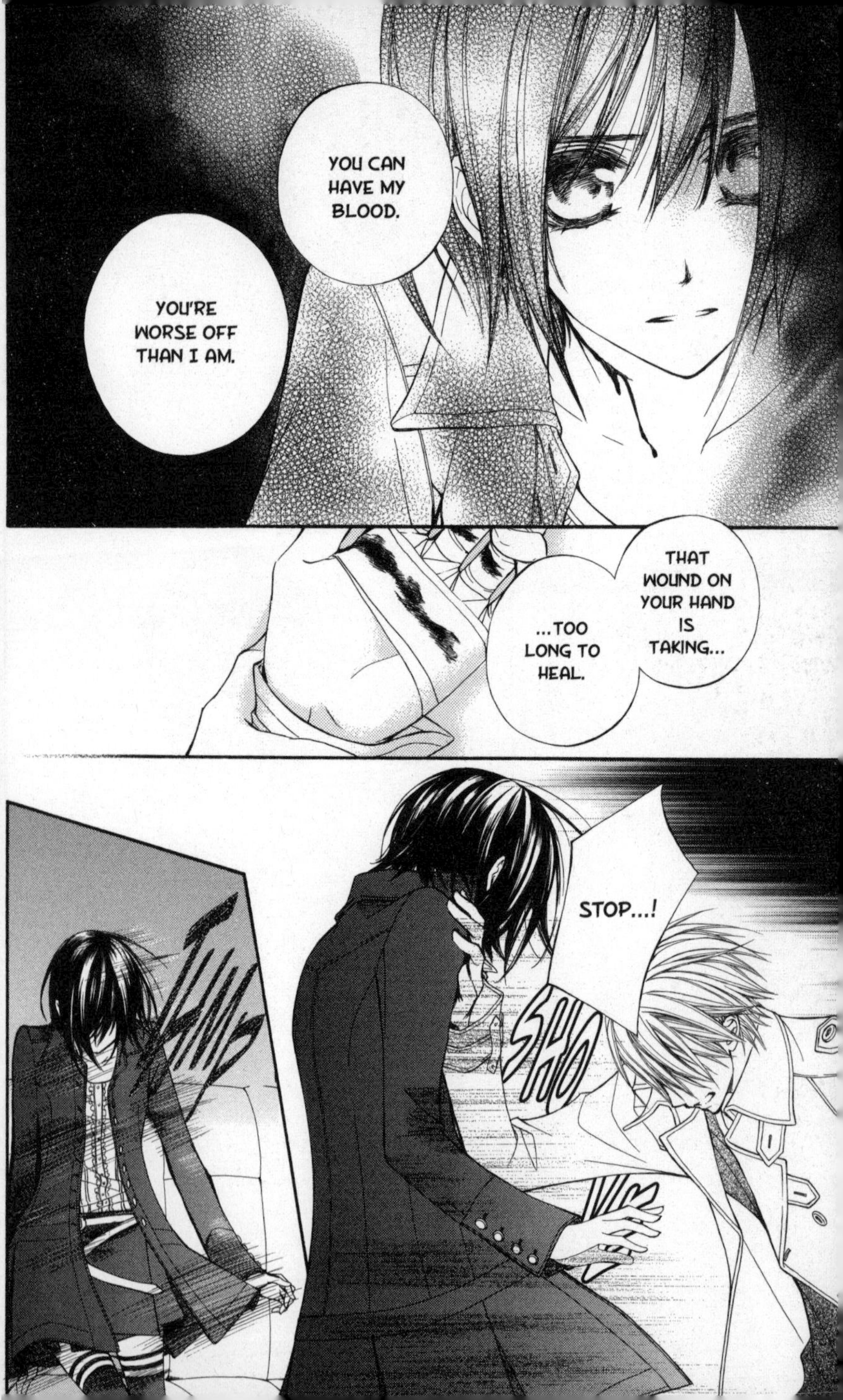
YOU CAN HAVE MY BLOOD.
YOU'RE WORSE OFF THAN I AM.
THAT WOUND ON YOUR HAND IS TAKING...
...TOO LONG TO HEAL.
STOP...!

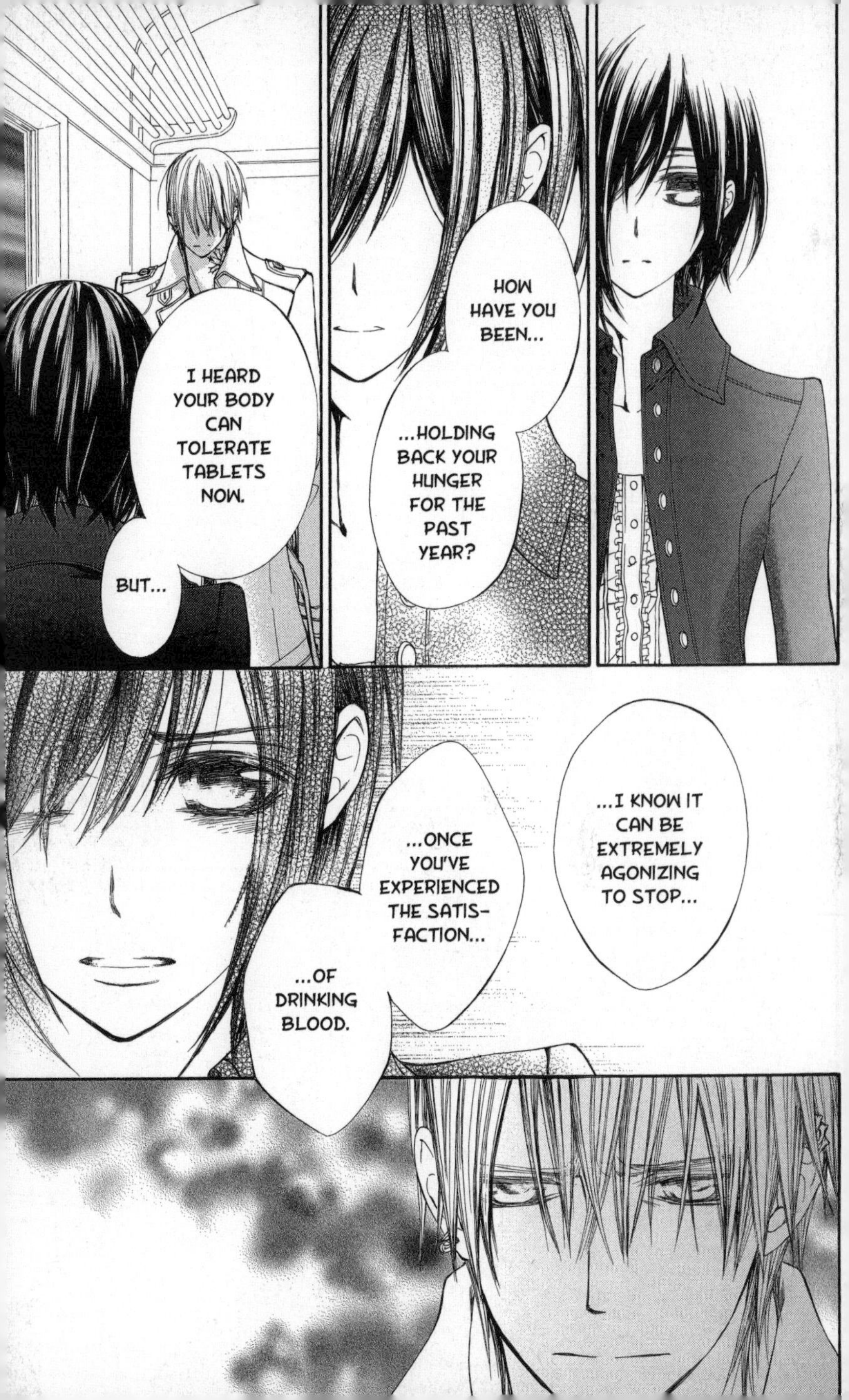
HOW HAVE YOU BEEN...
...HOLDING BACK YOUR HUNGER FOR THE PAST YEAR?
I HEARD YOUR BODY CAN TOLERATE TABLETS NOW.
BUT...
...I KNOW IT CAN BE EXTREMELY AGONIZING TO STOP...
...ONCE YOU'VE EXPERIENCED THE SATIS-FACTION...
...OF DRINKING BLOOD.

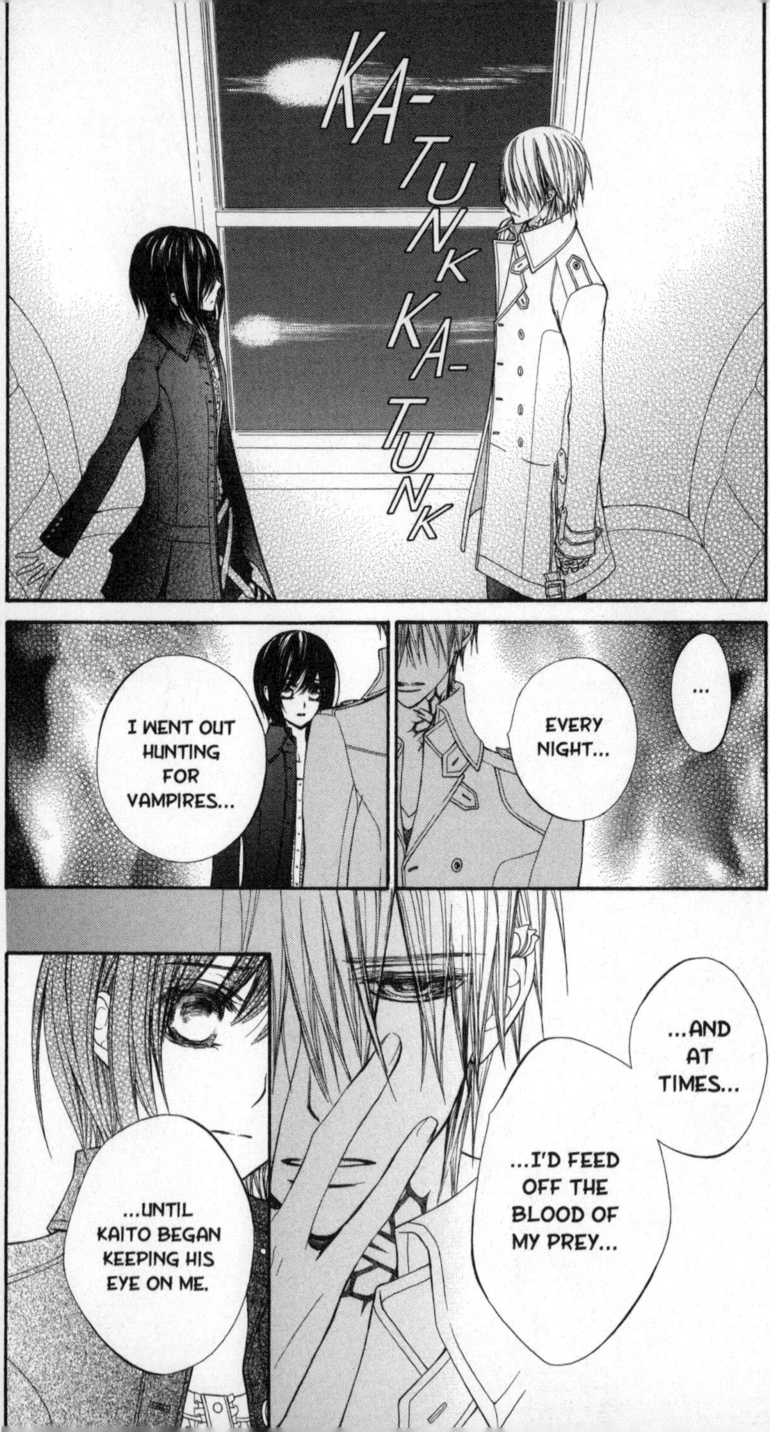
KA-TUNK KA-TUNK
...
EVERY NIGHT...
I WENT OUT HUNTING FOR VAMPIRES...
...AND AT TIMES...
...I'D FEED OFF THE BLOOD OF MY PREY...
...UNTIL KAITO BEGAN KEEPING HIS EYE ON ME.

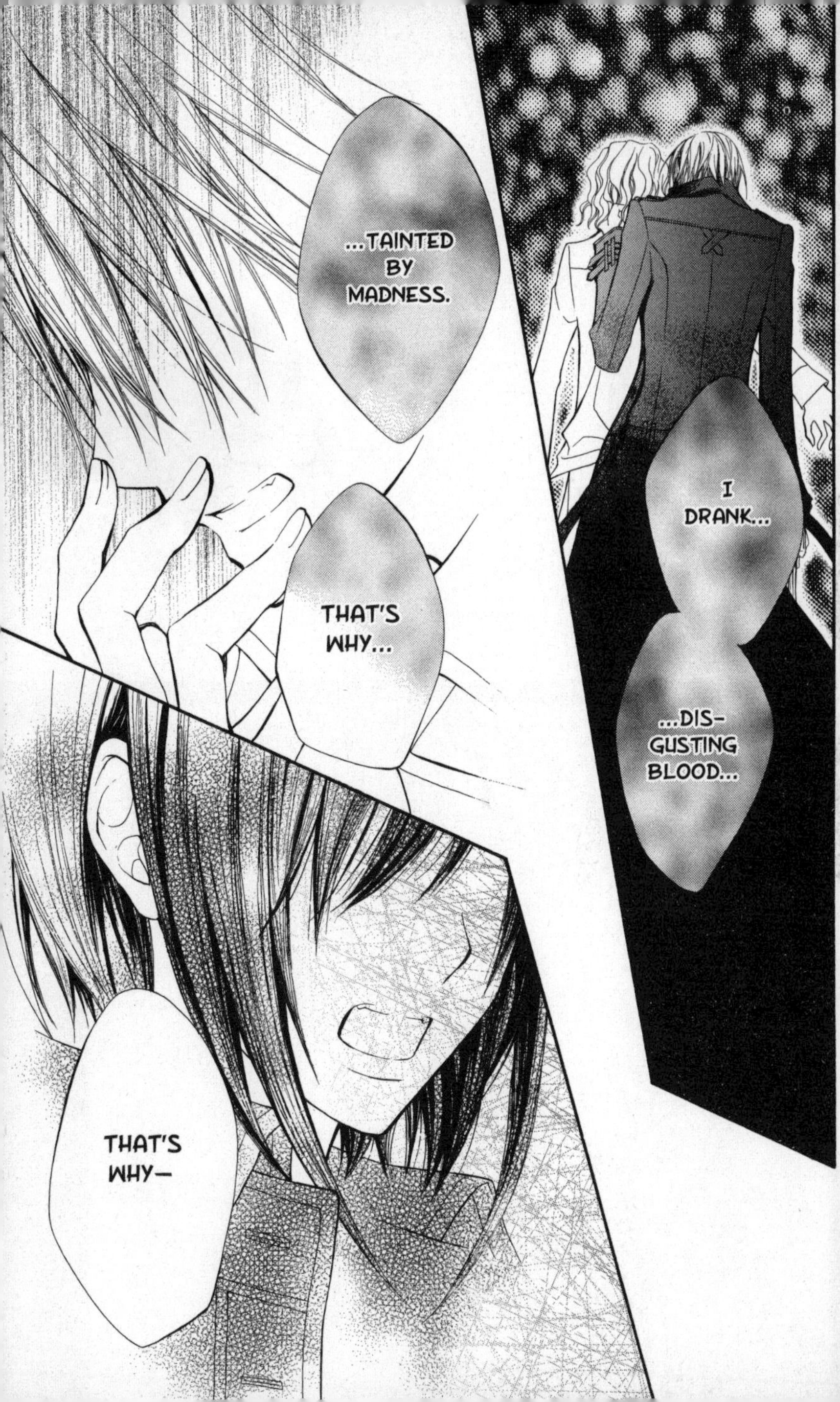
I DRANK...
...DIS-GUSTING BLOOD...
...TAINTED BY MADNESS.
THAT'S WHY...
THAT'S WHY—

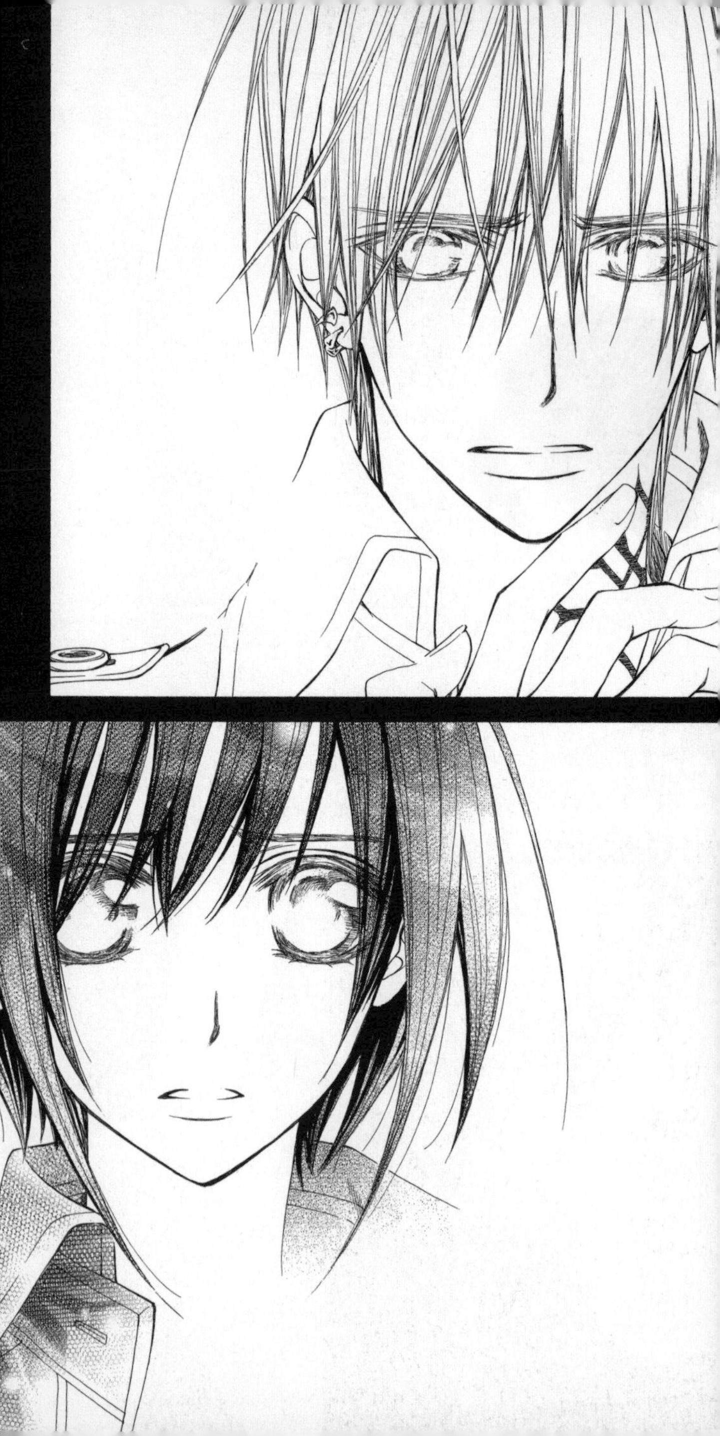

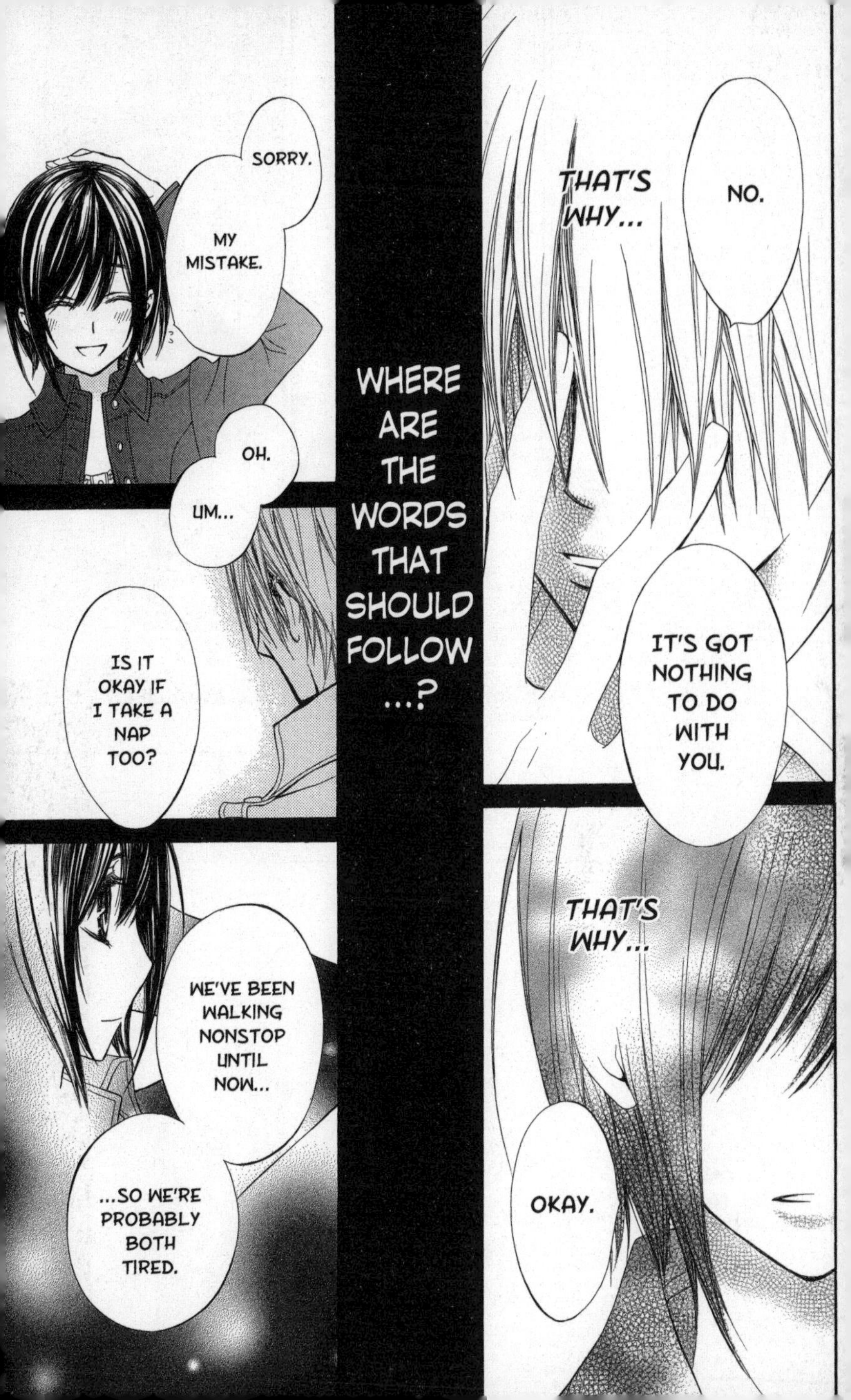
NO.
THAT'S WHY...
IT'S GOT NOTHING TO DO WITH YOU.
THAT'S WHY...
OKAY.
WHERE ARE THE WORDS THAT SHOULD FOLLOW ...?
SORRY.
MY MISTAKE.
OH.
UM...
IS IT OKAY IF I TAKE A NAP TOO?
WE'VE BEEN WALKING NONSTOP UNTIL NOW...
...SO WE'RE PROBABLY BOTH TIRED.

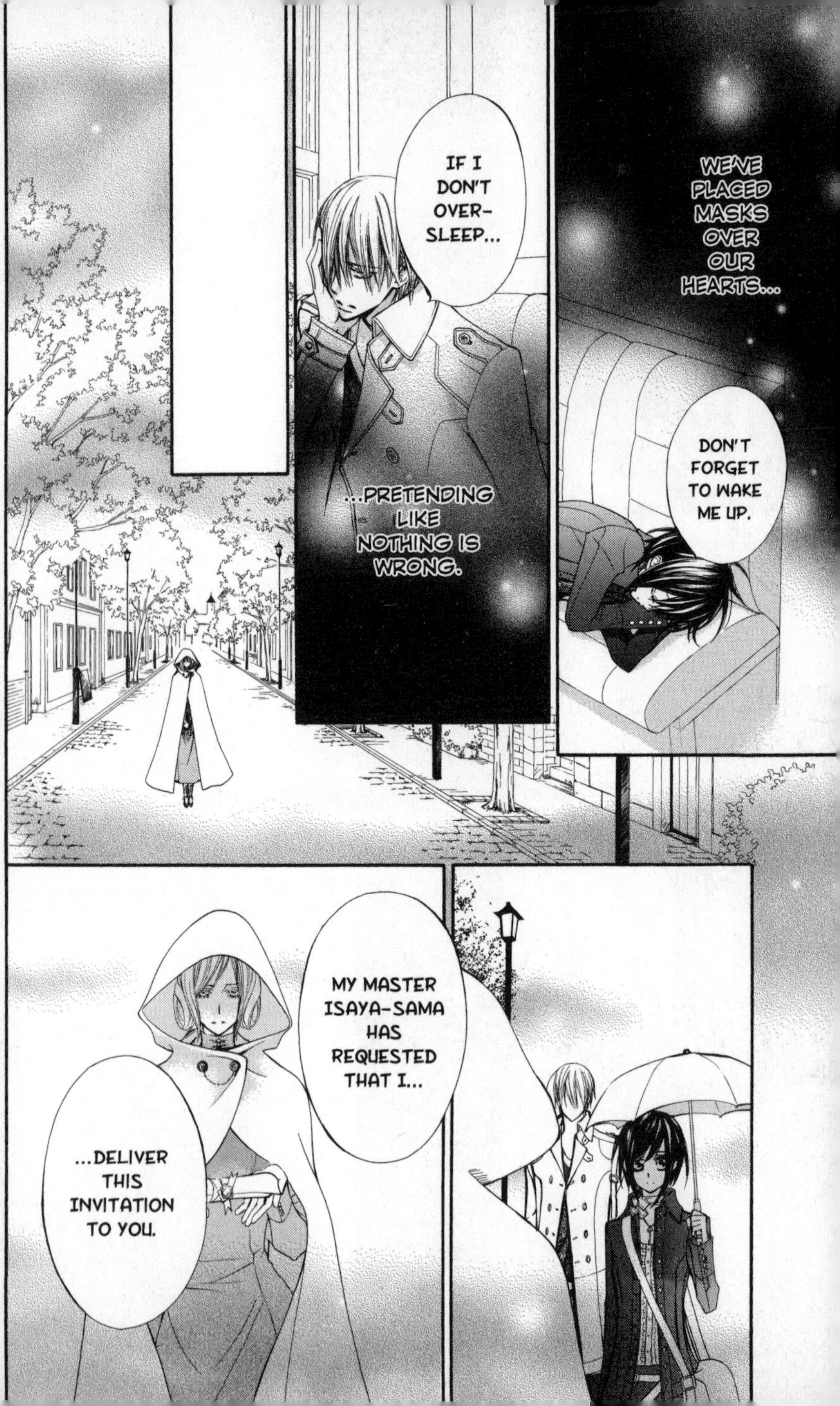
WE'VE PLACED MASKS OVER OUR HEARTS...
DON'T FORGET TO WAKE ME UP.
IF I DON'T OVER-SLEEP...
...PRETENDING LIKE NOTHING IS WRONG.
MY MASTER ISAYA-SAMA HAS REQUESTED THAT I...
...DELIVER THIS INVITATION TO YOU.

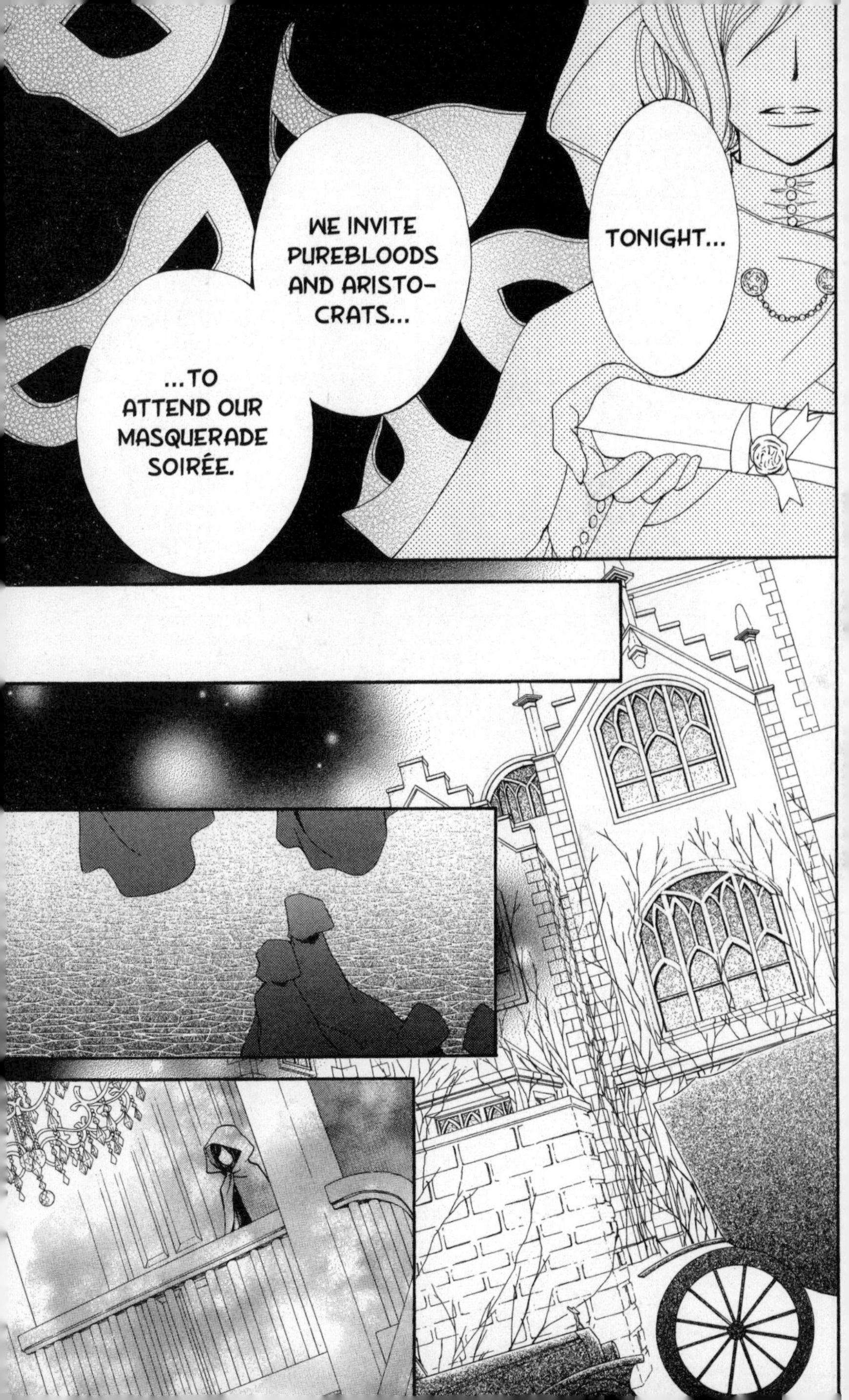
TONIGHT...
WE INVITE PUREBLOODS AND ARISTO-CRATS...
...TO ATTEND OUR MASQUERADE SOIRÉE.

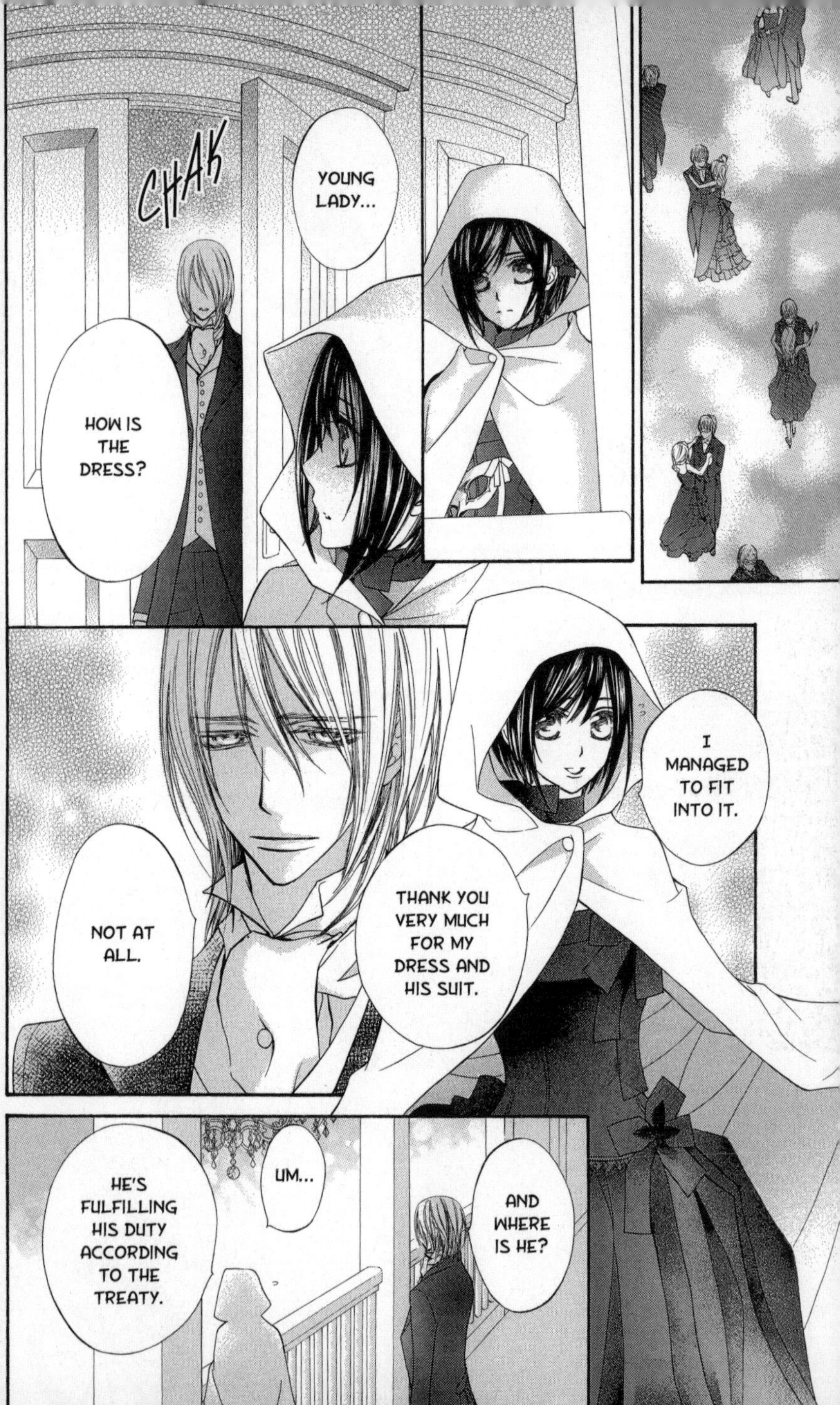
YOUNG LADY...
CHAK
HOW IS THE DRESS?
I MANAGED TO FIT INTO IT.
THANK YOU VERY MUCH FOR MY DRESS AND HIS SUIT.
NOT AT ALL.
AND WHERE IS HE?
UM...
HE'S FULFILLING HIS DUTY ACCORDING TO THE TREATY.

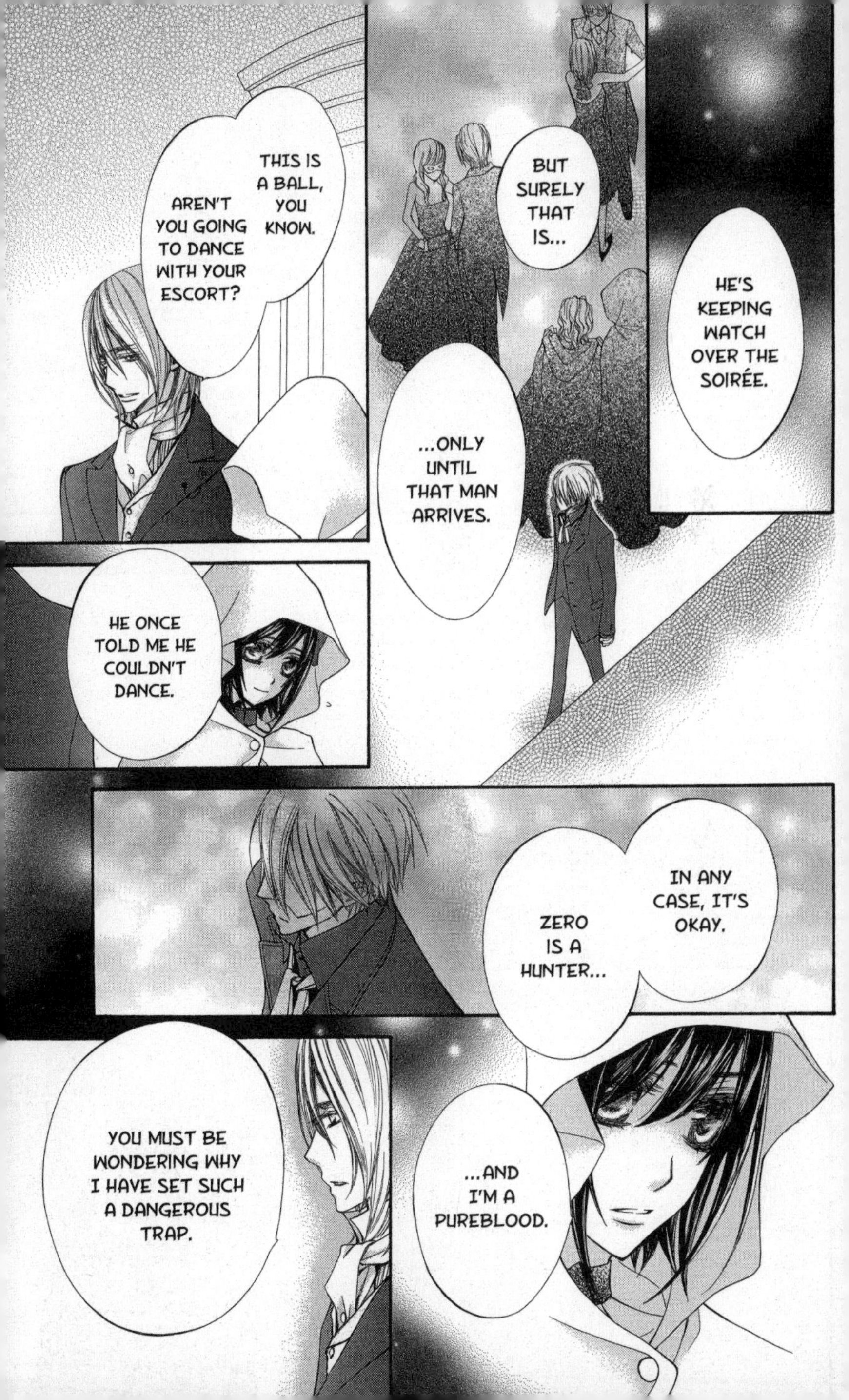
HE'S KEEPING WATCH OVER THE SOIRÉE.
BUT SURELY THAT IS...
...ONLY UNTIL THAT MAN ARRIVES.
THIS IS A BALL, YOU KNOW.
AREN'T YOU GOING TO DANCE WITH YOUR ESCORT?
HE ONCE TOLD ME HE COULDN'T DANCE.
IN ANY CASE, IT'S OKAY.
ZERO IS A HUNTER...
...AND I'M A PUREBLOOD.
YOU MUST BE WONDERING WHY I HAVE SET SUCH A DANGEROUS TRAP.

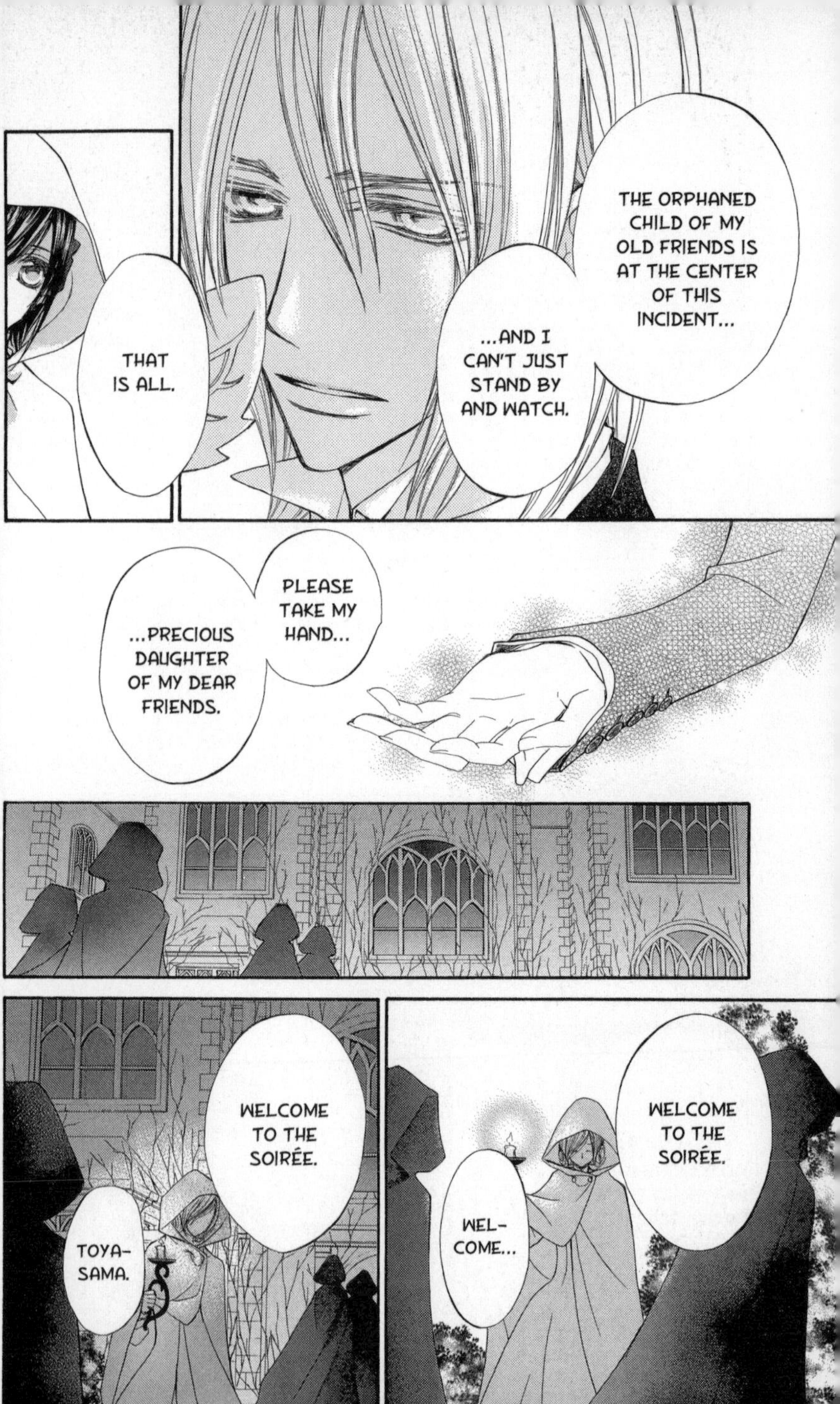
THE ORPHANED CHILD OF MY OLD FRIENDS IS AT THE CENTER OF THIS INCIDENT...
...AND I CAN'T JUST STAND BY AND WATCH.
THAT IS ALL.
PLEASE TAKE MY HAND...
...PRECIOUS DAUGHTER OF MY DEAR FRIENDS.
WELCOME TO THE SOIRÉE.
WEL-COME...
WELCOME TO THE SOIRÉE.
TOYA-SAMA.

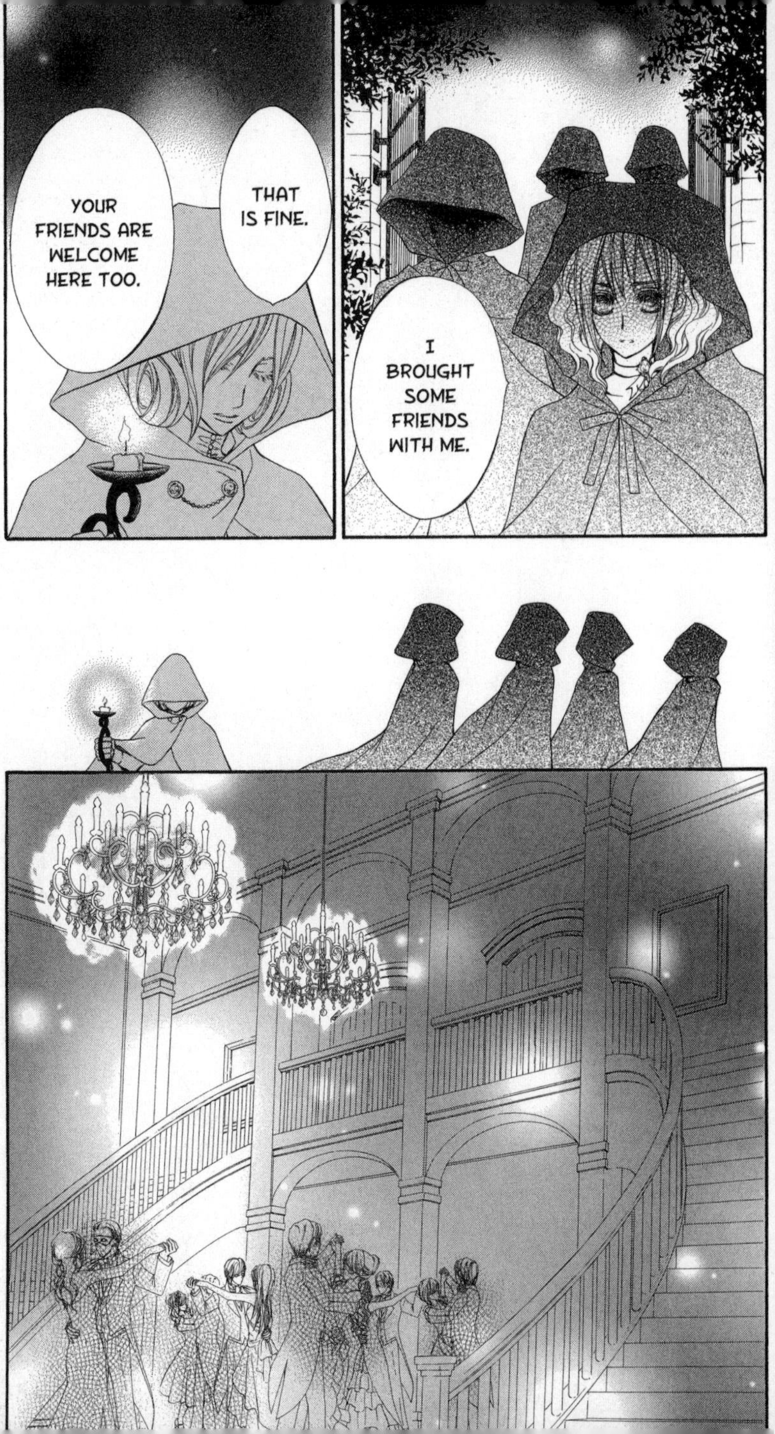
I BROUGHT SOME FRIENDS WITH ME.
THAT IS FINE.
YOUR FRIENDS ARE WELCOME HERE TOO.

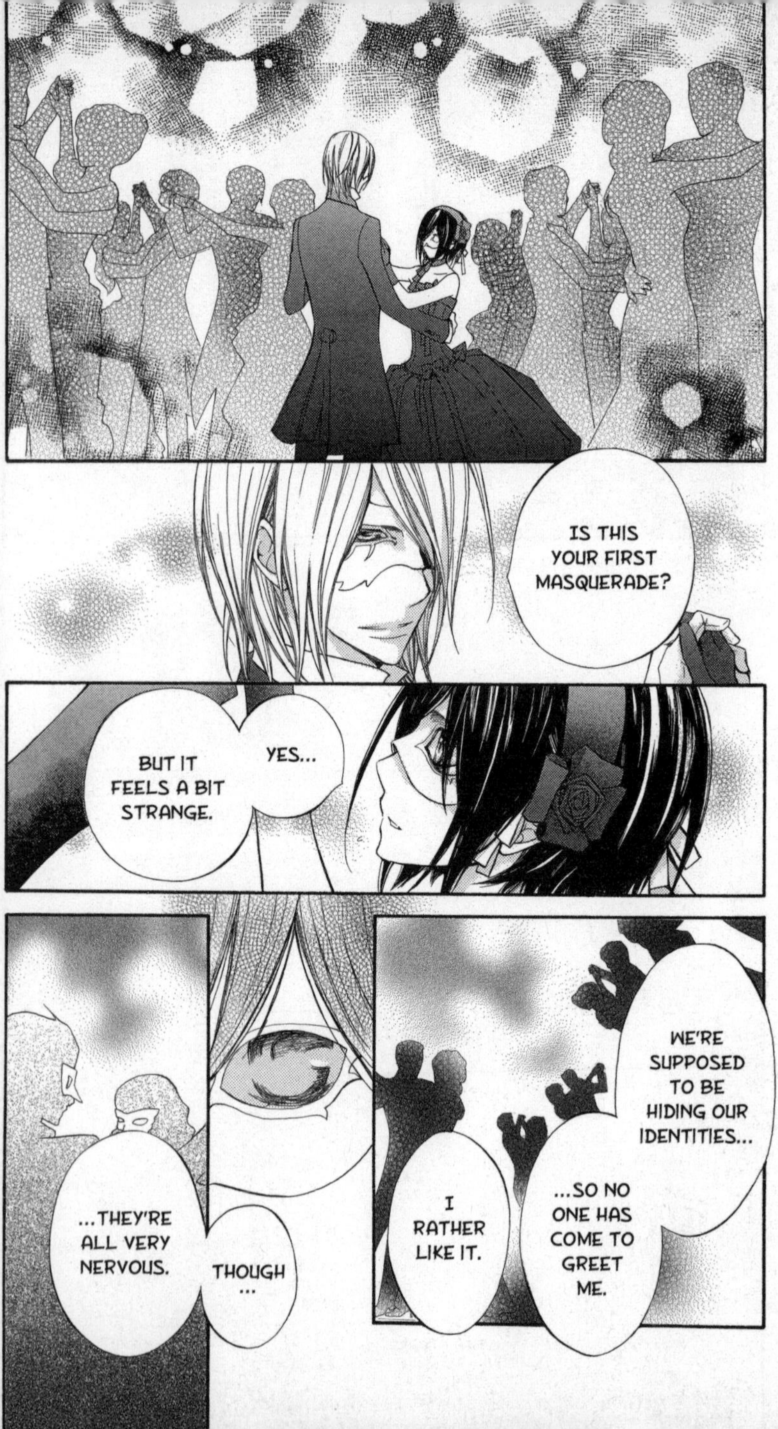
IS THIS YOUR FIRST MASQUERADE?
YES...
BUT IT FEELS A BIT STRANGE.
WE'RE SUPPOSED TO BE HIDING OUR IDENTITIES...
...SO NO ONE HAS COME TO GREET ME.
I RATHER LIKE IT.
THOUGH...
...THEY'RE ALL VERY NERVOUS.

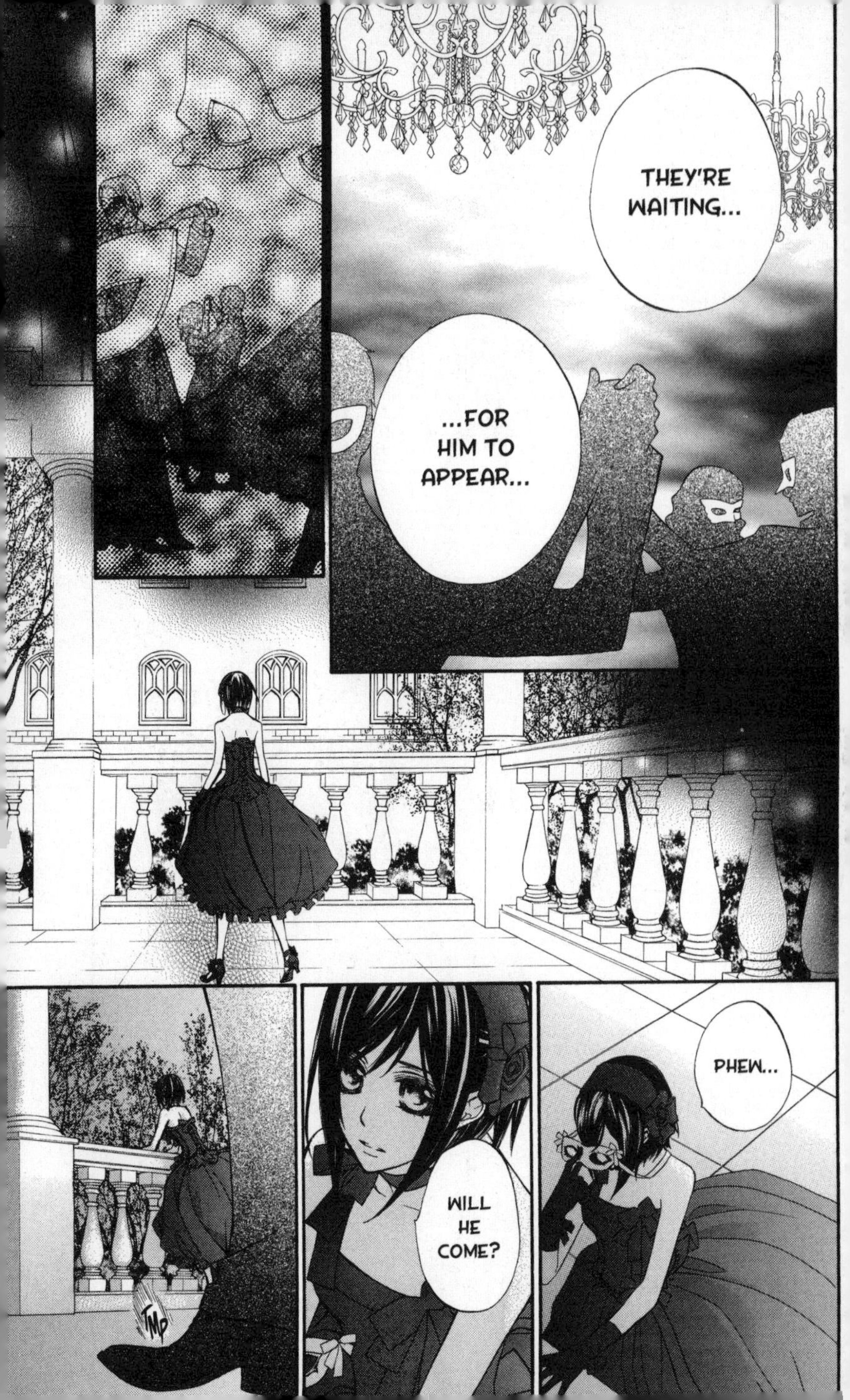
THEY'RE WAITING...
...FOR HIM TO APPEAR...
PHEW...
WILL HE COME?
TMP

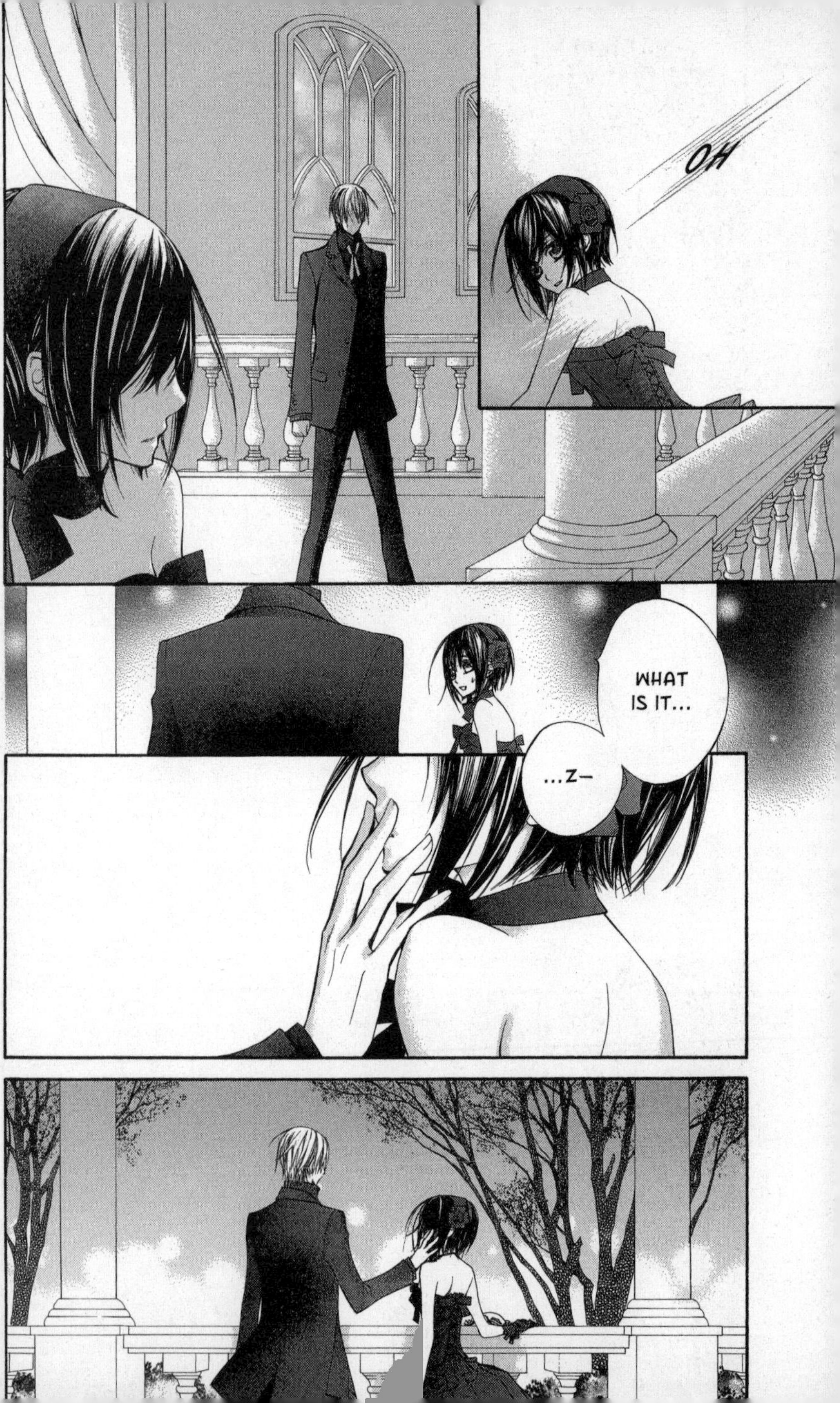
OH
WHAT IS IT...
...Z—

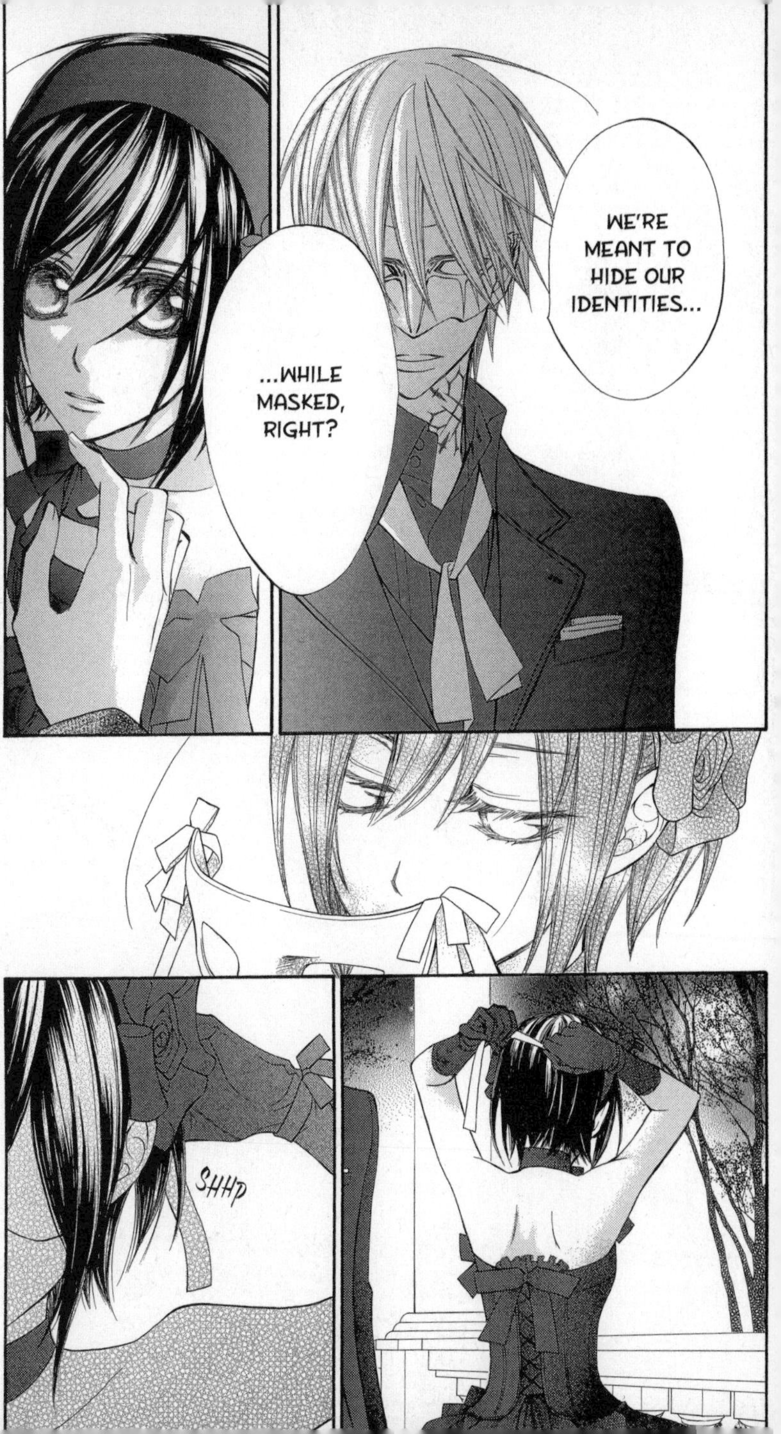
WE'RE MEANT TO HIDE OUR IDENTITIES...
...WHILE MASKED, RIGHT?
SHHP

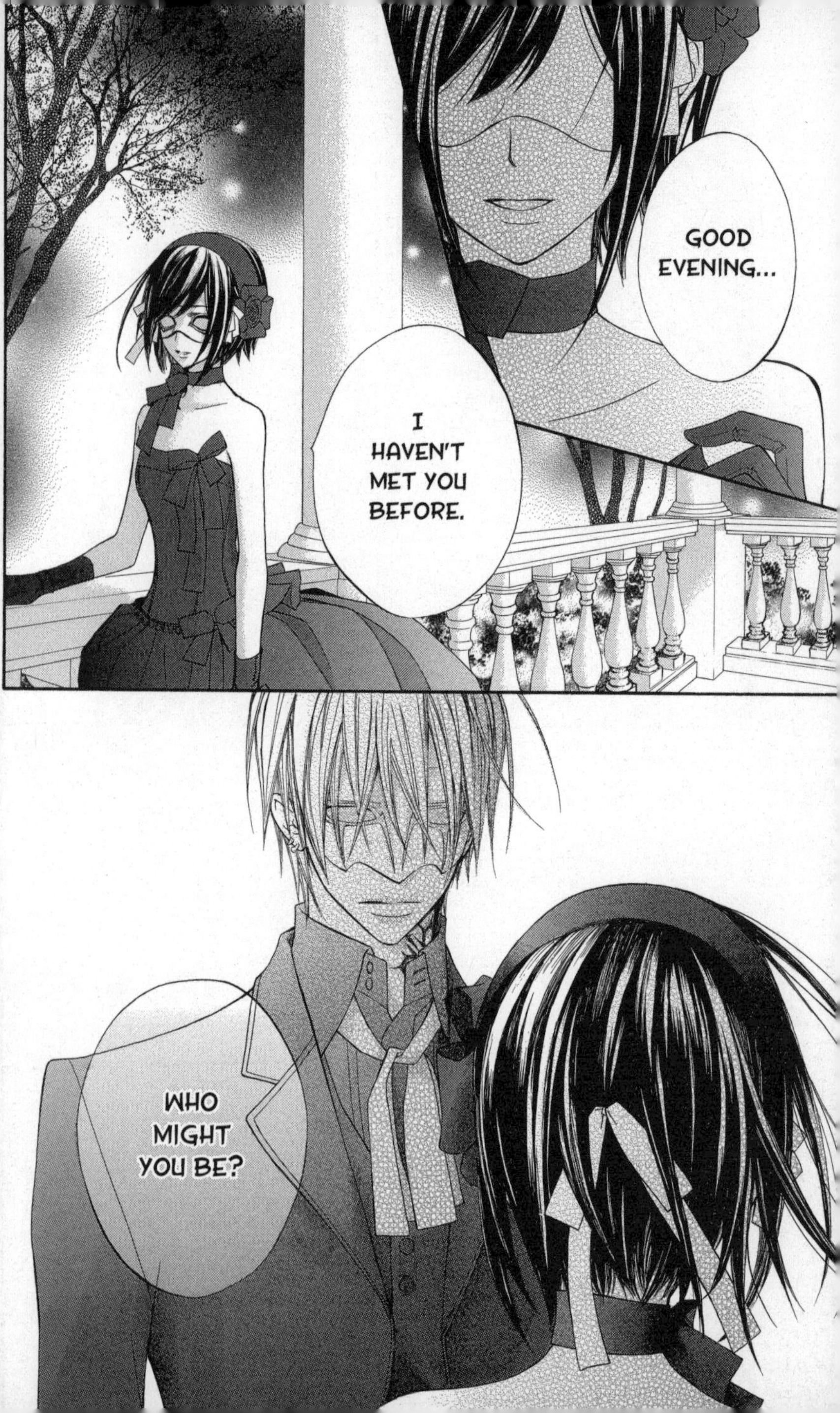
GOOD EVENING...
I HAVEN'T MET YOU BEFORE.
WHO MIGHT YOU BE?

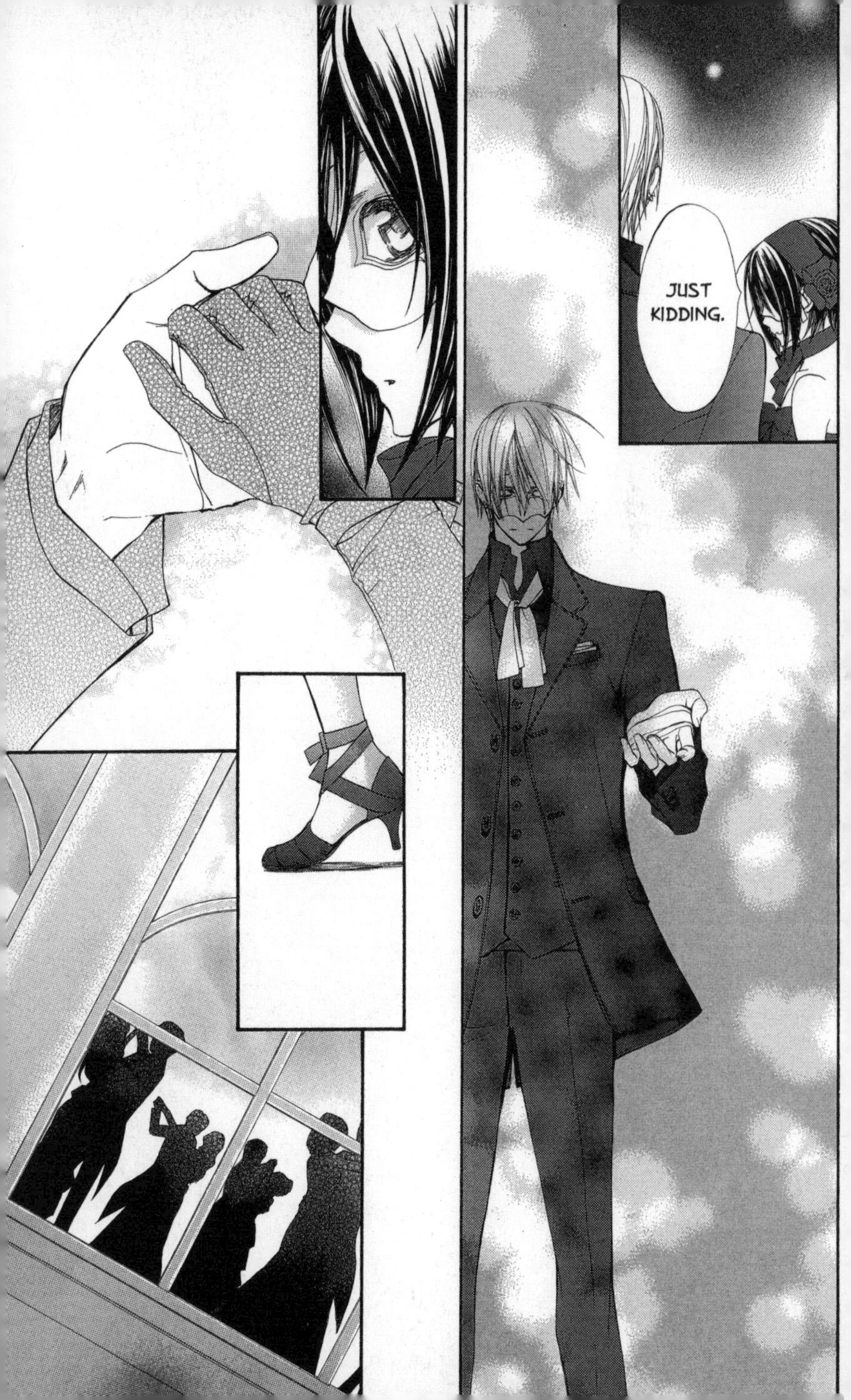
JUST KIDDING.

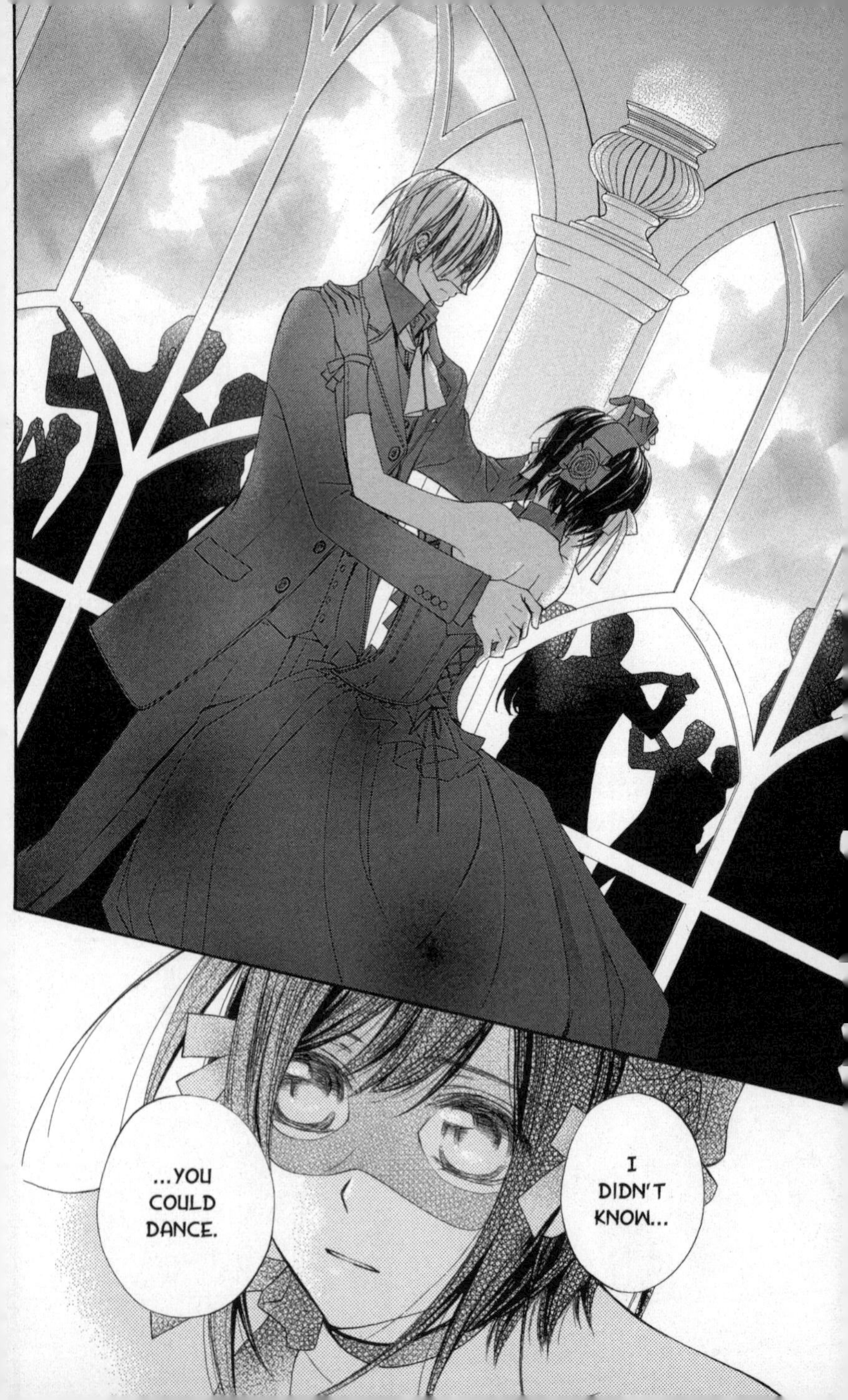
I DIDN'T KNOW...
...YOU COULD DANCE.

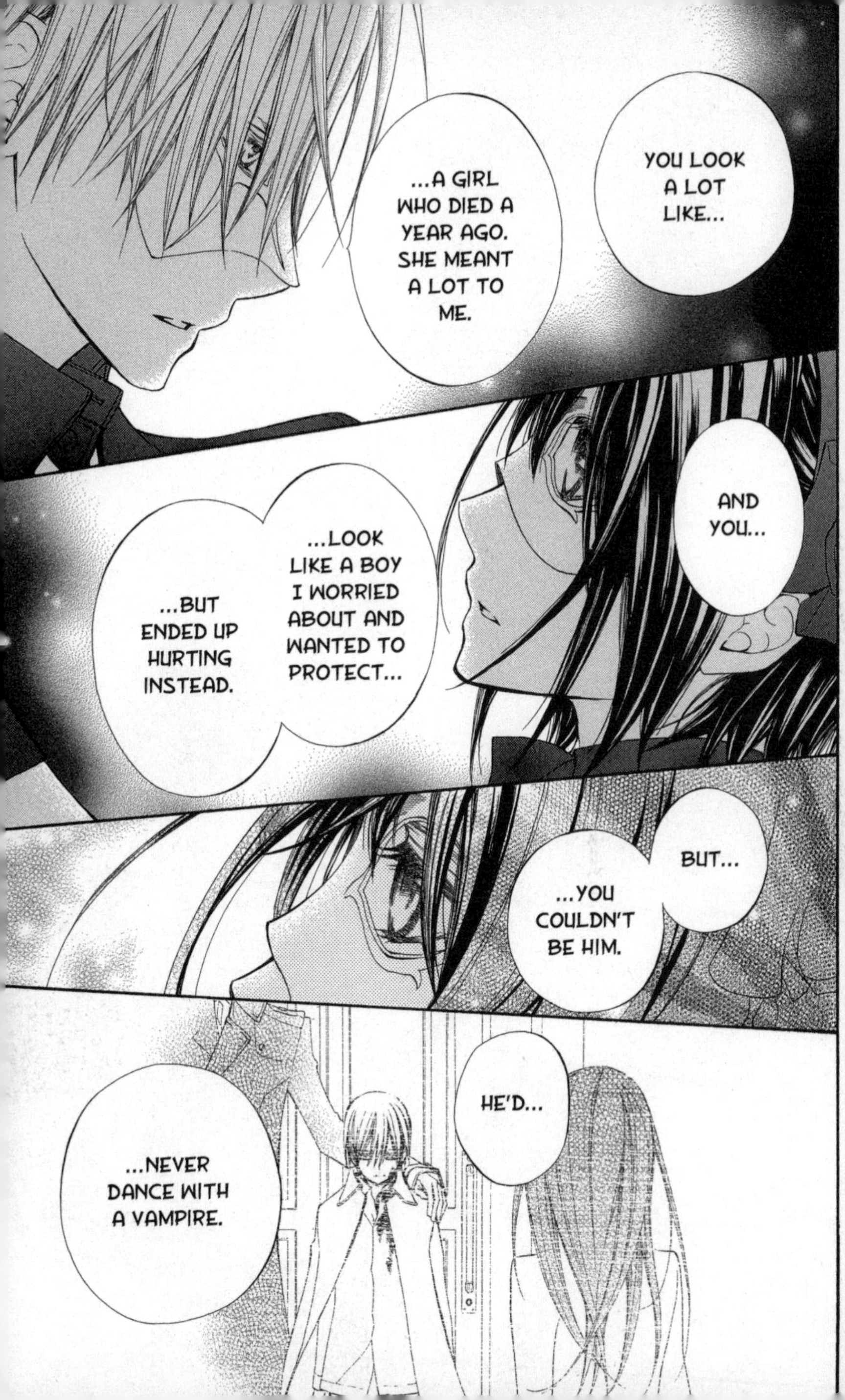
YOU LOOK A LOT LIKE...
...A GIRL WHO DIED A YEAR AGO. SHE MEANT A LOT TO ME.
AND YOU...
...LOOK LIKE A BOY I WORRIED ABOUT AND WANTED TO PROTECT...
...BUT ENDED UP HURTING INSTEAD.
BUT...
...YOU COULDN'T BE HIM.
HE'D...
...NEVER DANCE WITH A VAMPIRE.

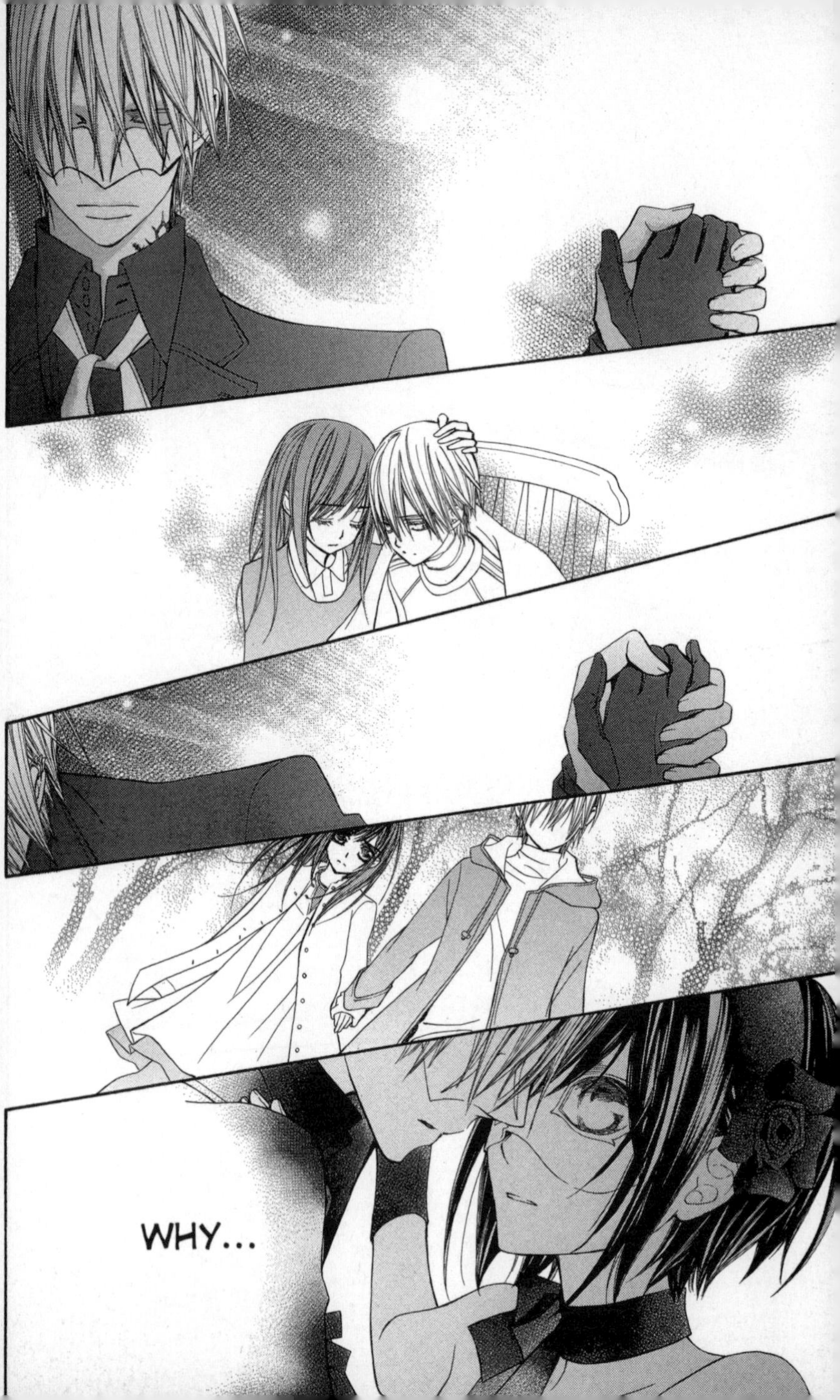
WHY...

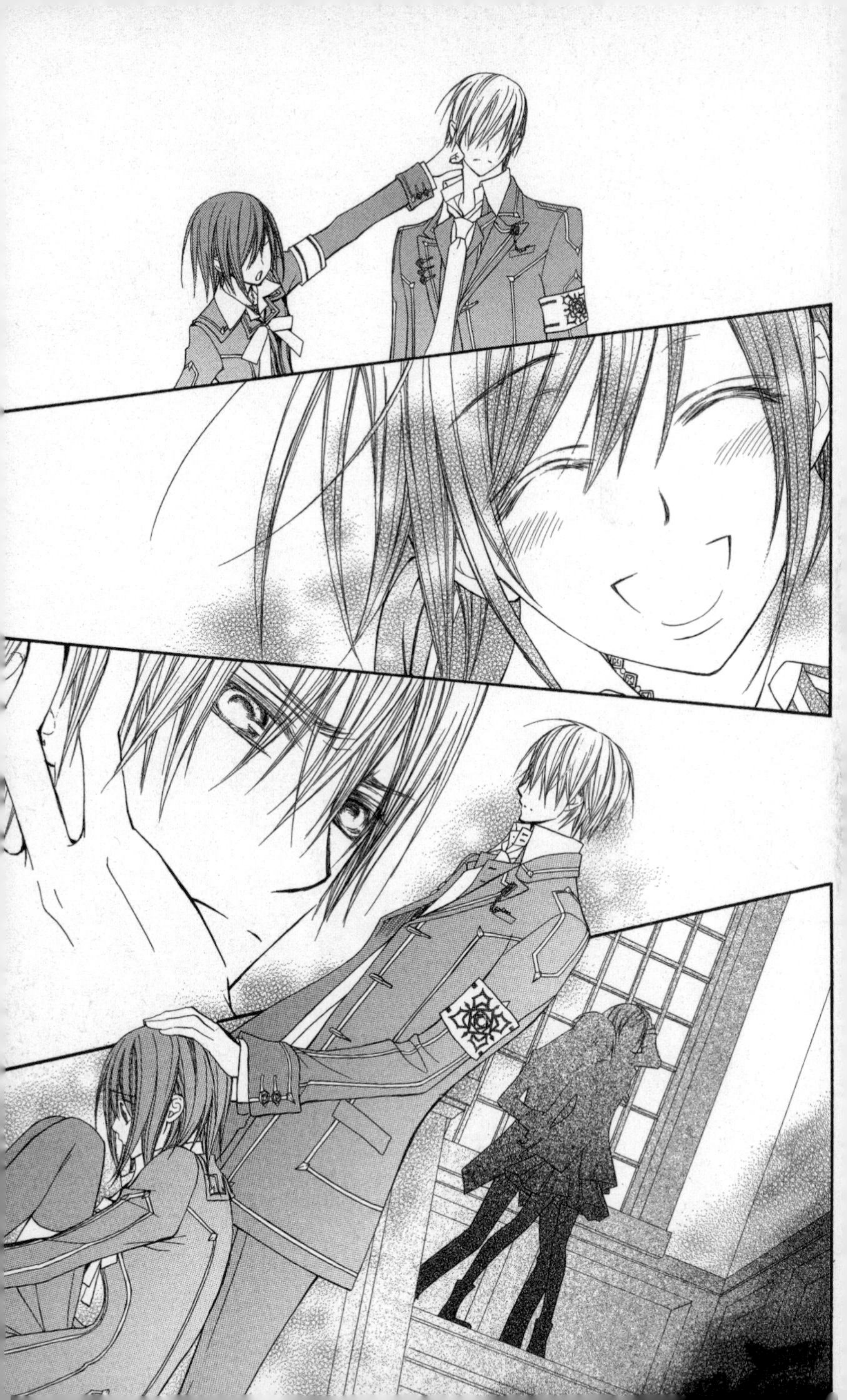

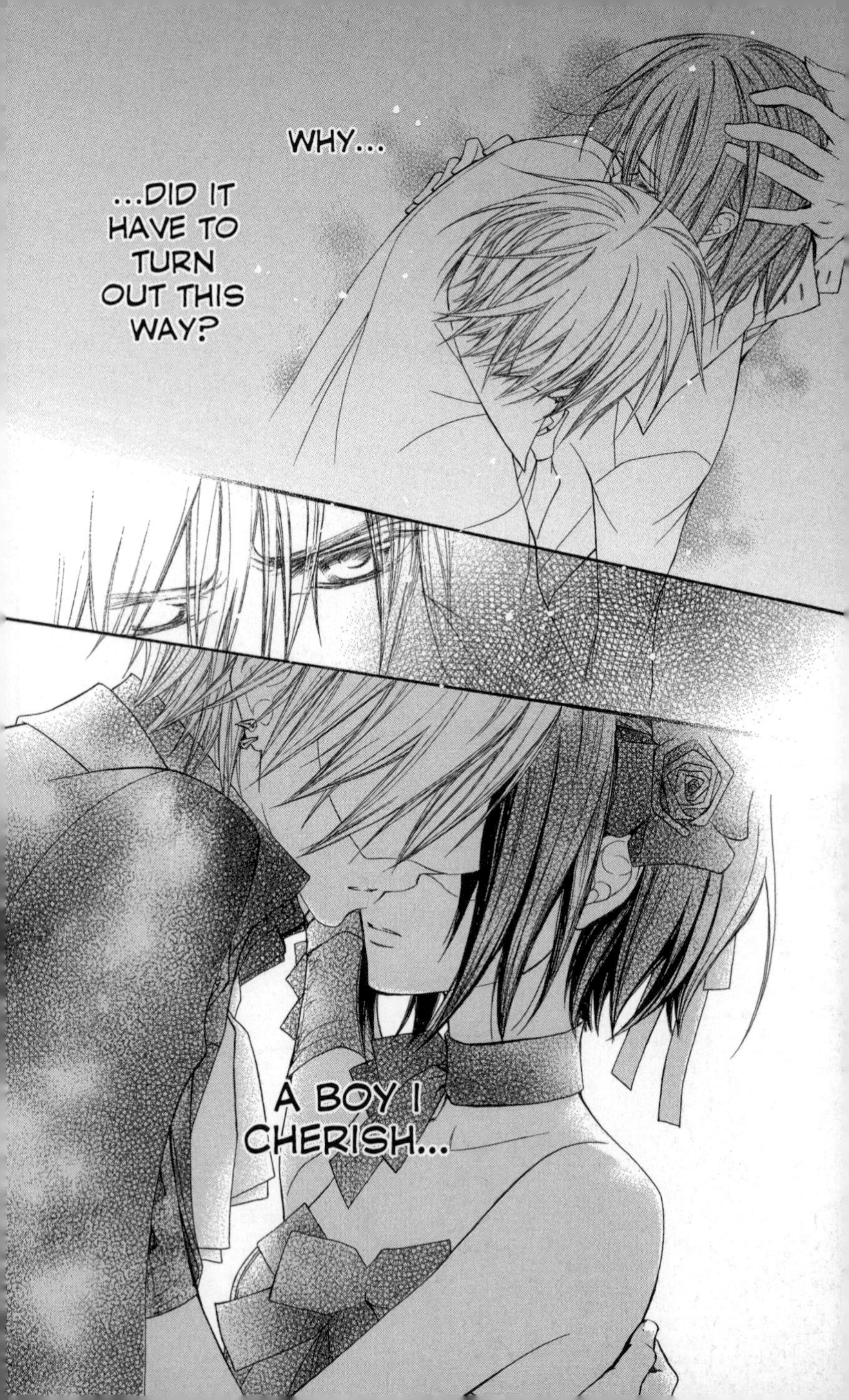
WHY...
...DID IT HAVE TO TURN OUT THIS WAY?
A BOY I CHERISH...

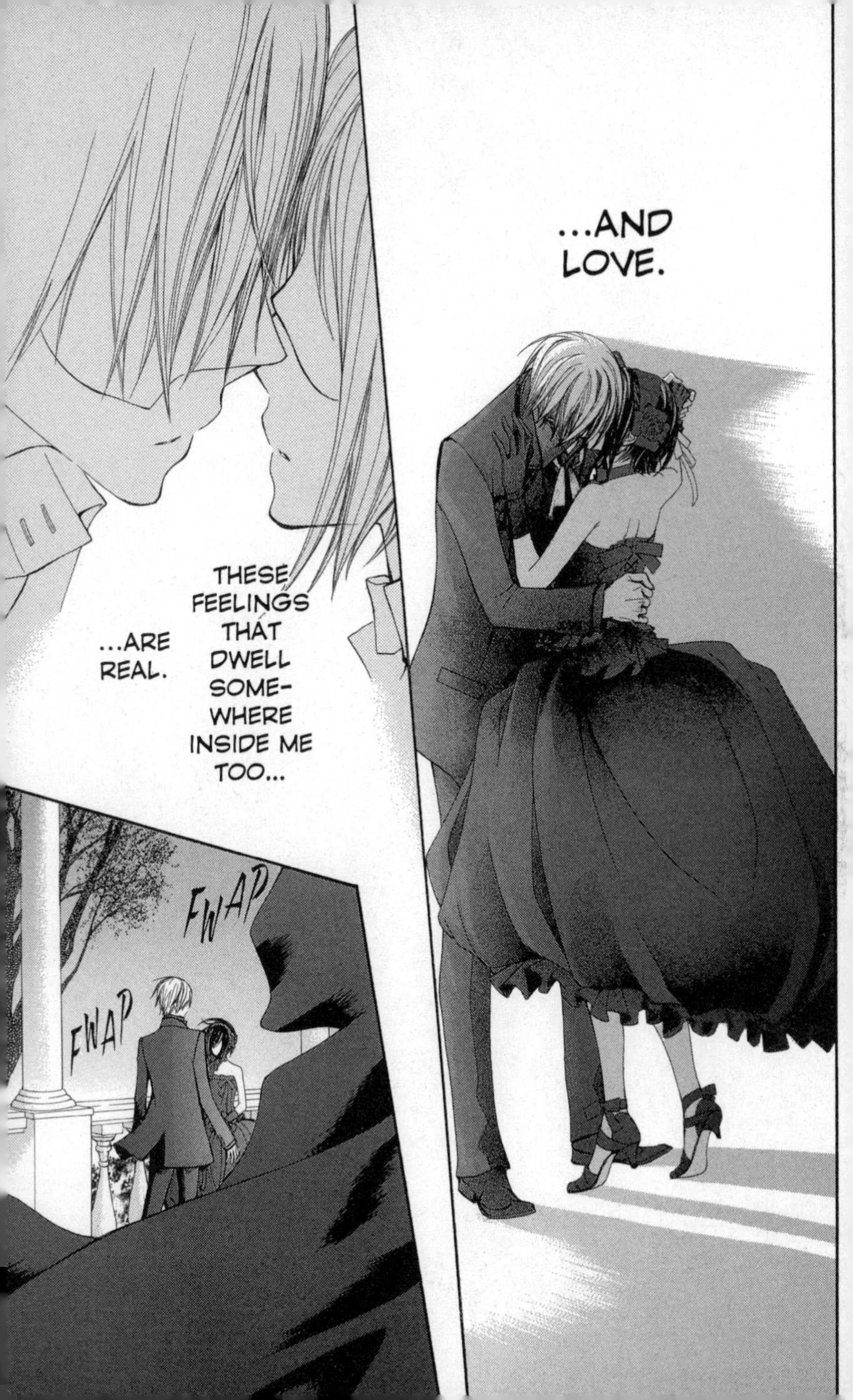
...AND LOVE.
THESE FEELINGS THAT DWELL SOME-WHERE INSIDE ME TOO...
...ARE REAL.
FWAP
FWAP

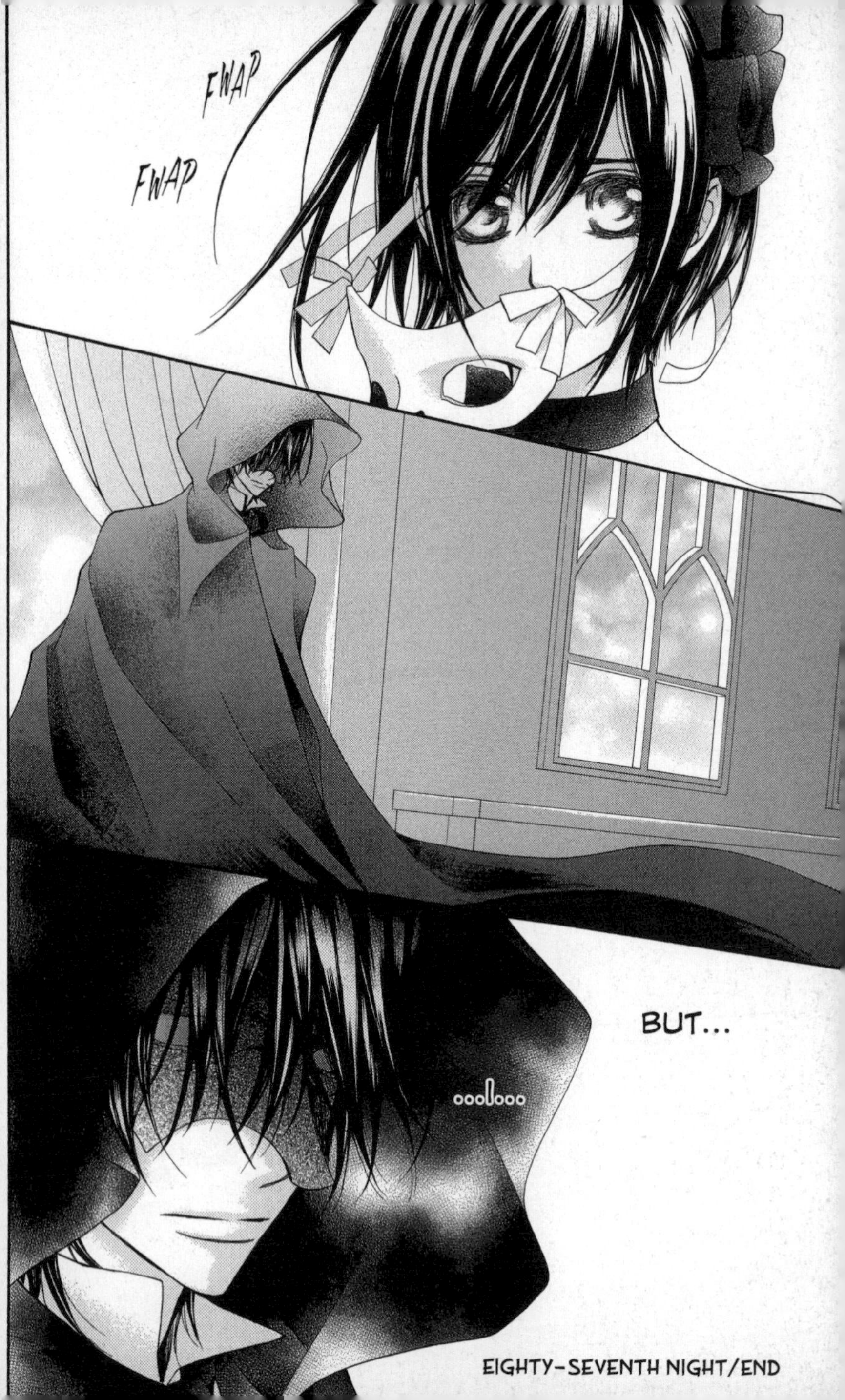
FWAP
FWAP
BUT...
EIGHTY-SEVENTH NIGHT/END

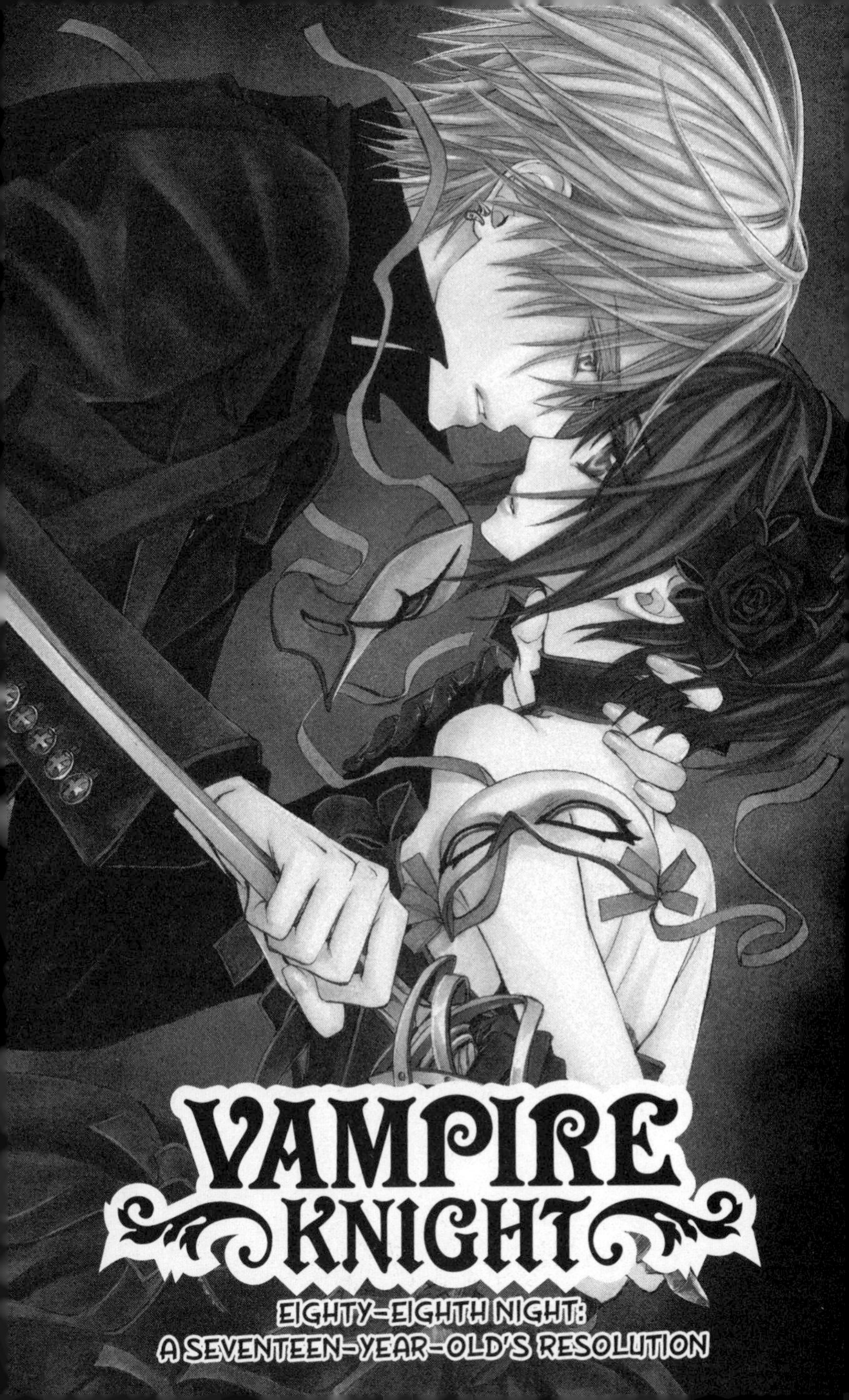
VAMPIRE KNIGHT
EIGHTY-EIGHTH NIGHT:
A SEVENTEEN-YEAR-OLD'S RESOLUTION

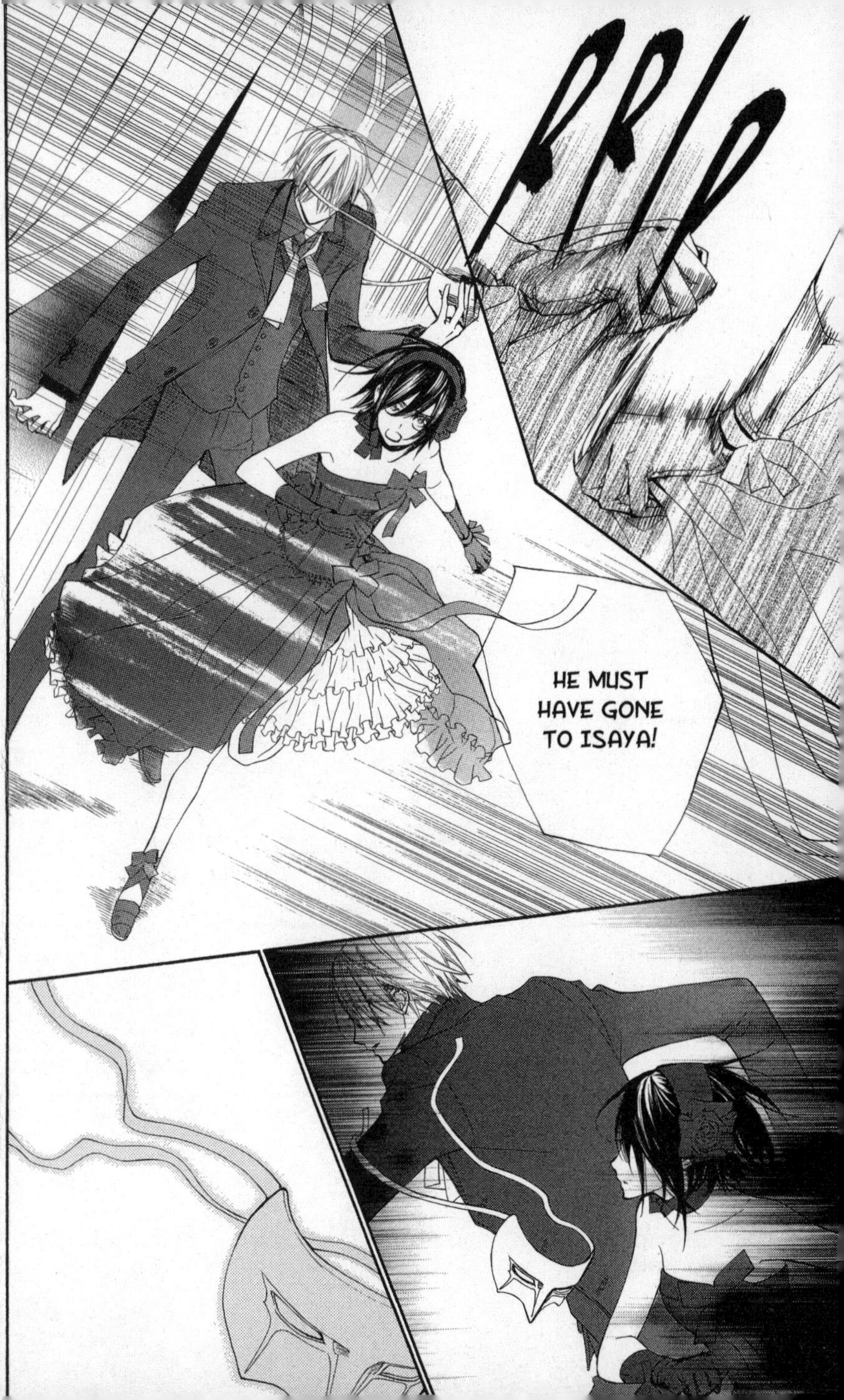
RRIP
HE MUST HAVE GONE TO ISAYA!

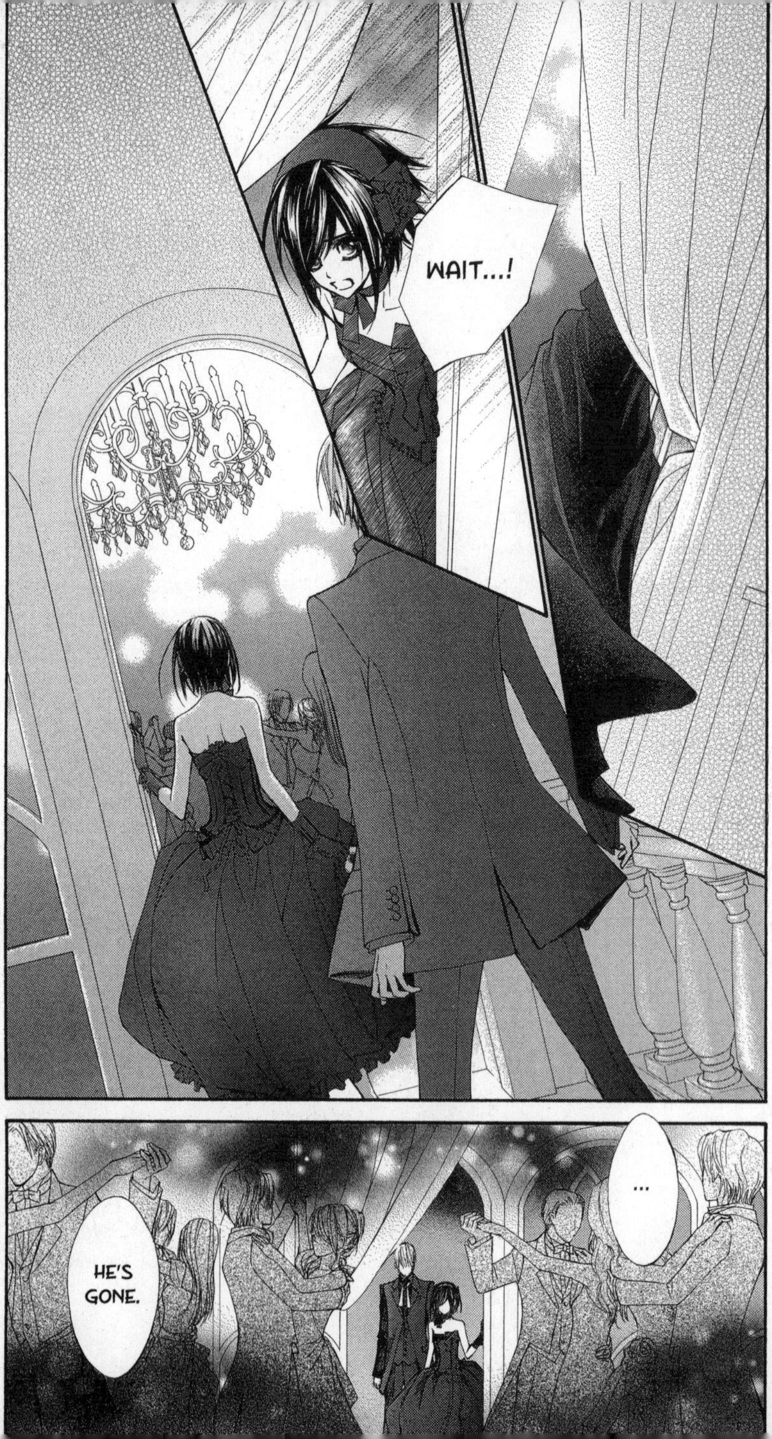
WAIT...!
...
HE'S GONE.

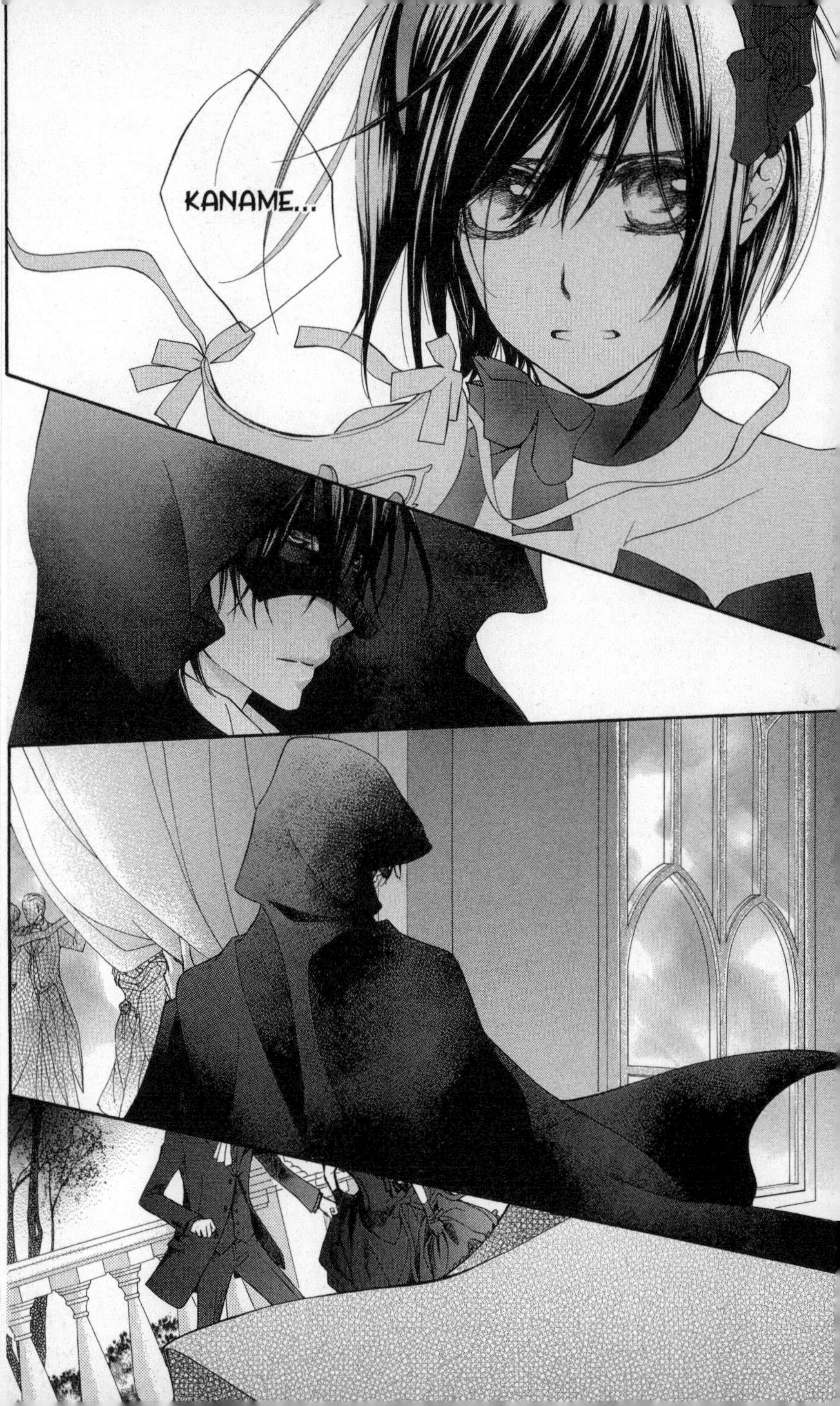
KANAME...

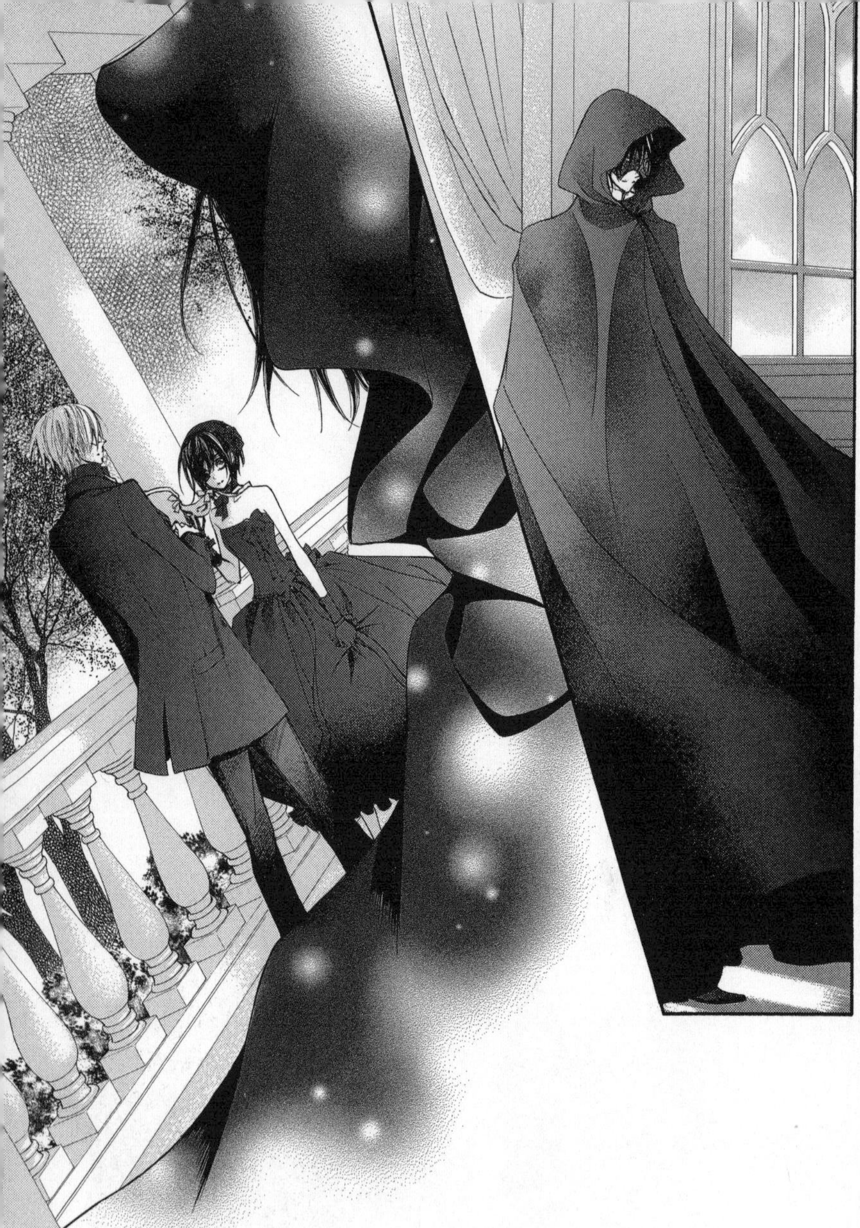

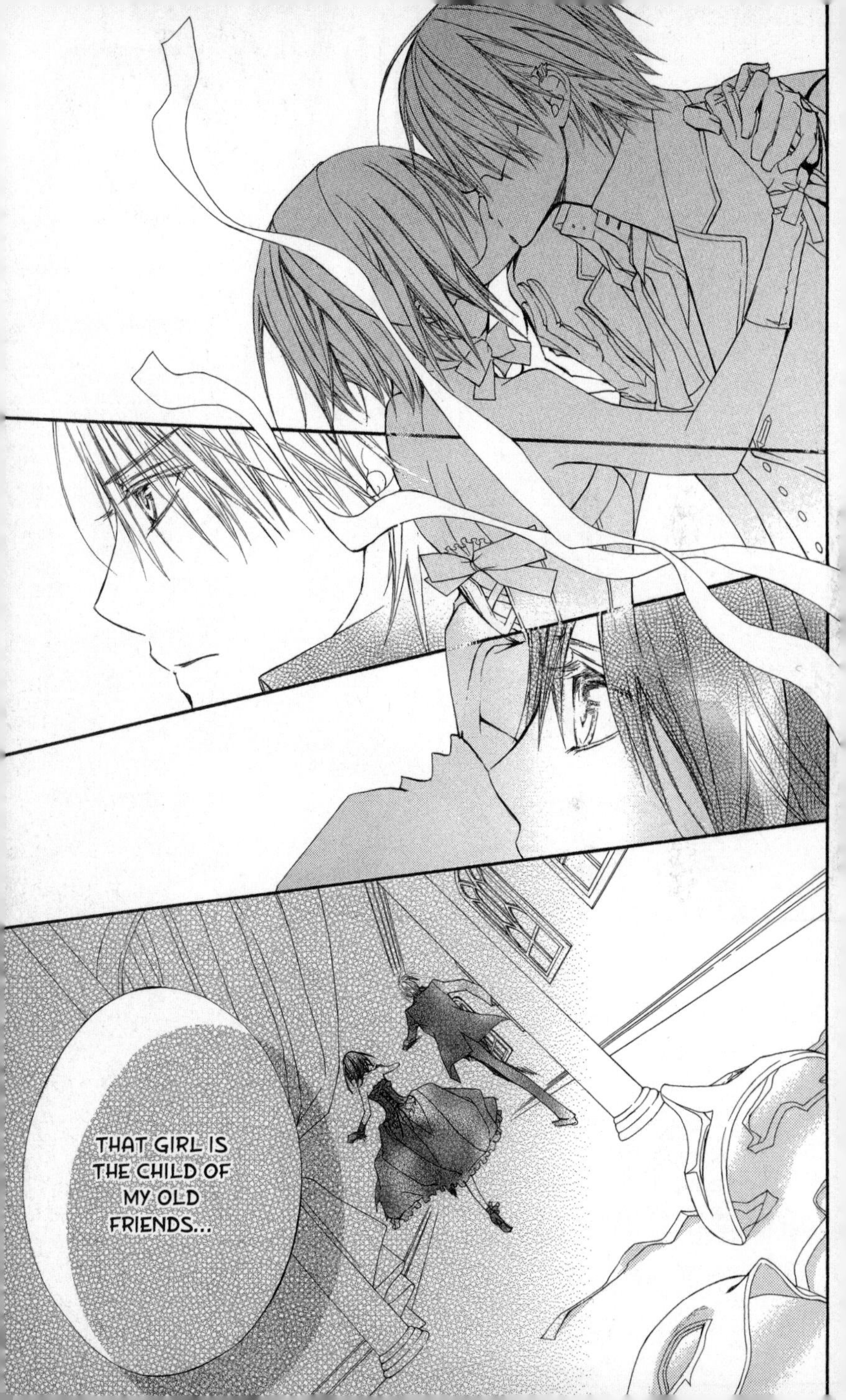
THAT GIRL IS THE CHILD OF MY OLD FRIENDS...

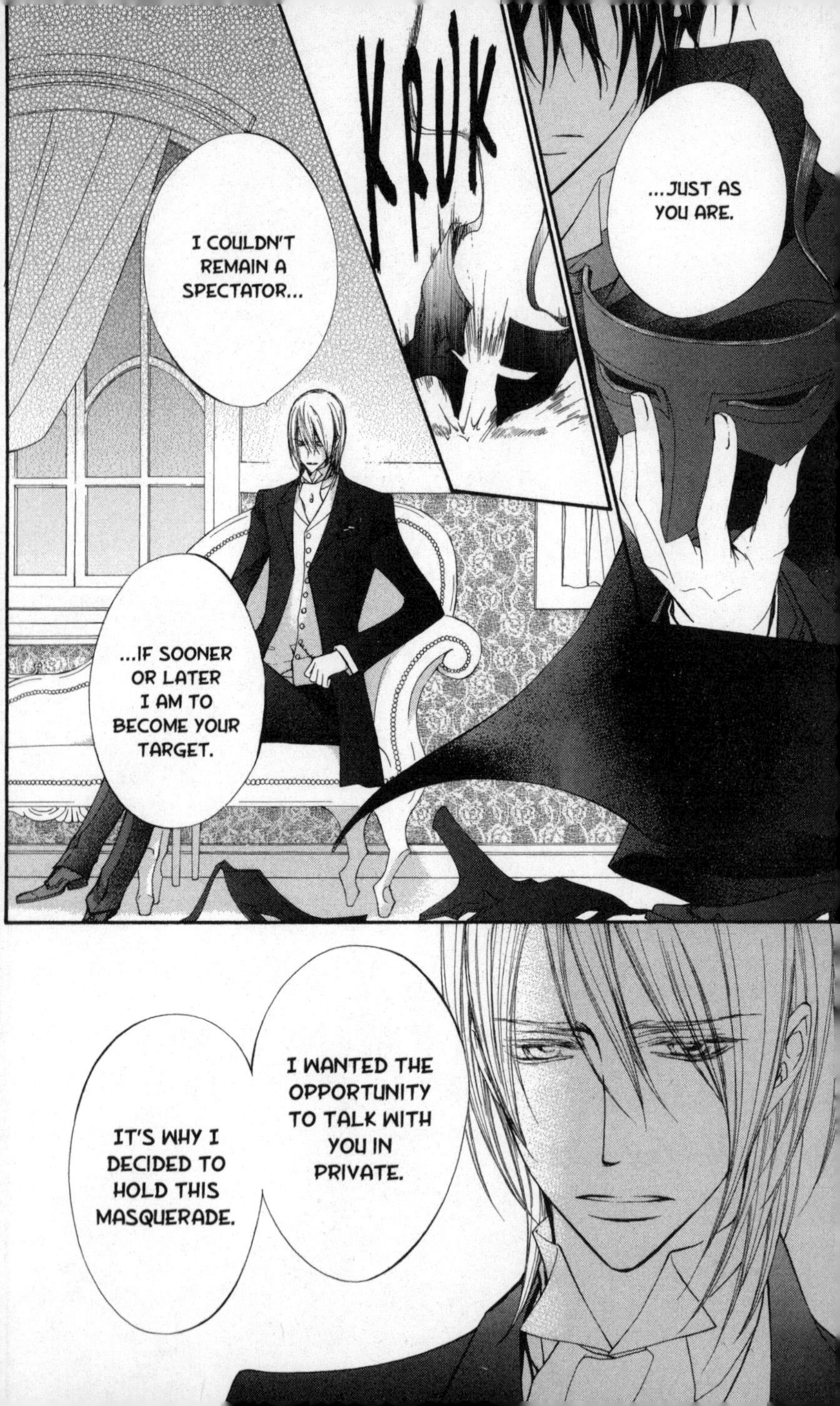
...JUST AS YOU ARE.
KRUK
I COULDN'T REMAIN A SPECTATOR...
...IF SOONER OR LATER I AM TO BECOME YOUR TARGET.
I WANTED THE OPPORTUNITY TO TALK WITH YOU IN PRIVATE.
IT'S WHY I DECIDED TO HOLD THIS MASQUERADE.

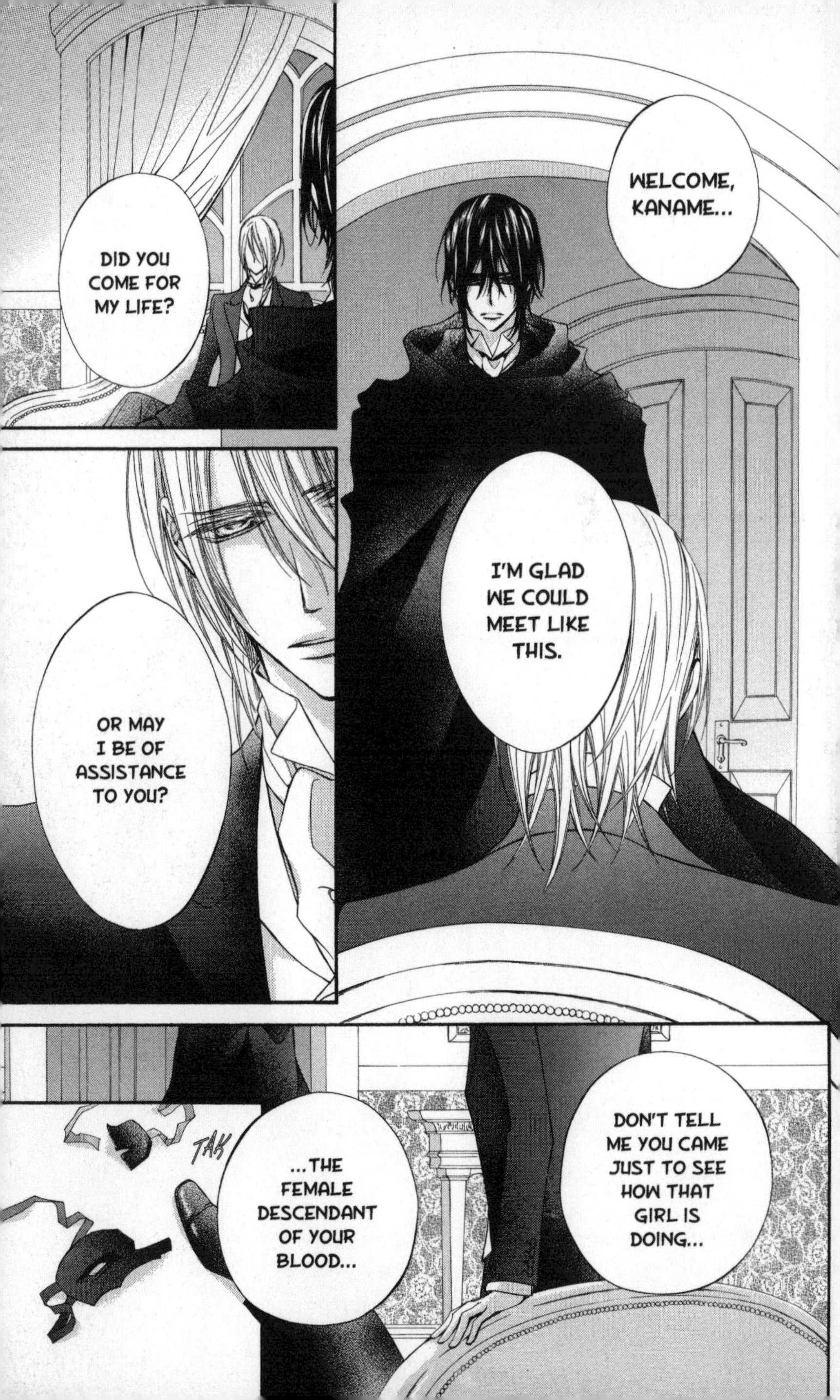
WELCOME, KANAME...
I'M GLAD WE COULD MEET LIKE THIS.
DID YOU COME FOR MY LIFE?
OR MAY I BE OF ASSISTANCE TO YOU?
DON'T TELL ME YOU CAME JUST TO SEE HOW THAT GIRL IS DOING...
...THE FEMALE DESCENDANT OF YOUR BLOOD...
TAK

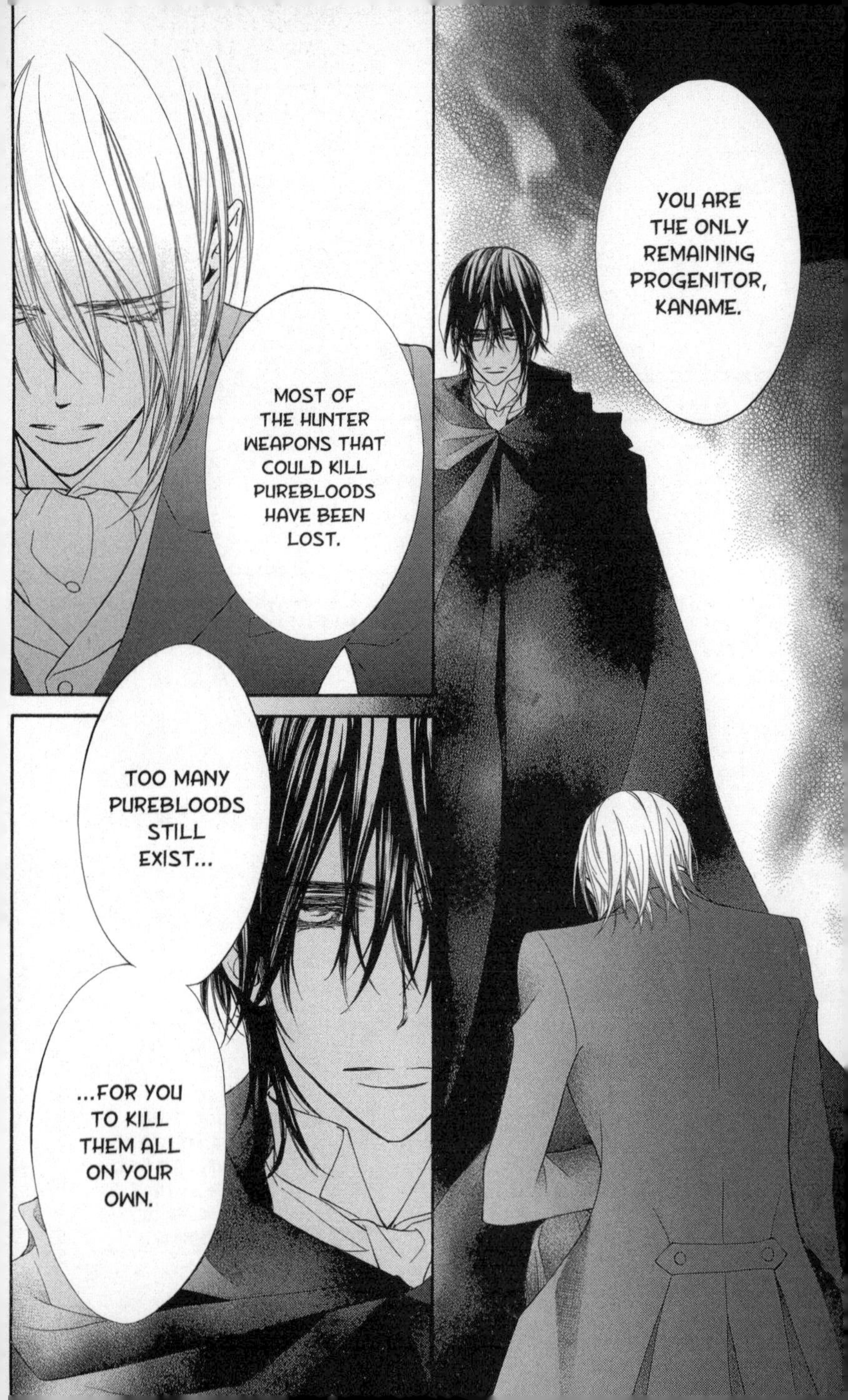
YOU ARE THE ONLY REMAINING PROGENITOR, KANAME.
MOST OF THE HUNTER WEAPONS THAT COULD KILL PUREBLOODS HAVE BEEN LOST.
TOO MANY PUREBLOODS STILL EXIST...
...FOR YOU TO KILL THEM ALL ON YOUR OWN.

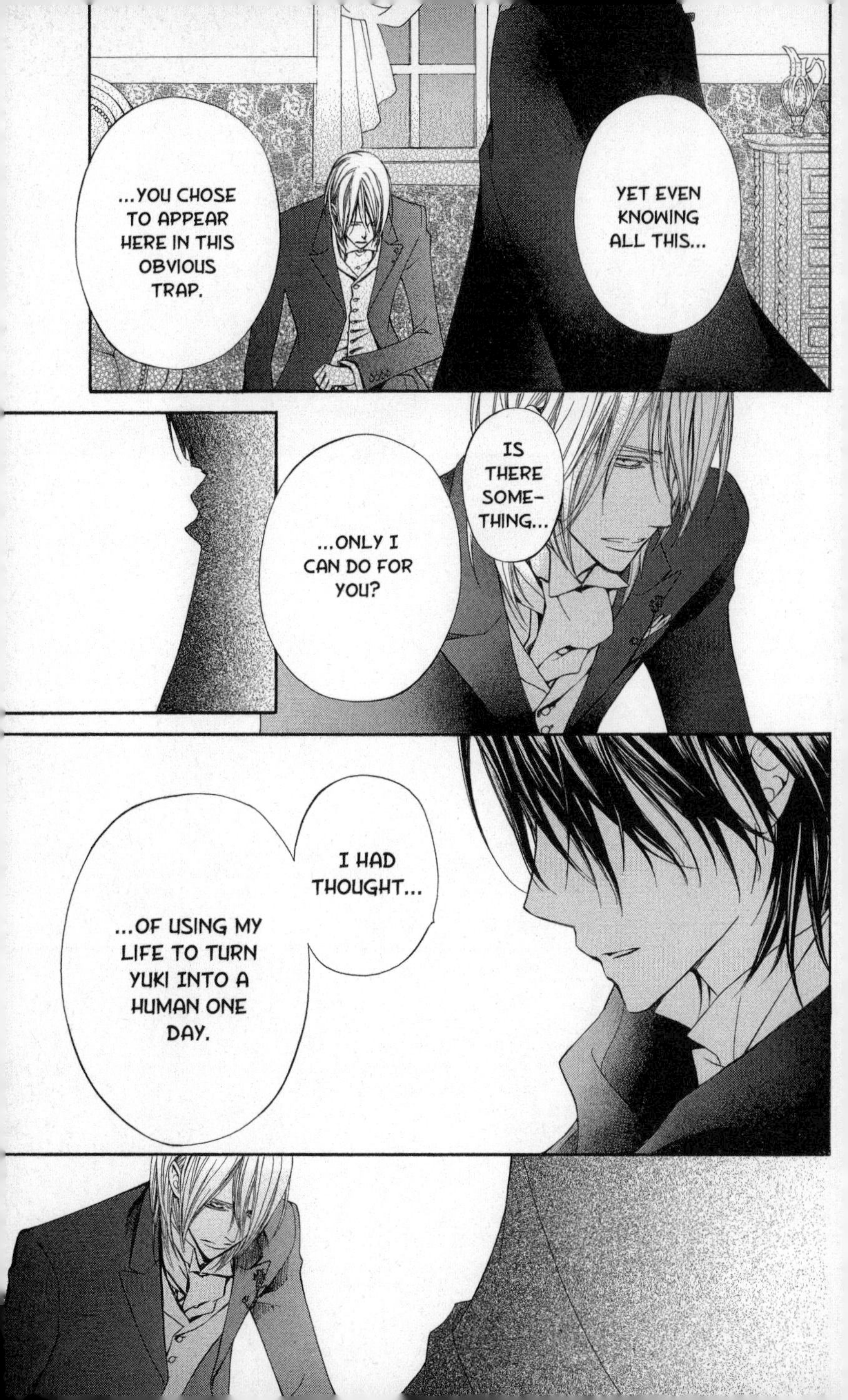
YET EVEN KNOWING ALL THIS...
...YOU CHOSE TO APPEAR HERE IN THIS OBVIOUS TRAP.
IS THERE SOME-THING...
...ONLY I CAN DO FOR YOU?
I HAD THOUGHT...
...OF USING MY LIFE TO TURN YUKI INTO A HUMAN ONE DAY.

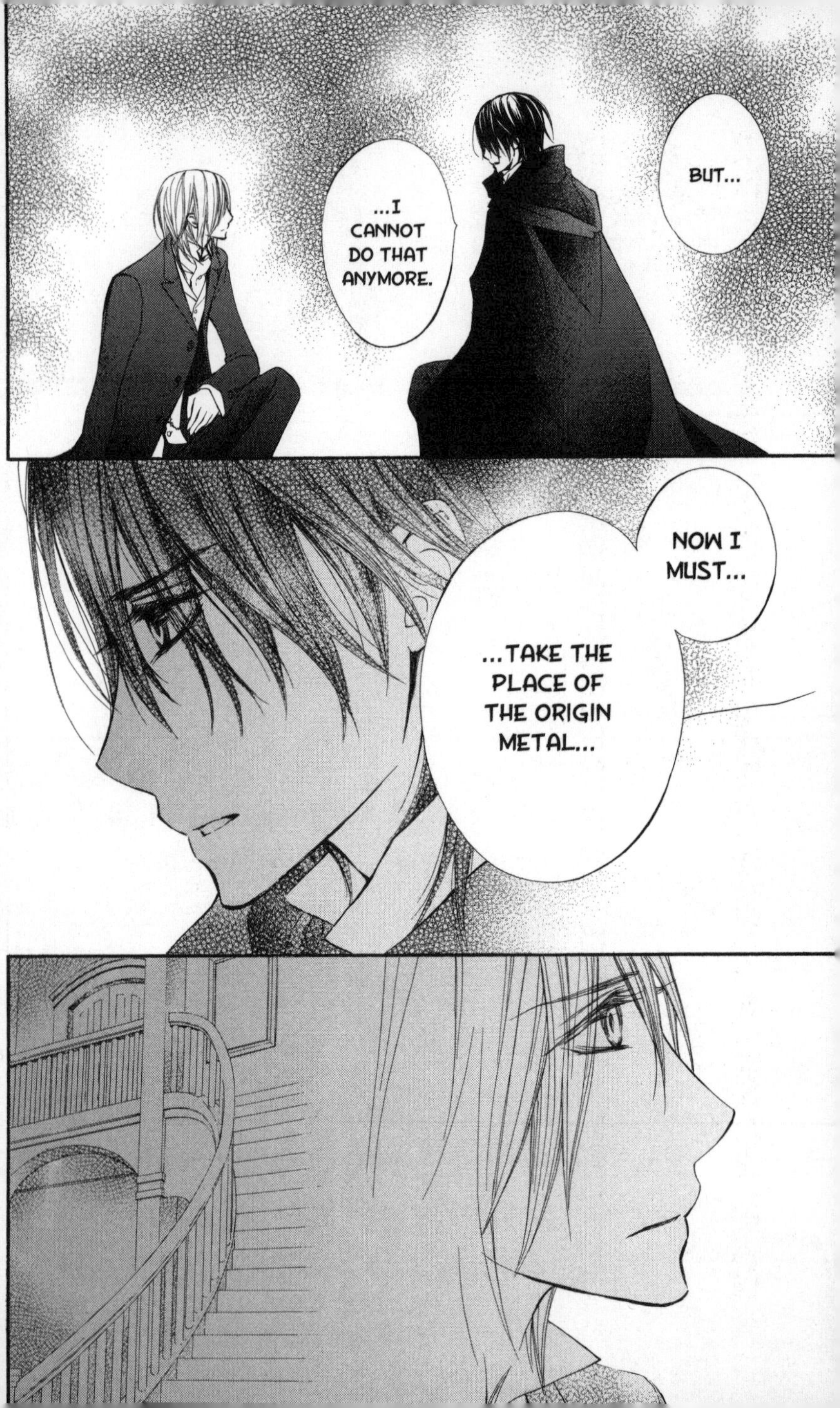
BUT...
...I CANNOT DO THAT ANYMORE.
NOW I MUST...
...TAKE THE PLACE OF THE ORIGIN METAL...

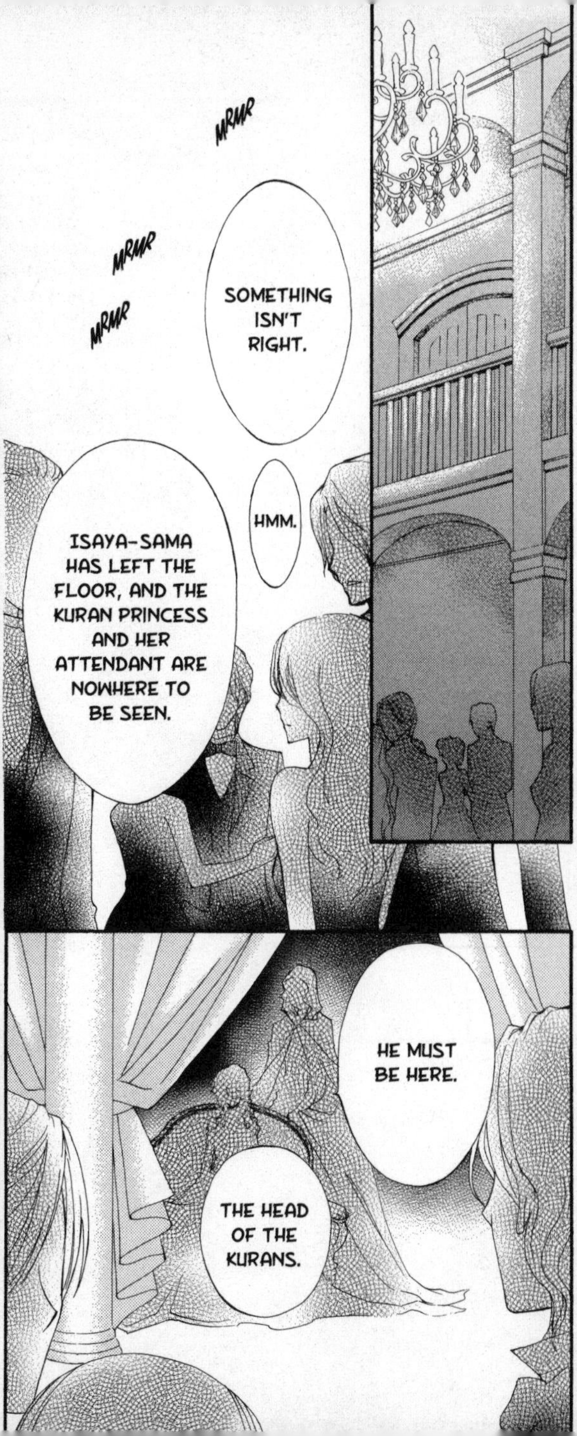
MRMR
MRMR
MRMR
SOMETHING ISN'T RIGHT.
HMM.
ISAYA-SAMA HAS LEFT THE FLOOR, AND THE KURAN PRINCESS AND HER ATTENDANT ARE NOWHERE TO BE SEEN.
HE MUST BE HERE.
THE HEAD OF THE KURANS.

Special Thanks.

O. Mio-sama
K. Midori-sama
I. Asami-sama
A. Ichiya-sama
&
My family and friends
&
My editor
&
Everyone else involved in the production of this book.

And I give my heartfelt gratitude to all the people who are reading this manga.

See you all in volume 19!

樋野まつり
Matsuri Hino

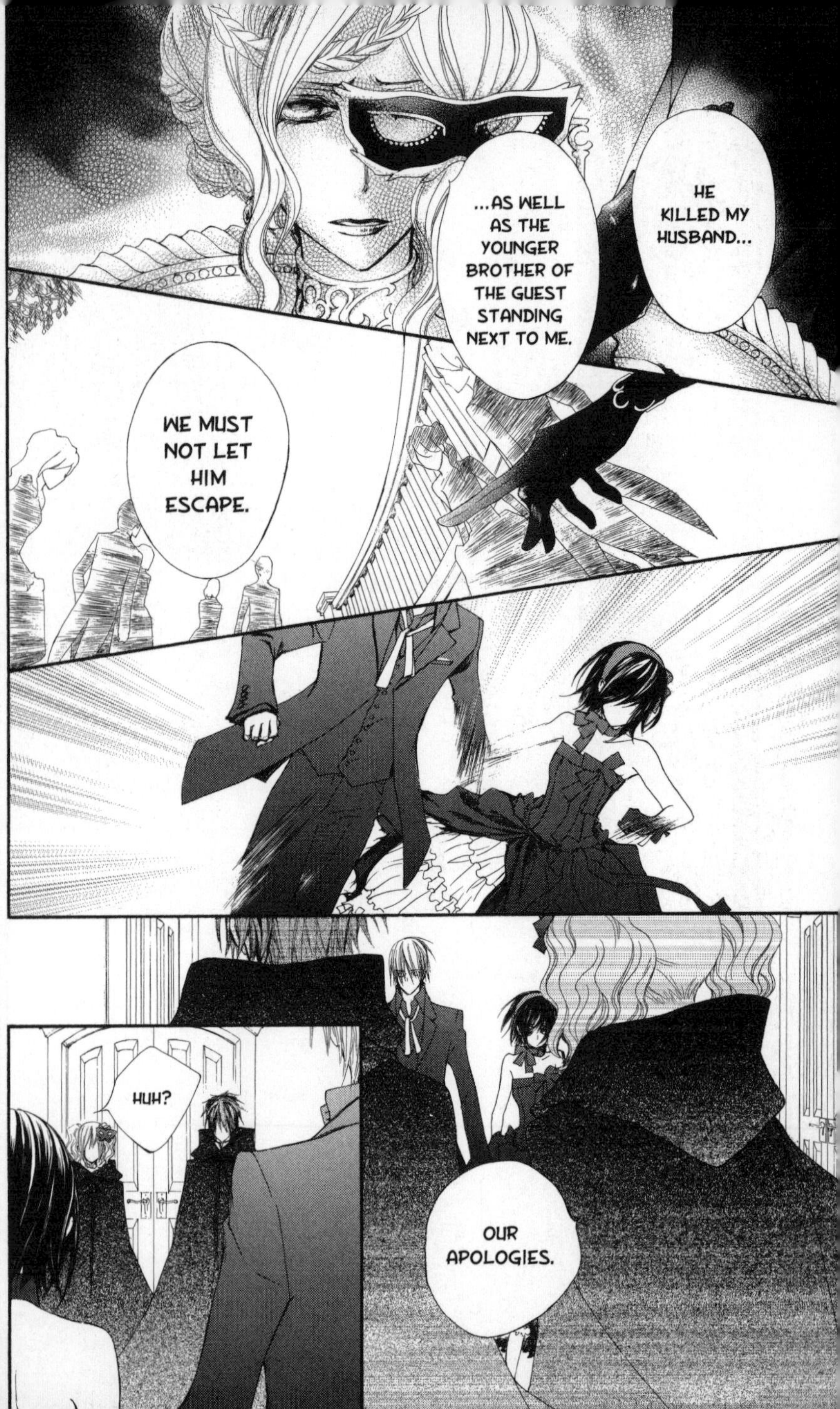
HE KILLED MY HUSBAND...
...AS WELL AS THE YOUNGER BROTHER OF THE GUEST STANDING NEXT TO ME.
WE MUST NOT LET HIM ESCAPE.
OUR APOLOGIES.
HUH?

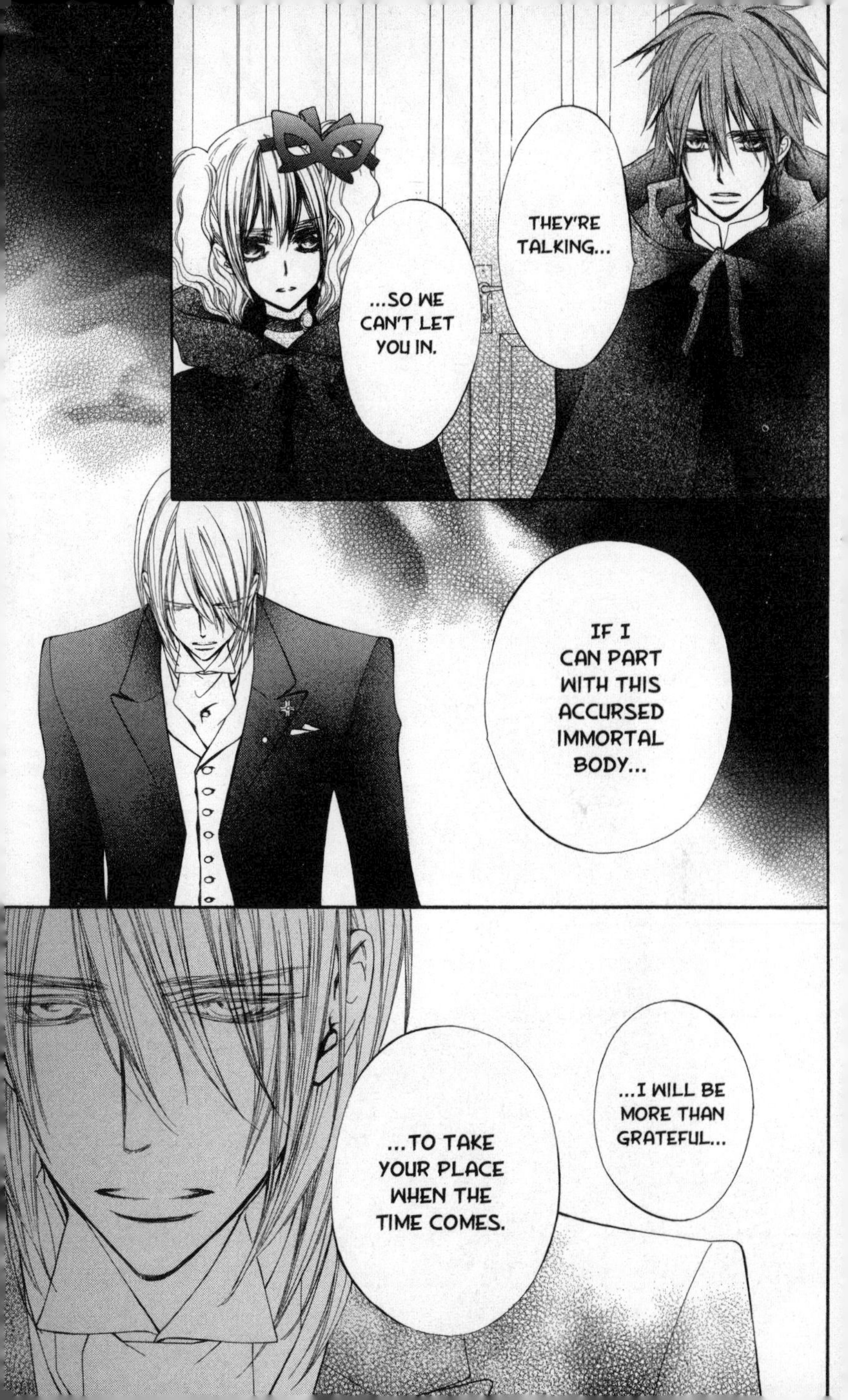
THEY'RE TALKING...
...SO WE CAN'T LET YOU IN.
IF I CAN PART WITH THIS ACCURSED IMMORTAL BODY...
...I WILL BE MORE THAN GRATEFUL...
...TO TAKE YOUR PLACE WHEN THE TIME COMES.

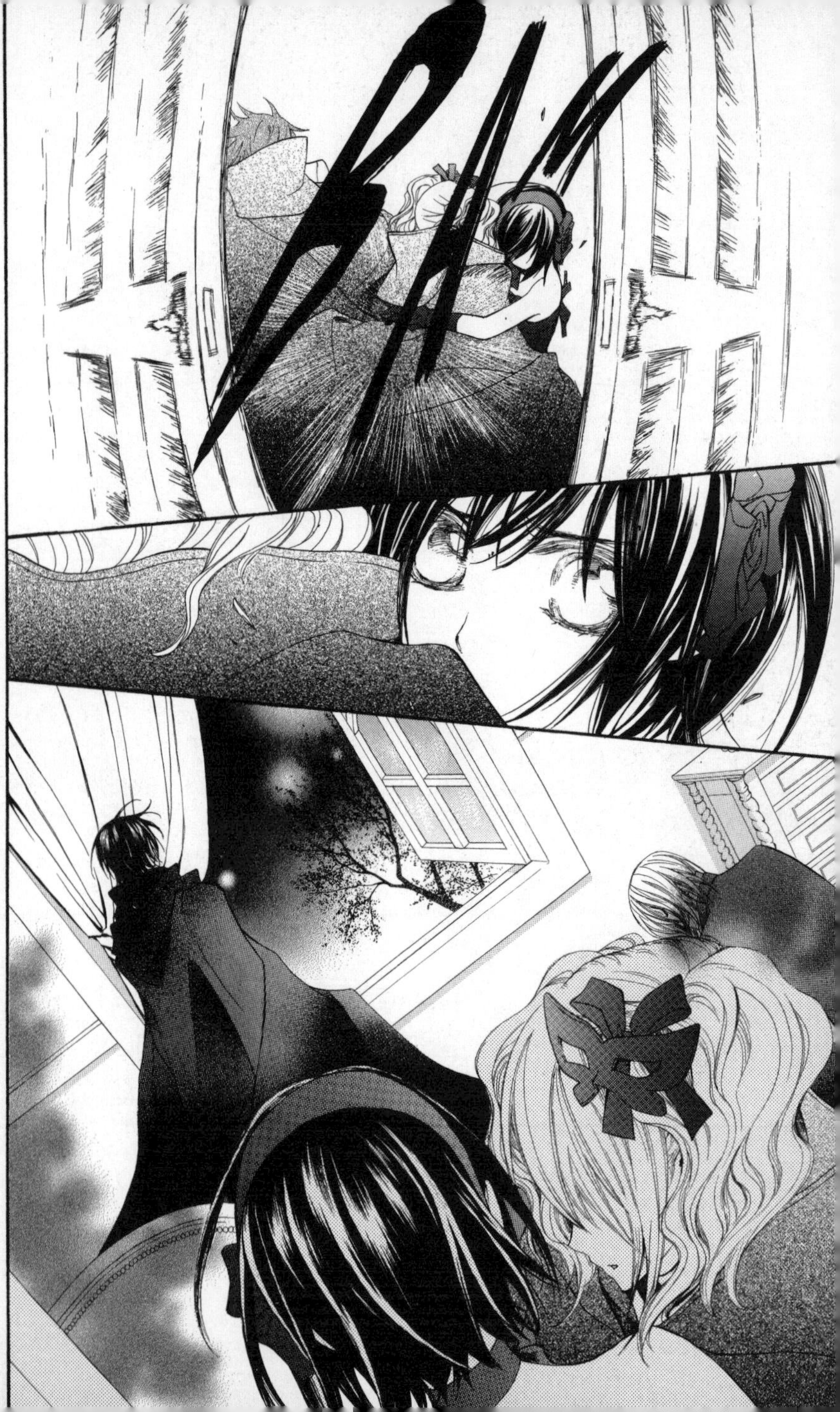
BAM

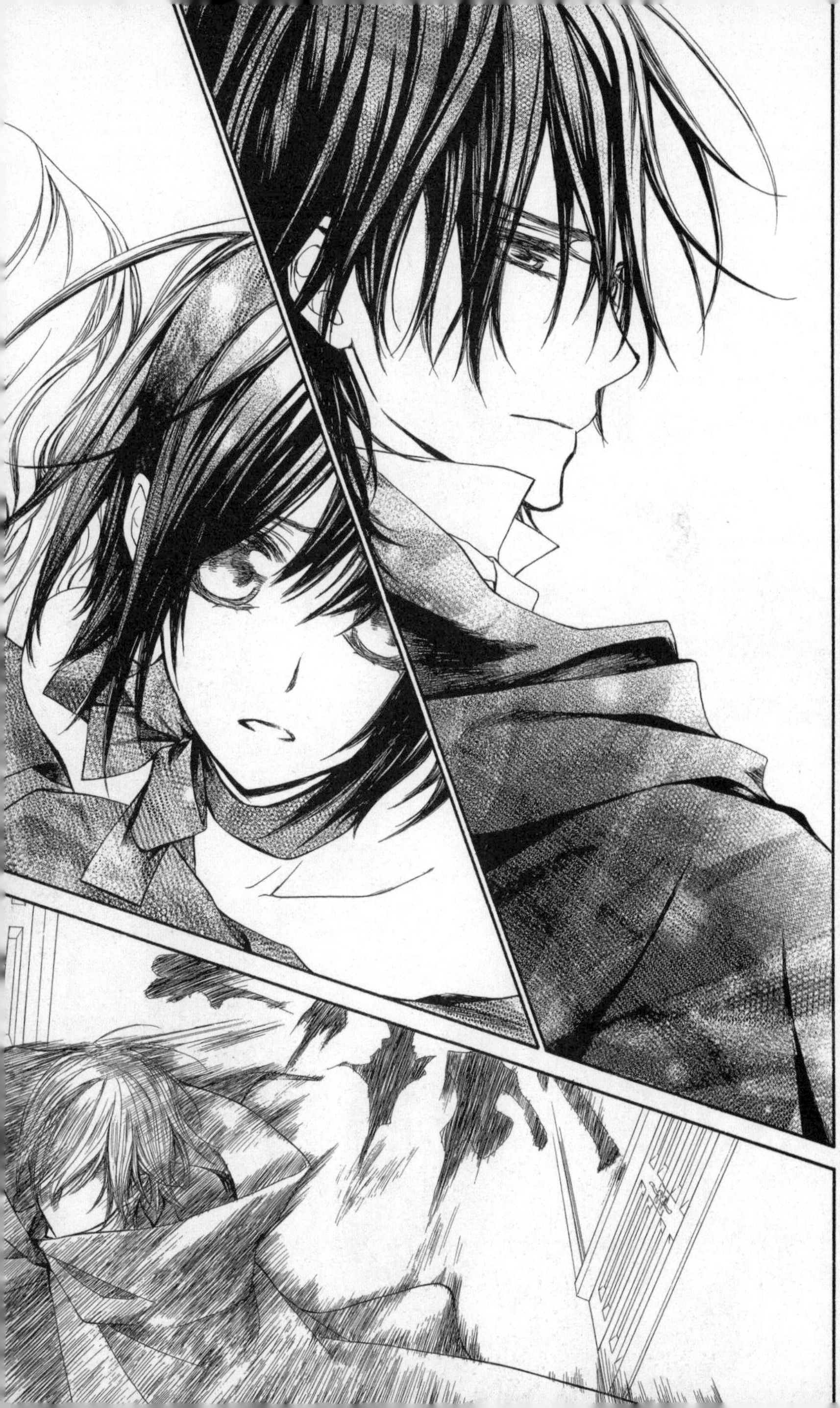

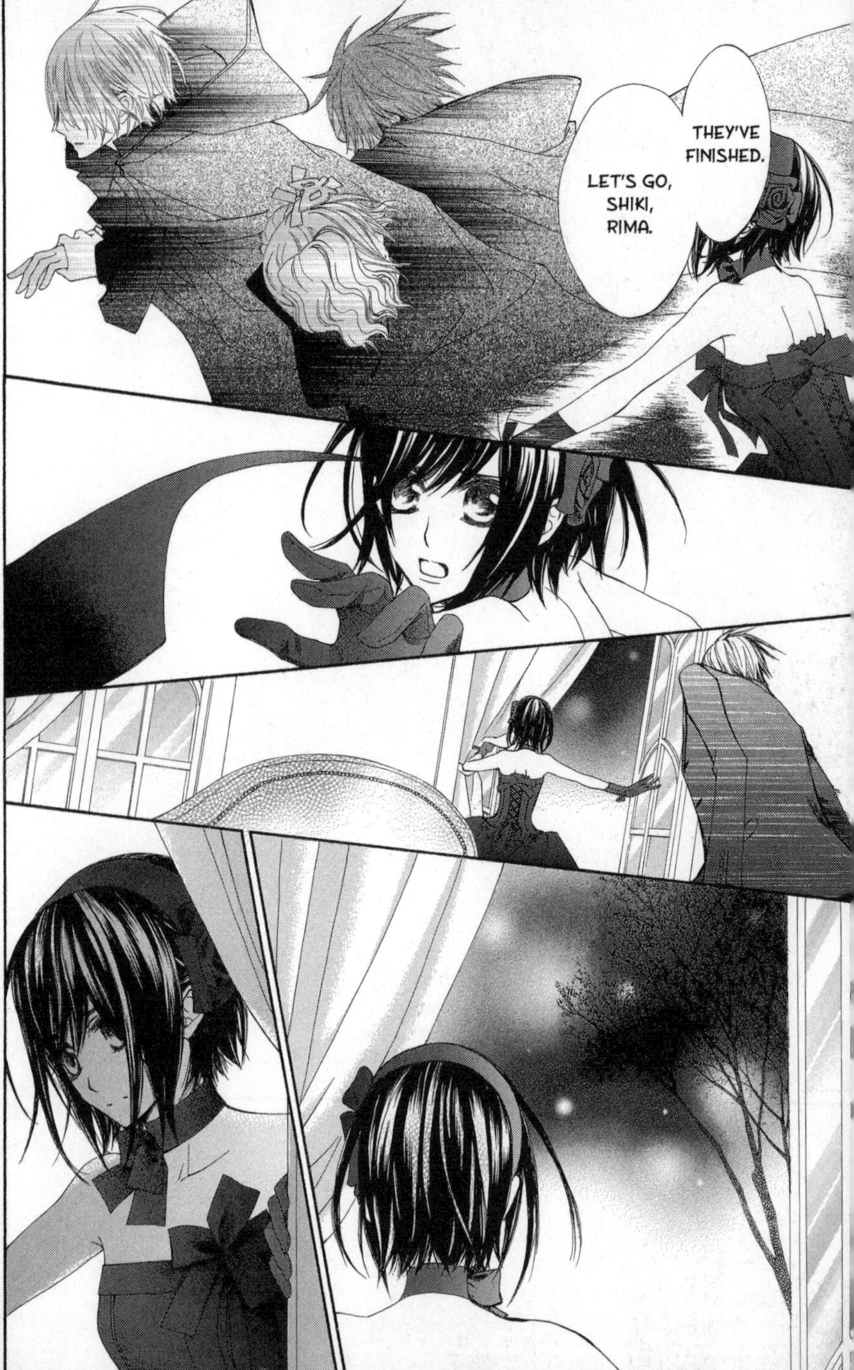
THEY'VE FINISHED.
LET'S GO, SHIKI, RIMA.

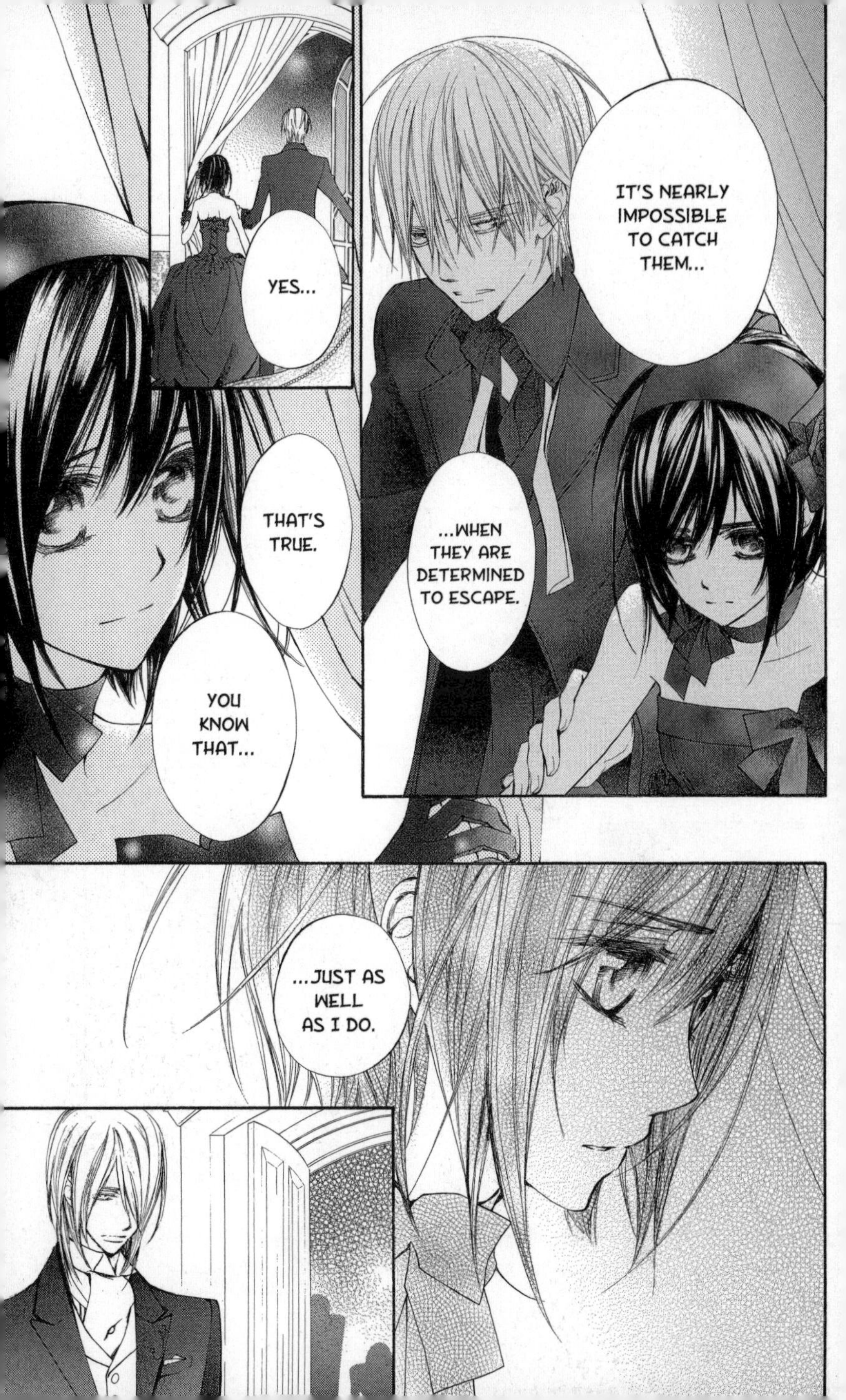
IT'S NEARLY IMPOSSIBLE TO CATCH THEM...
...WHEN THEY ARE DETERMINED TO ESCAPE.
YES...
THAT'S TRUE.
YOU KNOW THAT...
...JUST AS WELL AS I DO.

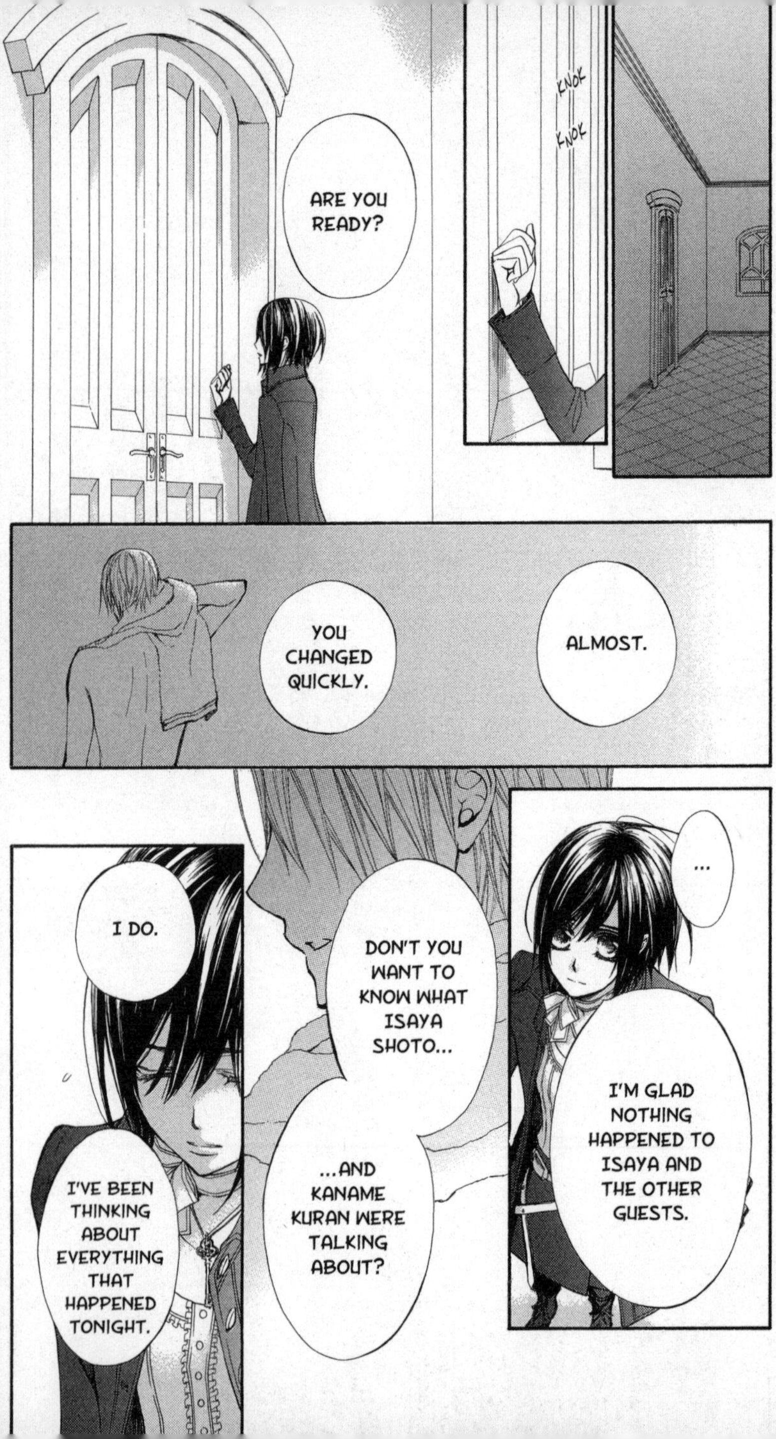
KNOK
KNOK
ARE YOU READY?
ALMOST.
YOU CHANGED QUICKLY.
...
I'M GLAD NOTHING HAPPENED TO ISAYA AND THE OTHER GUESTS.
DON'T YOU WANT TO KNOW WHAT ISAYA SHOTO...
...AND KANAME KURAN WERE TALKING ABOUT?
I DO.
I'VE BEEN THINKING ABOUT EVERYTHING THAT HAPPENED TONIGHT.

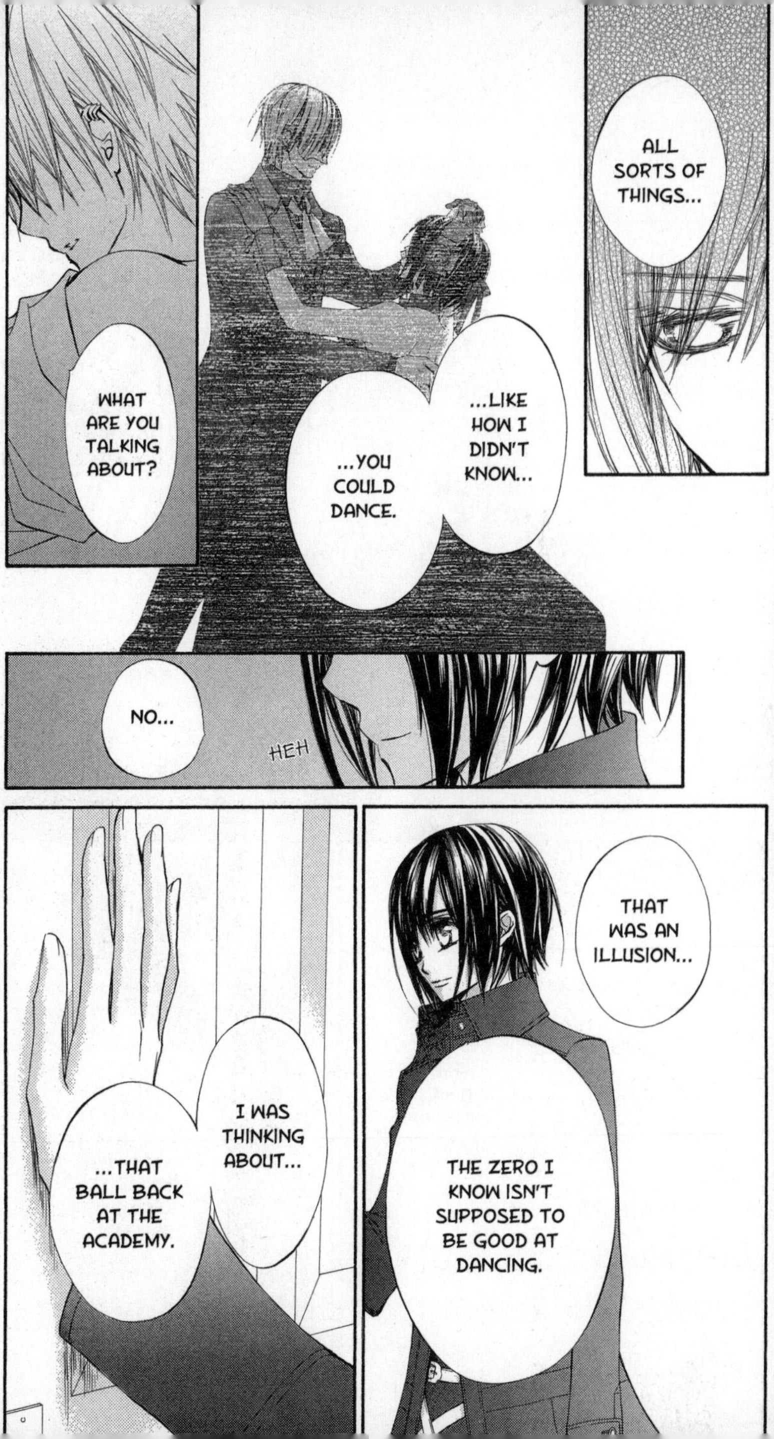
ALL SORTS OF THINGS...
...LIKE HOW I DIDN'T KNOW...
...YOU COULD DANCE.
WHAT ARE YOU TALKING ABOUT?
NO...
HEH
THAT WAS AN ILLUSION...
THE ZERO I KNOW ISN'T SUPPOSED TO BE GOOD AT DANCING.
I WAS THINKING ABOUT...
...THAT BALL BACK AT THE ACADEMY.

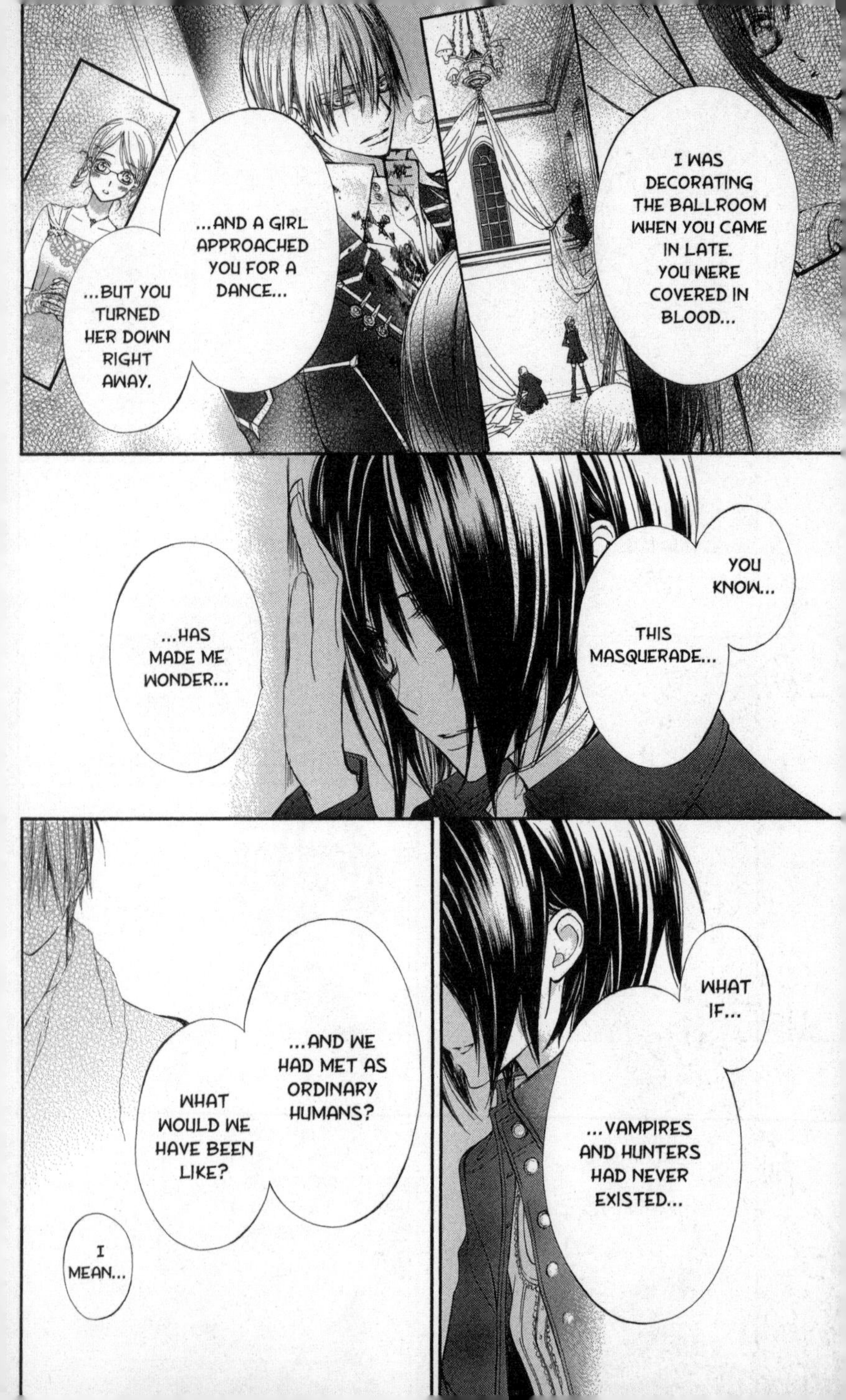
I WAS DECORATING THE BALLROOM WHEN YOU CAME IN LATE. YOU WERE COVERED IN BLOOD...
...AND A GIRL APPROACHED YOU FOR A DANCE...
...BUT YOU TURNED HER DOWN RIGHT AWAY.
YOU KNOW...
THIS MASQUERADE...
...HAS MADE ME WONDER...
WHAT IF...
...VAMPIRES AND HUNTERS HAD NEVER EXISTED...
...AND WE HAD MET AS ORDINARY HUMANS?
WHAT WOULD WE HAVE BEEN LIKE?
I MEAN...

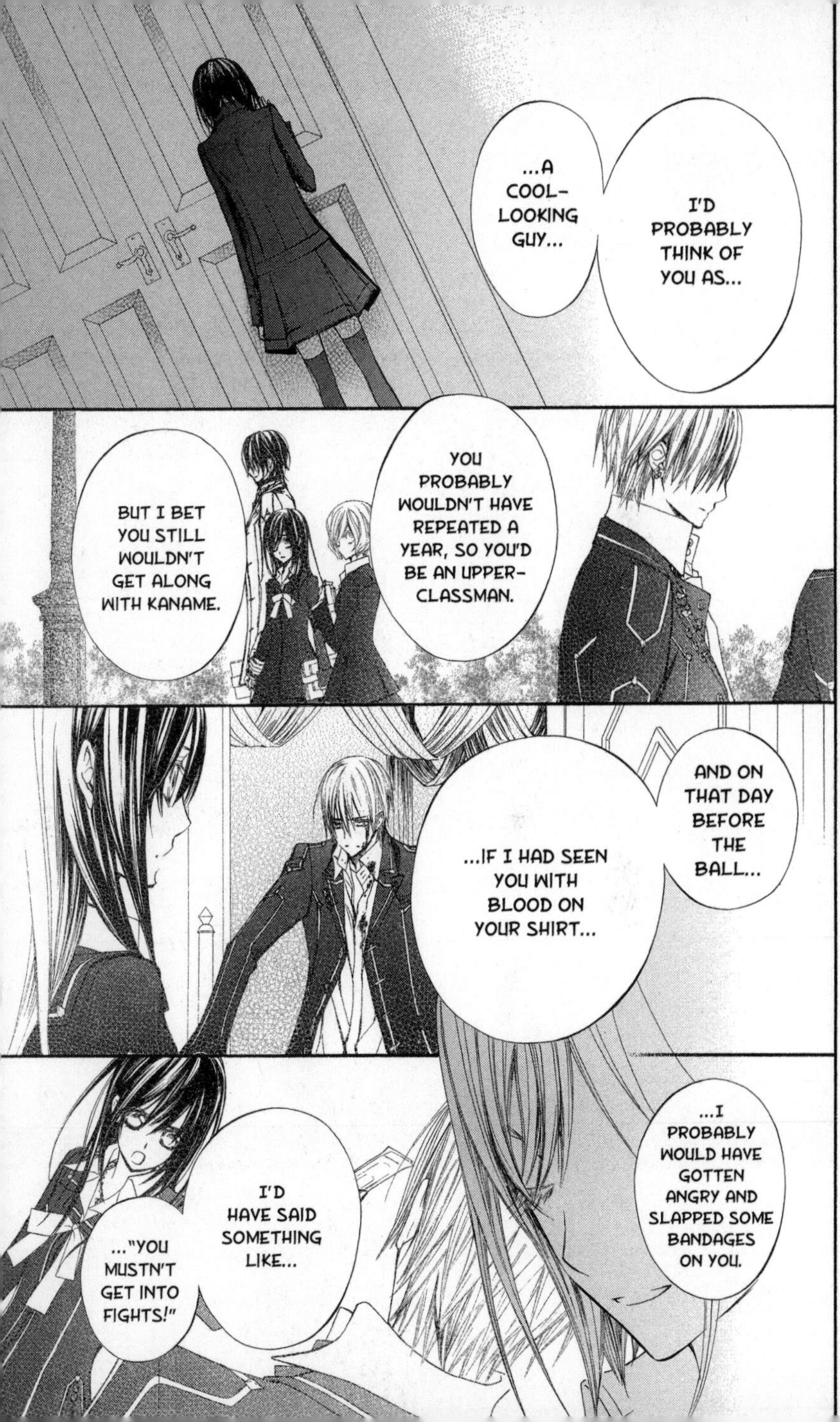
I'D PROBABLY THINK OF YOU AS...
...A COOL-LOOKING GUY...
YOU PROBABLY WOULDN'T HAVE REPEATED A YEAR, SO YOU'D BE AN UPPER-CLASSMAN.
BUT I BET YOU STILL WOULDN'T GET ALONG WITH KANAME.
AND ON THAT DAY BEFORE THE BALL...
...IF I HAD SEEN YOU WITH BLOOD ON YOUR SHIRT...
...I PROBABLY WOULD HAVE GOTTEN ANGRY AND SLAPPED SOME BANDAGES ON YOU.
I'D HAVE SAID SOMETHING LIKE...
..."YOU MUSTN'T GET INTO FIGHTS!"

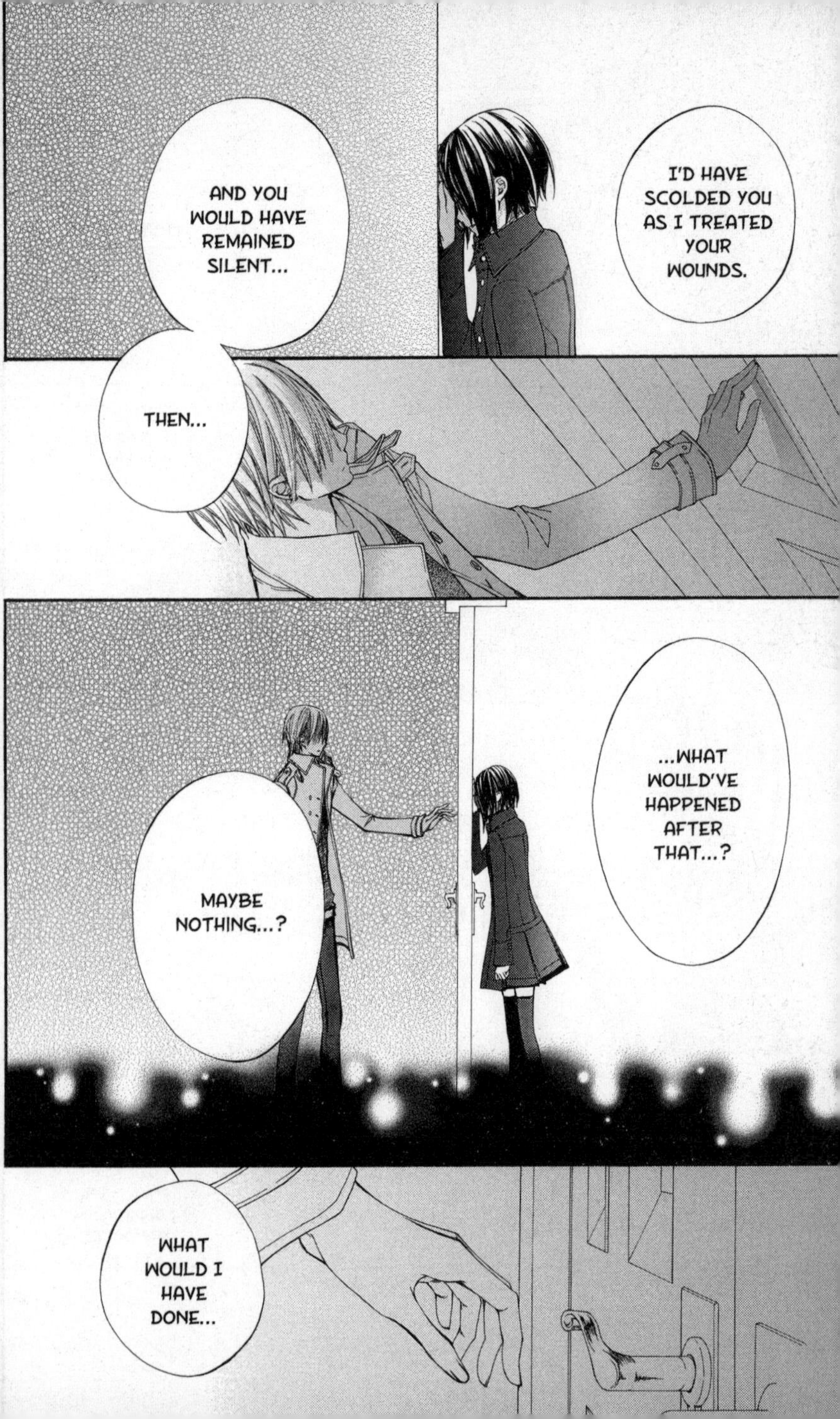
I'D HAVE SCOLDED YOU AS I TREATED YOUR WOUNDS.
AND YOU WOULD HAVE REMAINED SILENT...
THEN...
...WHAT WOULD'VE HAPPENED AFTER THAT...?
MAYBE NOTHING...?
WHAT WOULD I HAVE DONE...

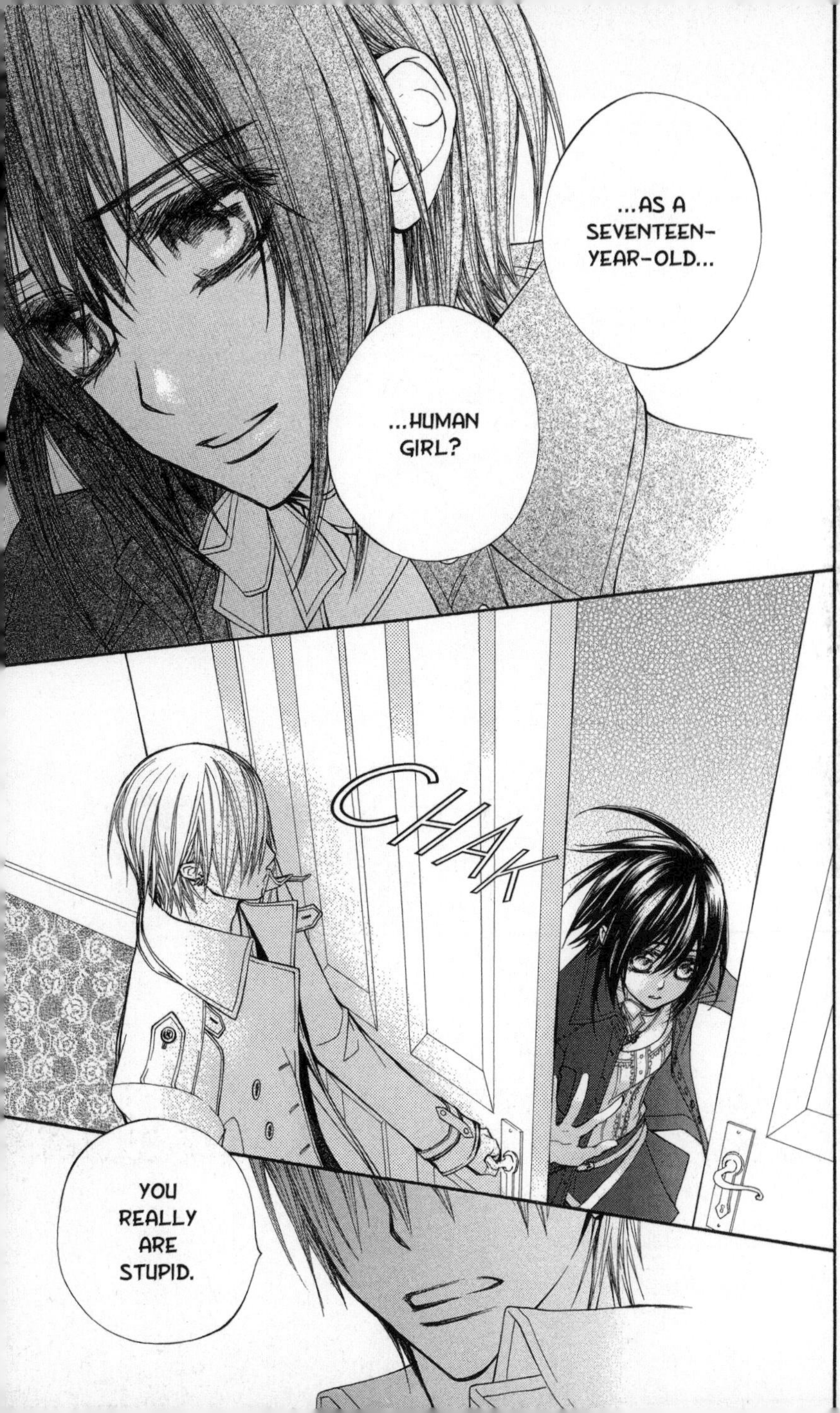
...AS A SEVENTEEN-YEAR-OLD...
...HUMAN GIRL?
CHAK
YOU REALLY ARE STUPID.

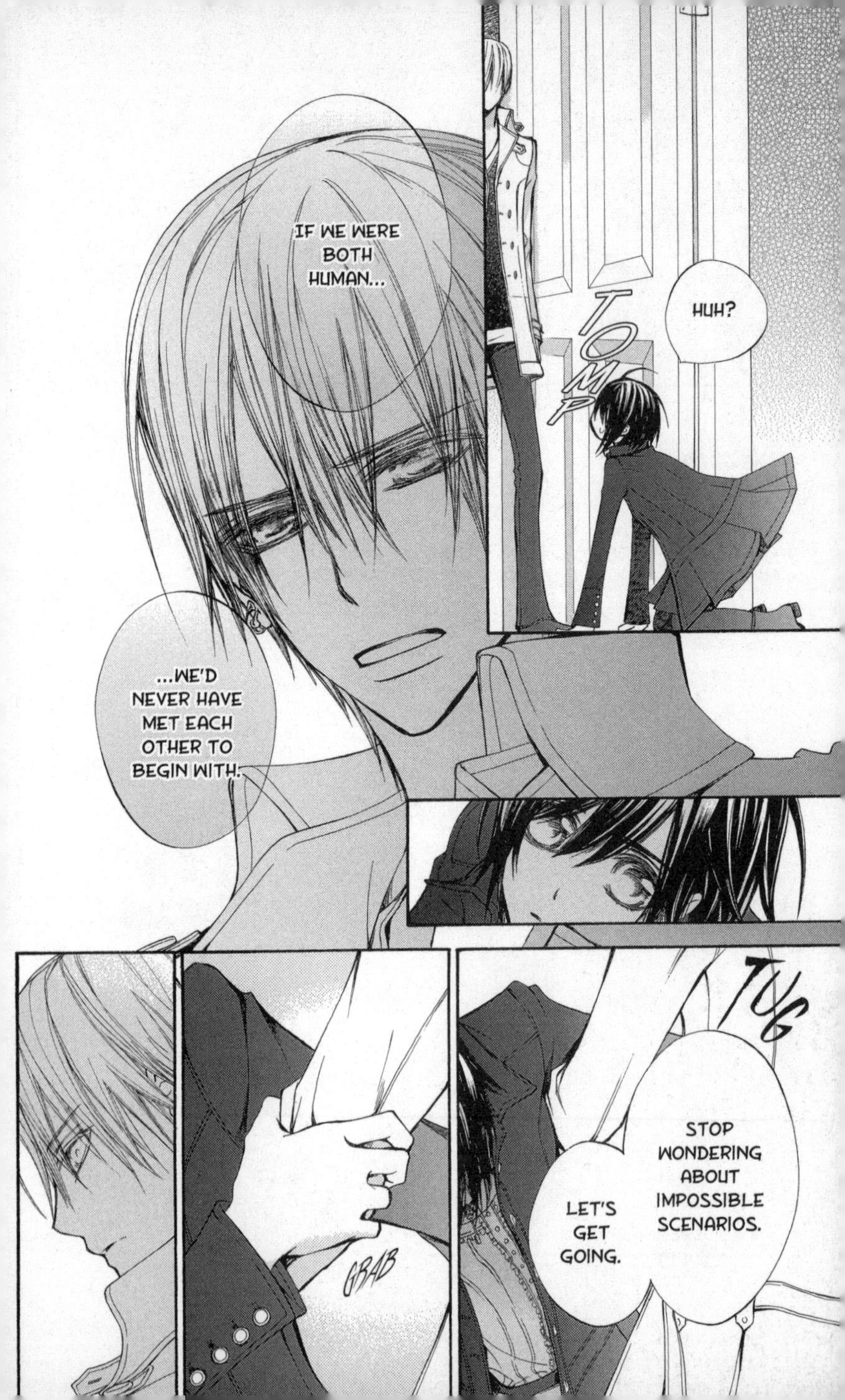
TOMP
HUH?
IF WE WERE BOTH HUMAN...
...WE'D NEVER HAVE MET EACH OTHER TO BEGIN WITH.
TUG
STOP WONDERING ABOUT IMPOSSIBLE SCENARIOS.
LET'S GET GOING.
GRAB

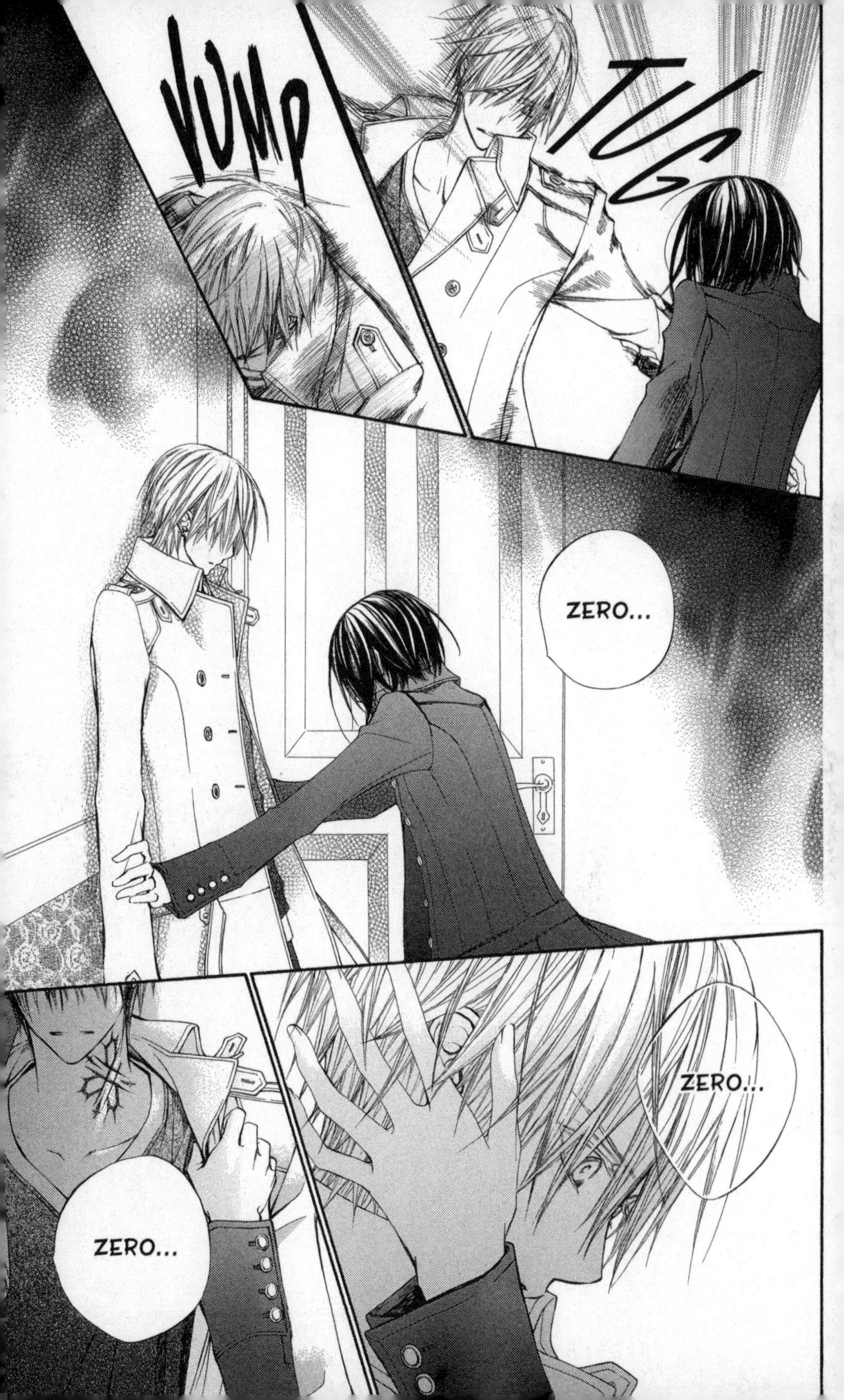
TUG
VUMP
ZERO...
ZERO...
ZERO...

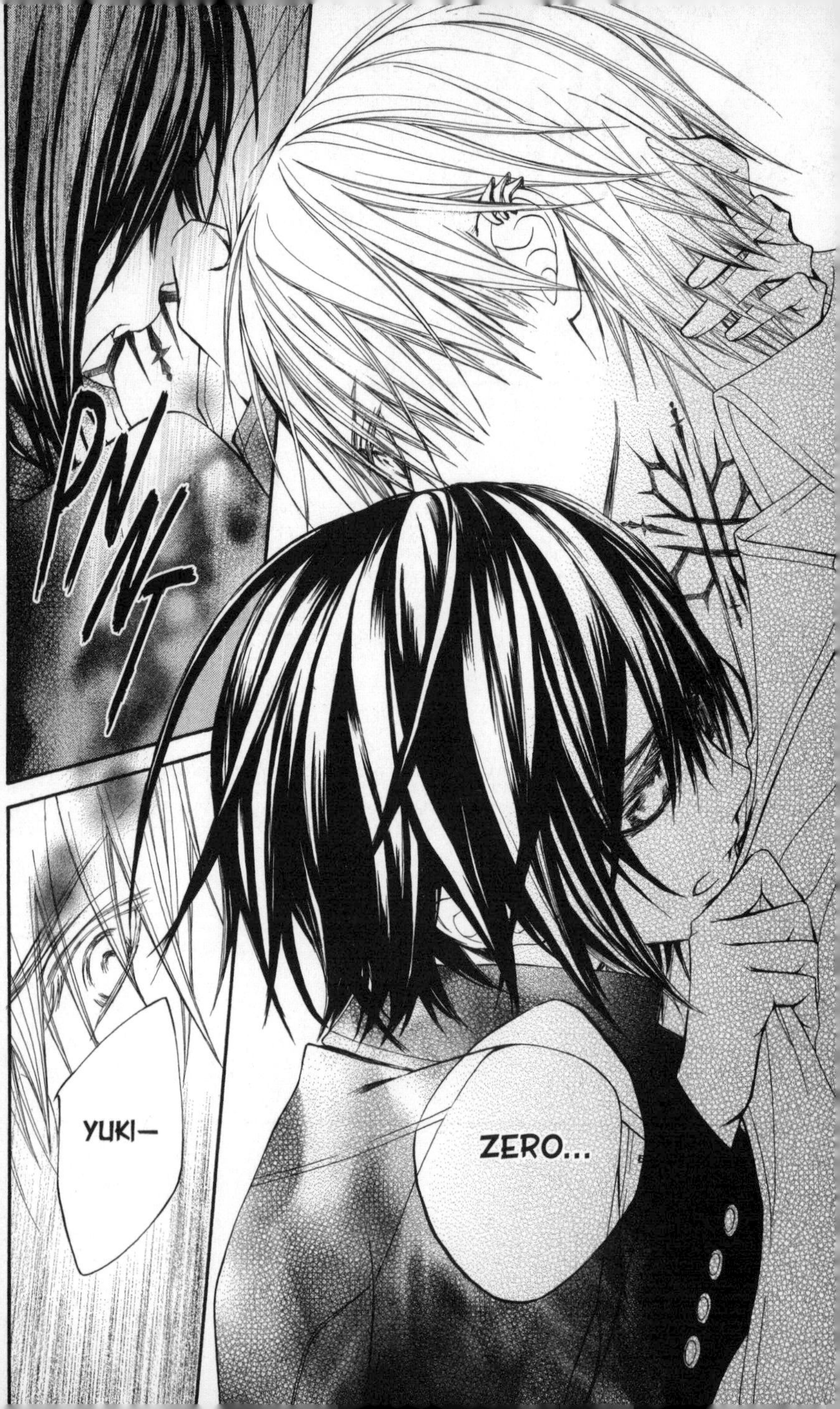
PNT
ZERO...
YUKI—

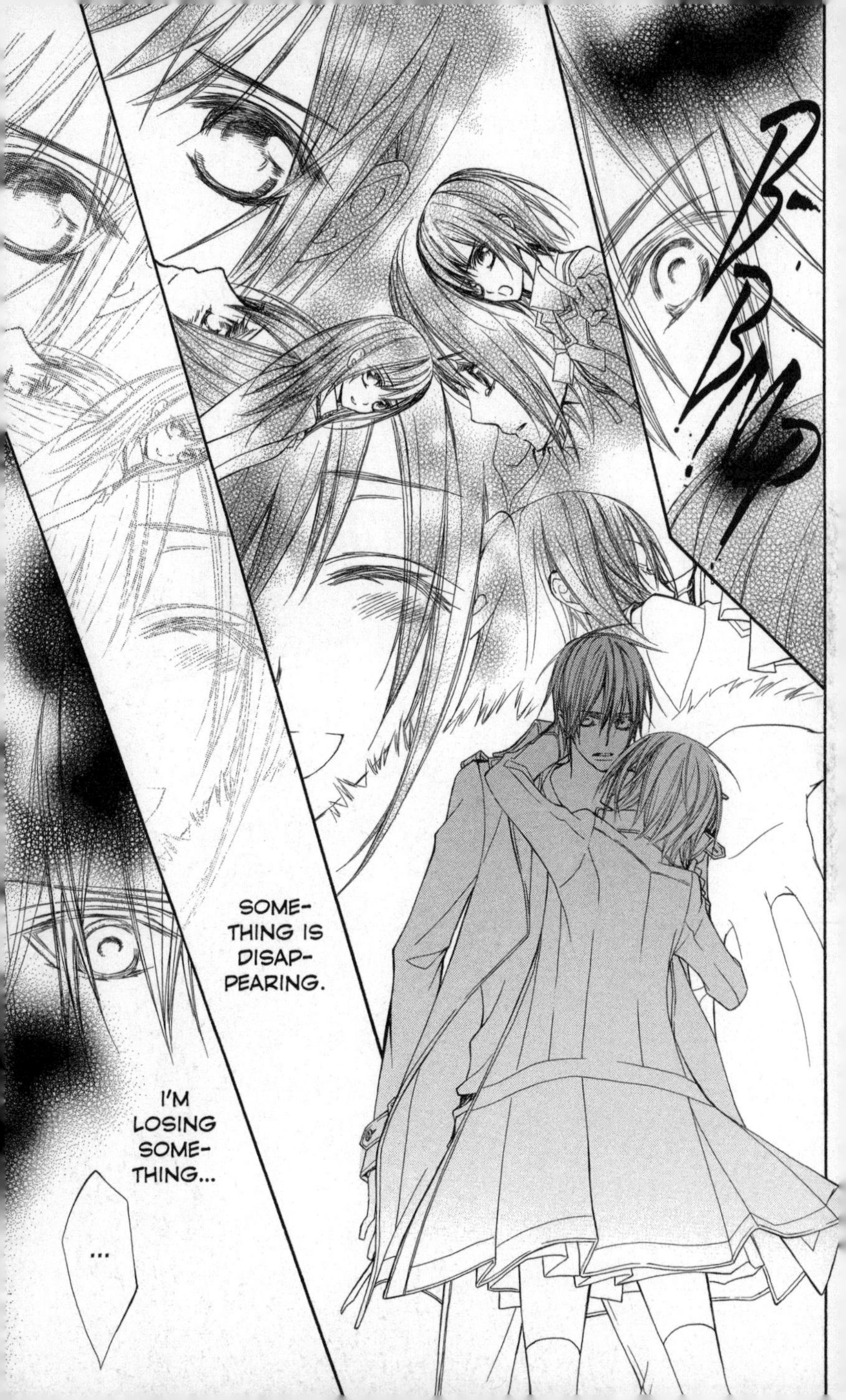
B-BMP!!
SOME-THING IS DISAP-PEARING.
I'M LOSING SOME-THING...
...

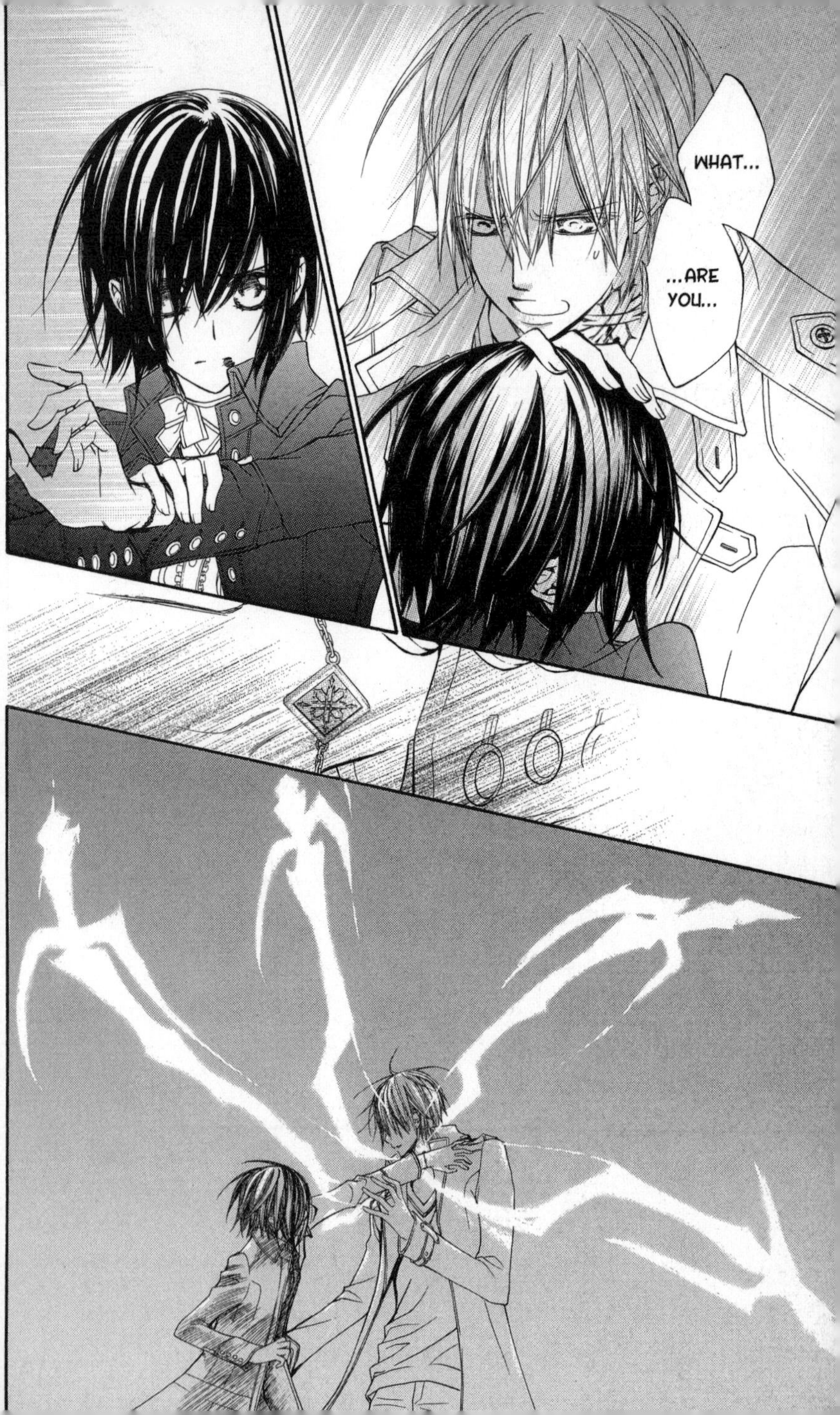
WHAT...
...ARE YOU...

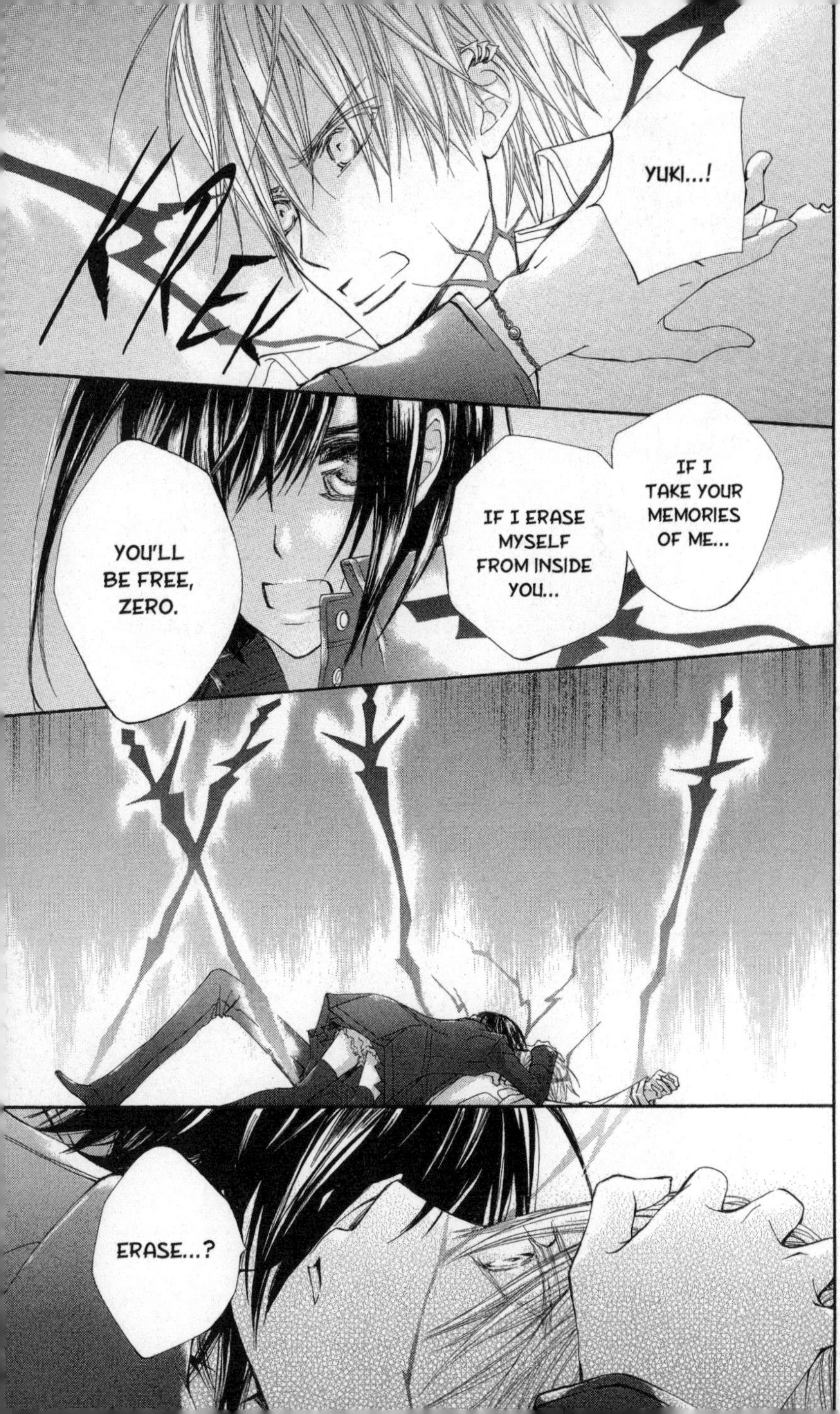
YUKI...!
KREEK
IF I TAKE YOUR MEMORIES OF ME...
IF I ERASE MYSELF FROM INSIDE YOU...
YOU'LL BE FREE, ZERO.
ERASE...?

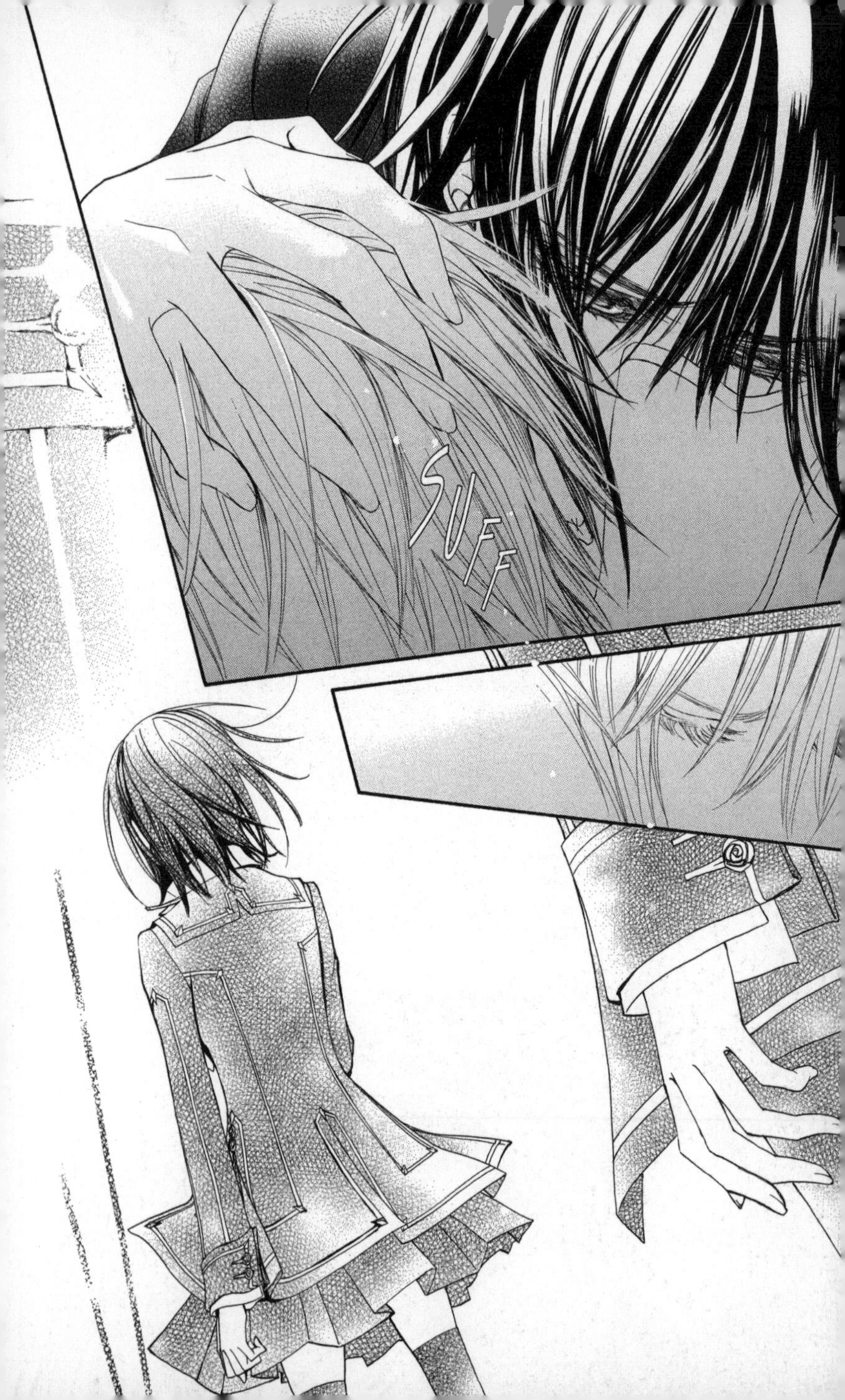
SUFF

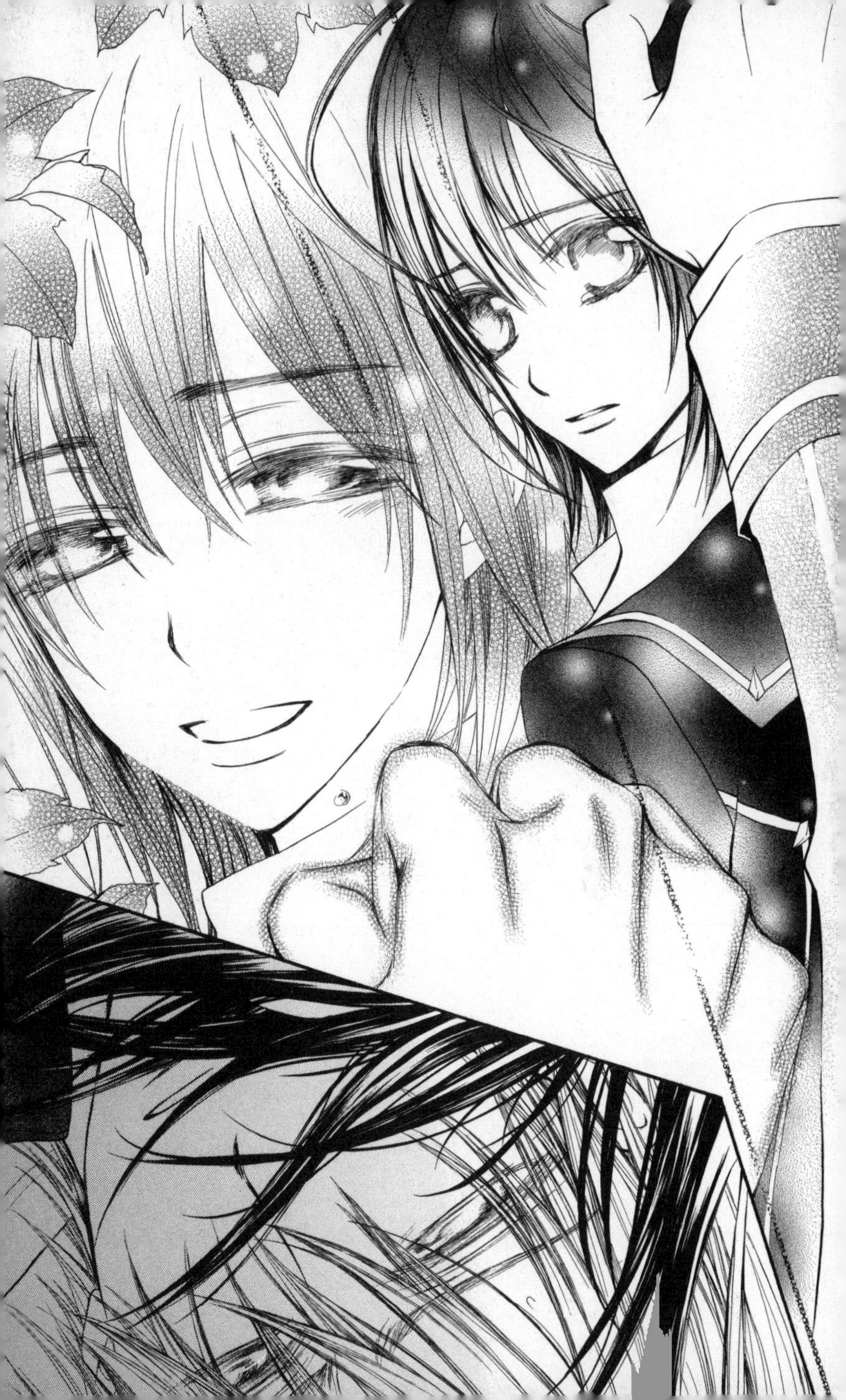

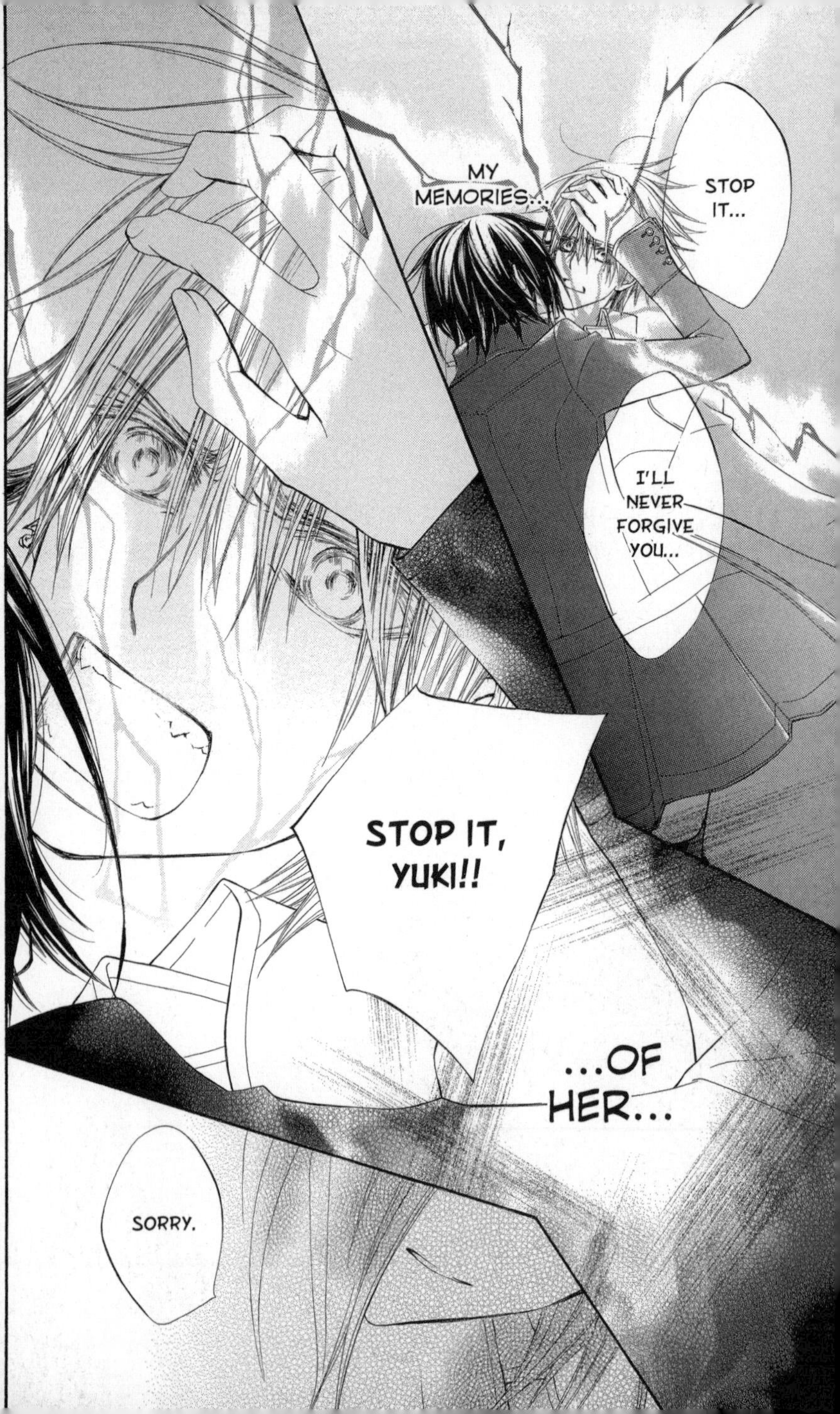
STOP IT...
MY MEMORIES...
I'LL NEVER FORGIVE YOU...
STOP IT, YUKI!!
...OF HER...
SORRY.

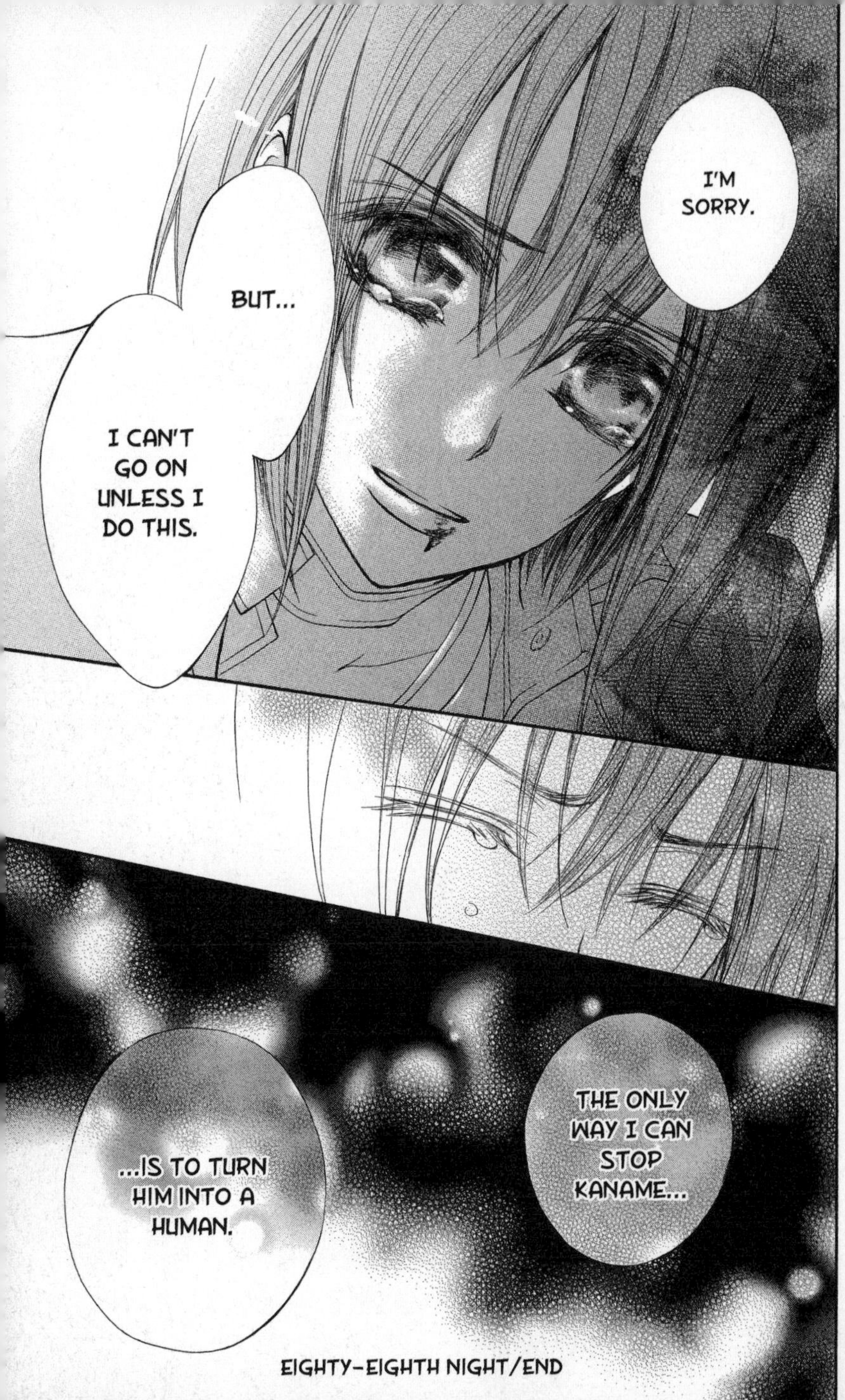
I'M SORRY.
BUT...
I CAN'T GO ON UNLESS I DO THIS.
THE ONLY WAY I CAN STOP KANAME...
...IS TO TURN HIM INTO A HUMAN.
EIGHTY-EIGHTH NIGHT/END

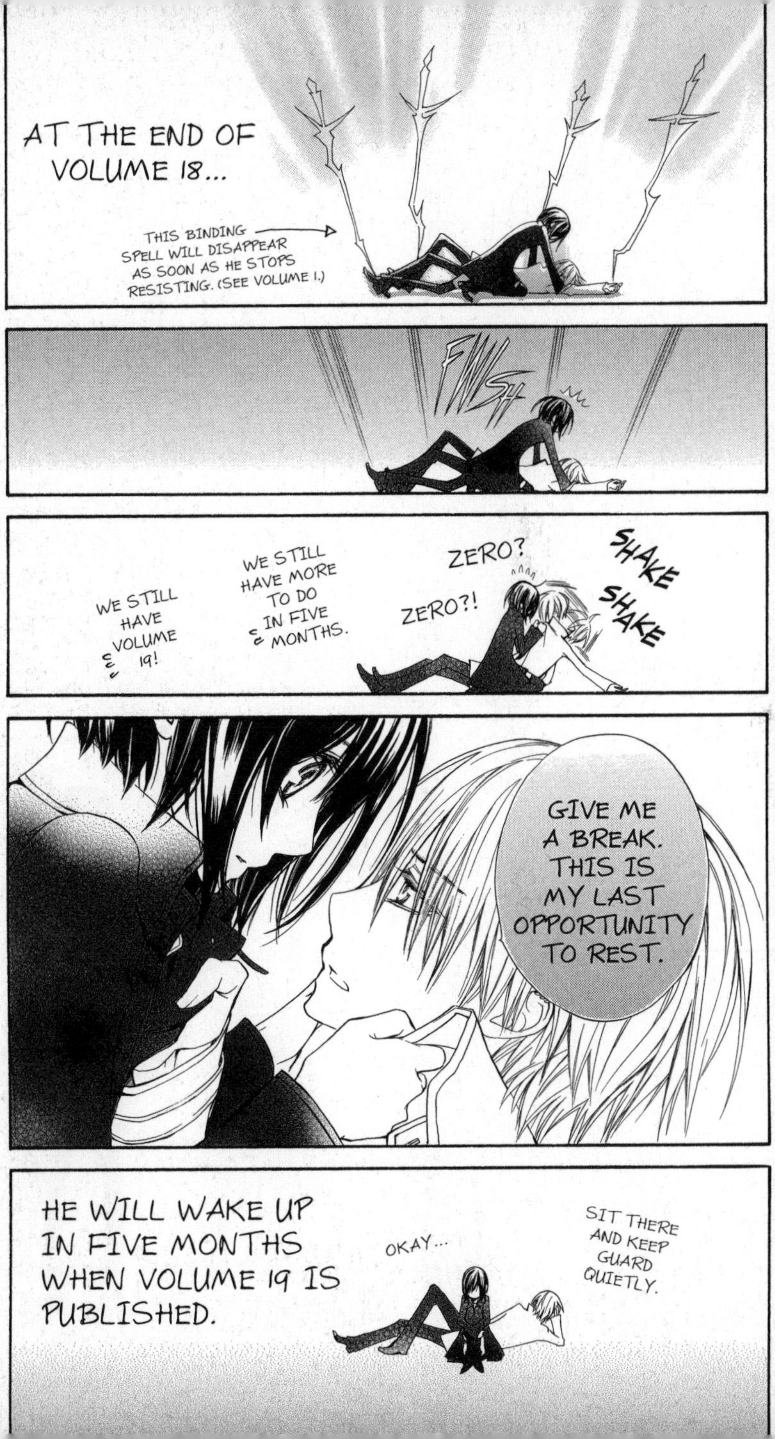
AT THE END OF VOLUME 18...
THIS BINDING SPELL WILL DISAPPEAR AS SOON AS HE STOPS RESISTING. (SEE VOLUME 1.)
FWISH
SHAKE
SHAKE
ZERO?
ZERO?!
WE STILL HAVE MORE TO DO IN FIVE MONTHS.
WE STILL HAVE VOLUME 19!
GIVE ME A BREAK. THIS IS MY LAST OPPORTUNITY TO REST.
SIT THERE AND KEEP GUARD QUIETLY.
OKAY...
HE WILL WAKE UP IN FIVE MONTHS WHEN VOLUME 19 IS PUBLISHED.

EDITOR'S NOTES

Characters

Matsuri Hino puts careful thought into the names of her characters in *Vampire Knight*. Below is the collection of characters through volume 18. Each character's name is presented family name first, per the kanji reading.

黒主優姫

Cross Yuki

Yuki's last name, *Kurosu*, is the Japanese pronunciation of the English word "cross." However, the kanji has a different meaning—*kuro* means "black" and *su* means "master." Her first name is a combination of *yuu*, meaning "tender" or "kind," and *ki*, meaning "princess."

錐生零

Kiryu Zero

Zero's first name is the kanji for *rei*, meaning "zero." In his last name, *Kiryu*, the *ki* means "auger" or "drill," and the *ryu* means "life."

玖蘭枢

Kuran Kaname

Kaname means "hinge" or "door." The kanji for his last name is a combination of the old-fashioned way of writing *ku*, meaning "nine," and *ran*, meaning "orchid": "nine orchids."

藍堂英

Aido Hanabusa

Hanabusa means "petals of a flower." *Aido* means "indigo temple." In Japanese, the pronunciation of *Aido* is very close to the pronunciation of the English word *idol*.

架院暁

Kain Akatsuki

Akatsuki means "dawn" or "daybreak." In *Kain, ka* is a base or support, while *in* denotes a building that has high fences around it, such as a temple or school.

早園瑠佳

Souen Ruka

In *Ruka*, the *ru* means "lapis lazuli" while the *ka* means "good-looking" or "beautiful." The *sou* in Ruka's surname, *Souen*, means "early," but this kanji also has an obscure meaning of "strong fragrance." The *en* means "garden."

一条拓麻

Ichijo Takuma

Ichijo can mean a "ray" or "streak." The kanji for *Takuma* is a combination of *taku*, meaning "to cultivate" and *ma*, which is the kanji for *asa*, meaning "hemp" or "flax," a plant with blue flowers.

支葵千里

Shiki Senri

Shiki's last name is a combination of *shi*, meaning "to support" and *ki*, meaning "mallow"—a flowering plant with pink or white blossoms. The *ri* in *Senri* is a traditional Japanese unit of measure for distance, and one *ri* is about 2.44 miles. *Senri* means "1,000 *ri*."

夜刈十牙

Yagari Toga

Yagari is a combination of *ya*, meaning "night," and *gari*, meaning "to harvest." *Toga* means "ten fangs."

一条麻遠, 一翁

Ichijo Asato, aka "Ichio"

Ichijo can mean a "ray" or "streak." Asato's first name is comprised of *asa*, meaning "hemp" or "flax," and *tou*, meaning "far off." His nickname is *ichi*, or "one," combined with *ou*, which can be used as an honorific when referring to an older man.

若葉沙頼

Wakaba Sayori

Yori's full name is Sayori Wakaba. *Wakaba* means "young leaves." Her given name, *Sayori*, is a combination of *sa*, meaning "sand," and *yori*, meaning "trust."

星煉

Seiren

Sei means "star" and *ren* means "to smelt" or "refine." *Ren* is also the same kanji used in *rengoku*, or "purgatory."

遠矢莉磨

Toya Rima

Toya means a "far-reaching arrow." Rima's first name is a combination of *ri*, or "jasmine," and *ma*, which signifies enhancement by wearing away, such as by polishing or scouring.

紅まり亜

Kurenai Maria

Kurenai means "crimson." The kanji for the last *a* in Maria's first name is the same that is used in "Asia."

錐生壱縷

Kiryu Ichiru
Ichi is the old-fashioned way of writing "one," and *ru* means "thread."

緋桜閑, 狂咲姫

Hio Shizuka, Kuruizaki-hime
Shizuka means "calm and quiet." In Shizuka's family name, *hi* is "scarlet," and *ou* is "cherry blossoms." Shizuka Hio is also referred to as the "Kuruizaki-hime." *Kuruizaki* means "flowers blooming out of season," and *hime* means "princess."

藍堂月子

Aido Tsukiko
Aido means "indigo temple." *Tsukiko* means "moon child."

白蕗更

Shirabuki Sara

Shira is "white," and *buki* is "butterbur," a plant with white flowers. *Sara* means "renew."

黒主灰閻

Cross Kaien

Cross, or *Kurosu*, means "black master." Kaien is a combination of *kai*, meaning "ashes," and *en*, meaning "village gate." The kanji for *en* is also used for Enma, the ruler of the Underworld in Buddhist mythology.

玖蘭李土

Kuran Rido

Kuran means "nine orchids." In *Rido*, *ri* means "plum" and *do* means "earth."

玖蘭樹里

Kuran Juri

Kuran means "nine orchids." In her first name, *ju* means "tree" and a *ri* is a traditional Japanese unit of measure for distance. The kanji for *ri* is the same as in Senri's name.

玖蘭悠

Kuran Haruka

Kuran means "nine orchids." *Haruka* means "distant" or "remote."

鷹宮海斗

Takamiya Kaito

Taka means "hawk" and *miya* means "imperial palace" or "shrine." *Kai* is "sea" and *to* means "to measure" or "grid."

菖藤依砂也

Shoto Isaya

Sho means "Siberian Iris" and *to* is "wisteria." The *I* in *Isaya* means "to rely on," while the *sa* means "sand." *Ya* is a suffix used for emphasis.

橙茉

Toma

In the family name *Toma*, *to* means "seville orange" and *ma* means "jasmine flower."

藍堂永路

Aido Nagamichi

The name *Nagamichi* is a combination of *naga*, which means "long" or "eternal," and *michi*, which is the kanji for "road" or "path." *Aido* means "indigo temple."

縹木

Hanadagi

In this family name, *Hanada* means "bright light blue" and *gi* means "tree."

影山霞

Kageyama Kasumi

In the Class Rep's family name, *kage* means "shadow," and *yama* means "mountain." His first name, Kasumi, means "haze" or "mist."

Terms

-sama: The suffix *sama* is used in formal address for someone who ranks higher in the social hierarchy. The vampires call their leader "Kaname-sama" only when they are among their own kind.

Matsuri Hino burst onto the manga scene with her series *Kono Yume ga Sametara* (When This Dream Is Over), which was published in *LaLa DX* magazine. Hino was a manga artist a mere nine months after she decided to become one.

With the success of her popular series *Captive Hearts* and *MeruPuri*, Hino has established herself as a major player in the world of shojo manga.

Hino enjoys creative activities and has commented that she would have been either an architect or an apprentice to traditional Japanese craft masters if she had not become a manga artist.

VAMPIRE KNIGHT
Vol. 18
Shojo Beat Edition

STORY AND ART BY
MATSURI HINO

Adaptation/Nancy Thistlethwaite
Translation/Tetsuichiro Miyaki
Touch-up Art & Lettering/Inori Fukuda Trant
Graphic Design/Amy Martin
Editor/Nancy Thistlethwaite

Printed in the U.S.A.

Published by VIZ Media, LLC
P.O. Box 77010
San Francisco, CA 94107

10 9 8 7 6 5 4 3 2 1
First printing, May 2014

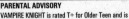

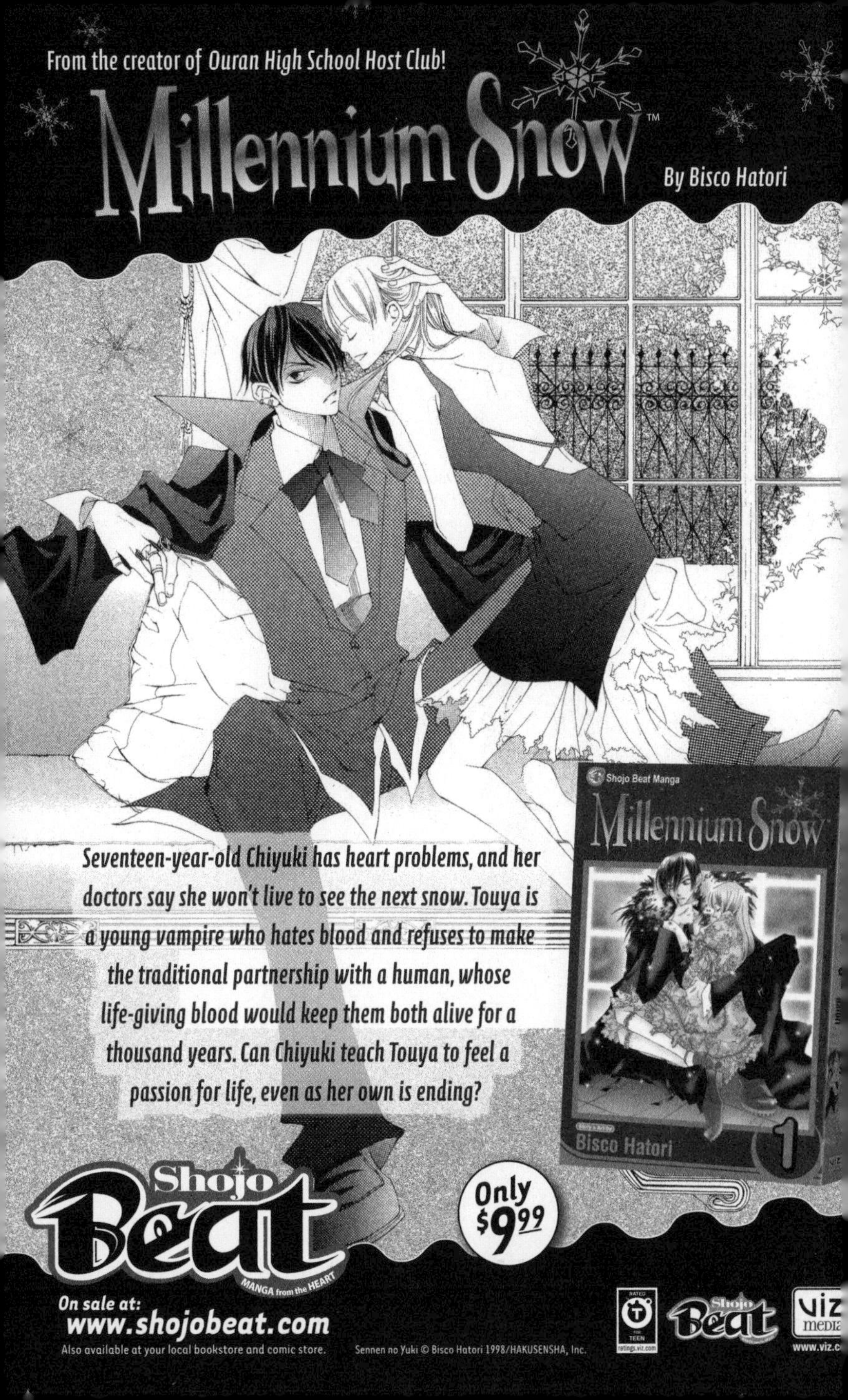
From the creator of Ouran High School Host Club!
Millennium Snow™
By Bisco Hatori
Seventeen-year-old Chiyuki has heart problems, and her doctors say she won't live to see the next snow. Touya is a young vampire who hates blood and refuses to make the traditional partnership with a human, whose life-giving blood would keep them both alive for a thousand years. Can Chiyuki teach Touya to feel a passion for life, even as her own is ending?
Shojo Beat Manga
Millennium Snow
Bisco Hatori
1
Shojo Beat
MANGA from the HEART
Only $9.99
On sale at:
www.shojobeat.com
Also available at your local bookstore and comic store.
Sennen no Yuki © Bisco Hatori 1998/HAKUSENSHA, Inc.
RATED T TEEN
ratings.viz.com
Shojo Beat
viz media
www.viz.c

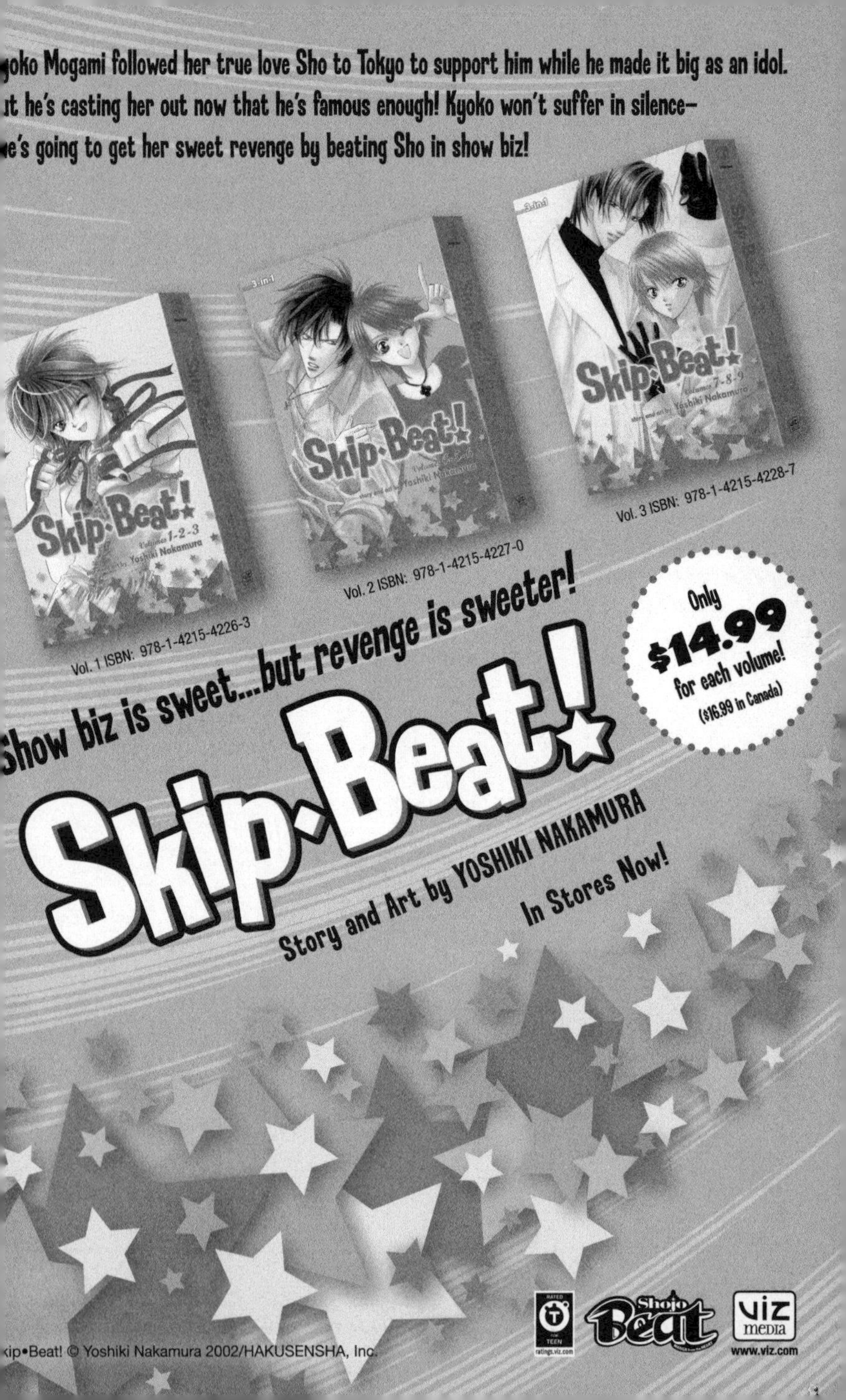
yoko Mogami followed her true love Sho to Tokyo to support him while he made it big as an idol.
ut he's casting her out now that he's famous enough! Kyoko won't suffer in silence—
e's going to get her sweet revenge by beating Sho in show biz!
Skip·Beat!
Volumes 1-2-3
Yoshiki Nakamura
Vol. 1 ISBN: 978-1-4215-4226-3
3-in-1
Skip·Beat!
Yoshiki Nakamura
Vol. 2 ISBN: 978-1-4215-4227-0
3-in-1
Skip·Beat!
Volumes 7-8-9
Yoshiki Nakamura
Vol. 3 ISBN: 978-1-4215-4228-7
Only
$14.99
for each volume!
($16.99 in Canada)
Show biz is sweet...but revenge is sweeter!
Skip·Beat!
Story and Art by YOSHIKI NAKAMURA
In Stores Now!
kip•Beat! © Yoshiki Nakamura 2002/HAKUSENSHA, Inc.
RATED T FOR TEEN
ratings.viz.com
Shojo Beat
VIZ media
www.viz.com

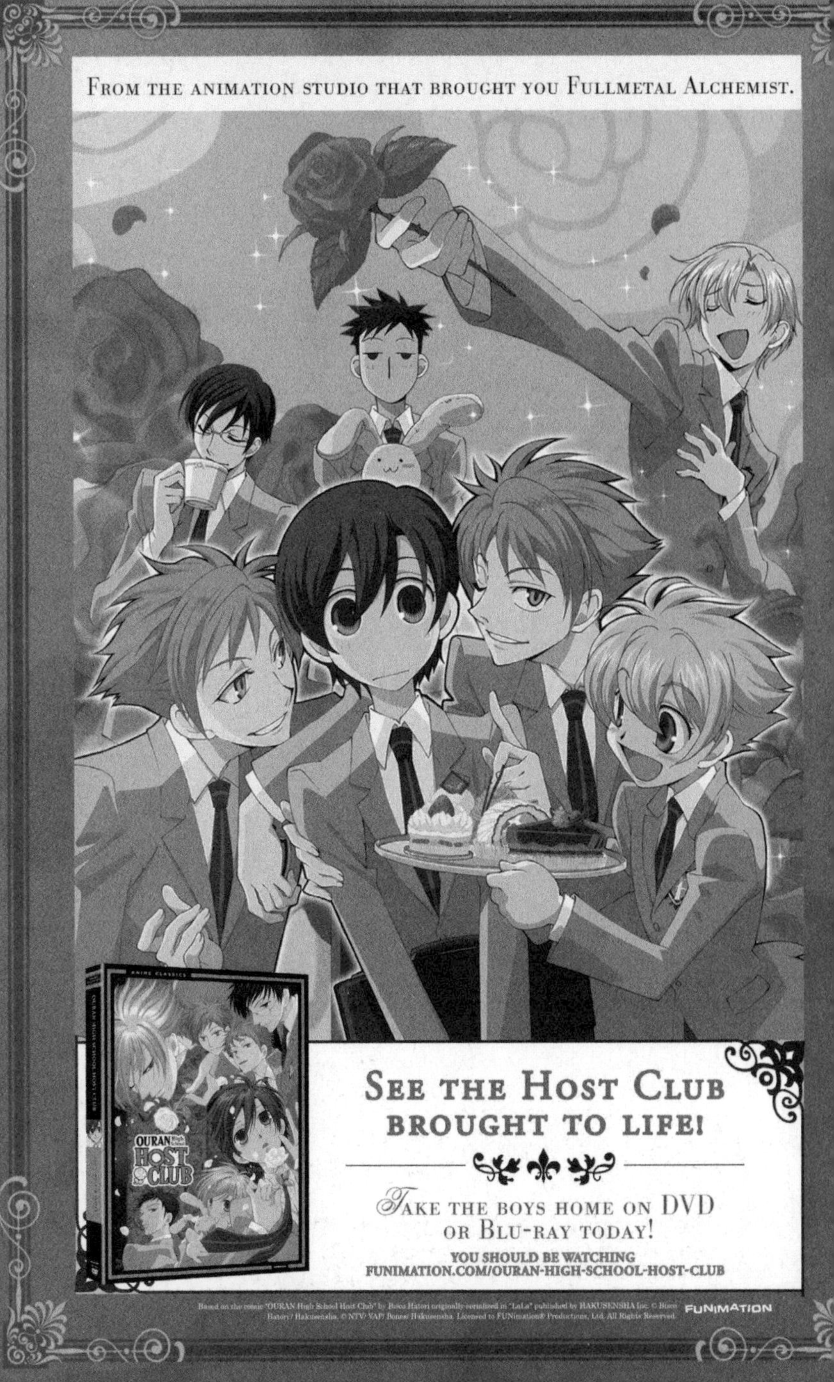

FROM THE ANIMATION STUDIO THAT BROUGHT YOU FULLMETAL ALCHEMIST.
OURAN High School HOST CLUB
SEE THE HOST CLUB BROUGHT TO LIFE!
TAKE THE BOYS HOME ON DVD OR BLU-RAY TODAY!
YOU SHOULD BE WATCHING
FUNIMATION.COM/OURAN-HIGH-SCHOOL-HOST-CLUB
Based on the comic "OURAN High School Host Club" by Bisco Hatori originally serialized in "LaLa" published by HAKUSENSHA Inc. © Bisco Hatori / Hakusensha. © NTV/ VAP/ Bones/ Hakusensha. Licensed to FUNimation® Productions, Ltd. All Rights Reserved.
FUNIMATION

ᑌIᘔᗰᗩᑎᘜᗩ
Read manga anytime, anywhere!

From our newest hit series to the classics you know and love, the best manga in the world is now available digitally. Buy a volume* of digital manga for your:

- iOS device (**iPad®, iPhone®, iPod® touch**)
  through the **VIZ Manga app**

- Android-powered device (**phone or tablet**)
  with a browser by visiting **VIZManga.com**

- **Mac or PC computer** by visiting **VIZManga.com**

VIZ Digital has loads to offer:

- 500+ ready-to-read volumes
- New volumes each week
- FREE previews
- Access on multiple devices! Create a log-in through the app
  so you buy a book once, and read it on your device of choice!*

To learn more, visit www.viz.com/apps

* Some series may not be available for multiple devices.
Check the app on your device to find out what's available.

SURPRISE!

You may be reading the wrong way!

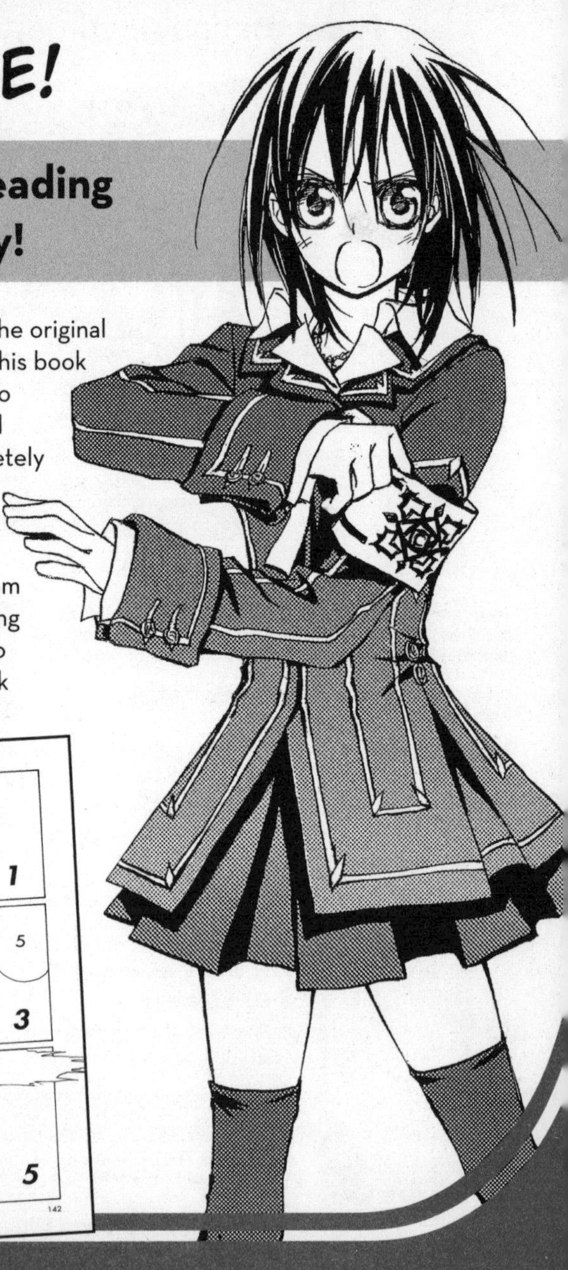

It's true: In keeping with the original Japanese comic format, this book reads from right to left—so action, sound effects, and word balloons are completely reversed. This preserves the orientation of the original artwork—plus, it's fun! Check out the diagram shown here to get the hang of things, and then turn to the other side of the book to get started!

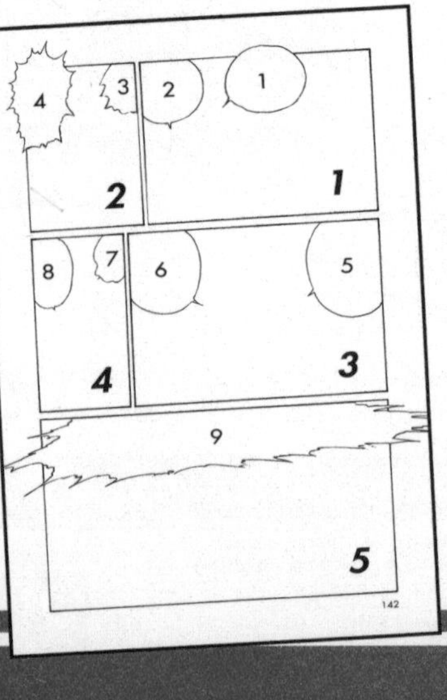